Mental
Mechanisms

Mental Mechanisms

Philosophical Perspectives on Cognitive Neuroscience

William Bechtel

Psychology Press
Taylor & Francis Group

New York   London

Lawrence Erlbaum Associates
Taylor & Francis Group
270 Madison Avenue
New York, NY 10016

Lawrence Erlbaum Associates
Taylor & Francis Group
2 Park Square
Milton Park, Abingdon
Oxon OX14 4RN

First Published by Lawrence Erlbaum Associates, Inc., Publishers
10 Industrial Avenue
Mahwah, New Jersey 07430

Reprinted 2009 by Psychology Press

Printed in the United States of America on acid-free paper
10 9 8 7 6 5 4 3

International Standard Book Number-13: 978-0-8058-6333-8 (Hardcover)

Library of Congress Cataloging-in-Publication Data

Bechtel, William.
    Mental mechanisms : philosophical perspectives on cognitive neuroscience /
William Bechtel.
        p. ; cm.
    "Taylor and Francis title."
    Includes bibliographical references and index.
    ISBN-13: 978-0-8058-6334-5 (paperback : alk. paper) 1. Cognitive
neuroscience--Philosophy. I. Title.
    [DNLM: 1. Memory--physiology. 2. Cognition--physiology. 3. Philosophy. WL 102
B392m 2008]

    QP360.5.B43 2008
    612.8'233--dc22

                                                              2007016047

Visit the Taylor & Francis Web site at
http://www.taylorandfrancis.com

Dedication

For Adele

Contents

Preface

How is it that we are able to see a sea lion climbing onto a rock? To remember our first romantic involvement? To plan a vacation to an exotic place? A variety of scientific disciplines have set as their task explaining these and other mental activities. All recognize that in some way these activities depend upon our brain. But until recently, the opportunities to conduct experiments directly on our brains were severely limited. As a result research efforts were split between disciplines such as cognitive psychology, linguistics, and artificial intelligence that investigated and modeled the activities of the human mind as revealed in behavior and disciplines such as neuroanatomy, neurophysiology, and genetics that experimented on the brains of nonhuman animals. In the 1960s the latter group of disciplines was integrated under the name *neuroscience* and in the 1970s the former cluster was integrated under the name *cognitive science*. Finally, in the late 1980s, with the advent of techniques for imaging activity in human brains, the term *cognitive neuroscience* began to be applied to the integrated investigations of mind and brain. This book is a philosophical examination of how these disciplines have and are pursuing the mission of explaining our mental capacities.

The term *mechanism* is ubiquitous when psychologists and neuroscientists offer explanations for mental activities. Surprisingly, philosophers addressing these disciplines have said little about what mechanisms are and how they serve to explain mental phenomena. In recent years, however, philosophers who have focused on various fields of biology have developed an analysis of mechanisms and mechanistic explanation. The mechanisms that explain mental phenomena are distinguished from many found in biology as what they must explain is how the operations occurring in our heads enable us to coordinate our thoughts and actions with the world outside us. Accordingly, they are often characterized as information-processing mechanisms because the operations within them produce and change informational vehicles in ways that correspond to the informational content they carry about things and events external to themselves.

The goal of *Mental Mechanisms* is to provide an account of how scientists investigating the mind–brain develop mechanistic accounts of mental activities. In chapter 1 I articulate the philosophical perspective I adopt, naturalism, according to which philosophers employ the same range of investigatory tools as other natural sciences and draw freely on the findings of those disciplines in conducting their own inquiries. Thus, rather than advancing an *a priori* or speculative account of what mind and brain must be, I focus on how various scientists investigate the mind–brain and advance a perspective on what they do. In this chapter I also develop accounts of mechanism and mechanistic explanation and focus, in particular, on characterizing the distinctive features of information-processing mechanisms. I conclude the chapter by detailing the investigatory strategies that are used by scientists to discover and evaluate proposed mechanistic explanations of mental phenomena.

Chapters 2 and 3 provide extended discussions of the development of mechanistic accounts of two mental phenomena, memory and vision. These case analyses reveal different ways in which investigators have developed accounts of mental mechanisms. In particular, chapter 2 addresses research into memory in which behavioral techniques of psychology played the leading role. I examine two ways in which psychologists have tried to decompose memory, phenomenal decomposition and mechanistic decomposition. The former distinguishes memory phenomena and has resulted in accounts identifying different memory systems. The latter emphasizes differentiating the operations that figure in producing memory phenomena. A serious obstacle to progress in this research is the lack of an understanding of what mental operations themselves are. I present parallels with research in biochemistry, which was only able to make progress in explaining physiological phenomena once the investigators understood the nature of biochemical operations. I then show how more recent research on neural processes involved in memory activities can provide guidance in decomposing memory operations, introducing the framework of the *heuristic identity theory*. One result of research into neural processes has been to suggest revisions in the initial differentiation of memory systems as a result of discovering that different memory phenomena rely on many of the same brain areas. I end by even considering research that suggests that the delineation of memory as a mental phenomenon distinct from vision, language processing, and reasoning may have to be revised, a revision I characterize as *reconstituting the phenomenon*.

Chapter 3 examines research on visual processing, a phenomenon initially thought to be localized in one region of the occipital lobe. The pattern in this research was to identify brain areas involved in visual processing and then to determine more precisely what operations were performed in each. This yielded the realization that the identified areas only performed specific operations required by the overall phenomenon of vision and prompted the search for additional areas and the attempt to determine what they contribute. To date, over 30 areas involved in visual processing have been found in the primate brain. These areas extend far into the parietal and temporal cortex. In many cases, however, the operation performed in the area has yet to be determined. Nonetheless, this differentiation of areas and operations has enabled researchers to begin to address another crucial part of mechanistic explanation, identifying the ways in which components are organized. I conclude by describing current ideas about how the visual system is organized.

One of the longest-standing philosophical issues about the mind concerns the relation between the mind and the brain. Investigators split over whether mental phenomena are reducible to brain activity or whether psychology and other cognitive sciences should pursue autonomous inquiries into mental phenomena. In chapter 4 I argue that this is a misguided dichotomy and that one of the virtues of understanding the nature of mechanistic explanation is that it reveals the importance of looking not only down to the parts and operations within a mechanism but also at the manner in which these are organized, and the context in which the mechanism is situated. Understanding a mechanism requires a multilevel perspective. Traditionally, arguments for the autonomy of psychology have appealed to the claimed multiple realizability of mental phenomena. I contend that there is no evidence for the sort of multiple realizability claimed, but that recognizing this does not undercut the case for autonomous inquiries at higher levels of organization as these are needed to understand the causal processes that determine the conditions under which mental mechanisms function.

In chapter 5 I turn to the concept of representation, which figures prominently in both cognitive science and neuroscience research. The importance of representation stems from the fact that mental mechanisms are information-processing mechanisms, and to understand them as such it is necessary to consider both the operations that occur within them and how what is operated on serves to stand in for things and events in the external world with which an organism is coordinating its behavior. This dual stance is captured by the distinction between the vehicle and content of a representation. I examine differences in the manner in which cognitive psychologists and neuroscientists have approached both the content and vehicle aspects of representation as well as a proposal, originating from proponents of dynamical systems theory, that the sciences of the mind–brain should abandon talk of representations. While rejecting the claim to abandon representations, I accept the challenge that it may be necessary to rethink issues about representations, and argue that a profitable framework for thinking about the representations results from viewing mental mechanisms as control systems. Such a perspective works well for many of the phenomena that have been the focus of neuroscience investigation, but seems more problematic for what have been taken as more prototypical cognitive activities such as problem solving and planning. I conclude by sketching a proposal about how representations grounded in perceptual and motor processing can nonetheless be utilized in concepts that can be deployed in activities such as reasoning and problem solving, in part by being brought under the control of language-using activities.

Although mechanistic explanations have provided extremely useful accounts of many phenomena in both biology and the cognitive and neurosciences, critics have faulted mechanisms as inadequate to account for some of the fundamental characteristics of living and thinking organisms. In chapter 6 I diagnose this problem as stemming from a conception of mechanisms as primarily reactive systems. Living organisms, including those with cognitive abilities, are inherently active. While some theorists view this as pointing to a fundamental failure of the mechanistic framework, I argue that mechanism has the resources to address the challenge. Realizing this potential requires emphasizing the mode of organization found in living mechanisms. Drawing upon theoretical research in biology, I develop first the notion of biological organisms as autonomous systems whose most basic activity involves recruiting and deploying matter and energy to build and repair themselves. I then focus on how additional mechanisms can make such systems agents that do things in their environment and adapt themselves to the specific conditions they confront, thereby arriving at the conception of autonomous adaptive agents. A key feature of autonomous adaptive agents is that they are inherently active and that sensory information about their environment modulates ongoing activity involved in maintaining the system as an autonomous system. I provide an example of recent computational modeling of visual processing in which internal dynamical processes underlie the behavior of the network even as it receives sensory inputs.

Humanist critics often allege that mechanistic accounts of mental activity in some way threaten our understanding of ourselves as agents with freedom and dignity. In the final chapter, I address these critics by arguing that, in fact, it is because of the mental mechanisms we possess that we are able to be agents with freedom and dignity. Although causality is often portrayed as undermining freedom and dignity, I contend that a free agent is one whose behavior is caused in appropriate ways by the agent's own mental states. The foundation to articulating the appropriate mode of causation lies in the characterization of autonomous adaptive agents developed in chapter 6. Autonomous systems are inherently active. What the evolution of mental mechanisms provides are resources for regulating the behavior of active organisms. Regulating ongoing activity involves deciding between alternatives and thereby valuing one rather than the others. These decisions are made by the autonomous agent as it confronts the contingencies of its environment. They are not imposed on the agent from without. Our functioning as autonomous adaptive agents is facilitated by a rich array of mental mechanisms. Some of these contribute to the development of a multifaceted conception of a self which is situated in a physical and social environment, which is able to remember its own past and anticipate its future, and which develops concepts about itself. These mechanisms are part of the regulatory system in the agent so that its plans and conception of itself can affect how the autonomous system behaves in the future. Far for undermining freedom and dignity, these mental mechanisms provide the resources for us to be free agents with dignity.

I began this book when I was invited to serve as the Chaire Cardinal Mercier at the Catholic University of Louvain in 2003. The six lectures I presented on that occasion articulated the basic themes that I have developed further here. I thank in particular Bernard Feltz and Gilbert Gerard for inviting me to present the Cardinal Mercier lectures and also the audiences at those lectures for discussions that furthered my thinking about these issues. Many of the ideas I develop in this book resulted from close interaction with a number of fellow-minded philosophers, including Andrew Brook, John Bickle, Carl Craver, Lindley Darden, Stuart Glennan, James Griesemer, Huib Looren de Jong, Fred Keijzer, Robert McCauley, Alvaro Moreno, Robert Richardson, Maurice Schouten, Paul Thagard, Cees van Leeuwen, and William Wimsatt. I am most thankful for these many interactions, as well as those with graduate students at Washington University (especially Chris Eliasmith, Pete Mandik, Jennifer Mundale, William Schoenbein, Jonathan Waskan, and Daniel Weiskopf) and at the University of California (especially Andrew Hamilton and Cory Wright), which have influenced my understanding of mechanism and the sciences of the mind–brain.

I offer a special thanks to Larry Erlbaum. He has been an invaluable friend not just to me but to the whole cognitive science community. He published my first two books when I was an assistant professor, and now that nearly 20 years later he has played a crucial role in bringing *Mental Mechanisms* to publication, albeit not under the Erlbaum imprint as originally planned. I hope that it reflects appropriate maturation. I also thank Lori Handelman of Lawrence Erlbaum associates and Paul Dukes and Jim McGovern of Taylor & Francis for their highly capable assistance.

Lastly, but most importantly, I thank my collaborator and spouse, Adele Abrahamsen. A great deal of my philosophical understanding of psychology and cognitive science developed through my interactions with her. She does not agree with all the views in the book, but her astute challenges have spurred my thinking. She also provided invaluable assistance with the editing of the book. I dedicate it to her.

One

Naturalism and Mechanism
Outlines of a New Philosophy of Science

René Descartes is perhaps the historical philosopher most strongly associated today with theorizing about the mind. Most people, when they think of Descartes' contribution, think first of his dualism—his insistence that minds are not physical and that mental activity is not to be explained in the same manner as physical phenomena. However, his greatest legacy arguably lies in his understanding of what constitutes explanation. Descartes was one of the foremost advocates of the new mechanical science of the seventeenth century, which sought to replace the ossified Aristotelian framework by explaining all phenomena of the natural world in terms of mechanical processes. This included not only ordinary physical processes but also processes in living organisms. Descartes even extended mechanistic explanation far into what is now the domain of psychology, explaining mechanically all animal behavior, and all human behavior that was comparable to that of animals.

Descartes lacked the research tools to take apart and experimentally investigate systems in nature. Instead he relied on "armchair" theorizing to find plausible mechanistic explanations. For example, he proposed to explain magnetism in terms of screw-shaped particles being drawn into threaded pores in the magnet. As fanciful as this seems now, it exemplified a working assumption that particles of the right size and shape, moving appropriately, would generate phenomena of interest in the physical world. He used more specific metaphors for living systems. For example, he proposed that the heart acts not as a pump, as Harvey had proposed, but rather as a furnace, reasoning that when blood was heated it would expand and hence move through blood vessels to various parts of the body. Although his specific proposals were superseded as scientists gained more adequate tools, Descartes' general program of mechanistic explanation has shaped scientific inquiry for centuries. Its success is especially obvious today in the life sciences: biologists routinely explain phenomena such as cell respiration, embryological development, and disease transmission by identifying the parts, operations, and organization of the responsible mechanisms in organisms.

For Descartes, this strategy broke down when he turned his attention to reasoning and language—abilities exhibited by humans alone among living beings.

These were phenomena for which he could not even begin to imagine a mechanism. How do humans produce such a variety of sentences, each appropriate to its context? How do they invoke knowledge to solve a wide variety of problems? The apparent lack of a mechanistic explanation for these abilities drove Descartes to dualism. By inexorable reasoning, if everything in the physical universe operated by mechanical processes, then those phenomena that defied mechanistic explanation could not be produced by anything in the physical world. Instead they must be attributed to a nonphysical substance—mind.

Here modern science has taken a different path, outdoing Descartes at his own endeavor by finding mechanistic explanations for mental as well as bodily phenomena. Cognitive scientists, and their predecessors and colleagues in such fields as psychology and neuroscience, assume that the mind is a complex of mechanisms that produce those phenomena we call "mental" or "psychological." The mind is to be understood by uncovering those mechanisms. That is, they have extended Descartes' mechanistic strategy to a domain he himself set aside as involving a special substance requiring special methods of inquiry. In embracing Descartes' mechanistic explanatory strategy, cognitive scientists reject his dualism. Often they speak of the "mind/brain," regarding the mind as what the brain does, rather than positing a mind and a brain as separate and dissimilar substances. Not everyone agrees with this expansion of the mechanist program. Descartes' dualistic assumption that mind and brain are distinct substances has been carried forward to the present day by humanist critics who reject the "mechanization" of mind as yielding the greatest indignity to humanity. Part of what lies behind this repudiation is a limited conception of mechanism that assimilates it to machines made by humans. Here the appeal by many in cognitive science to the computer as a model for the mind fuels the critics. The pejorative meaning of "robot" when applied to people exemplifies this negative view of the types of behavior of which machines are capable.

One of my objectives in this book is to counter this negative assessment of mechanism. The critics' first mistake, I will argue, is their assimilation of the notion of mechanism to human-made machines. Although it is true that scientists often draw their mechanical schemas from the technology of the period in which they are working, it is also the case that the mechanisms operative in the biological and psychological worlds are far more complicated than those produced by human engineering to date. Moreover, the complexity is not simply a matter of the number of components involved, but rather emerges from a particular mode of organization: Living systems not only react, they are inherently active systems. To stop acting is to die. A particular mode of organization is required to establish such active, autonomous agents. But, as I will develop in later chapters, understanding mechanisms within persons as organized to enable whole persons to function as active, autonomous agents provides the key to understanding how, despite being comprised of mechanisms, human beings are creatures with freedom and dignity. In fact, I will maintain, it is not in spite of being comprised of mechanisms, but in virtue of being composed of the right sort of mechanisms, that human beings are such creatures. At this stage in human inquiry there is no other positive account of what gives humans these properties.

The reason I defer to later chapters a discussion of how mechanisms can be organized to achieve active, autonomous agents is that a different conception of mechanism has figured in most biological and psychological inquiry. Traditionally, mechanisms have been viewed principally as responsive systems—that is, as systems that perform their activity when the conditions for such performance are met. Such a conception of a mechanism, although falling short of the goal of explaining how biological systems are active, autonomous systems and how humans are agents with freedom and dignity, has proved extremely productive in undergirding explanations about how the mind/brain operates.

If one listens to how cognitive scientists describe their research, they regularly talk of finding and describing the mechanisms responsible for phenomena exhibited by the mind/brain. Despite this, most philosophical accounts of scientific explanation, including philosophical accounts of explanation in psychology and neuroscience, hold that what scientists are seeking are the laws underlying behavior. This is a carryover from a framework that had wide appeal in the mid-twentieth century, the *nomological* (or *deductive-nomological*) account of science. It had its greatest applicability to fundamental physics, where explanation often does bottom out by identifying laws—for example, Newton's laws of motion.

The continued influence of the nomological perspective in the cognitive sciences is exemplified in the invocation of putative laws in accounts of folk psychology and the suggestion that the integration of psychology and neuroscience will involve the reduction of the laws of psychology to those of neuroscience. Folk psychology, as discussed by philosophers, is supposed to capture the way ordinary people talk about their own and other people's mental activity. On these accounts, mental states are characterized in terms of propositional attitudes—attitudes such as believing or desiring which are directed towards propositions. The belief that tomatoes are fruits, for example, would involve the attitude of belief directed towards the proposition *tomatoes are fruits*. Folk psychological explanations then explain either how actions arise from beliefs and desires or how the beliefs and desires a person holds are themselves changed as a result of reasoning from other beliefs and desires or from new experiences. The foundation of these explanations is taken to be laws that specify, for example, that someone with certain beliefs and desires will behave in a certain way or will develop specific other beliefs.

The key idea underlying nomological (law-based) models of explanation is that events in nature follow regular patterns and that it is sufficient to explain an event to show that it falls under such a pattern. Characterizing these patterns as laws appears to have originated with 17th – 18th century theorists who compared the patterns manifest in natural events to human-made laws. Recognizing that mortals cannot make laws that apply to inanimate objects, these theorists credited God with being the author of these laws. Although first developed by theorists with a theological orientation, the perspective was soon detached from the idea of God as the law maker (Giere, 1999, p. 13). What remained was the idea of laws of nature which in some sense prescribed the events of the natural world. However, there are considerable disanalogies between laws of nature and human laws. One of the foremost differences is that while humans can violate the laws set down by other humans, and societies have developed practices for punishing such violations, it does not make sense to think either of there being violations of laws of nature or of punishing such violations. Rather, laws of nature were viewed as inviolable generalizations. It is important to recognize that laws of nature are not just descriptions of what happens. They have a modal status, specifying what must happen if the stated circumstances are obtained.

The quest for mechanisms is very different than that for laws. In the search for laws, investigators are seeking principles of broad, even universal, applicability. Newton's laws of motion and the principles of thermodynamics are presumed to apply universally. Mechanisms, on the contrary, tend to be much more specific. A mechanism consists of a particular set of parts that carry out specific operations, organized so as to produce a given phenomenon. Moreover, the cognitive labor in understanding them is very different: Instead of abstracting general principles and applying them to specific cases, researchers focus from the beginning on the specifics of the composition and organization of a mechanism that generates a particular form of behavior.

I will develop the notions of mechanism and mechanistic explanation in more detail in section two of this chapter. First, though, I will discuss the broader context in which they became salient—the turn towards naturalism that has given philosophy of science new traction in recent decades.

1.1   THE NATURALISTIC TURN IN PHILOSOPHY OF SCIENCE

Historically, some philosophers of science have sought an independent platform, one from which they could prescribe the rules of scientific inquiry or epistemically evaluate the results of science. This is a project that W.V.O. Quine dubbed *first philosophy*. One example of the project of first philosophy is Descartes' endeavor to derive a method for scientific inquiry that would insure it obtained the truth. Arguing from his own existence to the existence of God and the claim that God would not deceive him, he concluded that whatever he or other investigators perceived clearly and distinctly would be true. The challenge for human cognizers, including scientists, was to identify clear and distinct ideas and reason from them. Although this Cartesian project of reasoning from clear and distinct ideas has attracted relatively few adherents in recent centuries, the project of identifying normative canons for science has remained popular.

The challenge for philosophy in advancing criteria independent of science for evaluating science is to articulate the resources it will employ in defending its evaluations. For an influential group of twentieth century philosophers, logic promised to provide such a resource. The logical positivists (later known as the logical empiricists) were like-minded clusters of scientists and philosophers working in eastern Europe in the early decades of the twentieth century. In arriving at their philosophical accounts of science, they drew upon the accounts of logic articulated by Frege, Russell, and Wittgenstein at the turn of the century. As deductive logic is simply a device for preserving truth (if the premises of a deductive argument are true, the conclusion must also be true), logical arguments must start from some foundation. As the terms *positivist* and *empiricist* suggest, experience—especially sensory experience—provided the foundation for these philosophers (see, for example, Carnap, 1936; 1937; Reichenbach, 1938; Hempel, 1962). Their strategy was to show how claims of science might be justified by being derived from sentences that could be confirmed or refuted by observation.

Sympathetic critics such as Karl Popper (1935/1959) objected that it was logically impossible to confirm or justify theories in such a manner, because theoretical claims extended beyond the particular observations used to support them. Subsequent observations could always prove the best-confirmed theory false. Popper argued for an alternative strategy in which scientists should strive to *falsify* hypotheses, especially bold ones that make strong claims about the world. Popper construed as corroborated those theories which best withstood the best efforts at falsification. The logic of falsification, however, is as problematic as the logic of confirmation. Any falsification always rests on a number of assumptions, and these, not the hypothesis being tested, can turn out to be problematic.

These complications with both confirmation and falsification led many philosophers to abandon the project of developing a logic of science. A related approach, however, does continue to garner significant support in philosophy. Instead of appealing to logical inference, this tradition appeals to probability theory and attempts to evaluate the probability of scientific hypotheses, given the evidence on which they are grounded. The best worked out of these approaches is based on Bayes' theorem, which provides a procedure for updating one's assessment of the probability that a hypothesis is true given new evidence (Maher, 1993).

In addition to attempting to articulate normative rules for scientific inquiry, there is another approach that some philosophers hope will give them knowledge of mental phenomena, one that is independent of the methods of science.

It involves an analysis of concepts in terms of their necessary and sufficient conditions. This has been one of the main modes of investigation in what is often known as analytic philosophy. The idea is that our concepts have a logical structure, often provided by definitions, and that by unpacking these definitions, we can secure knowledge. For example, if the concept *bachelor* means unmarried male, then it follows that a bachelor is unmarried. And if the concept *knowledge* means justified true belief, then we know that only true statements can be known. As concepts are thought, on this view, to be something any competent speaker of the language must know, proposed definitions of concepts are often tested against individuals' intuitions. Would, for example, a married man who is long separated from his spouse and living a bachelor lifestyle count as a bachelor? This approach to testing proposed definitions was soon elaborated into rather complex thought experiments (what Daniel Dennett, 1988 calls *intuition pumps*), some of which have been taken to reveal crucial features of the mind. The most famous example was offered by Hilary Putnam (1973). On the imaginary place known as *twinearth,* everything is the same as it is on Earth except that water is replaced by some other substance, XYZ. Putnam maintains that it is intuitive that the residents of twinearth mean XYZ and not H_2O when they use the concept *water* (including your doppelganger, who is indistinguishable from you except for having every H_2O molecule replaced by one of XYZ). Hence, he concludes, meaning is not a fact about what thoughts are in a person's head but instead about how the person is related to external objects.

A proponent of the naturalist perspective in philosophy, which I describe below, is deeply skeptical of such an approach. First, thought experiments are methodologically suspect. Although they have, on occasion, proven useful in advancing scientific inquiry (consider, for example, those of Galileo and Einstein), most philosophical thought experiments are underconstrained. Different people come to different conclusions from the same assumptions. Moreover, the capacity of thought experiments to reveal fundamental truths about the world is dubious. In science, what they show when successful are some of the unexpected consequences of a theoretical perspective. Then their status is no stronger than that of the theoretical perspective on which they are based.

Second, the attempt to identify truths by analyzing concepts assumes that concepts themselves constitute a secure foundation on which to build knowledge claims. Psychological investigations into human concepts over the past three decades give reason to be dubious that concepts provide such a foundation. Eleanor Rosch's early research on categorization indicated that human categories such as *bird* or *chair* have a prototype structure (items are judged to be better or worse exemplars of the category depending on their similarity to a prototype) and suggested that humans do not rely on definitions (Rosch, 1973; Rosch & Mervis, 1975). Although subsequent research has revealed a much more complex picture (Medin & Smith, 1984; Neisser, 1987; Keil, 1989; Murphy, 2002; Prinz, 2002), it does not support the view that human concepts provide epistemically sound access to truths about the world.

A prime motivation for rejecting the quest for first philosophy is that philosophy on its own lacks methods of investigation that are sufficient to realize its goals—to provide a method for science or to determine truths about the mind. As an alternative, the naturalist proposes that we should examine how scientific inquiry is conducted by actual scientists and in doing so avail ourselves of the resources of science. That is, the philosopher of science would focus on securing data about how scientists work and developing theoretical accounts that are tested against that data. Although such an approach cannot independently specify norms for doing science, it can draw upon scientists' own identification of cases that constitute good and bad scientific practice and use these to evaluate theories about how science works, as well as to evaluate work within the sciences that are the objects of study.

Rejecting first philosophy might seem tantamount to rejecting the project of philosophy itself. Whereas most philosophers find this prospect threatening, a few embrace it. A notable example is Wittgenstein (1953), who devoted the latter part of his career to flamboyantly dissolving various problems that other philosophers regarded as genuine and worthy of their attention. A less dramatic move is to reject first philosophy but hold onto the project of philosophy by proposing a new identity for it—one that aligns it more closely with science. Accordingly, Quine—whose focus was epistemology more generally, not just philosophy of science—proposed linking the project of epistemology with that of psychology. "Why not settle for psychology?" he asks (Quine, 1969, p. 75). If we take this as the project, then the epistemological inquiry itself becomes a scientific inquiry into the processes by which human beings acquire knowledge. Quine concludes that "Epistemology in its new setting ... is contained in natural science, as a chapter of psychology" (p. 83).[1]

If epistemology is simply a chapter within psychology, it might seem that there is little for philosophers to contribute, inasmuch as most philosophers lack

---

[1] In a widely quoted passage, he explains: "Epistemology, or something like it, simply falls into place as a chapter of psychology and hence of natural science. It studies a natural phenomenon, viz., a physical human subject. This human subject is accorded a certain experimentally controlled input—certain patterns of irradiation in assorted frequencies, for instance—and in the fullness of time the subject delivers as output a description of the three-dimensional external world and its history. The relation between the meager input and the torrential output is a relation that we are prompted to study for somewhat the same reasons that always prompted epistemology: namely, in order to see how evidence relates to theory, and in what ways one's theory of nature transcends any available evidence.... But a conspicuous difference between old epistemology and the epistemological enterprise in this new psychological setting is that we can now make free use of empirical psychology" (pp. 82–3).

training in experimental psychology. But Quine also suggests retaining the old relation between epistemology and natural science wherein natural science falls within the scope of epistemology:

> But the old containment [of natural science by epistemology] remains valid too, in its own way. We are studying how the human subject of our study posits bodies and projects his physics from his data, and we appreciate that our position in the world is just like his. Our very epistemological enterprise, therefore, and the psychology wherein it is a component chapter, and the whole of natural science wherein psychology is a component book—all of this is our own construction or projection from stimulations like those we are meting out to our epistemological subject (p. 83).

Quine himself does not make much of this later relation between science and epistemology. But for other philosophers who have adopted naturalism, this two-way relation is important. While happily adopting the investigatory tools of empirical inquiry, or invoking the results of those qualified to perform experimental investigations, naturalistic philosophers retain the focus of providing a philosophical perspective on empirical inquiry. Thus, the naturalistic philosophy of science attempts to make sense of the overall project of scientific inquiry, addressing such questions as:

- What are the objectives of inquiry?
- What methods are used to obtain the results?
- How are the methods and results of science evaluated?
- How do value issues impinge on the conduct of science?

For these purposes the empirical tools are sometimes those of the psychologist (Dunbar, 1995; Klahr & Simon, 1999), but often those of the historian or sociologist— analyzing the archival records of scientists or observing and interpreting their activities.

Although Quine made claims about scientific practice (e.g., about the role of nonepistemic factors such as simplicity in the evaluation of scientific theories) and about the limitations on scientific knowledge (e.g., the underdetermination of theories by all possible evidence), he generally did not engage science as a naturalist. For example, he did not study the investigatory strategies or reasoning employed by particular scientists or the specific explanations they advanced. But in the thirty years since Quine advanced the project of naturalized epistemology, numerous philosophers of science have taken up just this endeavor (for early developments of naturalism in philosophy of biology, see Callebaut, 1993). Many of these efforts involve examining the reasoning and inferential practices of particular scientists, although often with the goal of elaborating more general strategies.

For example, Nancy Nersessian (2002) has examined in detail the reasoning of physicists Faraday and Maxwell, especially their use of diagrams and invocation of analogies in developing explanatory models. Ronald Giere (1988; 2002) has not only examined how scientists construct models in their explanatory endeavors but also how epistemic efforts in science are distributed across multiple scientists and across the instruments they employ. Lindley Darden (1991; 2006) has focused on how scientists revise theories by localizing problems and employing specific repair strategies.

In addition to the theoretical reasoning of scientists, philosophers pursuing a naturalistic approach have also focused on the reasoning involved in the design and evaluation of new instruments and research techniques. One of the pioneering efforts of this sort was Ian Hacking's (1983) examination of the microscope and the manner in which scientists come to have confidence that they are confronting real phenomena, not just artifacts produced by their instruments. Hacking emphasized the importance of concurrence of results from new modes of intervention (e.g., electron microscopes, new stains for specimens) with existing ones (e.g., light microscopes, long-trusted stains). Later in this chapter I will discuss briefly the importance of experimental techniques for understanding how the sciences of the mind/brain have developed.

Naturalized philosophers are not alone in examining the actual practices of science. Historians, sociologists, and psychologists often pursue similar objectives. This broader, interdisciplinary inquiry into the activity of science is often referred to as *science studies*. In many cases it is difficult to draw any strong distinctions between the pursuits of naturalistic philosophers and other practitioners of science studies, although philosophers tend to focus on epistemology and the question of how the activities of scientists can be understood as productive of knowledge. Moreover, many retain the normative aspirations of earlier epistemology. That is, they hope that from an understanding of how scientific knowledge is actually procured, it will be possible to make recommendations for future practice. Of course, insofar as any such recommendations are based on understanding what has and has not worked well in previous science, the force of these recommendations is limited. We cannot guarantee that a strategy of reasoning that worked in the past will work for new problems. But in noting this I am merely recognizing that a naturalized pursuit cannot rise above its own naturalism.

One consequence of adopting the naturalist perspective is the recognition that not all sciences are the same. Many of the traditional philosophical ideas about science, whether developed by philosophers pursuing the *a priori* approach or the naturalist approach, were most applicable to domains of classical physics. But, starting in the 1970s and 1980s, certain philosophers who turned their attention to the biological sciences found that these frameworks did not apply all that well to different biological domains. Recognizing this, the naturalist is committed to developing accounts that work for specific sciences, postponing the question of determining what is in common in the inquiries of all sciences. In this sense, the naturalist is led to be a pluralist.

One of the most jarring results of joining a naturalistic perspective to a focus on the life sciences is that in many parts of biology one seems to look in vain for what philosophy has commonly taken to be the principal explanatory tool of science, that is, laws. The few statements that have been called laws in biology, such as Mendel's laws, have often turned out to be incorrect or at best only approximately correct. Some philosophers have offered explanations of the failure to find laws, such as: Laws are supposed to be universal in scope, and biological discoveries are restricted to the specific life forms that have evolved on this planet (Beatty, 1995; Sober, 1997). But that does not mean that biologists and psychologists are not developing explanations. If one investigates what biologists and psychologists seek and treat as sufficient for explanation, it often turns out to be mechanisms, not laws.[2]

At the center of the naturalistic account of the sciences of the mind and brain that I will be offering in this book is an understanding of scientists as engaged in the quest to understand the mechanisms responsible for particular phenomena. The term *mechanism* is widely used, not just in the cognitive sciences but across the life sciences. Until very recently, the notion of mechanism as it figures in the contemporary life sciences has not been much analyzed, but in the past fifteen years a number of philosophers have advanced characterizations of mechanisms. In the next section of this chapter I will present an account of mechanism and mechanistic explanation.

1.2   THE FRAMEWORK OF MECHANISTIC EXPLANATION: PARTS, OPERATIONS, AND ORGANIZATION

The idea that explanation of a phenomenon involves the quest to understand the mechanism responsible for it has deep roots in ancient history. It goes back at least as far as the fifth century BCE—prior to the idea of explanation in terms of laws—where it was prominent in the atomic theory by Leucippus and Democritus and in the writings of Pseudo Aristotle. The central explanatory strategy of the ancient atomic theory was to explain the features of observable objects in terms of the shape and motion of their constituents. At the time the opposition to mechanism was not from advocates of nomological accounts but from advocates of a

---

[2] Cummins (2000) observes that psychologists often refer to laws, although they typically call them effects (e.g., the spacing effect). But, he argues, these typically describe the phenomena to be explained rather than serving as explanations. Laws may continue to play a role in accounts of science that emphasize mechanisms, but they will not be central to explanation in the manner envisaged by the logical positivists.

teleological conception of nature such as that of Aristotelian philosophy. According to these teleological accounts, all phenomena in nature are directed toward an end, or *telos*, that was linked to what Aristotle called the *form* that determined the identity of a given object. Explanation then consisted in identifying the form of something and showing how it was directed towards its telos. Atomic theories, on the contrary, appealed only to an entity's constituents (especially their shape and motion) to explain what it did. No ends or purposes were involved.

Atomic theories were largely eclipsed by teleological theories, both in the ancient world and in the medieval world after the rediscovery of Aristotle. The atomist's project of explaining nature mechanistically was revived in the seventeenth and eighteenth century in the works of, among others, Galileo, Descartes, and Boyle. Their common objective was to show how natural phenomena could be accounted for in terms of the shape, size, and motion of elementary particles (Boas, 1952; Westfall, 1971). As with many other mechanists, Descartes' models for explanation were the machines humans built. He wrote:

> I do not recognize any difference between artifacts and natural bodies except that the operations of artifacts are for the most part performed by mechanisms which are large enough to be easily perceivable by the senses—as indeed must be the case if they are to be capable of being manufactured by human beings. The effects produced by nature, by contrast, almost always depend on structures which are so minute that they completely elude our senses (*Principia* IV, § 203).

Even if this were the only difference, it is an important one. Humans who design and build artifacts must know the nature of the building blocks before undertaking construction, but humans who seek to understand natural entities often can only speculate about their components. The mechanical scientists of the seventeenth century offered hypotheses about the existence and properties of unobservable "atoms" or "corpuscles" because these seemed necessary to explain observable macroscopic phenomena. In many domains of physics, such speculation came into disrepute, especially in the wake of Newton's articulation of a different approach according to which general laws, such as his three laws of motion, were shown to account for a broad range of natural phenomena, including the behavior of constituents in mechanical systems. These laws characterized forces operating over distance without requiring physical contact. Descartes' version of contact mechanism, however, remained influential in many fields including biology.

Descartes himself applied his mechanistic perspective not just to inanimate objects, but also to living organisms, including humans:

> I suppose the body [of a man/machine constructed by God] to be nothing but a statue or machine made of earth, which God forms with the explicit intention of

making it as much as possible like us. Thus, God not only gives it externally the colours and shapes of all the parts of our bodies, but also places inside it all the parts required to make it walk, eat, breathe, and indeed to imitate all those of our functions which can be imagined to proceed from matter and to depend solely on the disposition of our organs. We see clocks, artificial fountains, mills, and other such machines which, although only man-made, have the power to move of their own accord in many different ways. But I am supposing this machine to be made by the hands of God, and so I think you may reasonably think it capable of a greater variety of movement than I could possibly imagine of it, and of exhibiting more artistry than I could possible ascribe to it" (*Traité de l'homme,* AT XI, 120).

In developing his account of mechanisms in living organisms, Descartes appealed frequently to metaphors with human-made machines so as to suggest explanations of those features of biological systems that initially appear to set them apart. For example, to explain the ability of animals to initiate motion, he appealed to such artifacts as clocks and mills that succeeded in moving on their own. He further appealed to the hydraulically moved statuary in the Royal Gardens to provide a model of the ability of the nervous system to transmit sensory signals to and motor signals from the brain. Just as stepping on a stone could operate a valve that redirected hydraulic flow so as to move a statue, he proposed that in animals sensory input to the brain directed activity by altering the flow of very fine matter, the animal spirits, through the nerves.

The project of providing mechanistic explanations of living systems took off in subsequent centuries. It was discovered, for example, that electrical stimulation played a role in muscle contraction (Galvani, 1791) and that respiration was comparable to ordinary combustion in terms of heat released (Lavoisier & Laplace, 1780). The mechanistic perspective was actively embraced in the nineteenth century by physiologists such as Theodor Schwann, Hermann Helmholtz, Emil du Bois-Reymond, and Carl Ludwig. Schwann (1839), for example, proposed an account of cell formation on analogy with crystal formation and developed the idea that metabolic processes occurred in cells as a result of the specific concentration of materials found there. As I will discuss in chapter six, mechanists in biology were opposed by vitalists who doubted that mechanistic accounts could explain the phenomena of life. Nonetheless, by the end of the nineteenth century, mechanistic approaches to biology were thriving and vitalism had been dismissed from serious biology.

Although the project of explaining biological phenomena in terms of mechanisms has been central to biology since the nineteenth century, I have mentioned that it did not attract much attention from philosophers until recently. At best, mainstream twentieth-century philosophers would take note of the long-dormant vitalist-mechanist controversy, but in a way that assimilated mechanistic explanation to the dominant framework of nomological explanation (E. Nagel, 1961). One noteworthy exception was Wesley Salmon (1984), who advanced what he termed *causal/mechanical explanation* as an alternative to nomological explanation. Salmon was primarily interested in characterizing causal explanation and said little specifically about mechanisms. There is, however, a fundamental difference between explaining a phenomenon by identifying the responsible causal factors (e.g., explaining the contraction of a muscle as resulting from the neural signal impinging on the muscle cell) and explaining the coordinated operations within the system that enable it to respond in that way (e.g., the building of cross bridges between the myosin molecules of the thick filaments and the actin molecules of the thin filaments and the subsequent pulling action of the myosin on the actin to shorten the sacromeres).[3] Recently, a number of philosophers of science have advanced characterizations of such mechanisms (Bechtel & Richardson, 1993; Glennan, 1996; 2002; Machamer, Darden, & Craver, 2000). My own starting point is the following characterization:

> A mechanism is a structure performing a function in virtue of its component parts, component operations, and their organization. The orchestrated functioning of the mechanism is responsible for one or more phenomena (Bechtel & Abrahamsen, 2005; Bechtel, 2006).[4]

There are a number of features of this characterization that bear emphasis. First, mechanisms are identified in terms of the phenomena for which they are responsible (Glennan, 1996; Kauffman, 1971). The relevant notion of phenomena

---

[3] As this example suggests, in many causal processes one can explain the mediation between cause and effect in terms of a mediating mechanism.

[4] There are some salient differences between the various characterizations of mechanism currently on offer. With Robert Richardson (Bechtel & Richardson, 1993), I focused on the "functions" (operations) that parts perform, whereas Stuart Glennan focuses on the properties of parts in stating what he originally (1996) called laws and now (2002) calls "invariant change-relating generalizations." These are instantiated in "interactions" in which "a change in a property of one part brings about a change in a property of another part" (2002, p. S344). Peter Machamer, Lindley Darden, and Carl Craver (2000) pursue the metaphysical status of "entities" (parts) and "activities" (operations). James Tabery (2004) has proposed a partial synthesis in which activity and property changes are seen as complementary. I use the term operation rather than activity in order to draw attention to the involvement of parts that are affected by operations; for example, enzymes operate on substrates so as to catalyze changes in the substrates. Finally, Machamer et al. (p. 3) include a characterization of mechanisms as "productive of regular changes from start or set-up to finish or termination conditions." I am concerned that such an emphasis helps to retain a focus on linear processes whereas mechanisms, when they are embedded in larger mechanisms, are continuously responsive to conditions in the larger mechanism. For tractability scientists tend to focus on the conditions in which an operation is elicited and on its contribution to the behavior of the overall mechanism. However they often have to counter this analytical perspective to appreciate the dynamics at work in the system.

and the construal of them as targets of explanation has been developed by Bogen and Woodward (1988), who presented the focus on phenomena as an alternative to the then common view that explanations explained data. On their account, phenomena are occurrences in the world, and although they may be singular, as in the case of the big bang, they are often repeatable. Bogen and Woodward offered as examples of phenomena "weak neutral currents, the decay of the proton and chunking and recency effects in human memory" (p. 306). The importance of identifying mechanisms in terms of phenomena will become more apparent when we focus on parts and operations, as what count as parts and operations are just those components that, functioning together, are responsible for the phenomenon. For now I will simply note that a consequence of this approach to individuating mechanisms is that different mechanisms may reside in the same physical entity, such as the brain or the liver, if that entity is responsible for different functions. The idea that identifying mechanisms depends upon identifying phenomena does not mean that investigators must have a fixed idea of what a mechanism does prior to their investigation. Sometimes they will arrive at the characterization of the phenomenon itself only as they investigate the mechanism and will revise their characterization of the phenomenon as they develop a better understanding of the internal operation of the mechanism (Bechtel and Richardson, 1993, refer to this as *reconstituting the phenomenon.*)

Second, a mechanism consists of parts and operations. By *parts* I designate the structural components of a mechanism whereas by *operations* I refer to processes or changes involving the parts. I use the term *operation* to emphasize that in each operation not only is something performing an operation but something is operated on. In chemistry, investigators could identify the chemical substances (substrates) that are changed in a given reaction, and use that in characterizing the reaction. In the cognitive domain, investigators speak of *information processing*, suggesting that information is what is operated on, a topic to which I return in a later section of this chapter. To identify parts and operations, researchers must *decompose* the mechanism— that is, undertake a *mechanistic* decomposition—either physically as in a chemistry experiment or conceptually. Different research techniques are useful for decomposing a mechanism into parts (what I term *structural decomposition*) and into operations (*functional decomposition*), and historically these may be deployed by different communities of scientists. Yet, parts and operations are intimately connected. Parts of mechanisms are not just any physically separable part of a mechanism—rather, they are *working parts*, parts involved in the operations (Craver, 2007). I use the term *localization* for the process of linking parts and operations; to localize an operation is to assign it to a specific part. Although ultimately the goal is to identify the distinct part that performs an operation, often researchers must settle initially for situating the operation in a larger part (e.g., situating glycolysis initially in cells and later in the aqueous cytosol of the cell).

Let me briefly illustrate these ideas in the context of the sciences of the mind and brain. Efforts to identify parts of the brain go back many centuries, well before there were tools for assigning operations to particular parts. Nonetheless, the search for parts was guided by assumptions about how the brain functions. When the brain was thought to be involved in the circulation of fluids (as it was for both Galen and Descartes), the ventricles were thought to be the relevant working parts. In the eighteenth century researchers turned their attention instead to the grey matter constituting the cerebral cortex. Although initially the manner in which cortex was folded was thought to be random, as researchers discerned commonalities across individuals they began to assign names to particular sulci and gyri (see Clarke & Dewhurst, 1972). These came to be candidate working parts, and are still appealed to in contemporary efforts to localize mental operations (e.g., in the claims that the fusiform gyrus contains an area for recognizing faces). With the development of tools for analyzing cell structures in brain tissue, Korbinian Brodmann (1909/1994) determined that the cerebral cortex in mammals typically consists of six layers of cells (Figure 1.1). He further established that these layers differed in thickness in different parts of the brain. Thinking that the areas composed of the same types of neurons and exhibiting a similar layering structure were likely to share a function, he created his now famous maps of the cortex in many different species. Figure 1.2 shows his map of the human cortex. The numbering of areas in the map simply reflects the order in

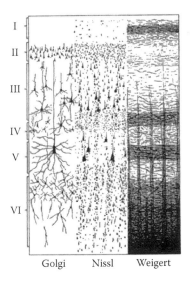

Figure 1.1   Brodmann's (1910) representation of the six-layer structure of the neocortex as revealed using three different stains.

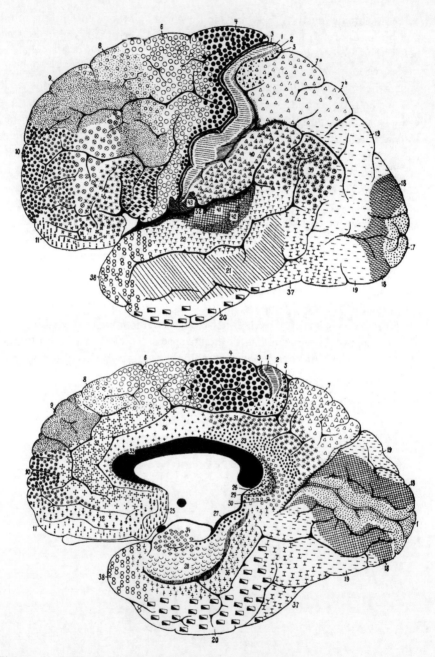

Figure 1.2   Brodmann's (1909) cytoarchitectonic map of the human cortex. The top shows the lateral view, the bottom, the medial view of the left hemisphere.

which Brodmann reported his observations. Proposed localizations of cognitive operations still make reference to Brodmann areas.

Psychologists, especially those adopting an information processing perspective, traditionally focused on the mind rather than the brain. Leaving aside questions of what brain areas are involved, they sought to identify the operations the mind would use in information processing, a project Robert Cummins (1975; 1983) referred to as *functional* analysis. Possible operations would be retrieving a piece of information from a memory store or comparing a representation of an occurrent event to one stored in memory. Analysis into such operations generally stemmed from hypothesizing ways in which information might be manipulated to perform a given task and testing such hypotheses against behavioral data—often reaction times (average response times) or error patterns across experimental conditions designed to share some operations but differ in others.

A third feature of mechanisms is important here: Their parts and operations must be organized appropriately. One reason organization is important is that the functioning of the mechanism requires the different operations to be linked to one another. This is already observed in simple linear organization such as is found on an assembly line. In living systems, as I will discuss in chapter six, far more complex modes of organization, such as cyclic pathways and feedback loops, are employed and are critical to understanding the phenomena exhibited by living systems. As I will discuss in chapter four, reductionistic research that focuses on the contributions of the parts and operations of a mechanism typically needs to be complemented by approaches geared to appreciating systemic properties such as how the parts and operations are organized and the difference that organization makes to the behavior of the components. Furthermore, the need to consider organization does not top out at the boundaries of the mechanism. A mechanism is always contextually situated. It functions in an environment, and its behavior is often altered by conditions in the environment. Often it is higher-level or special sciences that have the research tools and techniques to identify and characterize the causal factors affecting the mechanism as a whole. These autonomous higher-level inquiries provide information not accessible with the tools of more reductionistically oriented investigators.

1.3   REPRESENTING AND REASONING ABOUT MECHANISMS

So far I have focused on mechanisms themselves, but we need to consider what beyond the mechanism is involved in a mechanistic explanation. There has been a tendency among some philosophers who have emphasized the role of mechanisms in explanation to construe the mechanism in the world as itself providing explanation. Accounts such as that advanced by Machamer, Darden, and Craver (2000) try to downplay all epistemic features, including representations of mechanisms, and appeal directly to ontic factors: the component parts, operations, and organization of the mechanism.

Thus, in their account of electrochemical synaptic transmission, they appeal to the synthesis, transport, and vesicle storage of agonist/antagonist neurotransmitters and neuromodulators, their release and diffusion across the synaptic cleft, the process of binding with presynaptic autoreceptors and postsynaptic receptors, reuptake, depolarization, and so forth. They write: "It is through these activities of these entities that we understand how depolarization occurs" (Machamer, Darden, & Craver, 2000, p. 13).

The problem with this ontic view is that mechanisms do not explain themselves.[5] They are operative in the world whether or not there are any scientists engaged in offering explanations. Explanation is an activity of scientists who must contribute mental labor in advancing explanations. Even the advocates of the ontic perspective are unable to avoid invoking epistemic notions, although they try to minimize them. Machamer et al. sometimes refer to "giving a description of the mechanism" (p. 3) and "revealing ... productive relations" (p. 21), and Salmon uses such words as *exhibiting*. But these terms understate the cognitive labor involved. We can appreciate this by revisiting an example put forward by Michael Scriven that purports to show how minimal is the cognitive activity required for explanation. Criticizing Hempel's account in which explanation involves deduction from laws and initial conditions, Scriven says "Hempel's models could not accommodate the case in which one 'explains' by gestures to a Yugoslav garage mechanic what is wrong with a car" (quoted in Salmon, 1984, p. 10). If gesturing is successful in such a situation, however, it is only because the Yugoslav garage mechanic already possesses a large corpus of conceptual knowledge which he brings to the situation and to the cognitive activity in which he engages to understand the gesture.

One factor that motivates the ontic construal of explanation is the desire to resist a particular epistemic perspective on explanation, one that emphasized linguistic representations and deductive arguments. This framework drew its inspiration from the appeal to laws in explanation, as exemplified in Newton's appeal to force laws to explain the behavior of moving bodies, and became, as I noted above, the core of the D-N model of explanation advanced by the positivists. I have already noted that explanation via laws is problematic at least in the life sciences. Rejecting the D-N model, however, should not lead us to adopt an ontic account of explanation. Explanation is fundamentally an epistemic activity performed by scientists. One way to recognize this is to consider that many if not most of the explanations that are advanced in science turn out to be false. In the context of mechanistic explanation, this entails that there is a mismatch between the mechanism proposed and the mechanism actually responsible for the phenomenon. There is a straightforward way to account for this in the idiom of cognitive science: what the scientist advances is a representation of a mechanism—a construal of it—not the mechanism itself. She or he then evaluates the

---

[5] I thank Cory Wright for drawing my attention to the limitation of the ontic construal of mechanistic explanation. For further discussion, see Wright and Bechtel (2006).

representation by using it to reason about how such a mechanism would be expected to behave under a variety of circumstances and testing these expectations against the behavior of the actual mechanism. It is important to keep in focus that such representations and reasoning are *about* mechanisms taken to be operative in the world. In the sense articulated by Brentano (1874), the representations are intentional and may not accurately represent the mechanisms operative in the world.[6]

Although the account of mechanistic explanation needs to construe such explanations as due to epistemic activity, the characterization of the representations and reasoning involved may well be quite different from that of the D-N framework, according to which the representations are propositional and the reasoning is logical inference. Let's begin by considering how scientists present mechanistic explanations. Although they give talks and write papers (and thus employ language), they often resort to diagrams to represent the mechanisms they are proposing, much as engineers resort to diagrams in presenting their designs for new artifacts. Readers of scientific papers often focus on the diagrams first, relying on linguistic accounts (figure captions, text) to help them understand the diagrams. Diagrams are provided for many of the mechanisms discussed in this book, and readers are invited to reflect on how these contribute to their understanding of the various mechanisms. There are good reasons for the centrality of diagrams. A mechanism typically consists of multiple parts performing different operations, often in parallel with one another. By using two spatial dimensions (or with projection, three) to represent relations between parts of a mechanism, including spatial relations, a diagram can convey the organization of a mechanism more readily than text. Strategic use of arrows adds an additional resource that is often effective in representing causal or temporal relations in a mechanism. When these relations become complex, as they do when processes later in a causal chain feed back on those earlier, using arrows to indicate them in a diagram (as in Figures 6.2 and 6.3) enables readers to trace and retrace the various causal pathways as desired.

Diagrams are external representational devices that are used to convey accounts of mechanisms to other scientists, but how do scientists represent mechanisms in their heads? Self reports are notoriously unreliable guides to how our minds work (Nisbett & Wilson, 1977), but nonetheless it is worth noting that

---

[6] Craver's (2007) motivation for adopting the ontic perspective on explanation seems to be the desire to be able to specify the norms of explanation—a good explanation is one that presents a productively complete account of the operative mechanism. He is willing to embrace the view that an account that misrepresents the mechanism is no explanation at all. But there seems to be no reason Craver cannot adopt a representational perspective in specifying the norms for a good explanation. That is, a good explanation would be one that accurately represents the mechanism that actually produces the phenomenon. Moreover, it is difficult to see how to present his normative view without embracing a representational perspective—it is only the representational activities of scientists that can accurately or inaccurately present the mechanism.

many scientists report visualizing the proposed mechanism. There have been relatively few empirical studies seeking to uncover the processes involved in coming to understand a mechanism, but those that have been done support the idea that we rely on our sensory representational systems, especially our visual system, in representing mechanisms.[7] We should also note that scientists often insist on drawing diagrams as they think about mechanisms. Such drawings may not serve simply to convey information, but also to represent the mechanisms for their own further cognitive activity. By setting out the parts and operations in a diagram, scientists may realize there are additional relations that they had not thought about and, on occasion, may recognize that a given arrangement could not produce the phenomenon. In such cases, the diagram is the vehicle for representing the mechanism for the scientist and plays a critical role in his or her thinking.

I have focused so far on representations of mechanisms and have argued that diagrams are at least as important, and perhaps more important, than linguistic representations in scientists' reasoning about mechanisms. But we need to also consider how they reason about them. An important principle recognized by cognitive scientists engaged in modeling reasoning computationally is that it is essential to coordinate the modes of representation and procedures of inference. Philosophers since Aristotle have been so accustomed to thinking of inference as a matter of formal manipulation of propositional representations that it is difficult to conceive of a different mode of inference. As logic operates only on propositional representations, the reasoning of scientists by means of diagrams and visual images cannot be understood as logical inference. They must employ a mode of reasoning suitable to diagrammatic representations. The reasoning task for scientists is to determine how a mechanism generates the phenomenon of interest in virtue of its component parts performing their operations, organized such that the mechanism's activity is well-orchestrated. The kind of reasoning that is needed is reasoning that captures the actual functioning of the mechanism, including both the operations the parts are performing and the way these operations relate to one another.

We can recognize what is needed by noting that until recently most diagrams were static, set down once and then examined. They could not capture the mechanism's dynamics. A major advance in recent years has been the development of ways to animate diagrams so as to show how operations are orchestrated in real time and the effects at each time-step. Animation can thus be viewed as a reasoning tool. Prior to such animation, it was up to the viewer of the diagram to provide the animation mentally by imagining the parts in operation and tracking how they would be affected by one another. Mary Hegarty (1992), in one of the few empirical studies of reasoning

---

[7] As I will discuss in chapter five, the reliance on visual or modality-based representations may not be a special feature of scientific reasoning with diagrams, but may represent a general feature of mental representation.

about mechanisms, coined the phrase *mental animation* for the activity of inferring "the state of one component of the system given information about the states of the other system components, and the relations between the components." She emphasized the importance of mental animation to the activities of designing, troubleshooting, and operating mechanical devices. Obtaining reaction time and eye movement data while people solved problems about relatively simple pulley systems, she investigated the extent to which inference processes are isomorphic to the operation of the physical systems. One way they turned out not to be isomorphic is that the participants made inferences about different components of the system (i.e., individual pulleys) separately and sequentially even though in the physical system the components operated simultaneously. The participants found it considerably harder, however, to make inferences that required them to reason backwards through the system rather than forward, suggesting that they animated the system sequentially from what they represented as the first operation. In this respect they preserved isomorphism with the actual system.

Mechanistic explanation can, accordingly, be understood as an epistemic activity of scientists without restricting it to the sort of epistemic activity envisaged in the D-N approach to explanation. In addition to linguistic representations and inferences that can be characterized in logical terms, they may involve visual presentations and inferences that take the form of simulating the activity of the mechanism. Recognizing the expanded set of representational and reasoning tools available in presenting mechanistic explanations, moreover, will prove particularly fruitful when considering not just how scientists understand mechanisms but how they construct and assess hypotheses about mechanisms and design experiments upon them. A given way of diagramming a hypothesized mechanism, for instance, may suggest possible experiments and a means of simulating it may reveal shortcomings as well as ways to revise the hypothesis.

A final feature of mechanistic explanation that should be noted is that, insofar as it emphasizes the contributions made by parts of a mechanism to its operation, a mechanistic analysis is, in an important sense, reductionistic. However, insofar as it also recognizes the importance of the organization in which the parts are embedded and the context in which the whole mechanism is functioning, it not only sanctions looking to lower levels but also upward to higher levels. I will address the question of reduction in more detail in chapter four, but because the multilevel perspective is so important in understanding the mechanistic framework, I will make a few comments here. What often raises worries about reductionism is the assumption that a reductionist seeks to explain everything at the lower level, that is, in terms of the components that make up mechanisms. This assumes that there is a complete account of phenomena in terms of these components. But at the core of the mechanistic perspective is the assumption that different types of causal relations are found between the components of a mechanism and between the mechanism and things in its environment. A successful mechanistic analysis will identify the operations performed by the parts of a mechanism.[8] But the organization imposed on these operations is crucial. As a result of this organization, the mechanism as a whole is able to engage in its behavior. What it does is different from what its components do, and is described in a different vocabulary. The account of the mechanism straddles the two levels of organization (that of the mechanism and that of its component parts and operations). It involves showing how the mechanism, *when situated in appropriate contexts*, performs its function as a result of the organized set of operations performed by its parts. Thus, far from sanctioning only a focus downward on the components, a mechanistic perspective as well requires an account of engagements with other systems at the same level and, potentially, of the constraints imposed by being incorporated into a higher-level mechanism. In fact, therefore, the mechanistic perspective is inherently multilevel.

1.4   MENTAL MECHANISMS: MECHANISMS THAT PROCESS INFORMATION

The term *mechanism* is as ubiquitous in psychology, cognitive science, and cognitive neuroscience as it is in the domains of biology to which philosophers have appealed in articulating the account offered above of what a mechanism is. The key elements of the conception of mechanism already developed—component parts performing operations, organized so as to realize the phenomenon of interest—extend readily to the way mechanisms are understood in these sciences. Mechanisms identified as responsible for perception, attention, memory, problem solving, and language use all involve brain parts carrying out operations in an organized manner. But there are also some important differences. In most biological disciplines,[9] both the phenomena themselves and the operations proposed to explain them can be adequately characterized as involving physical transformations of material substances. For example, cellular respiration involves a series of reactions that oxidize foodstuffs to carbon dioxide and water while capturing energy in the form of ATP. In one of these stepwise

---

[8] Whether the lower level provides even a complete account of the behavior of the parts of a mechanism is itself in question. The behavior an entity exhibits is often dependent upon context and there is no reason to think that the account of an entity offered by any inquiry considers how it will behave under all conditions but only those which are the focus of inquiry. As engineers are well aware, how a component will behave when inserted into a particular kind of system often needs to be investigated empirically.

[9] Genetics represents a possibly important exception as it has been significantly influenced by an information perspective—genes are often characterized as coding information, which must then be processed in the activity of protein synthesis.

reactions, for example, oxidation of succinate to fumarate is coupled with the reduction of FAD to $FADH_2$.

The performance of a mental activity also involves material changes, notably changes in sodium and potassium concentrations inside and outside neurons, but the characterization of them as mental activities does not focus on these material changes. Rather, it focuses on such questions as how the organism appropriately relates its behavior to features of its distal environment—how it perceives objects and events distal to it, remembers them, and plans actions in light of them. The focus is not on the material changes within the mechanism, but rather on identifying more abstractly those functional parts and operations that are organized such that the mechanism can interact appropriately in its environment. Thus, mental mechanisms are ones that can be investigated taking a physical stance (examining neural structures and their operations) but also, distinctively and crucially, taking an information-processing stance. That is, cognitive scientists identify mental operations and consider how they contribute to the individual's functioning in its environment. Computer programs have provided an influential metaphor for the construal of mental operations, leading to information processing models in which symbolic representations are moved or transformed by symbolic operations. Quite different construals of how organisms function informationally also are possible and may ultimately prove more satisfactory.

To appreciate what is required for mental mechanisms, let us return to Descartes' refusal to apply the mechanical philosophy to the mind. He maintained that reasoning and language were phenomena that could not be accounted for mechanistically. Although he allowed that a mechanism could generate the sounds of a language in response to appropriate inputs (and thus a mechanism was responsible whenever an animal generated a sound in response to an appropriate stimulus), he denied that it could exhibit the flexibility involved in being able to respond to or construct novel sentences:

> For we can easily understand a machine's being constituted so that it can utter words, and even emit some responses to action on it of a corporeal kind, which brings about a change in its organs; for instance, if it is touched in a particular part it may ask what we wish to say to it: if in another part it may exclaim that it is being hurt, and so on. But it never happens that it arranges its speech in various ways, in order to reply appropriately to everything that may be said in its presence, as even the lowest type of man can do (*Discourse on Method*, 5).

Similarly, with respect to reason, Descartes' focus was not on providing an appropriate response to a particular stimulus, but the flexible ability to respond to any situation: "Reason is a universal instrument that can serve all contingencies."

I will return shortly to the emphasis Descartes put on the flexibility and universality exhibited in human reasoning and language use, but before doing so it is important to note a feature Descartes glossed over in the cases he dismissed as merely mechanical. In situations in which a mechanism (human made or animal) produces an appropriate response to a given stimulus, Descartes appealed to the statues in the Royal Garden which moved hydraulically when triggered. Using these as a model, he advanced a similar hydraulic account when he characterized the linkage between sensory stimulation and motor response as mediated by animal spirits. Although not emphasized by Descartes, let's consider the nature of the intermediaries in these cases. They are different in an important respect from the intermediaries in biochemical processes. In the biochemical case, the final products are made from the starting material, and the intermediate steps are all partial transformations of the starting material that culminate in the production of the final product. In contrast, the particular material character of the water in the pipes controlling the statues or the animal spirits in the nervous system controlling human or animal behavior is not itself important, as the later operations are not making something out of the water. Rather, what is important about the water is that it carries *information* about the stimulus so that the mechanism can produce its response even in the absence of direct physical contact with the stimulus. This informational perspective is clarifying for behavior but not for most investigations of material processes as such.

There are a number of different accounts of what information is,[10] but particularly useful in this context is Fred Dretske's (1981) characterization of information in terms of regular effects of a cause that make it possible to infer features of the cause from features of the effect. On this account, information is a causal notion, but when the interest is on the information an effect carries, the effect is of interest not for its own intrinsic properties but for the ability to identify or respond to the cause. The effect stands in or re-presents its cause, and hence is often called a *representation*. I will discuss representations and their use in cognitive explanations in more detail in chapter five, so here I will focus just on the most important features of representations that are required to understand the notion of an information processing mechanism. The intrinsic properties of a representation are often referred to as the *vehicle*, whereas that which it carries information about is the *content*. Thunder serves as a simple example: The sound

---

[10] The best known account is the theory of information developed by Claude Shannon (1948). Shannon, a mathematician employed by Bell Laboratories, provided a measure of the amount of information that could be transmitted over a channel such as telephone line in terms of the variability of the information being transmitted. In the simplest case he considered that, just two states of the signal, on and off, would be equally probable. He introduced the term *bit* (binary unit) for the information transmitted by selecting one of these alternatives rather than the other. A single bit could distinguish between two alternatives, two bits could distinguish between four alternatives, and three bits between eight. The channel capacity was then characterized in terms of the bits of information that could be successfully transmitted.

wave reaching a person's ear after lightning is the vehicle, and the information carried about the electrical discharge is the content.

What is critical to understanding an information processing mechanism is how content is changed as a result of causal operations that change vehicles, for it is in virtue of content that the mechanism is linked to the states outside the mechanism. The importance of focusing on content can be missed when focusing on very simple devices. Consider a classic thermostat, which employs a bimetallic strip that coils and uncoils depending on the ambient temperature. When the temperature cools to the point at which heat is desired, the metal makes contact with another piece of metal and completes the electrical circuit that controls the gas flow to the furnace. Tracing the causal process may seem sufficient for explaining the behavior of the furnace in going on and off, and we may overlook the fact that the content carried by the coiling of the metal is the ambient temperature. By way of contrast, consider a programmable thermostat, which adjusts the target temperature at different times of day. Here, there is a more complex relation linking the sensing of the ambient temperature and the control of gas flow, and just tracing the sequence of causal operations no longer suffices. One needs to understand how time of day is being tracked and how the mechanism that tracks it is coordinated with the mechanism tracking the temperature so as to produce an output that takes both types of information into account.

The need to adopt multiple points of view in understanding an information processing mechanism was highlighted in David Marr's differentiation of three modes of analysis. Marr introduced the need for adopting different modes of analysis by considering the relative stagnation he viewed as afflicting neuroscience research on vision by the 1970s. Research in the 1950s and 1960s had been successful in deciphering some of the information processing operations in the brain: Horace Barlow (1953) had identified ganglion cells in the frog's retina that served as bug detectors, David Hubel and Torsten Wiesel (1962; 1968) had demonstrated cells in primary visual cortex that functioned as edge detectors, and Marr (1969) himself had shown the capacity of Purkinje cells in the cerebellar cortex to learn motor patterns. Marr contended that the stagnation after the initial promise indicated the need to adopt a different perspective on what the brain is doing, which he characterized as a different *level*[11] *of understanding*:

> There must exist an additional level of understanding at which the character of the information-processing tasks carried out during perception are analyzed and

---

[11] There is a serious potential risk of conflating Marr's notion of level of understanding with the notion of level involved in characterizing levels of organization in mechanisms. Entities at different levels of organization stand in a part–whole relation to one another, whereas Marr's levels of understanding involve different perspectives or modes of analysis directed at the same entity or process.

understood in a way that is independent of the particular mechanisms and structures that implement them in our heads. This was what was missing—the analysis of the problem as an information processing task (Marr, 1982, p. 19).

The goal in adopting this perspective is to characterize the task being performed by the information-processing system, why it needs to be performed, and the constraints the task itself places on how it is performed. Marr referred to the resulting account as an abstract *computational theory*. This label can be misleading, as computational theory for Marr is concerned not with how computation is performed, but with the task requiring computation.

Since the computational theory addresses what the mechanism is doing, this is the perspective that focuses on the mechanism in context. The visual system receives information about wavelength and intensity of light reaching the retina and must, for example, determine the identity or trajectory of the object confronting the organism. The two other perspectives Marr proposed focus on the inside of the mechanism and how its components enable the mechanism to perform the task identified in the computational theory. Researchers targeting the level of *representation and algorithm* ask how the mechanism executes a computation—how the inputs and outputs are represented in the mechanism and the steps through which the mechanism transforms the input to generate the output. Those targeting the *hardware implementation* focus on the physical structures and processes the realize the representations and operations on them (see Table 1.1). Marr noted that the three perspectives are coupled, but only loosely: settling on a task and hardware constrains, but does not determine, the choice of an algorithm (e.g., a parallel algorithm can always be implemented on a serial machine.)

Table 1.1   Marr's Three Levels at Which Any Machine Carrying Out An Information Processing Task Must Be Understood

Computational Theory	Representation and Algorithm	Hardware Implementation
What is the goal of the computation, why is it appropriate, and what is the logic of the strategy by which it can be carried out?	How can this computational theory be implemented? In particular, what is the representation for the input and output, and what is the algorithm for the transformation?	How can the representation and algorithm be realized physically?

Source: Adapted from Marr, D.C. (1982). *Vision: A computation investigation into the human representational system and processing of visual information.* San Francisco, CA: Freeman, p. 25.

Figure 1.3   An information flow diagram in which the box designates an operation to be performed on the input information to produce the output information.

A somewhat different perspective on relating information processing accounts with accounts of underlying physical processes was offered by Stephen Palmer and Ruth Kimchi (1986). They began with the notion of an informational description of the mental process in which it is described as beginning with input information, performing an operation on it, and arriving at output information. They represent the process using an *information flow diagram* in which the operation is represented as a black box that transforms the input information into the output information (Figure 1.3). To arrive at an account of how information is processed, they introduced the notion of *recursive decomposition* according to which the overall mental process is decomposed into "a number of component informational events and a flow diagram that specifies the temporal ordering relations among the components" (Palmer, 1999, p. 74). Such decomposition is recursive in that the processes identified in a given decomposition can be further decomposed, until at some point one reaches "a flow diagram in which the boxes correspond to the functions performed by individual electrical components, such as resistors, capacitors, and transistors" (Ibid.). At this point one clearly identifies a *physical embodiment* (physical implementation) of the processes, but we should note that if the operations in the last iteration of decomposition are embodied, so are all of the ones generated in previous iterations, including the operation with which one started.[12] Figure 1.4 provides an illustration of such recursive decomposition of the mind as proposed by Palmer and Kimchi. It is noteworthy that although there is a dominant order from input to output in the operation of an information-processing device, Palmer does include recurrent processes that feed back and alter the processes that supply inputs to later processes.

---

[12] Palmer and Kimchi's account mirrors in some respects the account Daniel Dennett (1971) provided of the relation between two of the three stances he identifies as involved in understanding intentional systems. To account for the ability of a system to have intentional states such as believing something about the world (a characterization from the intentional stance), he argued that one must turn to the design perspective and specify the operations required to behave as someone with such a belief would. He called the components performing the various operations homunculi, and proposed that to show how intelligent intentional action is performed in a physical system one must repeatedly decompose homunculi into less intelligent ones until one reaches homunculi whose task can be performed by a simple physical device. At this point one has adopted the physical stance.

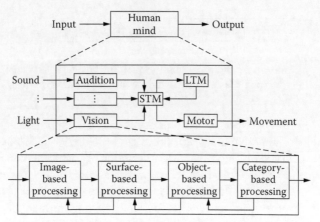

Figure 1.4 An example of the recursive decomposition of mental activity as proposed by Palmer and Kimchi (1986). A proposed decomposition of the mind into mental operations is shown in the middle, and a further decomposition of one of those operations, visual processing, into further operations is shown at the bottom.

In the discussion of Marr and of Palmer and Kimchi I have emphasized the linkage between the representational/algorithmic perspective and the physical perspective. The basic strategy for linking them is to maintain that operations in the ultimate algorithmic decomposition correspond to specifiable physical processes characterized in the implementational account. Discovering how to maintain such correspondences was one of the major feats in creating modern computers—the operations of physical switches that constitute the vehicles of representation are designed to correspond to relations between representational contents. But conceptually the roots of this idea are much more general than the application to computers and apply to a variety of ways in which humans have used symbol systems such as natural languages.

Rules of logical inference, as articulated both by Aristotle and by modern logicians, specify transformations on vehicles (symbol strings comprised of words) that appropriately respect the content (e.g., the resulting symbol strings will be true whenever the initial symbol strings are true). So as to avoid delving into the complications with unpacking the semantics of truth, let us consider a simpler example. A numeral is a vehicle whose contents might be the numerosity of the items being counted. Thus, the numeral "3" in the expression "3 apples" might be viewed as having the content that one could put the numerals *1, 2,* and *3* into a one-to-one mapping with the apples in the set. Rules of arithmetic allow for operations on numerals that respect the numerosity of those items so that, for example, performing the addition operation produces a result that corresponds to the process of enumerating the union of the two sets. Humans can learn the

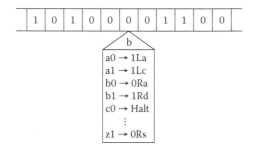

Figure 1.5   A schematic representation of a Turing machine. The read-head shown in the center reads the number (0 or 1) on the tape and, depending on the state it is in (shown in the triangle on the read-head), executes the appropriate rule. As in this case the machine is in state b and reading a 0 it writes a 0, moves one square to the right, and enters state a.

rules of arithmetic, and in the era before computers, some people were trained to execute complex routines by iteratively reading numerals written on paper, performing an operation, and writing new numerals on the paper. Such people were called *computers* and they, in fact, provided the inspiration for Turing (1936; see also Post, 1936) in developing his ideas of computation with a Turing machine.[13]

An individual Turing machine is simply a hypothetical mechanical device that carries out a specified series of operations on an input string (much in the manner of a human computer) to generate an output string. The input string is realized as a tape (the analogue of the paper on which the human computer writes) comprised of squares in which the symbols 0 and 1 are inscribed (one symbol per square). The operations are executed by a read-head that has a finite number of internal states and rules for responding to an input on the square being read. Depending on its current state, it responds by writing a new symbol on the tape, moving one square left or right, and changing or retaining its state (Figure 1.5).

---

[13] Systems of natural deduction in logic have the same character. The set of rules included in a system of natural deduction are designed to enable the derivation of any and only conclusions that are true whenever the initial premises are true. Truth is a semantic relation (that is, a relation between symbols and what they represent), but when constructing a proof from within a system of natural deduction it is not necessary to investigate what propositions are true or what makes them true. The natural deduction rules are simply applied to the propositions given as premises to generate the conclusion. (To determine which rules are truth preserving and hence candidates for inclusion in a system of natural deduction, one needs to step outside the syntactic framework and adopt a model theoretic perspective to show that in any model in which the statements to which the rule can be applied are true, the statement resulting from applying the rules will also be true.) Such rules are referred to as formal since they apply to statements in virtue of their syntactical form.

Turing's contribution was to demonstrate that for any well-defined series of formal operations (such as those of arithmetic) one could design a Turing machine that could carry it out. Also in the 1930s Alonzo Church independently proposed that any process for which there is a decision procedure could be carried out through such a series of formal operations. Accordingly, the Church-Turing thesis proposes that any decidable process can be implemented in a Turing machine.

Descartes might be intrigued to observe the operation of an individual Turing machine, given that it responds differently to different input strings, but ultimately he would probably not be particularly impressed. It has a richer repertoire of behavior than the statues in the Royal Gardens, but it still is limited in the set of responses it produces, and once one knows the range of states and the rules applying to them, its behavior is rather straightforward. But Turing also showed that, in principle, there existed a Turing machine, called the *universal Turing machine*, that could compute not just a single function, but any function that could be computed. The same transition from a machine designed to perform a single computation to one that could, in principle, compute any function, was played out in the development of actual computers in the 1940s and 1950s. The first electronic computer, ENIAC, had to be programmed by hand—technicians had to install electrical cables as needed to perform the desired computation. Once the cables were fixed, the computer was, in essence, a single Turing machine. But with the second computer, EDVAC, John von Neumann introduced the idea of storing programs along with data in the memory of the computer. Processing occurred in cycles in which both data and instructions were read from memory into the central processing unit (CPU), the specified operations were performed, and the results stored in memory. Such computers are universal in Turing's sense—but for limitations on memory, they could compute any computable function.

The Turing machine and the digital computer in principle answer Descartes' concern that a physical mechanism could only respond in a preset manner and not show the flexibility to comprehend novel sentences or solve new problems exhibited by humans. Assuming that comprehending a sentence or solving a problem involves computation, in principle a computer can execute the function (perform the behavior). Moreover, there are arguments that only a mechanism with the computational power of a universal Turing machine can exhibit the same range of responses as human minds. In some of his earliest work in linguistics, Chomsky (1956) showed that an automaton with the computational power of a Turing machine is required to generate the set of syntactic structures found in a natural language. The challenge of actually developing a computer that can comprehend the range of sentences humans can reason in the manner of humans remains unrealized, but the essential point that a machine can exhibit the requisite flexibility in performance is well-demonstrated.

As noted above, the cognitive tradition is often characterized as rooted in the computer as a metaphor for the mind. It is probably not incidental that the cognitive tradition in psychology developed at the same time as the creation of digital computers. The computer provided a powerful exemplar of a mechanism that engaged in processing information. Engineers designed computers to carry out tasks by operating on representations inside the computer that respected relations between the entities in the world that constituted the content of those representations. The initial motivation for developing ENIAC was to produce tables that would facilitate the proper targeting of artillery even when positioned on unstable terrain such as sand. Thus, computers provided a model of how to bridge Marr's computational and representational/algorithmic perspectives. Perhaps even more influential was the relation between software and hardware in a computer, which provided a model of how to bridge from the representational/algorithmic perspective to the implementational perspective. As long as there is a proper match between operations specified in the machine code into which a program is compiled and the physical operations in the computer itself, one could develop software to perform tasks and know that the computer once programmed would behave appropriately.

The computer, though, has also been a misleading model for thinking about cognition. One particularly misleading feature is the fact that computers have been engineered so that the same software can run on different hardware. Philosophers have characterized this relation as one of *multiple realization* and have sometimes drawn the inference that the realizations do not matter. Insofar as the information processing algorithms are the analogue of the software and the brain is the analogue of the hardware, the conclusion has been that the brain is not particularly relevant to the nature of mind—a mind could be built out of any hardware so long as it runs the appropriate software. I will return to the issue of multiple realizability in chapter four and argue there that it does not have the implications for understanding mental activity generally ascribed to it. For now it suffices to note that even with computers it is not the case that software runs the same on different hardware. Typically, different hardware makes some operations easier to perform and others more difficult, a difference that shows up in the time different hardware devices require to perform the same software operations. But more to the point is that general purpose computers have been designed to maximize the independence of information processing operations from the underlying hardware. There is little reason to think this is true of the brain. Brain components were not designed to be universal computing machines, but to perform particular tasks important to the organism. Brain mechanisms, accordingly, are far more likely to be structured and organized in ways particularly suitable to the tasks they must perform. As a result, the physical processes may provide highly useful guidance to scientists seeking to understand how the mind/brain works.

In fact, it is not the computer itself but the broader idea of information processing that proved influential in the development of the sciences of the mind/brain. What information processing requires is that the parts and operations within the mechanism be appropriate for the processing of information. The conception of an information processing mechanism was clearly articulated by Kenneth Craik (1943), who proposed that external phenomena were represented in words or other symbols, these were manipulated within the mechanism, and the transformed representations were decoded into external processes such as behavior:

> Thought is a term for the conscious working of a highly complex machine, built of parts having dimensions where the classical laws of mechanics are still very nearly true, and having dimensions where space is, to all intents and purposes, Euclidean. This mechanism, I have argued, has the power to represent, or parallel, certain phenomena in the external world as a calculating machine can parallel the development of strains in a bridge (p. 85).

As Craik worked out this view, the mind produces models of external events and can use these to predict future events and to plan accordingly. (For further development of this proposal see Washan, 2006.)

I will conclude with an example of research on mental activity that played an important role in the emergence of information processing theories but is not particularly linked to an understanding of computers. In 1953 Colin Cherry, working in an electronics research laboratory at MIT, investigated what he termed "the cocktail party effect," the ability of a listener to focus on one conversation even when in an environment, such as a cocktail party, in which many different people are all speaking. He did this using a technique known as *dichotic listening* in which a person, wearing headphones, hears different messages through the two ears. The person was required to shadow one message (repeat it back aloud), and Cherry found that his subjects noticed virtually nothing about the content of the other message (including when the language changed or the speech was presented in reverse), although they could detect changes in some of its physical features such as whether it contained speech or tones and whether the voice was that of a male or a female.

Cherry's research with dichotic listening was pursued by British psychologist Donald Broadbent, whose research developed out of the challenges faced by air traffic controllers to selectively focus their attention on the planes for which they were responsible. His 1958 book *Perception and Communication* was a pioneering work in cognitive psychology and served to make attention a focal area of research after a half-century hiatus during the era of behaviorism (whose influence was felt most acutely in the United States). In this book Broadbent advanced a model of how the mind works to explain Cherry's results and his own results obtained using the dichotic listening paradigm. The core of his model was the assumption that there is a limited capacity serial channel through which information can be processed.

The inputs from the two ears, however, arrive in parallel and so he proposed a filter (such as is used in audio equipment to remove undesired sounds) that restricted access to the limited channel. To explain Cherry's results, he posited that the filter would exclude the content from the unattended input but would allow information about the physical character of the signal to pass. In his own experiments, sequences of three digits were presented to each ear. One ear might be presented with 8 2 3 while the other would receive 6 9 4. The subjects were to repeat back all the numbers they heard, and Broadbent found that they strongly preferred to repeat the sequence to one ear and then the sequence to the other (e.g., 8 2 3 6 9 4) rather than the items of each pair successively (e.g., 8 6 2 9 3 4). To account for this, Broadbent proposed that prior to the filter there were buffers which held the contents from each channel temporarily so that first the content of one buffer was passed through the filter, then the contents of the other.

The virtue of Broadbent's model was that it made a number of specific predictions, many of which turned out to be false. Moray (1959) found, for example, that a subject would recognize and attend to his or her name when it appeared in the unattended channel, thus indicating that some of the content presented to it was processed. Anne Treisman (1964) created a situation in which the content of a story shifted from one channel to another, with the story in the second channel ending and a new one beginning on the first channel. When subjects were shadowing the first channel, they would spontaneously shift to the second channel at the crossover point before recovering and continuing with the new content on the first channel. This also indicated that content from the unattended channel was being processed. Treisman proposed a selectively tuned filter that could adjust its criteria depending upon processing later in the system. Such a filter might admit the contents of a story being heard. Other experiments produced results that seemed to require even greater modifications in the account. Gray and Wedderburn (1960) developed a variant on Broadbent's task which presented the sequence "mice two cheese" to one ear and "eight eat five" to the other. In this case, rather than reporting all the contents received by one ear before reporting those presented to the other, subjects would respond "mice eat cheese eight two five." This led Deutsch and Deutsch (1963) to conclude that the capacity constraint or bottleneck did not affect the processing of the stimuli but rather the response. Theirs was a late selection theory of attention in contrast to Broadbent's early selection theory.

Broadbent's theory of attention and the competitors to which it gave rise are all examples of accounts of information processing mechanisms in that the operations are characterized in terms of the changes they make in an informational structure. Some philosophical accounts construe neuroscience accounts as then providing the implementational side of information processing accounts, but in fact many accounts advanced in neuroscience are also information processing accounts.

In chapter three I will describe research that has largely been done by neuro-scientists in working out accounts of the processes involved in visual perception. Like information processing models in psychology, these accounts emphasize how information is transformed through the stages of processing visual input. They differ in emphasizing the parts of the brain that are performing the various operations, whereas cognitive psychology models, such as Broadbent's, are often silent with respect to the identity of the responsible brain parts.

If not neuroscience, what then provides the implementational perspective on these information processing accounts? The point to note is that the implemen-tation perspective is a different perspective on the same entities and processes described from the information processing perspective. In the language I used above, the implementational perspective focuses on the vehicle, not its content, whereas the representational and algorithmic analysis focuses on the content, not the vehicle. If the mechanism is appropriately designed to perform its informa-tion processing function, however, the vehicles and the operations they undergo must be appropriate for the content they carry. One could, in principle, equally track the processes in the mechanism in terms of the vehicles or the contents. However, insofar as the objective is to explain how the mechanism enables an agent (organism) to coordinate behavior with its environment, the characteriza-tion of processes in terms of content is usually the more informative.

1.5   DISCOVERING MENTAL MECHANISMS

In discussing reasoning about mechanisms above I focused on the situation in which scientists have already developed an account of a mechanism and are using it to explain a phenomenon of interest. Much of the excitement in science, however, comes from discoveries that go beyond what was already known. In the era in which the D-N model of explanation reigned, philosophers largely fore-swore any attempt to analyze discovery. Adopting Hans Reichenbach's distinc-tion between the *context of discovery* and the *context of justification*, they saw the latter as the proper venue for deploying the conservative, constrained tools of logical inference. The kinds of reasoning involved in discovery must instead be ampliative and diverse. Going beyond what is known calls upon imaginative resources in which analogy, mental images, "leaps of thought," etc., can play a key role. Recognizing that their favored tool of logic was at best incomplete as a tool for understanding discovery, and preferring precision, D-N philosophers targeted the context of justification. To them, limiting their focus in this way was a virtue.

When the quest for explanation is a quest for mechanisms, however, the pro-cess of discovery seems far more tractable. The very conception of a mechanism gives some guidance as to what needs to be done to arrive at an understanding of a mechanism. Insofar as a mechanism consists of parts performing operations in an organized fashion, what is needed to arrive at an account of a mechanism are means to identify the parts, determine the operations they are performing, and assess how they are organized. Although sometimes proposals for mechanisms may result from carefully observing mechanisms in operation and thinking creatively about what might be transpiring inside them, more often in real science they are the result of active experimental engagement with the mechanism—manipulating it in various ways so as to extract clues about what its parts are, what they are doing, and how they are organized.

Before considering experiments proper, it is worth examining observation more carefully. For the logical positivists and logical empiricists, who set the agenda for much of twentieth-century philosophy of science, observation, especially visual observation, played a critical role in procuring evidence. But these philosophers focused mostly on observation statements (Neurath, 1932; Carnap, 1936; 1937; Quine, 1969; 1973; 1975) and largely neglected the fact that scientists often must intervene on and alter the phenomena of nature before they even begin to record observations. As I noted above, one of the first philosophers to draw attention to this was Ian Hacking (1983) in his account of how investigators procure evidence through the light microscope. Although it is tempting to think of microscopes as simply magnifying an image to get better resolution, their complex optics can easily generate distortions, as most dramatically demonstrated by the severe chromatic and spherical aberrations of pre-nineteenth century microscopes. Moreover, in order to create images of sufficient contrast to be able to distinguish structures in biological specimens, researchers had to employ fixatives and stains. Each chemical altered the material in its own way, prior to any observation.

That such interventions are required to produce observational reports with instruments as apparently straightforward as the microscope opens the possibility that what is ultimately observed and reported is not an accurate reflection of the phenomenon being observed, but rather an artifact of the intervention. How to differentiate between reliable observations and artifacts is a major epistemological question scientists confront regularly, albeit one that is not often discussed in philosophy. Naively, one might think that this question could be answered by appealing to the theoretical understanding of how instruments work and are used to secure data. Often, however, scientists must make these judgments without such a theoretical understanding of the interventions through which the evidence was procured. The silver nitrate stain that Camillo Golgi (1873) introduced, which played a pivotal role in establishing that neurons were individual cells, provides an extreme but illustrative example. Silver nitrate stains only a small number of neurons in a preparation. Over a century and a quarter later, however, it is still not understood why it works in this manner. Moreover, even when scientists have a theory about how an intervention works, changes in that theory typically do not lead scientists to reassess the evidence based on it:

> Visual displays are curiously robust under changes of theory. You produce a display, and have a theory about why a tiny specimen looks like that. Later you reverse the theory of your microscope, and you still believe the representation. Can theory really be the source of our confidence that what we are seeing is the way things are? (Hacking, 1983. p. 199)

In place of theory, Hacking and others have focused on whether evidence produced by a new intervention agrees with that from other, generally already established interventions (Hacking, 1983; Wimsatt, 1981). We have learned from their investigations that converging evidence frequently plays a role in the assessment of new interventions, but there are two reasons to doubt the primacy of this criterion. First, the main interest in new interventions is that they produce evidence not obtained by other methods. In just these findings of greatest interest one cannot invoke agreement with other already accepted methodologies. Hence, at most the comparison with results of existing techniques represents a minimal check on the reliability of the new technique. For example, mid-twentieth-century scientists accepted new findings obtained from electron microscopes at high magnification, based on demonstrations that their results at low magnification were consistent with those from light microscopes. Second, relating the evidence generated with one instrument or technique to that produced by another frequently is not straightforward but depends upon a complex set of inferences. Researchers have to develop ways to bridge between techniques, often by modifying the new technique until it produces results appropriately aligned with the older technique. This undercuts the assumption that the two techniques are really independent. The fact that researchers have to work to bring a new technique into correspondence with results from more established techniques points to a different way to understand attempts to relate new techniques to older ones: Such attempts serve as means of calibrating the new technique (Bechtel, 2002). Not every technique can be calibrated to agree with another, so success in this enterprise does point to the reliability of the new technique (assuming, of course, that the old technique itself was reliable). But the main focus is calibration, not corroboration.

In other work (Bechtel, 1995; 2000; 2006; in press) I have identified two additional factors that seem to loom large in scientists' evaluation of whether an intervention produces reliable evidence or is compromised by artifacts. The first is that the intervention produces repeatable and well-defined results that exhibit a definite pattern. Although artifacts unfortunately can often pass this test, the *failure* of an intervention to produce clear and repeatable results is a clear deficiency that makes it suspect. The second factor is the degree to which the evidence produced through the intervention supports or coheres with what are regarded as plausible theories or models of the phenomenon.[14] Lacking a plausible theory that could explain the results often leads scientists to be skeptical of the results themselves. For example, one of the structures Golgi (1898) identified in cells was a reticular structure that came to bear his name: the Golgi body or Golgi apparatus. Many investigators, including two future Nobel laureates who later did important research on the Golgi apparatus—George Palade and Albert Claude (1949a; 1949b)—dismissed it as an artifact in the first half of the twentieth century (for details, see Bechtel, 2006, chapter four). Once the Golgi apparatus assumed a functional role in the mechanisms identified for exporting proteins from cells, claims that it was an artifact vanished. There is irony in the fact that scientists often evaluate evidence by whether it fits theories, as these theories are themselves supported by such evidence. This is a problem for a foundationalist philosopher who seeks to show how theoretical knowledge can be built up from or grounded in evidence. But insofar as it turns out that such a factor does figure in scientists' judgments, a philosopher committed to a naturalistic perspective in philosophy of science must take it seriously.

My concern here is less with how scientists rule out artifacts than with the insight that evidence is often generated through active intervention in the phenomenon being investigated. The interventions I have identified so far are ones required simply to secure observations. But in general, to discover the parts, operations, and organization of a mechanism requires a further kind of intervention, a kind commonly identified with experiments. In an experiment on a mechanism an investigator intervenes to alter its functioning so as to gain insight about what goes on in it when functioning normally. A major reason experimentation is required to understand mechanisms is that most mechanisms, whether naturally occurring or manufactured by humans, do not reveal their parts, operations, or organization to the observer or user. These are camouflaged in the smooth functioning of the mechanism. As a result, most of us cannot provide an accurate account of how things work—not even the computers, cars, and microwaves that we use daily. We are even less informed about biological mechanisms, in us or in plants or animals around us, although we often have a great deal of personal experience with them.

My focus will be on experiments directed towards figuring out how a mechanism operates, but it is worth noting that often experiments are required to delineate the phenomenon for which a mechanism is responsible. One reason for this is that it is not always clear what the are variables that influence how the mechanism operates and thus are crucial for the occurrence of the phenomenon.

---

[14] Note the difference between cohering with a theory of the phenomenon (as discussed here) and having a theory of the intervention (as discussed above).

Interventions that control the values of variables thought to affect the mechanism and record the effects these have on the functioning of the mechanism help provide a detailed account of the phenomenon to be explained. Sometimes refining the understanding of the manner in which the mechanism functions provides clues to its internal operation, but even when it does not do so, it provides critical information for evaluating proposed mechanistic explanations—if the hypothesized mechanism would not behave as the actual one does, then it falls short as an explanation of the phenomenon.

For an intervention to provide information about the operations within a mechanism, it must be coupled with a means for detecting the effects of the intervention. The informative effects may often be difficult to capture and require careful recording and analysis. By focusing on the points of intervention and detection, we can systematize the various ways of conducting experiments on mechanisms, as summarized in Table 1.2. To begin, there are two basic ways of intervening on a mechanism:

- Altering the input to the mechanism or the conditions under which it functions
- Going inside the mechanism itself and altering the operation of one or more of its component parts

Similarly, there are two levels at which the effects of such interventions may be detected:

- A change in the overall behavior of the mechanism
- A change in one of the component operations that together produce the overall behavior

Table 1.2   Strategies for Experimenting on Mental Mechanisms

	Detect change in component operation within the mechanism	Detect change in overall behavior of the mechanism
Intervene by altering the input to the mechanism or the conditions under which it functions	Single-cell recording, ERP, PET, fMRI experiments	Behavioral experiments using reaction times or error measures
Intervene by altering the operation of one or more parts of the mechanism	Lesion or stimulation experiments (detecting effect on another component)	Lesion or stimulation experiments (with global measure of effect)

Each of these modes of intervention and detection provides different information about mental mechanisms. None of them alone provides a direct and complete account; rather, each is partial and potentially misleading. Moreover, these techniques have been developed by practitioners in different disciplines and typically involve different subject populations. Cognitive psychologists have tended to remain at the periphery both for intervening and recording effects and generally have focused on normally functioning adult humans (often college undergraduates who are taking psychology classes). Neuroscientists, in contrast, tend to intervene or record directly from the brain (although most often if the intervention is directly on the brain, the effects are recorded in overall behavior, and vice versa). For ethical reasons, much of this research is carried out on nonhuman animals, often cats and monkeys, creating the challenge of relating the results to humans. In the last couple of decades, with the advent of techniques that enable recording, and sometimes intervening, on the brains of humans without causing permanent changes, a new interdisciplinary field known as *cognitive neuroscience* has developed that draws upon both the behavioral tasks designed by cognitive psychologists and means for intervening or measuring effects within the brain from neuroscience. In the sections below I will focus on how each of these modes of inquiry provides information about mental mechanisms while noting some of their limitations. (As the lower left cell in the previous table effectively combines the strategies identified in the upper left and lower right cells, and examples of such research are relatively rare, it is not discussed further.)

1.5.1   Behavioral Experiments

What distinguishes behavioral experiments is that the researcher does not *directly* manipulate or measure any of the operations within a mechanism. Rather the researcher manipulates the task posed to the subject in ways that differentially invoke internal operations. For example, in the dual task paradigm (Posner & Boies, 1981), a subject is required to perform two tasks simultaneously. If performance is reduced on either task, that indicates that the two tasks employed a common operation. Although sometimes the effects of interventions are measured in terms of accuracy, the most widely employed behavioral measure is the time required to perform an experimental task. The basic strategy was developed in the mid-nineteenth century by the Dutch psychologist Frans Cornelis Donders (1868). To determine the time it took a person to perform particular mental operations, such as making a decision, he measured the time required to perform a task that required a decision and subtracted from it the time required to perform an otherwise identical task in which no decision was required (this approach came to be known as the *subtractive method*). In his initial study, he presented shocks to the left or right foot and required subjects to respond by pressing a telegraph key with either the left or right hand. In the nondecision condition he informed subjects before each trial which foot would receive the shock, so all they had to do was react as soon as the shock was perceived. In the decision condition subjects did not know in advance which foot would be shocked. As a result, after experiencing each shock they had to decide which foot had been shocked before responding. Donders determined that it required an additional 1/15th of a second to respond in the decision condition.[15] He wrote of his accomplishment "This was the first determination of the duration of a well-defined mental process. It concerned the decision in a choice and an action of the will in response to that decision."[16]

A critical assumption of Donders' method is that additional operations involve a pure insertion into a sequence of cognitive operations without altering the execution of those other operations. To assess the validity of this assumption, Saul Sternberg (1969) proposed an extension of Donders' method. In what he called the *additive factors* approach, researchers used multiple manipulations, each of which should have an independent effect on the time required for a particular component operation. In his best-known paradigm, subjects memorized a list of items and then received a series of probe items for which a yes/no recognition response was required (push the "yes" button if the probe is on the memorized list; push the "no" button otherwise). Probe identification time could be affected by the number of items on the list to be memorized, and memory-scanning time could be affected by the degree of physical degradation in the probes used to test recognition. If the times added by each manipulation are additive (independent), that is taken as evidence that each elicits a separate process.

Confronted with the necessity of figuring out how a mechanism operates without direct access to its components, psychologists have devised ingenious tasks. Another example from Sternberg's research is illustrative (Sternberg, 1966). To study how symbolic information is retrieved from short-term memory he provided subjects with a list of digits, asked them whether a particular digit was on the list, and measured the time it took them to respond. He found that regardless of whether the probe item was on the list, it took subjects on average $392.7 + 37.9 s$ ms to respond, where s was the number of items on the list to be remembered. Sternberg drew two important conclusions from this research: (a) As the time required depended on the number of items on the list, items had to be recalled serially; and (b) as the time required was the same for positive and negative answers, subjects were performing an exhaustive search before answering, even if the probe item was the first recalled.

Patterns of responses in tasks such as those Sternberg used have been interpreted as revealing internal operations—in this case, a complete serial review of

---

[15] More typically the time for decision is found to be somewhat longer—approximately 250 milliseconds.

[16] From the English translation, Donders (1969, p. 419).

all stored representations prior to responding to a query. These inferences tend to be controversial. For example, when evidence is advanced that performing an additional task simultaneously with a task of interest affects performance, it is hard to avoid disagreements about which limited resource is responsible. It might be that what produces the increased reaction time in the task of interest is something peripheral to it. And when there is no such increase, that does not establish that the two tasks are not relying on a common resource. Instead, the common resource may be sufficiently plentiful that no decrement resulted when it was drawn upon in both tasks simultaneously.

Given the challenges in behavioral research, one might wonder why researchers seeking to identify the parts, operation, and organization inside a mechanism would choose to limit themselves in this way. If that is the goal, why not go inside the mechanism and examine the components directly? There are a variety of answers to this question. Sometimes, as in studies of the human mind, there are ethical limitations on using invasive interventions and measurements. Even when direct intervention on internal processes or measurement of them is possible, it often is not informative except in the context of knowing what the mechanism as a whole is doing. The art of designing good behavioral tasks is critical even in studies that record from within the brain. Finally, behavioral experimentation that focuses on what operations are required to generate a response given a stimulus is often successful on its own in providing critical information about what is going on inside.

1.5.2 Experiments That Manipulate Internal Operations

I turn now to strategies that perform manipulations inside the mechanism and measure the effect on the behavior of the mechanism as a whole. There are two obvious ways to manipulate an operation within a mechanism. First, the component part that performs the operation can be disabled either temporarily or permanently. Conversely the part can be stimulated so as to make the operation faster or more likely. In the context of studying the mind/brain, these strategies generally are undertaken by neuroscientists and are known as *lesion experiments* and *stimulation experiments,* respectively. In either case, researchers generally detect the consequences in the mechanism's output—i.e., in its behavior—although it also would be possible to detect the consequences for particular component parts and operations internal to the mechanism.

Brain lesions can originate either unintentionally from illness or injury or intentionally from interventions by neuroscientists that destroy or remove targeted areas of neural tissue. Lesion studies in humans generally involve cases of head injury or stroke—"experiments of nature" that can be difficult to interpret because they do not specifically target working parts of the brain. In stroke, for instance, whatever tissue receives its blood supply from a particular vascular bed is affected, and this does not map neatly onto areas of tissue regarded as working parts based on architectonics and function. In animals, and in human patients for whom there is hope of therapeutic benefit, surgical cutting or electrical current can target known or suspected working parts. Damage can be more extensive than intended, however, so neurotoxins that target specific cell types have been an important advance in recent years. For example, 6-hydroxydopamine targets cells whose axons are innervated by dopamine and norepinephrine. Regardless of the method used to experimentally induce a lesion, there are limitations to the use of animal models for human brain function. In many cases the behavior of interest is not exhibited in animals and even when it is, researchers must determine how to relate brain areas in other species to those in humans.

Whatever the source of a lesion, the researcher's goal is to identify a psychological deficit associated with it and then to infer from that deficit what contribution the damaged area made to normal psychological activity. A common way of construing lesion experiments is to infer that the damaged part of the brain was responsible for the activity that is impaired. In a celebrated early application of this approach, Paul Broca (1861) connected the first impaired function in his patient Leborgne (articulate speech) to the part of his brain that Broca claimed had sustained the earliest damage (long known as *Broca's area*). This presupposes a view of the mind as comprised of independent modules, a view espoused especially by evolutionary psychologists but widely criticized as inconsistent with what we know of brain organization and function. A much weaker interpretation is that the damaged area was in some way necessary to the normal performance of the affected activity, but that other areas may also be involved, perhaps much more directly. On this view, the fact that Leborgne experienced problems in speaking articulately licenses only the inference that Broca's area is somehow necessary for articulate speech; it may or may not be the central locus of this function. One problem for even this minimal interpretation is that the brain is a constantly adapting structure: once an area is removed, processing in other areas also is altered. The damaged area may even have nothing to do with the impaired activity; instead, the damage to it may have affected the area that is actually responsible for the activity or may simply have altered the signals it receives.

The converse problem with lesion studies is that the brain may recover much or all of the activity that was lost, perhaps because unimpaired areas of the brain were able to compensate.[17] For example, adults with damage in Broca's area

---

[17] A recently developed technique provides a strategy both for controlling more precisely the site of a lesion and preventing reorganization of processing after the lesion. This involves inducing temporary lesions through transcranial magnetic stimulation, a technique in which a strong but localized magnetic field is produced at the scalp so as to disrupt the activity in the immediately underlying brain regions. Early reports (Walsh & Cowey, 1998) indicate that one can disrupt very specific functions. If so, it will allow researchers to set side these worries and focus more directly on the question of what the affected area contributed to normal function.

often do exhibit some recovery of speech functions over time. More dramatically, young children who have experienced extensive loss of brain tissue in the left hemisphere, including in Broca's area, nonetheless tend to develop normal speech—often relying on corresponding areas in the right hemisphere. This counts against even the weaker claim that Broca's area is among those necessary for articulate speech.

Typically, however, the goal is not just to learn that a region is necessary for a function, but to determine what operations it contributed to performance of the function. To gain some appreciation of how difficult such an inference can be, consider trying to figure out how a radio (or a computer) operates by selectively removing parts and examining the resulting performance. As Richard Gregory (1968) noted, removal of a transistor from a radio may cause it to hum, yet it would be unwise to infer that the removed transistor was a hum suppressor. To begin to identify the operations that the damaged part actually performs, one needs to shift focus from the deficits manifested in the damaged system to the activity performed by the normal system and the component operations that would figure in that activity. In the case of mechanisms like radios, engineers designed them from knowledge of what operations components could perform. But in analyzing natural systems this basic engineering knowledge is unavailable. Researchers must therefore rely on less direct means of positing what operations might figure in the performance of the overall task—a process that involves much error, revision, and piecemeal progress.

A strategy that is widely deployed in lesion research is to attempt to dissociate two mental phenomena by showing that damage to a given brain part may interfere with one but not the other. Unfortunately, single dissociations do not prove that the damaged brain part is involved only in the impaired activity. It could be that the two activities differ in the demands they make on that part. If so, more extensive damage might produce interference with both activities. Researchers therefore prefer to find double dissociations, in which damage to one area causes disruption in one activity (while leaving the other largely unaffected), and damage to a second area disrupts the second activity (while leaving the first largely unaffected). For example, one lesion may impair spatial navigation but not affect discrimination learning, whereas another lesion impairs discrimination learning but not spatial navigation.

Double dissociations are often taken as compelling evidence that the two activities are performed separately in the brain (Shallice, 1988). However, they do not establish complete independence. Double dissociations can arise even if the two activities share a number of component operations. The discovery of a double dissociation encourages researchers to think comparatively about the two activities, asking what operations each requires and whether all are distinct or certain of them potentially are shared. Such a strategy is a productive way to generate a decomposition of a task into more basic operations.

The double dissociation can then be explained in terms of impairment to opera-tions not shared by the mechanisms responsible for the two activities.[18]

The second strategy for manipulating operations within a mechanism is to stimulate the parts. In the case of the brain, this generally involves supplying an electrical or chemi-cal stimulus to a targeted area. The aim is to elicit the same kind of sensory, motor, or other response as the organism would normally generate itself. Thus, in the earliest stimu-lation studies, by stimulating areas in what we now refer to as the motor cortex research-ers were able to elicit motor responses from animals (Fritsch & Hitzig, 1870; Ferrier, 1876). In humans being prepared for neurosurgery, stimulation was found to elicit sensations comparable to those normally elicited by sensory input (Penfield & Boldrey, 1937; Penfield & Rasmussen, 1950). In chapter four I will describe a somewhat more sophisti-cated use of the stimulation strategy in which researchers, by appropriate stimulation, influence the behavior of an organism when presented with ambiguous stimuli.

Stimulation experiments are commonly interpreted as showing that the area stim-ulated is responsible for the response generated. A pioneer in this approach, Ferrier (1876), regarded stimulation studies as especially appropriate for demonstrating that an area is *sufficient* to produce a given type of response, complementary to the use of lesion studies to demonstrate that it is *necessary*. Since a given brain region is connected to other regions and activation of one may lead to activation of other areas which contrib-ute to the behavior, such sufficiency should be interpreted in the context of a normally connected brain. But then the question arises as to just what the stimulated area is con-tributing. It may only perform the ancillary function of eliciting activity in these other areas that carry out the most significant operations in generating the behavior.

Whereas both lesion and stimulation studies provide important clues as to the operations performed in brain areas, these clues are often not sufficient in them-selves to reveal the operations being performed. This is one reason researchers often try to relate results from these studies with results from studies that detect activity in these brain regions during various tasks posed to the organism.

1.5.3   Experiments That Measure Internal Operations

Once researchers in the nineteenth century identified the brain as operating in part on electrical principles, they sought to measure this electrical activity by recording

---

[18] Recent investigations with neural networks and other dynamical systems have shown that double dis-sociations can result from differential damage to single network systems that do not employ different subsystems for performing different tasks, e.g., applying rules for pronouncing words versus looking up pronunciations in a lexicon (Hinton & Shallice, 1991; van Orden, Pennington, & Stone, 2001). Although such results seem to count against the claim that double dissociations are evidence for separate systems being responsible for separately impaired activities, they are compatible with the strategy just outlined of focusing on what elementary operations figure differentially in the two tasks. The double dissociations in these networks are generated by lesioning different parts of these networks, and it is plausible to construe these parts of the networks as responsible for different elementary operations.

from implanted electrodes. The challenge was that the electrical impulse in individual neurons is very weak, and it took investigators such as Edgar Adrian, Joseph Erlanger, and Herbert Gasser over 30 years to succeed in recording from individual neurons. But in the late 1930s and 1940s researchers began to record, first in anesthetized and later in awake cats and monkeys and even in humans, while different tactile, visual, and auditory stimuli were presented (Marshall, Woolsey, & Bard, 1937; 1941; Penfield & Boldrey, 1937). To make sense of the electrical activity in the brain, it was necessary to relate it to stimuli presented to the organism. For vision, investigators started by recording from retinal ganglion cells and the thalamus as they varied where in the visual field a stimulus was presented. Finding that individual cells were responsive to stimuli in particular regions of the visual field, Haldan Keffer Hartline (1938) coined the term *receptive field* for the part of the visual field that would elicit a response, a term still in use though with disagreements about its construal.

The information we receive from our senses is not just that something is present in a particular sensory field, but information about what is present. Thus, researchers began to systematically vary stimuli to determine which stimulus characteristics produced responses. An influential perspective was that cells were feature detectors; that is, they would respond most vigorously to stimuli with the feature they were designed to detect (Barlow, 1969; 1972). In an extremely influential paper entitled "What the frog's eye tells the frog's brain," Jerome Lettvin and his colleagues recorded from retinal ganglion cells from the frog. Finding that moving dark spots of light elicited strong responses from the cells, they concluded: "Could one better describe a system for detecting an accessible bug?" (Lettvin, Maturana, McCulloch, & Pitts, 1959, p. 258).

In chapter three I discuss in detail the pioneering work of Hubel and Wiesel which resulted in identification of the preferred stimuli for cells in the primary visual cortex, research which other researchers emulated in developing an account of the overall processing of visual information. Working in the auditory cortex of the cat during the same period as Hubel and Wiesel, Clinton Woolsey (1961) identified cells at different locations that responded to sounds of different frequencies. Cell recording has also been used to identify cells engaged in tasks further removed from the sensory and motor periphery; for example, Goldman-Rakic (1987) has identified cells that perform a short-term memory function by continuing to fire after a stimulus has been removed when it is necessary for the animal to retain information about the stimulus for a short interval before performing an action.

Single-cell recording is an invasive procedure that requires exposing the brain, and typically it injures or destroys the cells from which recordings are made. As a result, such recordings are usually made on humans only if they are candidates for particular kinds of brain surgery (e.g., to remove a tumor or the origin point of epileptic seizures). The recordings, although of scientific interest, are undertaken primarily to guide the surgery by mapping regions involved in such critical functions as sensory or motor control or language, which surgeons are loathe to remove. During the same period in which techniques for single-cell recording were being developed, other researchers found a noninvasive technique for detecting brain activity that involved placing electrodes on the skull (or sometimes on exposed cortex). In 1924 Hans Berger, a German psychiatrist, adapted methods designed to record the much stronger electrical signal from the heart muscle to produce recordings (electroencephalograms or EEGs) from the skull of his 15-year-old son.

Berger (1929) himself began the project of distinguishing different wave patterns in EEG recordings. These have turned out to be useful for studying sleep–wake cycles, identifying brain damage, detecting the origin of epileptic tumors, and monitoring the depth of anesthesia. However, the basic EEG technique has been of limited use for studying information processing in the brain, as recorded EEG activity is a combined measure of many different neural processes. To employ EEG for studying information processing, it was necessary to isolate the effects in the EEG of particular information-processing operations. This was accomplished when G.D. Dawson (1951) adapted a procedure originally designed for detecting lunar tides in the atmosphere by averaging over a large number of cases. Over many cases in which the same stimulus was presented, background noise would likely be randomly distributed whereas any specific response to the stimulus would stand out. In applying this averaging procedure to EEG, researchers set up multiple trials of a known stimulus type and onset time and averaged the responses to extract event-related effects in the EEG. The resulting electrical response pattern across a small temporal window is known as an *evoked response potential* (ERP).

ERPs provide high-resolution temporal information about brain activity, but are unable to provide detailed information about the locus of this activity in the brain. Two techniques developed in the 1980s and 1990s, *positron emission tomography* (PET) and *functional magnetic resonance imaging* (fMRI) have enabled researchers to localize brain activity with relatively high spatial resolution. These techniques are often used to obtain static images of structure, but by using a signal that is related to metabolic processes in neurons, can also be used to reveal functional activities in the brain (thus the name *functional neuroimaging*).[19]

---

[19] The physiological source of the signal, especially in the case of fMRI, remains controversial. MRI depends upon what is termed the blood oxygen level dependent (BOLD) signal, which involves an increase in blood flow in excess of oxygen utilization (Fox, Raichle, Mintun, & Dence, 1988). Raichle (1998) traced inquiry into the relation of brain activity and blood flow to nineteenth-century researchers such as Angelo Mosso, but showed that the mechanism responsible for increasing blood flow is still not known. The fact that the increase in blood flow exceeds the metabolic demands for neuronal activity makes the relationship particularly puzzling, although recent research has begun to elucidate the responsible mechanism (Raichle & Mintun, 2006). The details of the relationship will likely ultimately be important for understanding particular uses of fMRI, and some researchers are very concerned about the current deficit in our understanding (see Fitzpatrick & Rothman, 1999 for a report on a McDonnell Foundation sponsored conference devoted to this issue).

To relate brain activity to cognitive operations, researchers typically use neuroimaging techniques to measure brain activity during different tasks. One widely employed strategy adapts the *subtractive method* Donders initially developed for reaction time studies (see previous text).[20] Subjects are imaged while performing each of two different tasks, selected so that one is thought to require the same cognitive operations as the other plus an additional operation (or very small number of additional operations). The average activation at each cortical location during the simpler task is then subtracted from that of the more complex task. The result is a difference image showing the added (or reduced) activation elicited by the more complex task at a fine spatial grain across all cortical areas. The level of difference (or the statistical significance level associated with the difference) is color-coded on the brain images commonly shown in neuroimaging papers. The area(s) of additional activation in the difference image are taken to be the locus of the additional operations. As the signal of brain activity recorded in PET or MRI studies is relatively weak, researchers commonly must average over multiple events. In early studies they commonly employed a block design in which subjects performed one task for a number of trials, then performed another task for another set of trials. More recently a procedure has been developed that parallels that used in ERP studies in which brain responses can be linked to individual event types (e.g., stimuli that were later recalled and those that were not), thereby avoiding the limitation that items of the same type be presented in blocks (Rosen, Buckner, & Dale, 1998).

Studies recording internal brain activity, whether by recording from individual neurons or through ERP, PET, or fMRI, require a careful analysis of the tasks subjects are being asked to perform. Only in light of such analyses can the resulting brain activity be linked to operations in mental mechanisms. Some neuroimaging studies have failed to attend sufficiently to this problem; at worst, there may be no serious task analysis at all but simply running subjects through a task "to see what lights up." A result is that researchers end up, much in the tradition of phrenology, making claims that a particular brain area is responsible for the whole of a cognitive task. Petersen and Fiez, however, emphasized a sharp distinction between task and *elementary operations*:

> . . . elementary operations, defined on the basis of information processing analyses of task performance, are localized in different regions of the brain. Because many such elementary operations are involved in any cognitive task, a set of distributed functional areas must be orchestrated in the performance of even simple cognitive tasks.... A functional area of the brain is not a task area: There is no "tennis forehand area" to be discovered. Likewise, no area of the brain is devoted to a very complex function; "attention" or "language" is not localized in a particular Brodmann area or lobe. Any task or "function" utilizes a complex and distributed set of brain areas (Petersen & Fiez, 1993, p. 513).

---

[20] Alternative approaches are being developed (see, for example, Frith & Friston, 1997).

The difficult challenge of figuring out what operations are involved in mental mechanisms will be the focus of the next chapter.

1.6 SUMMARY

In this chapter I have laid out the basic framework I will be using in offering a philosophical analysis of the sciences of the mind and brain in the chapters to come. My approach is naturalistic, my primary objective being to characterize accurately the explanatory framework employed in these sciences. Unlike most philosophical accounts of these sciences, I do not assume that explanation involves the discovery of laws. Rather, following the language used in both biology and the sciences of the mind and brain, it involves primarily the discovery of mechanisms. The basic idea of mechanism, which is employed widely in biology, is that a mechanism consists of a set of parts performing operations that are organized so as to realize the phenomenon of interest. Mechanistic explanation consists in representing (verbally or in diagrams) the parts, operations, and organization, and showing (often via mental or computational simulations) how such a mechanism realizes the phenomenon in question. Mental mechanisms share these features, but operate not just to transform physical substrates but to process information. Hence, we will find that mental mechanisms are often most usefully described in terms of the content they carry, not their intrinsic physical features.

In the next two chapters I will discuss examples of research directed to uncovering the mechanisms responsible for mental phenomena in two different domains—memory and visual perception. I have chosen these domains because they illustrate two different approaches to discovering mental mechanisms. Both, however, happen to focus on identifying operations, not representations, within those mechanisms. After discussing reduction in chapter four, I will turn to questions of representation in chapter five. Finally, I turn to ways of construing mechanisms as active rather than passive in chapters six and the implications of doing so for understanding human freedom and dignity in the final chapter.

Two

From Mental Phenomena to Operations
Delineating and Decomposing Memory

In chapter one I characterized mechanistic explanation as requiring the decomposition of a whole mechanism associated with a phenomenon into its components. I also noted that in the attempt to discover mechanisms, psychologists most often conduct behavioral experiments and focus on human subjects, whereas neuroscientists prefer to manipulate or measure internal operations directly in nonhuman animals. In this chapter and the next I will describe research directed towards the discovery of mechanisms underlying two bodies of mental phenomena, memory and vision, which reveal different patterns of investigating mental mechanisms. In the case of memory, behavioral inquiries initially played a leading role and yielded competing taxonomies; success in identifying responsible brain areas and linking these to cognitive operations came more recently. In the case of vision (see chapter 3), the identification of operations and responsible brain areas played a more central role early on, leaving for later the task of figuring out how the whole system is organized.

Behavioral research on memory has emphasized decomposing it, but the decomposition is not always into operations. Sometimes the decomposition differentiates only among phenomena, not the operations responsible for them. This was the strategy adopted in faculty psychology as it was developed in the eighteenth and nineteenth centuries.[1] We will see that it is also the strategy that has

---

[1] In one standard view that had roots in Plato, the mind is comprised of three faculties: the will, the emotions, and the intellect. Through Christian Wolff, this demarcation of faculties influenced Kant (Radden, 1996). Faculty psychology was often eclipsed by the associationist tradition (drawing upon Locke and Hume), which focused on a general capacity for association and disavowed the division of the mind into faculties. Yet faculty psychology continued to be developed by some prominent theorists such as Thomas Reid (1785), who divided the mind into active (affective and conative) and intellectual powers. Among the latter, he distinguished memory, attention, and moral taste.

mostly dominated work on memory in the twentieth century, with researchers vying to identify distinct memory systems thought to be responsible for different clusters of phenomena. Such decomposition does not directly advance the goal of explaining how the mind actually produces these phenomena. It does, though, serve the important preparatory role of delineating the phenomena to be explained. To distinguish these two approaches to decomposition, I will refer to *phenomenal decomposition* when decomposition yields distinct types of phenomena, and *mechanistic decomposition* (or use the more specific terms *structural* or *functional decomposition* introduced in chapter 1) when component parts or operations of the mechanism producing the phenomenon are the focus. In the current chapter on memory, the initial emphasis is on phenomenal and functional decomposition. In chapter 3, on vision research, structural decomposition initially played the leading role.

Although much research on memory has focused on phenomenally decomposing memory systems, not all cognitive psychologists have accepted this agenda. A minority have focused instead on uncovering the processes or operations underlying different memory activities. This approach has the potential to produce mechanistic accounts of memory, but it confronts a serious challenge of articulating just what are the operations underlying cognitive activities such as memory. This is a serious challenge not just for memory research, but for cognitive psychology and cognitive neuroscience more generally. As I will develop in the third section of this chapter, cognitive investigators seeking to identify operations have generally either remained too close to the phenomena to be explained (drawing upon folk characterizations of mental life), or reached too low (focusing on systems made of neuron-like processing units). I suggest that neither of these approaches is sufficient to reveal the sorts of operations that figure in the mechanisms responsible for memory or other cognitive functions.

Psychologists have sometimes extended their behavioral techniques to study memory in patients with brain damage. Until recently, however, this research has served primarily as evidence for particular decompositions of memory into distinct systems and sometimes to localize (or at least situate) these memory systems in different brain regions. But localization research can play a much more important role—helping to differentiate mental operations. This requires not just identifying brain areas associated with cognitive tasks but using such identifications as heuristic guides to understanding how the brain performs those tasks. In section four I describe this approach, which Robert McCauley and I have dubbed *heuristic identity theory*. In sections five and six I review recent cognitive neuroscience research, which is beginning to offer insight into the operations that figure in memory mechanisms, suggesting new delineations of memory phenomena.

Most research on memory has tacitly assumed that memory is largely veridical. In memory tests, recalling something other than what was presented is usually construed as an error and an indication of a failure of memory. But evidence from a variety of sources suggests that memory is considerably less accurate than often assumed. One way to respond is to continue to treat veridical recall as the phenomenon and treat nonveridical recall as evidence of the shortcomings of the responsible mechanisms. Another is to question whether veridical reinstatement of the past correctly describes what an optimally functioning human memory system, in fact, is doing. I will end the chapter (section seven) by presenting some of the evidence for the nonveridical nature of memory and sketch the way some researchers are proposing to reconstitute the phenomenon of memory itself in light of it.

2.1 PHENOMENAL DECOMPOSITION OF MEMORY INTO TYPES OF MEMORY

Folk theorizing about memory has a long history. Plato in the *Theaetetus* compared memory to an aviary in which birds were kept. Successful retrieval was akin to grabbing the intended bird, and mistaken retrieval to grabbing the wrong bird:

> [L]et us now suppose that in the mind of each man there is an aviary of all sorts of birds—some flocking together apart from the rest, others in small groups, others solitary, flying anywhere and everywhere.... We may suppose that the birds are kinds of knowledge, and that when we were children, this receptacle was empty; whenever a man has gotten and detained in the enclosure a kind of knowledge, he may be said to have learned or discovered the thing which is the subject of the knowledge: and this is to know. . . . [Error occurs] when the various numbers and forms of knowledge are flying about in the aviary, and wishing to capture a certain sort of knowledge out of the general store, he takes the wrong one by mistake, that is to say, when he thought eleven to be twelve, he got hold of the ringdove which he had in his mind, when he wanted the pigeon (*Theaetetus*, Parts V and VI).

In addition to theorizing about the nature of memory, the ancients offered strategies for improving memory performance, such as the method of loci, attributed by Cicero to the poet Simonides. To remember a list of items, this method advises mentally traversing a well-known path and at each landmark making a mental image that associates it with the next item on the list. For example, if the first three landmarks between your home and the grocery store are a mailbox, lamppost, and stop sign, the first three items on your shopping list might be remembered by imagining a huge loaf of bread sticking out of the mailbox, bananas dangling from the lamppost, and milk spilling all over the stop sign. To recall the items after arriving at the store, you mentally retrace your steps and are pleased to find them one by one at the landmarks.

Memory finally advanced from folk theories and how-to guides to become an object of scientific investigation thanks to Hermann Ebbinghaus (1885), who developed painstaking procedures for measuring memory across time. Using only himself as a subject, he learned lists of nonsense syllables (e.g., "zok") until he could repeat them perfectly. He then measured forgetting after a given interval of time in terms of how many repetitions he needed to relearn the material to the same standard. By testing himself many times in each experimental paradigm and pooling the data, Ebbinghaus established a number of regular patterns. For example, he determined that forgetting exhibits a logarithmic function against time: forgetting is greatest just after learning and then tapers off. He also discovered the spacing effect, according to which better retention is obtained when study is spaced out than when it is massed into one learning period. Around the same time, but based mainly on introspection, William James (1890/1950) distinguished between immediate (*primary*) memory and longer-term (*secondary*) memory. However, any further consideration of memory as a mental phenomenon was pushed aside in American psychology by the emergence of behaviorism early in the twentieth century.[2] It also did not fare well as a focus of neural research, especially after Lashley's (1929; 1950) celebrated failure to find a location in the brain where memories are stored.[3]

Although Lashley challenged the idea that memories involved discreet encodings in the brain, his theorizing about serial order effects—the ability of learners to recognize sequential structure in serially presented items—marked the rebirth of appeals to internal representational structures as needed to account for learning. In a much-cited paper published late in his career, Lashley (1951) argued that associative chaining of the sort favored by behaviorists could not explain serial order effects. Instead, he maintained that this required higher-order representations. Once psychologists began focusing on such representations, memory more generally became a focus of study. Much of this research focused on short-term memory (or the related construct, working memory) and its capacity limits. For example, George Miller (1956) determined that over short periods of time during which they were not distracted, individuals could retain approximately seven chunks (meaningful units) of information. In contrast to such short-term memory, people can retain over the long term extremely large amounts of information.

---

[2] While memory was eclipsed by learning in American psychology, researchers elsewhere in the world were developing strategies to study it empirically. Especially noteworthy was Bartlett's (1932) naturalistic study of how an individual's memory of a story changes over time or how recall of a story is altered when it is retold successively by a series of individuals.

[3] Lashley referred to the *engram* as the hypothetical memory trace that was to be localized in the brain. The term *engram* was barrowed from Richard Semon, who had introduced the modern view of memory as involving encoding, storage (engram), and retrieval (see Schacter, Eich, & Tulving, 1978).

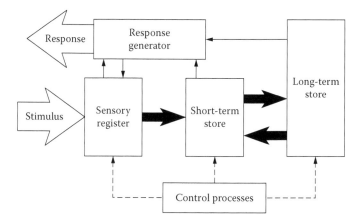

Figure 2.1   Adapted from Atkinson and Shiffrin's (1968) memory model involving three different stores (sensory register, short-term store and long-term store), plus control processes that regulate use of the memory stores and transfer of information between them. Adapted from Shiffrin and Atkinson (1969), p.180.

James' ruminations thus were revived in mid-century researchers' distinction between short- and long-term memory, and improved upon as they found tasks that enabled them to make inferences about internal memory mechanisms from purely behavioral data (Broadbent, 1958; Waugh & Norman, 1965; Neisser, 1967). Sperling (1960) showed that for very brief periods after a visual presentation people could, if appropriately cued, access any row or column in an iconic representation of items where the total number of items exceeded the limitations of short-term memory. This finding led to a three-store conception of memory and a model, articulated by Atkinson and Shiffrin (1968), in which attentional and other control processes helped direct the flow of information between memory stores (see Figure 2.1). Research in subsequent decades has further developed and generated revisions in this account. One influential development was the reconstrual by Baddeley and Hitch (1974; Baddeley, 1986) of short-term memory as a working memory system comprised of a central executive and modality-specific buffers, one phonological and one visuo-spatial. In what follows, though, I will focus on the more elaborate tale of long-term memory and its reconstruals.

2.1.1   Distinctions Within Long-Term Memory

Although long-term memory was treated as a single type of memory in these early psychological accounts, neuroscientists soon found that memory for different kinds of information could be differentially affected by brain damage. In an attempt to control severe epileptic seizures in a patient designated "H.M.,"

William Scoville removed much of his medial temporal lobe.[4] The surgery was successful in relieving H.M.'s epilepsy, but left him severely amnesic (Scoville & Milner, 1957). In particular, after the surgery he was not able to learn new information or remember events in his life since the surgery (anterograde amnesia). Moreover, he experienced graded loss of memory for several years of his life preceding the surgery (retrograde amnesia). Nonetheless, H.M.'s short-term memory was unimpaired—if not distracted he could retain information for several minutes. One result of the line of research that began with H.M., to which I will return below, was the hypothesis that the hippocampus plays a critical role in memory. But equally important was that behavioral experiments with H.M. showed that he could acquire new skills even though he had no memory of learning them (Corkin, 1968). This suggested that skill memory was a distinct type of long-term memory.

Shortly thereafter, Endel Tulving (1972) proposed a further fractionation of long-term memory in which he distinguished "two parallel and partially overlapping information processing systems" (p. 401). One, *episodic memory*, is concerned with events or episodes in a person's own life, specifying information about the time and place of their occurrence and permitting the person to "travel back" to reexperience them. The other, *semantic memory*, is concerned with information that typically is retrieved independently of recalling the time and place in which it was acquired (e.g., word meanings, general knowledge, scientific facts). One difference between these types of memory is that episodic memory closely involves the self, whereas semantic memory seems more removed. That is, remembering a significant event in your own life involves you in a fundamentally different way than does your knowledge about Plato. James captured this aspect of episodic memory: "Memory requires more than the mere dating of a fact in the past. It must be dated in *my* past ... I must think that I directly experienced its occurrence" (James, 1890/1950, p. 612).

Tulving introduced the term *autonoetic awareness* for the access one has to episodic memories. Autonoetic awareness involves being able to move around in the temporal dimension of one's life (Tulving often speaks of episodic memory as involving "mental time travel") and reexperiencing events that one has previously experienced (a capacity that, like memory more generally, is error-prone: people sometimes have compelling memories of events that never happened). Tulving quoted James to capture the affective aspect of autonoetic awareness—its "feeling of warmth and intimacy." He contrasts such remembering with knowing, which he regards as characteristic of semantic memory. One may know about a number of events in one's life (e.g., that one was born in a particular place) without reexperiencing the event.

---

[4] Scoville thought he had removed H.M.'s hippocampus, but later neuroimaging studies revealed that the lesion spared much of the hippocampus proper, although it subsequently atrophied as a result of loss of its normal inputs from surrounding cortical structures (Corkin, Amaral, González, Johnson, et al., 1997).

Such recollections count as semantic, not episodic, memories. Tulving has articulated a number of additional distinctions between these two kinds of memory. For example, episodic memory is oriented towards the past, whereas semantic memory applies information learned in the past to the present. Episodic memory, moreover, is evolutionarily more recent—he contends that there is no evidence of episodic memory in any species other than humans—and it develops later in ontogeny (Tulving, 1999a).

In his initial formulation, Tulving proposed that different types of tasks measured episodic and semantic memory performance. His tests of episodic memory involved recall and recognition of recently studied events, whereas semantic memory was tested by such tasks as generating words from a fragment or from a definition, identifying words from brief tachistoscopic displays, and making lexical decisions (i.e., presented with a series of letter strings, deciding whether each constitutes an English word). In one experiment, Tulving and his collaborators tested episodic memory by measuring recognition of words presented in a list-learning task. Either one hour or seven days later, they tested semantic memory by asking the same subjects to fill in the missing letters in incomplete words, such as _o_ma__c. Although completing such a word fragment can be difficult, it was rendered much easier if the target word (here, "dogmatic") was on the list used earlier in the episodic-memory task. Success in fragment completion remained roughly constant over the one-week interval, whereas recognition performance declined dramatically. Such dissociation between results is often construed as evidence that the psychological processes are independent. In a further analysis, it was established that the probability that subjects could complete a given fragment was stochastically independent of the probability that they could recognize it as having been on the study list (Tulving, Schacter, & Stark, 1982), providing additional evidence that different processes were involved. Subsequently Tulving emphasized that the difference in the kind of information remembered (general facts versus personally experienced events) was more fundamental.

Although Tulving advanced the distinction between episodic and semantic memory on behavioral grounds, he found powerful confirmation in studies of the patient "K.C.," who became profoundly amnesic following a closed-head injury in 1981. Whereas H.M. suffered substantial loss of both semantic and episodic memory, K.C. lost all episodic memory (retrograde and anterograde), while retaining much of his semantic memory:

> The outstanding fact about K.C.'s mental make-up is his utter inability to remember any events, circumstances, or situations from his own life. His episodic amnesia covers his whole life, from birth to the present. The only exception is the experiences that, at any time, he has had in the last minute or two. It does not matter how much and how specific information is given to him about any particular event from further back in the past, how memorable the event is by ordinary standards, how long

its duration, or how many times he has been asked about it before. He always denies any recollection and does not even acknowledge any sense of familiarity with the event (Tulving, 2002, p. 14).

K.C. nonetheless retains his factual knowledge, including knowledge of facts about himself: he can report the date of his birth, the names of many of the schools he attended, the make and color of a car he had owned, etc. In reporting these he relies on semantic memory—he does not remember experiencing any of these but simply knows about them. Moreover, with extensive training, K.C. has been able to learn both new skills and new semantic information. He thus presents a dissociation between episodic and semantic memories.

An even stronger dissociation of episodic and semantic memory was reported by Faraneh Vargha-Khadem et al. (1997). This involved three patients who suffered bilateral damage to the hippocampus at ages ranging from birth to nine years of age. All suffered severe impairments in episodic memory, especially for events of their daily lives (where they had left an item, what television show they had watched, what conversations they had had). Nonetheless, all have been successful in school. They have developed language skills commensurate with their age and are able to learn and reason about information that involves semantic memory (Squire & Zola, 1998).

Tulving's distinction between episodic and semantic memories was not the only taxonomic distinction developed during this period. Neal Cohen and Larry Squire (1980) approached the fractionation of long-term memory in a way that emphasized what episodic and semantic memories have in common. In particular, people can report semantic knowledge and episodic memories linguistically. But there are other memories people can acquire with experience but cannot report linguistically, such as the ability to ride a bicycle or solve crossword puzzles (these are the sorts of skills H.M. and K.C. could both acquire). Typically, people cannot explain in words how they perform these skills. Philosopher Gilbert Ryle (1949) characterized the distinction between skill knowledge and semantic knowledge as *knowing how* versus *knowing that*; Cohen and Squire characterized it in terms of *procedural* versus *declarative* information. As an individual could report both semantic and episodic memories in language, both counted as declarative for Cohen and Squire.[5]

---

[5] An important difference between Cohen and Squire's approach and Tulving's is that Cohen and Squire were guided in part by work on animal models. At first it may seem surprising to consider declarative memory in organisms who cannot report their memories in language. But animal investigators have found ingenious ways to detect declarative memories in animals. One approach involves testing whether the animal recognizes a previously presented stimulus. Researchers, for example, can present a monkey with a stimulus, remove it, and then present two further stimuli, one of which matches that presented before. The monkey can then be trained to select the new stimulus (this procedure is referred to as *delayed nonmatching to sample*). Researchers have found that hippocampal damage in monkeys impairs ability on such tasks (Zola, Squire, Teng, Stefanacci, & Clark, 2000).

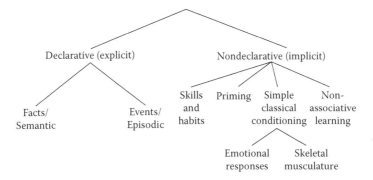

Figure 2.2   Squire and Knowlton's (1995) taxonomy of memory systems.

An important aspect of declarative memories is that they involve a representation of external objects and events and accordingly can be evaluated in terms of whether they provide a true or false representation of those objects or events. Procedures, on the other hand, may be appropriate or inappropriate, but are not judged as true or false. Moreover, although procedures generally take practice to acquire, declarative memories can sometimes be acquired in a single exposure. Finally, declarative memories can be flexibly expressed in multiple forms (verbal reports, problem solving), whereas procedures are often far less flexible and transferable to other expressions.

Once researchers extended their attention beyond declarative memory, they came to realize there are subtypes of nondeclarative memory and that some (e.g., skills and habits) more clearly relate to the procedural notion than others. Figure 2.2, adapted from Squire and Knowlton (1995), is representative of the taxonomies proposed. As indicated there, the original dichotomy has been reconceptualized as a contrast between explicit and implicit memory, often characterized in terms of whether conscious awareness is involved. Daniel Schacter (1987), for example stated: "Implicit memory is revealed when previous experiences facilitate performance on a task that does not require conscious or international recollection of these experiences" (p. 501). This raises the question as to whether there is any cohesiveness to the category of implicit memory (Willingham & Preuss, 1995). Schacter's statement emphasizes a subtype of implicit memory called *priming*. In priming, exposure to a stimulus that is not explicitly remembered may, nonetheless, bias responses in later situations. It is often assessed using a variation of the fragment completion task, the stem completion task, in which a subject will be asked to complete a stem such as sal___ with the first word that comes to mind. If the word *salary* was on a list of words that subjects had previously read, then even if they could not remember or recognize that *salary* had been on the list, they would still be more likely to complete the stem with *salary* than if it had not been on the list. Priming exhibits a different behavioral profile than explicit memory. For example, factors such as typeface are more likely to affect priming than explicit recall (Roediger & McDermott, 1993). Moreover, priming is often spared in patients with amnesia (Squire, 1987). Priming, however, appears not to be a single phenomenon. Researchers have found dissociations between perceptual priming, which is linked to a specific sensory modality (Church & Schacter, 1994) and conceptual priming, which is revealed in tasks requiring semantic analysis such as generating exemplars for a category (Hamman, 1990). Moreover, forms of priming can be dissociated from skill learning, which is preserved in Alzheimer patients who exhibit deficits in priming tasks (D. P. Salmon & Butters, 1995).

Closely linked to the notion of implicit memory is that of implicit learning, a concept first developed by Arthur Reber (1967) to characterize the ability of people to learn complex skills without conscious awareness. Reber developed artificial grammars in the form of finite state automata (often referred to as *Reber grammars*) used to create strings of letters. Subjects were presented with some number of strings generated by the grammar (e.g., TSSXS and PTTSS) and then asked to determine whether additional strings presented to them (e.g., TSXXS) followed the same rules. Even though subjects were not able to figure out the rules, they were significantly above chance in distinguishing strings that fit the grammar from strings that did not.

2.1.2   Memory Systems

In his initial presentation of the semantic/episodic distinction, Tulving maintained that it was "primarily for the convenience of communication, rather than as an expression of any profound belief about structural or functional separation of the two" (1972, p. 384). In the 1980s, though, in addition to incorporating procedural (implicit) memory into his scheme, Tulving began to speak of different *memory systems*:[6]

> Memory systems constitute the major subdivisions of the overall organization of the memory complex. They are organized structures of more elementary operating components. An operating component of a system consists of a neural substrate and its behavioral or cognitive correlates. Some components are shared by all systems, others are shared only by some, and still others are unique to individual systems. Different learning and memory situations involve different concatenations of components from one or more systems (Tulving, 1985, p. 387).

---

[6] Different theorists seem to speak differently of memory systems. For example, Squire and Zola-Morgan (1991) referred to a medial temporal lobe memory system (involving the hippocampus plus the entorhinal, perirhinal, and parahippocampal cortex) that is involved in developing long-term memories. In this case, there are neuroanatomical pathways linking the components, and researchers have more recently developed highly suggestive computational models of how these structures combine in the process of encoding long-term memories (Rolls & Treves, 1998).

He also proposed what he called a *monohierarchical* arrangement of the systems:

The system at the lowest level of the hierarchy, procedural memory, contains semantic memory as its single specialized subsystem, and semantic memory, in turn, contains episodic memory as its single specialized subsystem. In this scheme, each higher system depends on, and is supported by, the lower system or systems, but it possesses unique capabilities not possessed by the lower systems (p. 387).[7]

Although in this characterization Tulving acknowledged that memory systems can share components and he has continued to allow that different situations may recruit components from more than one system, there is a tendency, both by Tulving and others,[8] to treat them as relatively independent. At the extreme, memory systems are comparable to modules, characterized by Jerry Fodor (1983) as processing information from specific domains, operating rapidly, relying on a fixed neural architecture, and exhibiting characteristic patterns of acquisition and breakdown. Most important for Fodor is what he terms *information encapsulation*. Information processing is encapsulated when processing can only employ information obtained within the module and it has no access to information stored elsewhere in the mind. As most thinking activities do not exhibit encapsulation, but rather can make use of any information the person knows, Fodor denies that what he terms *central cognition* is modular. Fodor offers sensory processing and language processing as his only examples of modular processing systems. Other theorists have adopted Fodor's view of modules and generalized it to all cognition.[9] Although he does not characterize memory systems as modules, some of the features Tulving identifies with memory systems are at least consistent with Fodor's criteria for modules. He comments, for example, that "each system differs

---

[7] In other writings, Tulving has construed episodic memory as a uniquely human capacity and hence as a late evolutionary development: "Episodic memory is a recently evolved, late-developing, and early-deteriorating past-oriented memory system, more vulnerable than other memory systems to neuronal dysfunction, and probably unique to humans" (Tulving, 2002, p. 5). Although in the passage cited in the text he treats episodic memory as a subsystem of semantic memory, he sometimes treats it as involving a network that goes beyond semantic memory: "Episodic memory is subserved by a widely distributed network of cortical and subcortical brain regions that overlaps with but also extends beyond the networks subserving other memory systems" (p. 5).

[8] In setting up their challenge to the memory systems view, Rajah and McIntosh attribute the following view to Tulving: "A memory system is thought to consist of a distributed neural network that is anatomically connected and functionally integrated. Each memory system is believed to process a different type of information, use unique operations, and be neurologically discrete and independent in its function" (Rajah & McIntosh, 2005, p. 476).

[9] Evolutionary psychologists, in particular, view the whole mind as modular, and advance accounts according to which modules can be independently evolved (D.D. Cummins & Allen, 1998; Shettleworth, 2000).

in its methods of acquisition, representation, and expression of knowledge" as well as the sort of conscious awareness it provides[10] (Tulving, 1985, p. 387).

Subseqently, and partly in response to evidence generated by critics of Tulving's memory systems approach, Tulving and Schacter (1990) expanded Tulving's taxonomy of memory systems to include a perceptual memory system that operates at a presemantic level and accounts for the results of various priming experiments. They treat this system as distinct from procedural memory, insofar as it has access to semantic information. Unlike the semantic memory system, the perceptual memory system operates unconsciously and is sensitive to information about the perceptual presentation of stimuli (e.g., the font in which text is written or the voice with which it is spoken).

Tulving sometimes portrays what are now four different memory systems as distinct and operating in parallel:

> While working memory operates on the incoming information ... other memory systems in the complex, massively parallel computational machine that is the brain are also involved, separately from the process of working memory. Thus, PRS, the perceptual representation system, encodes and stores information about the features of the visual objects represented by the letter strings AARDVARKS EAT ANTS. The semantic memory system, or a set of its (presumably numerous) subsystems, encodes and stores propositional information about the feeding habits of animals named aardvarks. The episodic system integrates, registers, temporally dates, and spatially localizes the rememberer's experience of the experience of being present and witnessing the sentence appearing on and disappearing from the screen" (Tulving, 1999b, p. 20).

The tendency to view memory systems as sharply independent is particularly manifest when Tulving (1985) promotes stochastic independence (a relation between two events in which their joint probability is equal to the product of their individual probabilities) as more compelling than what he terms functional independence (in which one dependent variable varies as a function of an independent variable but the other does not). Functional independence, he maintains,

---

[10] Tulving (1984) advanced his most detailed account of memory systems when he proposed that memory systems could be distinguished in terms of:
- Different behavioral and cognitive functions and the kinds of information and knowledge they possess
- Operations according to different laws and principle
- Different neural substrates (neural structures and neural mechanisms)
- Differences in the timing of their appearance in phylogenetic and ontogenetic development
- Difference in the formation of represented information (the extent to which the after-effects of information acquisition represent the past or merely modify future behavior or experience)

is compatible with a two-stage processing view in which a common stage explains the positive correlation and the additional stage explains the functional independence. Stochastic independence, he claims, is incompatible with such a view:

> Stochastic independence cannot be explained by assuming that the two comparison tasks differ in only one or a few operating components (information, stages, processes, mechanisms). As long as there is any overlap in those operating components that are responsible for differences in what is retrieved, some positive dependence between the measures should appear. Perfect stochastic independence implies complete absence of such overlap (1985, p. 395).

The strategy of seeking separate memory systems advances a view of the mind similar to that proposed in faculty psychology in which each mental activity is attributed to a separate processing system. Although this might be one way to design a mind, it is an unlikely way for evolution to have done it. Instead, evolution more commonly reuses already evolved components even when recombining them to realize new phenomena. What is more important, for our purposes, is that merely identifying a system responsible for a given memory phenomenon does not serve to advance the goal of explaining it. Even if the mind is highly modular, explaining how each module works requires taking it apart and identifying the operations that are employed in it—i.e., achieving not just a phenomenol decomposition, but a mechanistic one. It may then turn out, as Tulving at times acknowledges, that different types of memory activity invoke some of the same operations. The key explanatory activity will involve identifying these operations and their organization, not merely identifying the different systems that utilize them.

There is, though, an important contribution made by advocates of separate memory systems. By distinguishing different kinds of memory activity, they serve to clarify the phenomena that require explanation. Failing to differentiate phenomena that are really different from each other can result in proposed explanations that fail to adequately account for the full character of the phenomena. Hence, taxonomies of memory systems, and phenomenal decompositions in other cognitive domains, play an important role as a prolegomenon to explanation. Moreover, recalling the point from the first chapter that the search for mechanisms starts with characterization of the phenomena to be explained, there is a close affinity between a memory system and a memory mechanism. Those component parts and operations that are organized so as to realize a given phenomenon constitute the mechanism responsible for the phenomenon. As long as we keep clearly in focus that the parts and operations identified in one mechanism (system) may overlap substantially with those that figure in another mechanism (system), there is no harm in speaking of memory systems. But, as I have emphasized, identification of such systems does not explain but only identifies what needs explanation.

2.2   MECHANISTIC DECOMPOSITION OF MEMORY INTO COMPONENT PROCESSES/OPERATIONS

The memory systems approach has frequently been criticized by investigators who defend a focus on *processes* or *procedures* rather than systems. These are roughly equivalent to what I call operations and, like operations, might be identified only at a very general level early in inquiry (e.g., the process of retrieving a memory) and at a finer grain later (e.g., two of the processes by which a memory is retrieved, given a cue, might be spreading activation from the cue and assessment of the strength of a retrieved item). Roediger, Buckner, and McDermott characterized the process approach as follows, highlighting Paul Kolers' role in its development.[11]

> The hallmark of the procedural approach, harking back to Bartlett and Neisser, was that performance on memory tasks could be described as skilled performance and that one should look to the procedures of mind to explain cognitive performances. Many experiments can be interpreted as supporting the procedural approach, including several revealing dissociations in performance on tasks that all measured recognition of words. In particular, Kolers' experiments showed that transfer from one task to another benefited to the degree that the procedures underlying performance on the two tasks were similar (Roediger, Buckner, & McDermott, 1999, p. 42).

The challenge for the process approach is how to identify processes (operations). Much of the research focuses on establishing that performance in different

---

[11] In large part, Kolers construed his process approach as opposed to a structuralist approach in which memory was viewed as involving stored representations, and the mind was populated with different structural components. Kolers and Roediger (1984) stated: "We will show in some detail that distinctions between mental representation and mental process, between 'symbol' and 'skill,' are of questionable worth for psychology and may indeed actually misrepresent psychological processes" (p. 429). Instead of drawing a dichotomy between structuralist and proceduralist accounts, however, it is perhaps more fruitful to construe Kolers' project as recommending a corrective in the symbolic/linguistic account of mental representations and recognizing a broader range of mental representations and processes on them. Kolers and Roediger's positive statement of their view, in fact, maintains the distinction between representations and operations, but shifts the focus to operations (skills): "We will argue that knowledge is a matter of skill in operating on symbols, that the latter are of many kinds, that the kinds are not perfectly correlated, and that knowledge is, as a consequence, means dependent" (p. 430). One feature of the corrective, though, may be the recognition that there is not just one set of representations on which different operations are performed, as suggested for example by Anderson: "Representations that do not preserve the exact perceptual structures of the events remembered are the mainstay of long-term memory. It is important to appreciate that these meaning representations are neither linguistic nor pictorial. Rather they encode the meaning of pictures and linguistic information" (Anderson, 1990, p. 122). One alternative to consider is that in many cases representations may be grounded in the sensory modalities through which we acquire knowledge of the world; as discussed in chapter 5, there is growing evidence that modality-specific representations are reactivated in thought processes.

tasks relies on different processes rather than characterizing the processes themselves. Kolers, for example, developed a strategy for establishing that different processes were involved by examining whether learning one kind of task (reading inverted text) transfers to performance on another (reading reversed text). If performance of the two tasks drew upon similar processing operations, then there should be transfer from learning to perform one to learning the other, but not otherwise (Kolers & Ostry, 1974; Kolers & Perkins, 1975).[12]

A similar approach was employed by John Bransford and his collaborators (Bransford, Franks, Morris, & Stein, 1979) in advancing the idea of *transfer-appropriate processing*. The idea is that recall performance would be affected by similarity between the processes used in acquiring information and those required in recall. Performance would be better if the learning and recall tasks both involved semantic processing than if learning involved phonemic processing whereas recall emphasized semantic processing. If the recall task involved a phonemic judgment (e.g., "Does this word rhyme with a word seen during encoding?"), then performance would be better if the learning also required phonemic processing.

As in the memory systems literature, advocates of processing approaches relied on findings of dissociations. The difference is that they used dissociations to distinguish, not entire systems, but component processes involved in one task from those used in another task. Roediger and his colleagues (Roediger, Weldon, & Challis, 1989) developed a set of principles that they hoped would point the way to a processing-based account of a wide range of dissociation data:

1. Performance on memory tests benefit to the degree they invoke the same processes required in encoding
2. Explicit and implicit memory tests tend to invoke different processes
3. Most (but not all) explicit memory tests (free recall, cued recall, recognition) depend primarily on semantic and conceptual processing
4. Most (but not all) implicit memory tests depend primarily on perceptual processing[13]

---

[12] Kolers and Roediger described the approach: "Our view, transfer of training and savings methods, properly applied, constitutes a fundament upon which to construct an empirically based cognitive psychology. The techniques would be applied as measures of skills acquired in one cognitive task and expressed in performance on another. Degree of transfer from one task to the second or, as in Nelson's (1978) work, the more subtle measurement of savings, can aid in diagnosing the underlying cognitive operations. The idea is that any complex event is composed of a number of component activities, and the more alike they are, the more alike the behavior will be (Kolers & Perkins, 1975). Judicious experimentation may allow one to infer their identity" (p. 443). They proceeded to talk of developing a taxonomy of "trainable capabilities" that can be organized in the performance of different tasks.

[13] As Roediger et al. acknowledged, there is not a sharp distinction between perceptual and conceptual processes; they proposed, instead, a continuum.

By comparing performance on implicit memory tests that required semantic vs. perceptual processing, Blaxton (1989) obtained dissociations within implicit tasks. Specifically, she showed that generating words from conceptual cues as opposed to simply reading the words led to better recall on conceptual tests than on perceptual tests, whether episodic or semantic, whereas reading produced better recall on perceptual tests than conceptual ones, whether episodic or semantic. However, researchers also found dissociations between tasks thought to employ conceptual processes (Cabeza, 1994), evidence that did not fit well with the existing procedural accounts. In response, advocates of the procedural approach proposed subdividing the perceptual and conceptual processes into finer-grained processes (Roediger, Gallo, & Geraci, 2002).

The advocates of the processing approach viewed themselves as providing compelling evidence against the systems approach. Kolers and Roediger (1984) reasoned: "If dissociations are found among tests tapping the same memory system, then the discovery of dissociations between tasks cannot be taken as evidence for different memory systems" (p. 438). Nonetheless, advocates of the systems approach persisted in developing and refining their view. For example, in response to Blaxton's results noted above, Tulving and Schacter (1990) proposed their fourth memory system: the perceptual representation system.

One advantage the memory systems approach seemed to offer was an account of the overall capacity to perform a task. Performance on a given task was simply the result of the application of a whole memory system. The process approach seemed to offer only a hodgepodge of processes. Morris Moscovitch (1994) offered an alternative perspective that emphasized the integration of operations, an approach he termed *components of processing*. As the term *processing* in its name suggests, the components of processing framework is a descendent of the memory processes approach. It adds the idea that different tasks may draw differentially upon memory processes to create a processing network. If two tasks can be dissociated (by showing that a manipulation affects performance on one task but not on the other), then there must be at least one component process that figures differently in the two tasks (Hintzman, 1990). Within this framework, dissociations are no longer used to tease apart whole systems, but only differences in reliance on components.

Some researchers have denied that there is opposition between the memory systems and the components of processing approaches. Tulving, for example, maintains that "the classification approach *complements* the process-oriented approach to memory; it is not an alternative to it" (1991, emphasis in original). Indeed, when the components of processing advocates talk of recruiting different processes in performing a particular memory task, they can be construed as describing the building up of a memory system or mechanism. But the emphasis that components of processing researchers place on constituent operations constitutes an important difference in research objective. Their project is directed at mechanistic decomposition, not just phenomenal decomposition. Even so, however, the components of processing approach has provided little in the way of a specific account of what operations are involved in performing various memory tasks. This is not very surprising because, as I argue in the next section, this is a generic problem for cognitive science.

2.3   WHAT ARE THE MENTAL OPERATIONS?

In chapter one I noted that what is distinctive of mental mechanisms is that they process information. Attempts to account for mental mechanisms have raised a number of thorny questions regarding mental representations and the operations presumed to act on them. Deferring discussion of mental representation to chapter five, here I focus on a basic question: What are the specific mental operations that we deploy? Process-oriented views of cognition rely on dissociations and other evidence to determine when performance on different tasks involves different operations. But what are these operations? What changes do information-processing operations make in the representations they act on? Determining *that* an operation has been performed is different from determining *what* operation has been performed. Until we know what these operations are, we won't have explained how the mind is capable of performing cognitive tasks.

As I have discussed, researchers often rely on dissociations between tasks to argue for differences in the operations involved. The most compelling evidence is usually assumed to result from double dissociations in which different perturbations of the system have opposite effects on two overall tasks: One impairs one task more than the other, and the other impairs the other task more (Shallice, 1988). Evidence of dissociations would be compelling if such dissociations could result only from differences in operations. But one of the consequences of research with connectionist models has been to show that double dissociations are possible in networks in which activity in the same set of units can achieve two different tasks (Rumelhart & McClelland, 1986a; Hinton & Shallice, 1991). Guy van Orden and his collaborators (van Orden, Pennington, & Stone, 2001) have argued that double dissociations are an artifact of the research strategies investigators adopt and do not necessarily reflect different component operations in a mechanism. To answer these critics, positive evidence of the component operations is needed— not just evidence of dissociations between tasks.

To illustrate what it would be to identify operations, and some of the challenges confronted in doing so, I will consider another discipline—physiological, or biological, chemistry—which faced a similar quandary and failed to advance as a science until it identified the relevant operations in terms of which it could explain its target phenomena. The chemical revolution at the end of the eighteenth century, in which Lavoisier was the central figure, brought a revised assessment of what is a basic element.[14] With a new conception of elements, researchers were able to characterize the chemical composition of organic compounds. Lavoisier (1781) himself determined that carbon, hydrogen, and oxygen are constituents of organic substances, while Berthollet (1780) identified nitrogen as another frequent component. This permitted a clear specification of some of the overall chemical processes performed in living organisms. For example, alcoholic fermentation was determined to involve the following overall reaction (in modern symbolic format):

$$C_6H_{12}O_6 \rightarrow 2C_2H_5OH + 2CO_2$$

Similarly, respiration was determined to involve the complete "burning" of glucose to yield carbon dioxide and water:

$$C_6H_{12}O_6 + 6\,O_2 \rightarrow 6\,CO_2 + 6\,H_2O$$

With an understanding of the overall reactions, the challenge was to explain how such reactions took place in the animal body.[15] It was assumed by most researchers that these overall reactions consisted of a sequence of simpler reactions. Two strategies presented themselves for describing these component reactions. One, pursued prominently by Justus Liebig (1842), was to focus on the atoms that might be added or removed from a molecule in a given reaction, writing chemical formulae that would lead from a starting substance (glucose) to the final products (carbon dioxide and water). Liebig made what seemed like perfectly reasonable assumptions that guided his search: (a) as plants synthesized all complex organic forms, animals would not synthesize new substances but would break down (catabolize) what they received from plants and (b) animals would incorporate proteins in the diet directly into their bodies, later breaking them down as needed to produce work. Neither of these assumptions turned out to be correct, and Liebig's accounts were ultimately rejected. The other strategy was to test possible intermediate substances (such as the three-carbon

---

[14] The previously dominant phlogiston chemistry treated phlogiston, the element of fire, as a basic element and explained such phenomena as combustion, rusting, and animal respiration as involving the removal of phlogiston from compounds. In the case of rusting, iron was treated as a compound of calx and phlogiston; what remained after rusting was the calx. Lavoisier's alternative was to treat oxygen, iron, and carbon as elements, with combustion, rusting, and respiration resulting in the generation of compounds incorporating oxygen.

[15] Lavoisier and Laplace (1780) used a calorimeter to establish that the same heat was generated by metabolizing glucose in an animal and by ordinary burning of it. Part of the challenge was to explain why substances could be "burned" in living organisms at temperatures at which they would not ordinarily be burned. The chemist Jacob Berzelius (1836) named the responsible agent a *catalyst* and many chemists hoped that catalytic chemical changes could account for the reactions in living organisms.

compounds produced by treating glucose with alkalis) in appropriately prepared animal tissue to see if they generated the correct end products. The problem was to characterize the reactions that might lead to these substances or from them to the end products. In the case of fermentation, researchers spoke of the intermediates being themselves *fermented*.

Neither of these strategies produced a successful biochemistry. In retrospect, we can see that the first strategy focused on too low a level to identify the relevant reactions while the second stayed at the same level as the overall phenomenon rather than identifying operations of lower-level components. Progress was not made until organic chemists figured out that organic substances consisted of various groups of molecules, such as amino (NH_3^+), carboxyl (COO^-), hydroxyl (OH^-), and phosphate (PO_4^-) groups that were bound to a carbon ring backbone (F. L. Holmes, 1992). This provided a new way to understand many of the component chemical operations that made up the overall physiological processes of fermentation and respiration; they involved the addition or removal of whole chemical groups to a substrate molecule. (Other reactions might involve splitting a large molecule into two molecules.) With this characterization of the basic operations, biochemists were positioned to develop detailed accounts of the basic processes of life (see Bechtel, 2006, chapter three).

Cognitive scientists are in a position comparable to that of physiological chemists in the nineteenth century, attempting to develop accounts of information processing operations at either too low or too high a level. This is most clearly seen by considering the two strategies most commonly deployed in developing computational models of cognition. Starting with investigators such as Warren McCulloch and Walter Pitts (McCulloch & Pitts, 1943; Pitts & McCulloch, 1947), Donald Hebb (1949), and Frank Rosenblatt (1962) many theorists have tried to build models of cognitive operations out of units that are sometimes called *artificial neurons*. These connectionist (or neural network) modelers have convincingly shown that connected networks of such units can exhibit many of the characteristics of cognitive systems. However, as discussions of distributed representations make clear, the relevant informational structures are at a larger scale than individual neurons.[16] Connectionist modeling is a framework in which it is

---

[16] In one sense, work in basic physics spells out elementary operations in terms of which all phenomena in nature are comprised. But this is typically not the level at which we find the operations that are to figure in the explanation of a given phenomenon. To explain how a car generates locomotion we do not jump immediately to quantum mechanics. Rather, we appeal to parts at one level of decomposition down from the whole car—the engine, drive shaft, axles, etc. Each of them makes a contribution which we can understand in light of the goal of generating locomotion—transforming chemical energy to mechanical energy, etc. We might then want to explain how the engine works by taking it apart into the next level of parts—the cylinders, pistons, rods, etc. What is needed for mechanistic explanations, then, are the parts at a level of organization immediately below the level of the phenomenon.

possible to implement networks of various designs. One simple design involves three layers of units and two layers of weighted connections, with each unit in one layer sending input to all units in the next. As long as they are provided with sufficient units in the intermediate or hidden layer, such networks can learn any desired mapping of inputs into outputs. With each unit involved in each activity of the network, there is no sharp division of labor. As a result, such networks are problematic from the perspective of mechanistic explanation: No definitive account can be offered of what different parts and their operations are contributing to the behavior of the whole network (Bechtel & Richardson, 1993, chapter nine). Connectionist modelers concerned with complex tasks have commonly explored modular networks in which different subnetworks are responsible for different subtasks (Miikkulainen, 1993; for discussion, see Bechtel & Abrahamsen, 2002, chapter seven). In such networks, the parts carrying out the relevant component operations are not the individual units, but the modules. The challenge for researchers pursuing such an approach is to determine in a principled manner how to decompose the overall task to arrive at the particular operations that should be assigned to different modules. This is the modelers' version of the problem I am addressing in this section. So far, decisions as to how to divide tasks into subtasks for modules is typically handled in an ad hoc manner or by drawing insights from the alternative perspective I describe next.

Working from the other end, theorists who defend symbolic modeling take as their basis for theorizing about cognition overall activities of cognitive agents. Recall that Turing drew his inspiration for the Turing machine from the activities of human computers who applied a finite set of rules to symbols written on paper. When Newell and Simon (1956) designed Logic Theorist, the first operating AI program, they first assigned humans to carry out the operations that became the steps of the program. This appeal to activities performed by agents continued as Newell and Simon pursued the project of devising problem solving strategies by taking protocols from human subjects who were required to talk aloud as they solved problems. The steps they identified became component operations in their production system models (Newell & Simon, 1972). Other investigators developing symbolic models are more skeptical than Newell and Simon regarding the informativeness of protocols from human subjects, but nonetheless characterize the cognitive operations underlying overall cognitive performance in the same language as we use to characterize human subjects. For example, stages in memory are characterized as *encoding, storage,* and *retrieval.*

Symbolic theorists are in a position comparable to physiological chemists who characterized possible intermediates in fermentation as undergoing fermentation, whereas connectionists are in a position comparable to chemists who tried to describe fermentation in terms of atomic changes. The case from biochemistry suggests that what cognitive inquiry needs is to identify operations at the appropriate level of organization. If the analogy holds true, what investigators should seek to identify are a set of basic types of operations on information that would be comparable to operations on chemical groups. To find those actually used to perform cognitive tasks is a monumental challenge. The discovery of biochemical groups guided biochemists to the sorts of reactions that could explain the overall reaction, thereby constraining the search for the particular set of operations used to achieve metabolism in living systems. Because for the most part cognitive inquiry lacks tools for identifying the information-bearing states in the brain directly, it cannot use such results to guide the search for possible operations.

The challenge for cognitive science is not an ordinary empirical challenge of figuring out what sorts of evidence might adjudicate whether a particular operation was deployed in performing a particular task. It is, rather, a conceptual challenge; investigators need to figure out the type of operations that are appropriate for explaining cognitive activity. If the example from biochemistry is applicable in this case, the operations in question will be of a different type than either the manipulations cognitive agents perform on external symbols or the operations that individual neurons perform. They likely will be characterized in a new vocabulary, one we do not now possess. Only equipped with such concepts will it be possible to fill in the components of processing accounts described in the previous section. Only then can cognitive scientists move beyond appealing to dissociations and other evidence in arguing that the same or different processes (operations) are involved in different tasks. Instead, they can advance proposals as to what these processes are.

2.4   USING LOCALIZATION TO HELP IDENTIFY OPERATIONS: HEURISTIC IDENTITY THEORY

So far I have focused on attempts in cognitive science to identify operations in the mind using purely behavioral tools. I noted that, largely for pragmatic reasons, cognitive science had developed without neuroscience playing much of a role. A major reason was that few tools existed for studying brain activity as humans perform cognitive tasks. This situation changed dramatically when positron emission tomography (PET), and later functional magnetic resonance imaging (fMRI), became available to noninvasively determine which human brain regions were most active for different cognitive tasks. My contention in this section is that this does not obviate the need to perform the hard conceptual work of figuring out what the operations are, but it does provide valuable constraints that can assist in this endeavor.

Underlying attempts to localize cognitive operations in brain structures is the assumption that there is an identity relation between particular mental mechanisms and neural mechanisms. Asserting that it is the same thing that is described in mental and neural or physical terms is the characteristic claim of one of the traditional philosophical stances on the mind–body problem, the

Mind–Brain Identity Theory (Place, 1956; Smart, 1959; Armstrong, 1968). Beginning in the 1970s, the identity theory was largely supplanted in philosophy of mind by a position known as functionalism, largely based on an argument (which I discuss and criticize in chapter four) that mental states are multiply realizable and so not identical with any given physical or neural state. Instead, mental states can, on this view, only be characterized in terms of their functional relations with one another.[17] In its heyday, however, the identity theory faced another objection, one that is relevant to the current question as to how localization can facilitate identifying cognitive operations. This was the claim that the evidence put forward for identity claims can never support more than the claim that mental states and brain states are correlated. Kim presented the claim crisply:

> ... the factual content of the identity statement is exhausted by the corresponding correlation statement. ... There is no conceivable observation that would confirm or refute the identity but not the associated correlation (Kim, 1966, p. 227).

Since correlation claims are easily accommodated even by dualists, to assert identity when the evidence consists only of correlations is to engage in metaphysical presumption.

This objection, however, lifts identity (or localization) claims out of the context in which they commonly are introduced in actual science. Identity claims (e.g., that water is H_2O or pain is C-fiber firing) are not advanced as conclusions of an inferential process, but are assumptions made at the outset of investigation, often on the basis of a limited number of correlations. Assuming identity entails a very strong conclusion: if two things, x and y, are really identical, then everything that is said about x applies to y, and vice versa. This is often referred to as Leibniz's law of the *indiscernability of identicals*.[18] Assume for a moment that Leibniz's law seems to be violated—that what is true of something under one description (e.g., a

---

[17] Some philosophers have resisted the forced choice between the identity theory and functionalism, maintaining that mental processes could both be characterized by their interactions with other mental processes and be identical with brain processes (Armstrong, 1968; Lycan, 1979). Such a view is highly compatible with the mechanistic perspective which embraces both functional and structural decomposition and localization as linking structures with functions.

[18] In the debates over the identity theory, Leibniz's law was frequently appealed to in order to argue against identity claims. For example, philosophers argued that we are introspectively aware of our mental states but not of our brain states. Therefore, mental states are not identical to physical states. In response to such objections, proponents of the identity theory commonly maintain that although we may not know that our mental states are brain states, if they are, then in fact we do know about our brain states introspectively, and there is no violation of Leibniz's Law (see, for example, Lycan, 1972).

functional description) is not true of it under another (e.g., a structural description). Then one has a choice: Either reject the identity claim, or carry out further research to show that what is true under the two descriptions matches. The latter strategy is a common discovery strategy in science. From assuming that genes are pieces of chromosomes, the Morgan school of genetics engaged in a highly productive research program that yielded new discoveries about both genes and chromosomes (Darden & Maull, 1977; Darden, 1991). To capture the fact that identity claims are tools of discovery, Robert McCauley and I have dubbed the version of the identity theory we endorse as the heuristic identity theory (Bechtel & McCauley, 1999; McCauley & Bechtel, 2001).

Heuristic identity claims are particularly useful for relating functional and structural decompositions of a mechanism. If, at the time the identity is advanced, there are structural properties which have no functional correlates, or functional relations with no structural correlates, that prompts research to determine if the corresponding parts and operations can be found. One of the virtues of viewing identity as a heuristic claim is that it can guide not only the elaboration of the two perspectives which are linked by the identity claim, but it can use each to revise the other. Thus, mechanistic research does not require that investigators identify the component operations correctly before they attempt to localize them in the brain. As long as the initial hypothesis as to the operation performed is even roughly in the right ballpark, an identity claim can play a fruitful role in generating evidence that leads to revisions and refinements of the initial claim.

2.5   USING BRAIN STRUCTURES TO GUIDE THE SEARCH FOR MENTAL OPERATIONS

Cognitive research into memory operations yielded little direct empirical evidence about the operations involved in memory.[19] In this section I will describe how recent research that is directed towards identifying the brain structures involved when people perform various memory tasks can play a heuristic role in identifying the mental operations involved. This is not to suggest that brain research supplants the need for cognitive research that attempts to decompose memory operations. If we are to understand memory mechanisms, it is necessary to characterize the information processing operations that figure in them. The focus, accordingly, is on how information about which neural structures are involved in particular tasks can help with the project of identifying key mental operations (and, less often so far, also help settle issues about the nature of the

---

[19] Computational models using such architectures as productions systems or semantic networks, offer detailed proposals regarding specific operations. Such models are often evaluated in terms of whether the overall behavior corresponds to the target system being modeled, rather than seeking evidence that people employ the same operations.

mental representations that the operations are presumed to act upon). I begin with the hippocampus and related structures that constitute the medial temporal lobe, which have been the focus of multiple lines of inquiry over the past half century.

2.5.1   Identifying the Operations Performed by Medial Temporal Lobe Structures

Above, I introduced the case of H.M., whose hippocampus Scoville resectioned in the attempt to alleviate severe epilepsy. This resulted in both partial temporally graded retrograde and complete anterograde amnesia. The pattern of deficits led to the view that the hippocampus was the locus of the mental mechanism that encodes episodic memories (but not of the long-term storage mechanism, given that H.M. could remember events from several years before his surgery). Subsequent studies revealed that it is not just the hippocampus proper but also adjoining areas, including the entorhinal, perirhinal, and parahippocampal cortices, that are involved in memory encoding. These areas, together with midline diencephalic structures such as the medial thalamus and the fornix, comprise what is referred to as the *medial temporal lobe* (MTL). Among the significant features of the MTL is that it receives inputs from numerous cortical and subcortical regions that are known to involve the end-stages in the processing of sensory and emotional information as well as motor planning and spatial navigation information, suggesting that its inputs involve already highly processed information.

One of the intriguing questions that emerged from studies of H.M. and other patients with hippocampal damage is why they experienced graded retrograde amnesia, severely affecting memory for events up to a few years preceding damage. The phenomenon suggested that the hippocampus was not just a gateway to long-term memory but played a more extended role in creating long-term memories, a process referred to as *consolidation*. Why should the process of laying down long-term memories occur on a timescale of years? James McClelland, Bruce McNaughton, and Randall O'Reilly (1995) proposed that the answer had to do with the way in which information is stored in neocortical areas (likely in the other parts of the temporal lobe than the MTL). They proposed that the neocortex works much like a standard feed-forward connectionist network. Although such networks can be trained to perform any task (as long as sufficient hidden units are available), they suffer what is known as catastrophic interference. That is, their ability to perform an already-learned task is compromised when they are trained to perform new tasks but not provided with continued training on the initial task (McCloskey & Cohen, 1989; R. Ratcliff, 1990). McClelland and colleagues proposed that the hippocampus helped avoid this problem by training the neocortex slowly over an extended period during which already-learned information was also rehearsed. Although they did not model the hippocampus per se, they developed a procedure for training a network representing neocortex that they regarded as a good approximation to the training procedure employed by the hippocampus. They showed that when the training procedure was interrupted, their network exhibited retrograde amnesia, hence simulating the effects of hippocampal damage on human patients and in animal studies.

McClelland et al.'s simulation, together with existing empirical data, provides a first step in decomposing memory encoding. It is not one operation, but at least two operations: rapid encoding (achieved by neural activity in the hippocampus) and longer-term consolidation (achieved by other neural activity involving both the hippocampus and some part of neocortex). This raises a question: How is the hippocampus able to both quickly learn new patterns and later recreate them so as to supply training signals to neocortex? In a separate paper, O'Reilly and McClelland (1994) identified what initially appeared to be two inconsistent requirements: (a) to ensure that new memories are formed for new events, the hippocampus needs to separate incoming items by giving each a distinctive encoding, but (b) to retrieve existing memories from imperfect cues (for current use and/or to reinstate them in the neocortex), the hippocampus needs to be able to perform pattern completion.

The hippocampus has a highly distinctive neuroarchitecture that provides suggestive clues as to how it might be capable of such dissimilar memory encoding operations. Overall, the hippocampal complex offers a set of loops through which activity elsewhere in the cortex is funneled (Figure 2.3). At its center is the *Cornu Ammonis* (Ammon's horn), which consists of three separate regions of cells known as CA3, CA2 (not shown), and CA1. The dentate gyrus (DG) is sometimes included in the hippocampus and viewed as a separate structure. These structures, together with the subiculum (and sometimes the fornix, not shown), constitute what is often referred to as the *hippocampal formation*. These areas plus three additional areas, the parahippocampal gyrus, the perirhinal cortex, and the entorhinal cortex (EC), constitute the hippocampal system or medial temporal lobe (MTL). The loops through the hippocampal formation begin in the EC. One loop projects first to the granule cells of the DG—which has ten times as many neurons as EC, but in which fewer fire in response to a given input—and then to the pyramidal cells of CA3, in which an even smaller percentage of cells fire in response to a given input. CA3 also receives some inputs directly from EC, and is similar to DG (and to CA1) in its number of excitatory neurons; all areas also have smaller numbers of inhibitory interneurons. CA3's pyramidal cells are highly interconnected via recurrent connections (indicated by a small looping arrow), and the same cells also send activation forward to the pyramidal cells in CA1 via the small CA2 area. Output from CA1 projects back to EC directly or via the subiculum.

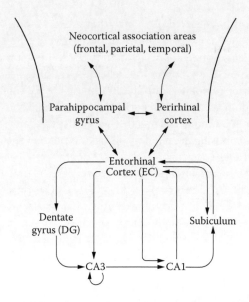

Figure 2.3   Schematic diagram of the hippocampal system. Information from widespread areas of neocortex converge on the parahippocampal region (parahippocampal gyrus, perirhinal cortex, and entorhinal cortex, EC) to be funneled into the processing loops of the hippocampal formation. The tightest loop runs from EC into the core areas of the hippocampus (CA1 and CA3) and back; the loop through the dentate gyrus and the recurrent connections in CA3 are also important; and the subiculum, which is not part of the hippocampus proper, provides an alternative return to EC. Not shown are a number of subcortical inputs and details of pathways and their synapses.

O'Reilly and McClelland (1994) fingered CA3 as capable of reinstating learned patterns so that they could be repeatedly sent out as training signals to neocortex. The principal neurons in CA3 send extensive projections to other CA3 neurons, with each cell connecting to between five and twenty percent of the other CA3 cells. O'Reilly and McClelland proposed that these connections within CA3 create a dynamical system in which attractor basins arise that serve to fill in partial patterns. This idea is supported by other research. Studies in the hippocampus beginning in the 1970s have also revealed a striking form of synaptic plasticity known as *long-term potentiation* (LTP). *N*-methyl-d-aspartate (NMDA)-mediated LTP, in particular, has been linked to memory functions in the hippocampus (Martin, Grimwood, & Morris, 2000). One proposal is that LTP among the recurrently linked cells in CA3 results in associative connections in which synapses at each of the activated cells would be enhanced for an extended period (Bliss & Collingridge, 1993). Such a mechanism would support rapid learning of patterns as well as the ability to perform pattern completion whenever parts of already learned patterns were reinstantiated.

To explain the pattern separation that is required in order to learn new patterns, O'Reilly and McClelland noted that inputs also traverse the less-direct pathway from EC to CA3 via DG. They proposed that the small number of DG neurons firing in response to inputs serve to differentiate patterns. They also proposed that separation could be increased without reducing completion by also decreasing the weight on any connection between an inactive input unit and active output unit. Although controversial, others have proposed neural mechanisms for long-term depression (LDP) in the hippocampus (Levy, Colbert, & Desmond, 1990). In addition, Lisman (1999) has proposed how the two pathways into CA3 together serve to reinstantiate patterns representing sequences of events. This line of research supports both the proposal of McClelland et al. that the MTL serves to train other cortical areas and the suggestion that doing so requires procedures for separating patterns as well as completing patterns from partial patterns. These are promising steps toward decomposing memory encoding into component operations.

This suggested decomposition of memory encoding seemed plausible and appealing, but animal research in the years after H.M. generated a rather different account of the functions of the hippocampus. Rats with hippocampal lesions were found to exhibit profound deficits in spatial navigation. In the Morris water maze, for example, a rat swims to reach a submerged platform on which it can stand. A normal rat who has found the platform from one starting position will, when released from a different location, swim directly towards it. When a rat with its hippocampus lesioned is released from different locations, it searches anew for the platform each time (R. G. M. Morris, Garrud, Rawlins, & O'Keefe, 1982). The deficit is not apparent if the rat is regularly released from the same starting point, presumably because it can rely on a memorized route. O'Keefe and Nadel (1978) concluded that without a hippocampus, the rat can still navigate by landmarks using what they termed *taxon* navigation. To swim directly to the submerged platform from novel locations, they proposed that the rat requires an allocentric representation of space (that is, a representation not based on relations to the rat itself). It must then be able to represent its current location in that allocentric representation and plot an appropriate route. This capacity they attributed to the hippocampus. O'Keefe and Dostrovsky (1971) identified cells in the CA3 fields of the hippocampus (the same areas that on the above account served to complete old patterns and learn distinct new ones) that fired selectively for different locations, leading them to designate these cells *place cells*. These results raise the prospect that encoding of explicit memories and navigation rely on similar operations.

Recently, some theorists starting from these different perspectives on the hippocampus have begun to converge in their accounts of its function. From a consideration of animal navigation, Redish (1999) proposed that the hippocampus' role in spatial encoding provides the foundation for it to play a role in encoding declarative memories. In particular, both navigation and encoding of declarative memories require rapid reinstantiation of previous patterns, and both benefit from replaying previously acquired patterns.[20] Starting instead from a focus on declarative memory, Eichenbaum and his collaborators (N. J. Cohen & Eichenbaum, 1993; Eichenbaum, Otto, & Cohen, 1993) proposed that what is crucial about declarative memory (and what the hippocampus accomplishes) is establishing relationships between information items that can be accessed in a flexible manner. They suggested that spatial memory is just one example of this kind of memory.

Research on the hippocampus points to two ways in which identifying working parts of a neural mechanism can serve a heuristic role in identifying mental operations. First, focusing on the distinctive cytoarchitecture of the components of the hippocampal formation provided clues as to the types of operations (separating patterns and completing patterns) that might figure in encoding of explicit memories. Second, the identification of what initially seemed rather different functions associated with the same structure (encoding explicit memories; navigation) focused investigators' attention on operations that might subserve both activities. The eventual goal is a multilevel account that links two explanatory perspectives both focused on the hippocampus. First, the account of the hippocampus as a neural mechanism should include a structural decomposition into parts such as DG and of those parts down at least to neurons; a characterization of the neural activity of each part, such as the sparse firing in DG; and an understanding of the function served by the activity of each part. The second account is couched in the language of mental mechanisms, with most of the proposals to date focusing on their component operations rather than the nature of the representations operated upon. The neural and mental mechanisms are regarded,

---

[20] Not all animal researchers concur in this attempt to relate the human and animal results. When memory impairments were discovered in human patients such as H.M., animal researchers sought to replicate the deficit in animal models, especially monkeys. Mishkin (1982) created lesions in the medial temporal lobes of monkeys that resulted in severe impairment in object recognition. He found that they could still associate rewards to stimuli (Malamut, Saunders, & Mishkin, 1984). This marked a difference from the human case, as similar lesions in humans do not spare reward learning. In attempting to resolve this puzzle, Gaffan, Parker, and Easton (2001) found that sectioning three axon pathways running in the white matter of the medial temporal lobe of the monkey produced the deep amnesia effects exhibited in humans. These pathways all involve ascending axons from the basal forebrain and midbrain. The researchers concluded that it was these axons, not the medial temporal lobe structures, that were involved in the long-term memory deficits reported in human patients. Gaffan (2002, p. 1112) concluded from this research: "In brief, many non-spatial aspects of memory function are substantially independent of the hippocampus and fornix, and the main role of the hippocampus in primates as well as in rodents is in spatial information processing rather than in memory *per se*."

at least heuristically, as being in an identity relation. In particular, the proposed mental mechanisms provide an explicit account of functions served by the neural mechanisms.

2.5.2   Identifying Operations Performed by Frontal Lobe Structures

Although the hippocampus was one of the first brain structures to be associated with declarative memory, others have been identified as well. The prefrontal cortex was traditionally discounted as insignificant for memory, since lesions there did not seem to impact memory performance.[21] More recently it has emerged as a locus for memory mechanisms, partly as a result of PET studies performed by Tulving and his colleagues.[22] These indicated a role for prefrontal cortex in the encoding and retrieval of episodic memories for words in a list-learning task. The researchers hoped that neuroimaging would enable them to distinguish areas involved in encoding from those involved in retrieval; hence, they imaged subjects during both encoding and recall tasks. As imaging using the subtractive method focuses on differences in activation between tasks thought to differ in specific respects, Tulving and his collaborators (Tulving, Kapur, Markowitsch, et al., 1994) began by comparing blood flow during tasks they thought would require semantic processing (categorizing a noun as referring to a living or nonliving thing) with blood flow during tasks requiring perceptual processing (determining whether a word contained an *a*). That semantic tasks would involve deeper processing, and hence better encoding of the learning episode, was called the *depth of processing effect* by Craik and Lockhart (1972) and is well established. PET imaging revealed that semantic processing produced greater activation in left dorsolateral prefrontal areas than did perceptual processing, suggesting that these areas played a role in the encoding of episodic memories (Kapur et al., 1994). Tulving and his collaborators then imaged subjects during a sentence recognition test, subtracting activation for novel sentences from that for previously heard sentences. There was increased activation in right anterior prefrontal cortex for previously heard sentences. From these results Tulving and his collaborators advanced the hemispheric encoding/retrieval asymmetry (HERA) hypothesis according to which the left prefrontal cortex is more involved than the right in encoding information about novel events (and in

---

[21] Later investigations, though, identified deficits on a number of more demanding episodic memory tasks in patients with frontal lobe damage (see Gabrieli, 2001, for a review).

[22] Although memory deficits were not specifically targeted, Luria (1973) described how patients with damage in prefrontal cortex are reluctant to engage in reflection on themselves or introspection. Instead of being deeply and personally engaged when reporting on events in their lives such patients are detached, as if they are casual observers of their lives (Wheeler, Stuss, & Tulving, 1997).

retrieval of information from semantic memory[23]), while the right prefrontal cortex is more involved than the left in tasks involving retrieval of episodic memories (Tulving, Kapur, Craik, Moscovitch, & Houle, 1994).

Although in some statements of HERA Tulving and his collaborators simply note that left and right prefrontal areas are differentially active in encoding and retrieval, they and others also present these areas as the locus of encoding and retrieval operations, respectively. For example, in their table summarizing various PET studies, they report results as simply showing involvement of brain areas in encoding and retrieval. In summarizing their findings they say:

> We suggest that left frontal activation signals the involvement of the left-frontal cortical regions in the encoding of novel information into episodic memory, at least for verbal or verbalizable materials.... we suggest that right frontal activation indicates the involvement of the right frontal cortical regions in the retrieval of information from episodic memory (p. 2018).

Especially in this form, HERA is a bold hypothesis implying that different brain areas are responsible for the operations of encoding and retrieval of episodic memories. It constitutes an important step towards developing a functional decomposition into component operations of the overall mechanism presumed responsible for episodic memory. As is often the case, such initial steps do not settle the matter, but prepare the way for further research.

2.6   REVISING INITIAL DECOMPOSITIONS OF MEMORY PROCESSES

An important merit of Tulving's HERA model is that it provides a strong set of claims about the operations localized in different brain areas. It is an exemplar of a heuristic identity claim. One of the virtues of advancing such claims is that researchers expand the body of relevant evidence that can be used in assessing the functional decomposition employed in their mechanistic models. In this case cognitive psychologists had long differentiated the operations of encoding and retrieval and, as I have detailed in earlier sections, had phenomenally decomposed memory into different phenomena: short-term or working memory and four types of long-term memory—procedural, perceptual, semantic, and episodic. HERA is specifically a heuristic identity claim about encoding and retrieval of episodic memory representations. Do these mental activities really rely on distinct mental operations? In this section, I will begin by discussing challenges specifically to Tulving's HERA model. The strategy exhibited in advancing these challenges can be applied more generally (not only to HERA), and in

---

[23] Tulving et al. also reported greater activation in left prefrontal areas during semantic recall, and explained the common activation of these areas in semantic recall and episodic encoding as due to the fact that the deep episodic encoding task required recall of semantic information.

the remainder of this section I briefly point to evidence that challenges the distinctions between episodic and semantic memory, between short- and long-term memory, and between memory and other cognitive functions.

The key claim of the HERA model is that the processes involved in encoding and retrieval are different. To show the differences, Tulving and his collaborators relied on subtraction images comparing a focal task condition with a baseline condition. Areas that were active in both conditions are eliminated from the final images due to the subtraction. Yet, they presumably played a role in both the focal task and the baseline task. Buckner (1996) pointed out what subtraction conceals in such cases, and argued for attention to areas whose activation is subtracted out as well as areas whose activity survives subtraction; presumably they work together in performing the task. Looking at the activation during the episodic retrieval task prior to the subtraction, one sees activation not only in right prefrontal cortex but also in left prefrontal cortex. Viewed this way, episodic retrieval seems to require all the processes involved in the episodic encoding task (which was also a semantic retrieval task). This brings into question the assumption that encoding and retrieval are really distinct operations (although, of course, they may each rely on some distinct operations, as well as shared ones, at a lower level of analysis).

Because of the limitations of PET, Tulving et al. had to rely on a rather indirect assessment of encoding—examination of activations during performance of a task that was expected to result in good encoding. The development of event-related fMRI provides a much better way of assessing neural activity during encoding. This technique allows subtracting activation recorded during individual encoding trials for items which the subject later failed to recognize (unsuccessful encoding) from activation recorded during encoding trials for items which the subject later succeeded in recognizing (successful encoding). Utilizing this technique in an experiment in which subjects were required in all cases to perform the same task—make a concrete versus abstract judgment—followed by a test of memory for the words that had been judged, Wagner et al. (1998) found activation in several left prefrontal areas (posterior and anterior left inferior prefrontal gyrus and left frontal operculum) on successful encoding trials. This basically accords with HERA.

In summarizing evidence for HERA in their initial paper, Tulving et al. noted they had used only verbal stimuli. Using event-related fMRI, John Gabrieli and his colleagues presented pictures as stimuli and found activation of right inferior frontal cortex as well as the hippocampus (bilaterally) on encoding tasks (Brewer, Zhao, Desmond, Glover, & Gabrieli, 1998). Right hemisphere activation for encoding conflicts with HERA and suggests that the finding of left hemisphere activation for encoding might have been contingent on the use of words (vs. pictures) as stimuli. Similar results were procured by Kelley et al. (1998) using unfamiliar faces. With line drawings of nameable objects they found bilateral activation, and proposed that the left hemispheric activations might reflect the activation of semantic processing areas as the subject supplies linguistic labels. Both results seem to seriously challenge HERA. First, left localization may be due simply to activating semantic processing of language stimuli. Second, both the left and right activations may have more to do with processing the stimulus than with encoding into episodic memory. Nonetheless, Nyberg, Cabeza, and Tulving (1998) continued to defend the HERA model, arguing that the hemispheric differences represented a statistical, not absolute, difference, and proposing that the discrepant results may have been due to the short presentation times used in the Kelley et al. study.

2.6.1   Do Episodic and Semantic Memories Rely on Different Systems?

Although HERA is presented as advancing a contrast between encoding and retrieval of episodic memory, the encoding studies used to defend HERA require semantic memory retrieval. Hence, the results can be interpreted as supporting an asymmetry between semantic and episodic retrieval, with semantic retrieval being localized to left prefrontal cortex and episodic retrieval to right prefrontal cortex. This distinction between semantic and episodic memory is fundamental to the memory systems approach that Tulving and others have defended, with the hippocampus and right prefrontal cortex being claimed as central contributors to the episodic encoding system. Recently, a variety of types of evidence have been advanced challenging the sharpness of the distinction and especially the idea that different memory systems are involved. Typically, hippocampal damage does manifest itself primarily in failure of episodic memory. However, children who suffer hippocampal damage early in life exhibit deficits in both semantic and episodic memory retrieval, although the deficits are greater for episodic retrieval (Squire & Zola, 1998). Moreover, in tension with Tulving's HERA hypothesis, damage to left prefrontal cortex results in deficits on some episodic retrieval tasks, such as remembering the source of a memory. In an imaging study, Wiggs, Weisberg, and Martin (1999) found activity in left prefrontal cortex on an episodic retrieval task. The deficit and imaging results regarding left prefrontal cortex engagement in episodic retrieval suggest that it is not as distinct from semantic retrieval as Tulving has proposed.

Given such evidence that areas presumably involved in the alternative memory system were involved in episodic and semantic memory tests, Rajah and McIntosh (2005) set out to test whether the differences between episodic and semantic retrieval that had been found in other studies really supported the multiple systems hypothesis or could be better explained as involving differential activation of common components. They did not collect new data, but subjected to a different analysis the imaging data from Düzel et al.'s (1999) study, which had been taken by the authors as supporting the left/right distinction between semantic and episodic retrieval. Instead of relying on subtraction, Rajah and McIntosh employed the technique of structural equation modeling (SEM). This is a form of multivariate analysis that in this application interpreted correlations in activation between different areas as evidence that those areas are linked in a common causal network. Even though the network models they tested were based on "nodes that showed maximal differences in regional activity during episodic versus semantic retrieval tasks," the analysis failed to yield significant differences between the two retrieval tasks. The authors note that a failure to find significant differences (to reject the null hypothesis) does not usually suffice to support a claim of no difference, but maintain that the "striking similarity of the majority of the paths in the present model (the observed value for the X^2_{diff} and degrees and freedom were very close)" does support the claim of "an actual overlap in the pattern of interactions among brain regions across episodic and semantic retrieval" and that "episodic and semantic retrieval were mediated by a single network" (p. 476). There are, the authors grant, differences in the behavior of the network in different tasks, but these differences do not support the claim of separate networks.

Rajah and McIntosh's analysis lends further credence to the arguments considered above against the memory systems approach. Although it remains reasonable to distinguish semantic and episodic memory phenomena, the overlap in neural processing areas involved in each suggests not looking for separate systems but rather focusing on how different tasks place different demands on operations performed in different processing areas. Moreover, insofar as the recruited areas are not viewed as parts of a prewired system, there must be some means by which they are organized or organize themselves to operate together in performing a given task. This presents a new explanatory task.

2.6.2   Are Short- and Long-Term Memory Really Distinct?

One of the earliest distinctions in modern memory research is that between short- and long-term memory. Although H.M. had exhibited severe deficits in encoding new long-term explicit memories, he performed normally on short-term memory tasks requiring delays of only a few seconds. Other patients were identified who exhibited impaired short-term memory but intact long-term memory (Shallice & Warrington, 1970). This suggested that there are distinct short- and long-term memory systems (or in more recent formulations, distinct working memory and long-term memory systems). However, there remained a contingent of investigators who rejected the construal of short-term or working memory as a separate system (Cowan, 1995), and recent studies have suggested that short- and long-term memory rely on some of the same brain areas and, hence, presumably similar operations.

From the initial studies of H.M., areas in the MTL, including not just the hippocampus but also the perirhinal, parahippocampal, and entorhinal cortices, have been viewed as essential for the encoding of long-term episodic memories. As patients with damage to these areas have been reported to perform normally on short-term tasks with simple visual features or shapes (Cave & Squire, 1992), researchers have concluded that these regions figure in encoding long-term but not short-term memories. But, as Ranganath and Blumenfeld (2005) note, previous studies employed relatively simple stimuli. These researchers report a number of deficit and single-cell recording studies on monkeys and deficit studies with humans. The results indicate a role for MTL areas in short-term memory when complex and novel stimuli are employed. The reverse dissociation has also been claimed in earlier studies: subjects with perisylvian lesions exhibit impaired phonological short-term memory but unimpaired long-term memory. But Ranganath and Blumenfeld note that most studies use stimuli that could be encoded semantically or visually as well as phonologically, and so do not provide a comparable measure. They identify other studies of long-term memory in which the stimuli could only be encoded phonologically. In these studies deficits in long-term memory do arise with perisylvian lesions. They thereby claim that the full range of findings undermines the claim of a dissociation between short- and long-term memory.

2.6.3   Is Remembering Really a Distinct Mental Activity?

The decomposition of mental life into activities such as perception, memory, and decision making provided the takeoff point for the development of cognitive accounts of the mind. Textbooks and courses on cognition have traditionally divided the subject matter into such categories. One of the most potent contributions of the attempt to localize memory and other activities in the brain may be the realization that such decompositions may not reflect how the brain organizes its functioning. When a variety of mental operations have been convincingly identified and localized in the appropriate brain areas, it may turn out that the characterization of the operations are orthogonal to these long-standing categories of mental phenomena.

Already in their original paper, Tulving, Kapur, Craik, et al. (1994) drew attention to the fact that the areas active in their episodic encoding task were very close to those Steven Petersen and his colleagues had found in their pioneering PET study using a task in which subjects were asked to generate a verb appropriate to a noun (Petersen, Fox, Posner, Mintun, & Raichle, 1989; Petersen, Fox, Posner, Mintun, & Raichle, 1988). The focus of Petersen and his collaborators was to identify brain areas involved in different language processes, including semantic processing. The fact that the same area is active in a memory task raises the question as to whether the operation the area performs is best understood as a language operation or a memory operation. Tulving and his collaborators took the view that the verb-generate task was, in fact, a semantic recall and episodic encoding task and that the operation of the area in left prefrontal cortex belongs to memory:

> The verb generation task and the noun repetition task perform two functions concurrently: retrieval of information from semantic memory and encoding of information into episodic memory. For the subject to be able to respond with an appropriate verb to a presented stimulus noun, he or she must retrieve relevant information from semantic memory. But information about the event of doing so also is encoded into episodic memory: the subject, with a certain probability, can subsequently remember the event of hearing "car" and saying "drive" (p. 2017).[24]

Rather than settling whether the left prefrontal cortex is a language or memory area, another perspective is to view it as performing an operation deployed in both types of mental activity. Further evidence for this interpretation is provided by the fact that the same areas are active in working memory tasks, and their activation increases parametrically in relation to memory load in working memory tasks (Braver et al., 1997). Gabrieli, Poldrack, & Desmond (1998), in reviewing some of this evidence, concluded that the "operations may be the same whether they are considered in the context of language, working memory, episodic memory, or implicit memory. The left prefrontal cortex thus serves as a crossroads between meaning in language and memory" (p. 912).

Although the view that memory involves storing information in a location separate from where it might be processed (as references to memory *stores* suggest) seems compelling from the perspective of devising an artificial mind, it looks increasing less plausible when considering the range of areas that seem to be activated in memory tasks as well as in other cognitive activities. An alternative view is that remembering is simply one aspect of various mental phenomena; that as the mind performs the operations that generate those phenomena, it is altered in ways that alters future performance and in some cases allows it to remember what has happened to it. This is the view advanced by theorists such as Robert Crowder under the label *proceduralism*: "Proceduralism, in memory theory, is the idea that memory storage for an experience resides in the same neural units that processed that experience when it happened in the first place" (Crowder, 1993, p. 139). If such a view should turn out to be right, the

---

[24] In other research, Tulving and his collaborators demonstrated that subjects exhibited high levels of episodic recall for words they generated in the verb-generate task (Kapur et al., 1994; Tulving, Kapur, Craik., et al., 1994).

operations involved in memory will have more in common with those involved in other cognitive activities than generally acknowledged.

2.7   DO WE NEED TO RECONSTITUTE THE PHENOMENON OF MEMORY?

Through this chapter I have followed the mainstream tradition in the mind/brain sciences in treating memory as a distinct psychological phenomenon concerned with reinstating in the present or future what was learned in the past, whether in the form of skills, semantic knowledge, or episodic recall. The suggestion introduced at the end of the previous section—that memory may not be as distinct from other mental activities as commonly assumed—points to a significant reassessment of that assumption. A yet more radical challenge to the traditional conception of memory has also emerged in recent years—a challenge to the characterization of memory as primarily concerned with veridically reinstating what was experienced. This challenge has arisen most sharply with respect to episodic memory, in part as a result of examining the role frontal areas play in memory retrieval.

One reason frontal areas were not traditionally associated with memory is that damage to them does not result in the pervasive memory deficits characteristic of amnesia, but rather in deficits that arise only in contexts that seem to require effortful processing. Two suggestive findings of patients with frontal lobe lesions is that they often have higher than normal claims to recall stimuli that had not been presented (Schacter, Curran, Galluccio, Millburg, & Bates, 1996) and to confabulate when asked to recall an event (Moscovitch, 1989). Buckner and Schacter (2004) linked this evidence with neural imaging results on recall to support the case that the frontal areas are engaged in a controlled *constructive* process, as follows: (a) the greater the difficulty of the memory challenge, the more anterior are the areas activated (Buckner, 2003); (b) these activations are independent of accuracy of the recall; and (c) activity in frontopolar cortex in particular exhibits extended activity, not tied to specific memory events, in a manner that suggests it plays a role in maintaining attention during retrieval. In contrast to these frontal areas, regions in left parietal cortex seem to track "the perception or decision that information is old" (Buckner & Schacter, 2004), whether or not the information provides the correct response to the current memory task (McDermott, Jones, Petersen, Lageman, & Roediger, 2000).

It is worth noting that Buckner and Schacter are advancing a functional decomposition in interpreting the areas they identify with specific operations. What is different is that the operations do not involve the activation of stored engrams, but rather the effort to create a response to a memory query and to evaluate whether the information presented in the response is information the subject has encountered before. Subjects in these conditions seem to recognize that they should be able to answer the memory probe and are trying to synthesize a plausible response from accessible information. To appreciate what this might involve, imagine that three days ago you met an old friend and later related to someone else how much weight your friend had lost. Then the person asks you what your friend was wearing. Lacking a vivid image of your friend's clothing, you engage in an effortful activity of reconstructing what your friend was wearing. Unless you met your friend in a sauna, it is likely he or she was wearing clothes, so there must be some answer to this question. Rather than admitting that you didn't see your friend's clothes while noticing the loss of weight, you construct a plausible answer from indirect information such as the fact that your friend proclaims to prefer wearing shorts to long pants whenever possible. Soon you construct an image of your friend wearing a white t-shirt and blue shorts, and you answer. You may not have any sense that you were "making up" the answer (after all, the answer feels right in the end), but the psychological processes were engaged in constructing the answer, not just accessing a stored memory.

On the view that Buckner and Schacter develop, in demanding recall tasks frontal areas are engaged with parietal and especially occipital and temporal cortical areas that were involved in initial processing of information. For example, Wheeler and Buckner (2003; Wheeler, Petersen, & Buckner, 2000) found that when subjects had to recall the context in which items had been presented to them during study and determine whether they were presented as sounds or as pictures, they reactivated a subset of the areas initially involved late in the processing of the sounds or pictures. Buckner and Schacter comment: "Reactivation during remembering may rely on a top-down cascade of neural activity that includes sensory areas that process relatively high-level perceptual attributes while sparing early areas that process primitive attributes. Such a retrieval process is both elegant and efficient." (Note that this finding accords well with the suggestion at the end of the previous section that memory is not a mental activity distinct from others such as perception.)

From this account of the range and pattern of processing areas active in recall tasks, Buckner and Schacter advance a view of recall as an active, constructive process. This view receives support from considering how frequently what is recalled is not a veridical representation of the original experience but in various ways misrepresents the original experience. An early example of a focus on memory that is not necessarily veridical is found in a study in which Frederic Bartlett (1932) intentionally presented to his British subjects a culturally unfamiliar native American folk tale, "The War of the Ghosts." He anticipated correctly that his subjects would revise the story to fit models from their own culture. Subsequent research has shown that people tend to recall the gist of narratives they hear, but typically not the exact words. Moreover, they often flesh out or add information that goes beyond what was initially presented to them. In their research on memory for narratives about eating in restaurants, Schank and

Abelson (1977) found that their subjects might add details, such as that the waiter gave the person a menu, that was not in the initial story they heard.[25]

Over the past forty years evidence for the inaccuracies of memory has arisen from a number of research paradigms. Often people think the vividness of memory is indicative of its reliability. Among the most vivid memories people tend to report are *flashbulb memories*, so named by Brown and Kulik (1977) as these memories of highly charged emotional events (e.g., learning of the assassination of President Kennedy) seemed to be fixed in a person's mind as if captured by a flash camera. Psychologist Ulric Neisser became interested in flashbulb memories largely as a result of reflecting on his own flashbulb memory of hearing the news of the bombing of Pearl Harbor:

> For many years I have remembered how I heard of the news of the Japanese attack on Pearl Harbor, which occurred on the day before my thirteenth birthday. I recall sitting in the living room of our house—we only lived in that house for one year, but I remember it well—listening to a baseball game on the radio. The game was interrupted by an announcement of the attack, and I rushed upstairs to tell my mother. This memory has been so clear for so long that I never confronted its inherent absurdity until last year: no one broadcasts baseball games in December! (Neisser, 1982),

To study the reliability of such memories in other people, Neisser developed the strategy in which, shortly after such a major news event (e.g., the explosion of the space shuttle Challenger), he had subjects fill out questionnaires that include details of how they learned of the event. Then several months later they answered the same questions. Neisser found surprising discrepancies between the initial and later reports (Neisser & Harsch, 1992; Neisser et al., 1996). Presumably by the time of the later report subjects were reconstructing, not just reporting, on the event. A highly plausible explanation for some of the differences is that by the time they gave their second report the subjects had rehearsed the events in discussions with friends and that these retellings supported the reconstructed story and gave it great vividness.

Support for the idea that information received after an event can alter a person's memory for the event is provided by a very influential line of research focusing on the reliability of eyewitness testimony that was initiated by Elizabeth Loftus in

---

[25] A particularly compelling example of how people modify details in recalling events, but capture the gist of the original, is provided by John Dean's testimony about Watergate at a congressional hearing. Dean's testimony was particularly compelling as he seemed to have a complete recollection of conversations, specifying explicitly what Nixon and the others had said in numerous conversations. After his testimony the tapes of conversations in the Oval Office were discovered, and it was possible to compare the tapes with the testimony. Neisser (1981) found that while Dean reported accurately on the gist of the meetings, he was wrong about many of the details. Presumably as he was testifying, Dean was reconstructing events in his mind and reporting those reconstructions.

the 1970s. In early studies she had subjects watch a film of a traffic accident. After watching the film she asked the subjects questions that were suggestive or misleading. For example, she asked subjects how fast a sports car was traveling when it went past a barn on the country road even though there was no barn in the film. When later asked to recall what they had seen, many subjects who had been asked the misleading question included content from the question in their recollection of the event (Loftus, 1975; Loftus & Palmer, 1974). Subsequent research by a variety of memory researchers has shown that it is relatively easy to lead subjects to misreport previously experienced events through such questioning.

In 1959 James Deese published a procedure for reliably inducing false recognition of words that were not on a list of words just presented (Deese, 1959). Roediger and McDermott (1995) revived and modified this procedure. They constructed lists of words that are close cognates of a target word, such as *sweet*, but did not include the target word on the list. An exceptionally high proportion of subjects (up to 80%) identify the target word as being on the list. These findings have been replicated and extended in a variety of ways, suggesting that the procedure taps a mechanism for generating memory reports that are robustly nonveridical. Patients with damage to the MTL or diencephalic areas surprisingly were less subject to this effect, although they produced many false alarms to unrelated lures (Schacter, Verlaellie, & Pradere, 1996).

A common conclusion from these and many other findings, one encouraged by the reference to these as studies of *false memory*, is that our memory mechanisms are poorly constructed. But another approach is to treat these findings as supporting the constructive account of memory suggested by Buckner and Schacter. When asked to recall an event, a person engages in mental activity to construct a plausible account of it. A host of factors at different times between the occurrence of the event and the recalling of the event may influence how the person does this.

The picture of episodic memory as involving recording and veridical playback of experienced events has been severely challenged by a number of research findings: experimental findings such as those just reviewed that point to particular, sometimes surprising, memory phenomena as well as results of investigations into the mechanisms involved in memory such as those I focused on earlier. I have emphasized retrieval, but reconstructive processes may be involved even in the encoding process. What a person attends to and their background knowledge at the time of the event can influence how they process it. It seems likely that as they first heard *The War of the Ghosts*, Bartlett's subjects tried to westernize it. When watching a videotape of a traffic accident, one is not simply passively recording what one sees but is trying to understand what is going on. The characterization of the phenomenon of memory as storing items away and later retrieving them, prevalent since Plato put forward the aviary metaphor, is called into question, requiring a recharacterization of the phenomenon of memory as well as an explanation of it.

Reconstituting our understanding of memory does not negate the value of research directed toward understanding the mechanisms of memory that adopted a different understanding of memory phenomena. The conclusions of that research may need to be reinterpreted in light of revised accounts of the phenomena, but often they are still informative. As I have described the work on memory mechanisms in this chapter, the major focus has been on differentiating types of memory. Even if memory is reconceived as a constructive activity involving close connections with other mental activity, there are still differences between episodic and semantic memory and between short-term and long-term recall, both in terms of how subjects perform such activities and in terms of the ways in which brain areas are recruited in them. The recent identification of brain areas involved in different memory tasks provides additional resources to employ in trying to characterize the operations involved. Finding that the same brain areas are recruited in activities not previously counted as involving memory in fact helps advance the project, as investigators can now focus on what would be common operations employed in these different activities. Although still far from providing a detailed account of the operations responsible for various memory phenomena, many of the needed ingredients are now in place for developing such an account. The mechanisms of vision to be discussed in the next chapter, for which researchers have now produced a detailed sketch (albeit one with many details to be filled in), provides a model of what subsequent research on memory mechanisms can hope to yield.

Three

From Working Parts to Operations
Decomposing Visual Processing

Having examined in chapter two research on memory in which behavioral research initially played the leading role, I turn now to research on visual perception in which investigators first identified brain regions that were involved and then tried to figure out the visual operations that were performed in each region. A common first step in such research is to attribute to a part of the system that produces a given phenomenon full responsibility for that phenomenon (in Bechtel & Richardson, 1993, we referred to this as direct localization). In the case of vision, this involved treating an area of the brain as the visual center. Such attributions of complex activities to single components of a system seldom turn out to be correct. As heuristic identity claims, however, they often contribute to productive research by facilitating the discovery that in fact the area is associated with only one or a few of the component operations required to produce the phenomenon. This can spur the search for other areas that are parts of the mechanism responsible for the phenomenon, as well as research directed toward determining what visual operations are localized in each part. In the case of vision, this strategy of *complex localization* was played out through several iterations over the course of more than a century.

Once multiple brain areas and their associated visual operations were identified, researchers faced the further challenge of understanding how they were organized. As a result of this research, the mechanisms of vision (in primates) are now among the best understood mental mechanisms. The responsible brain areas are delineated and substantial progress has been made both in figuring out what different areas do and how they are organized. As with memory, vision researchers eventually recognized that they were not dealing with a single phenomenon. But in this case the route to differentiating phenomena is rather different, as the initial insight stemmed from an understanding of the (neural) parts and (visual) operations in the responsible mechanisms.

To appreciate what was gained by beginning with direct localization and revising the account as needed, it is worth considering how more behaviorally oriented researchers approached vision by trying to decompose it functionally in the manner discussed in the previous chapter. When first considered, visual processing seems like a straightforward way of gaining immediate access to the world about us. We assume there is some sort of direct transmission of light to our eyes and then some process of recognizing what it is that we see. Even Marvin Minsky, a pioneer in artificial intelligence (AI), thought in 1966 that writing a computer simulation of visual perception was a suitable summer project for an undergraduate. Although his choice of a student to confront the task, Gerald Sussman, was inspired, Minsky grossly underestimated the challenge. In 1973 neurophysiologist David Marr visited Minsky's laboratory. Impressed with the approach of AI, and frustrated with the approach of building up from an interpretation of neuroanatomical and neurophysiological findings, he became first an extended visitor and then a permanent member of the laboratory. There, he set about developing an algorithmic approach to vision according to which a visual representation of a scene is built up from the retinal input in stages. First a primal sketch is constructed where various properties of the scene, such as edges, are represented. From this is constructed a two-dimensional sketch that provides a viewer-centered representation of surface properties and geometry. This in turn is the basis for a three-dimensional model of the world, a model which describes shapes and their organization in terms of volumetric and surface primitives, is constructed. Marr's impressive conceptual and modeling work was published posthumously (Marr, 1982) and provided a powerful spur to research in computational vision. It had very little impact, though, on the neuroanatomists and neurophysiologists whose work he had left behind, and it only roughly fit the accounts they developed of visual mechanisms using the strategy he spurned—that is, decomposing the brain into relevant parts and determining the perceptual operations performed in each.

Working from the parts to the operations performed in them requires an initial identification of the working parts of the system—that is, those brain areas whose patterns of neural activity realize visual operations. This initial partitioning might later be revised or refined, but should be accurate enough that manipulating those parts will have an interpretable impact on perception. Not all decompositions into parts identify working parts. Smashing most machines will break them into parts, but not necessarily working parts. In devising his brain regions (Figure 1.2), Brodmann (1909/1994) explicitly appealed to features he thought would be relevant to the mental operations these areas might perform, for example, the types of neurons present and the thickness of cortical layers. Subsequent efforts at brain mapping have likewise emphasized what are likely to be functionally significant features such as patterns of connectivity between neurons (see Mundale, 1998). Once researchers identify potential working parts, new strategies are needed to determine the mental operations actually performed in them. In chapter one I described the techniques available to researchers in addressing this issue: lesion and stimulation studies that manipulate the working parts themselves, and single-cell and neuroimaging studies which detect the changes in neural activity of a working part when different stimuli are presented. The combined use of these tools over the course of the twentieth century culminated in a complex but still incomplete account of the mechanisms that subserve vision. Following the various steps in the story provides an illuminating perspective on how mechanistic explanations of other mental phenomena might be developed.

3.1   LOCALIZING VISUAL PROCESSING IN STRIATE CORTEX

The first clues as to which brain parts perform visual operations came from analyzing patients with visual deficits stemming from brain damage. Bartolomeo Panizza (1856), who studied patients experiencing blindness after stroke-induced occipital lobe damage, proposed that the occipital lobe was the cortical center for vision. He corroborated his human findings by creating lesions in the occipital lobes of animals of several other species including ravens, chickens, and ducks, and showing that blindness resulted. His findings were largely ignored, perhaps because they were published in Italian and perhaps because of lingering opposition to the sorts of localization proposed by phrenologists in the early decades of the nineteenth century.[1] Eventually, though, other investigators started reporting visual deficits in humans who had experienced injury or disease in the occipital lobe (Henschen, 1893; Wilbrand, 1890) and in animals after lesions to the occipital lobe (Munk, 1881; Schäfer, 1888b). Hermann Munk's findings were particularly important, as he had developed techniques for selective removal of small amounts of tissue. In addition to finding a site in the occipital cortex where a bilateral lesion produced what he termed *mind-blindness* (Figure 3.1b), he found an area in the temporal lobe where a bilateral lesion resulted in *psychic deafness.*[2]

---

[1] Phrenology was an approach to relating mental phenomena to the brain advanced by Franz Josef Gall and his collaborator Johann Gaspar Spurzheim (Gall & Spurzheim, 1810–1819/1835) that decomposed the mind into faculties (one for number, one for language, etc.) and then linked these to brain areas based on correlations with cranial bumps or depressions (claimed to reflect the size of underlying brain areas). In the wake of lesion studies by Pierre Flourens (1846) that failed to identify specific deficits following removal of areas of cortex in pigeons as well as theoretical arguments that emphasized the unity of the mind, phrenology fell into widespread disrepute among scientists, although retaining considerable popularity with the public.

[2] Munk also described a gradual recovery of function: "It could be demonstrated that the motor disturbances as well as mind-blindness always disappeared gradually and completely without the least trace within four to six weeks, so that the operated animals could no longer be distinguished in any way from the normal ones. In the animals affected with mind-blindness, one could follow in minute detail how these animals learned to see again exactly as in their earliest years" (Munk, 1877). Munk tried to conduct a second round of ablations around the locus of the first to determine whether that was the area responsible for the recovered function, but discovered that the dogs could not recover sufficiently to allow for careful assessment. One possible explanation for these results is that the area in the occipital lobe that Munk lesioned was more lateral and anterior than the primary projection areas along the calcarine fissure.

(a)   (b)

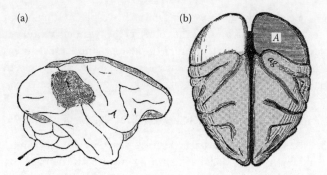

Figure 3.1 Competing proposed localizations of visual processing based on lesions made in monkeys. (a) David Ferrier claimed that lesions to the angular gyrus resulted in blindness. (b) Hermann Munk argued that it was lesions to the occipital lobe that generated blindness.

These results from lesion studies were supported by neuroanatomical evidence reported by Pierre Gratiolet (1854) and Theodor Meynert (1870), which indicated that the optic tract projects from the eye to an area of the thalamus known as the *lateral geniculate nucleus* (LGN) and from there to the occipital lobe. Meynert traced the projections more specifically to the area surrounding the calcarine fissure.

Not everyone agreed with these findings. In particular, David Ferrier (1876), a pioneer in combining electrical stimulation and lesion studies to localize functions in the brain and recognized by many as the leading neurologist of the period, rejected occipital cortex as the site of vision. He maintained that the angular gyrus, an area in the parietal lobe, was its locus (Figure 3.1a). In arguing his case, Ferrier relied in part on lesion studies which, he claimed, showed that bilateral lesions to the angular gyrus resulted in blindness, whereas even large lesions in the occipital lobe produced little impairment. In addition, he found that mild electrical stimulation of the angular gyrus caused monkeys to move their eyes toward the opposite side. Ferrier (1881) later moderated his opposition to an occipital lobe locus, allowing that both the angular gyrus and the occipital lobe figured in vision and that only lesions to both could produce complete and enduring blindness.

Such disagreements over the locus of the mechanism responsible for a given phenomenon are quite common in science (Bechtel & Richardson, 1993). Noting them, though, draws attention to the fact that mechanisms in nature do not come prelabeled. In this case the neuroanatomical information concerning the projection pathways of the optic tract, plus the overwhelming number of lesion results favoring the occipital lobe, resulted in Ferrier's proposal being rejected.[3] By the 1890s there was general consensus that the occipital lobe was the locus of visual processing.

Already, by this time, neuroanatomists had begun to make distinctions among parts of the occipital lobe. Francesco Gennari (1782) had observed an unusual striation pattern in part of the occipital lobe in the course of examining frozen sections of human brains, and reported similar observations in several other species including sheep and cat (Glickstein & Rizzolatti, 1984; Glickstein, 1988). Paul Flechsig (1896) identified the striated area in particular as the target of the projections from the LGN and hence as the locus of visual processing. Named *area striata* by Grafton Elliot Smith (1907), the area is now often referred to as the *striate cortex*. When Brodmann deployed cytoarchitectural tools to map brain areas, he found this area to have a distinctive neuroarchitecture and assigned it the number 17. (Much later, when researchers had recognized that additional areas also figure in visual processing, the terms *primary visual cortex* and *V1*, for *visual area 1*, came into use for Brodmann area 17.)

Localizing visual processing in the striate cortex does not itself provide a mechanistic explanation for vision, as it offers no decomposition into the operations that are involved in seeing. If correct, it only informs us as to where that perceptual mechanism is situated. Yet, right or wrong, it was an important step towards developing such an explanation, in that it provided a focus for further empirical investigation. It is an example of a heuristic identity claim that, as discussed in the previous chapter, earns its keep by fostering further inquiry. The requisite further investigation addressed the question, What does the striate cortex actually do? In large part this was facilitated by finding further structure within the striate cortex.

3.2   FIGURING OUT WHAT VISUAL OPERATIONS ARE LOCALIZED IN STRIATE CORTEX

One possible result of proposing that the striate cortex was the locus of vision would have been the discovery of all the requisite parts needed to process visual information in that region. If so, then the challenge would be to figure out how

---

[3] In retrospect, it appears that the reason Ferrier's lesions of the angular gyrus produced deficits in vision was that his incisions cut deeply and severed the nerve pathways from the thalamus to the occipital cortex (Finger, 1994). Moreover, his failure to eliminate vision with occipital lobe lesions was due to incomplete removal of the visual processing areas in the occipital lobe. But these shortcomings in his technique were only established much later and did not figure in settling the conflict. Moreover, one should not just infer that Ferrier misapplied the lesion techniques because he cut too deeply. Before this could be regarded as an error, the difference between the underlying white matter and the grey matter had to be appreciated and standards for conducting lesion research developed. Standardized methods are often the outcome of such scientific controversies—they cannot be appealed to in settling the controversies.

the requisite operations could all occur within it. This would require discovery of different structures or areas within the region that performed different operations that together provided the ability to see. But in this case it turned out that the striate cortex constitutes just one part of the mechanism of seeing, with many other cortical areas also involved. To discover this, however, researchers had to figure out what cells in the striate cortex actually do. A first step was to discover an arrangement of cells (or, as it later turned out, columns) in which cells in different locations were responsive to different parts of the visual scene, with a systematic mapping from regions of the visual field onto areas in the striate cortex.

Salomen Henschen (1893) was the first to find hints of organized structure in the occipital lobe when he identified sites within it that, when damaged, produced vision deficits in humans. His first claim, based on one patient with a very circumscribed lesion, was that damage to the area around the calcarine fissure, and only it, produced complete hemianopsia.[4] On the basis of anatomical analysis of the neural pathways to the calcarine fissure, he further proposed that different parts of the retina projected to different parts of the calcarine fissure in a manner that preserved the topology of the visual field; as a result, he referred to the area around the calcarine fissure as the *cortical retina* (Henschen, 1903). He further speculated that single ideas or memories would be linked to individual cells. Henschen's account had the projection sites laid out in the reverse of the manner supported by subsequent research. Although it might seem surprising that someone could discover a topological structure, and yet get all the locations reversed, such developments are surprisingly common in the history of science. It is indicative of how difficult it is to extend beyond individual highly suggestive findings to generate a systematic account.

Working with dogs, Mechyslav Minkowski (1911) provided additional evidence that lesions along the calcarine fissure resulted in blindness by showing that complete bilateral removal of the area produced complete and permanent blindness. He further refined Henschen's proposal as to how the retina mapped the cortex, but rejected Henschen's claim of a one-to-one mapping:

> There exists a constant projection of the retina upon the cortical retina, and in such a manner that the upper parts of the retina are located in its anterior portion, the lower parts in the posterior. However, the projection is not of a geometrical but of a physiological nature: each identifiable element of the retina is not connected with one, but with an entire area of identifiable elements of the cortical retina, although with some of

---

[4] Henschen (1924, p. 30) later summarized his conclusion, emphasizing the localizationist claim and its revolutionary character: "The kernel of my researches and conclusions can be formulated as follows: *The visual field coincides with the area striata.* These words include, for the present, the statement that our senses have a peculiar and sharply limited anatomical seat and organization in the brain, *the statement also including, at the same time, a revolution of earlier views and also an important progress in our knowledge of the organization of the brain and its functions.*"

these more closely than with others. This area is the larger, the stronger the physiological claims to the respective elements of the retina, or the closer it is to the point of central vision; the latter is represented like an island within the area of the cortical retina, but in a particularly extensive area. The corresponding parts of both retinas have a common projection field within the confines of the cortical retina (p. 306).[5]

Minkowski also applied mild electrical stimulation in the vicinity of the lesions he had induced in dogs, and determined that in response they still moved their eyes. From this he concluded that sensory inputs terminate solely within the striate cortex but that an optical motor area lies outside it but in the same vicinity.

During the Russo-Japanese War, Tatsuji Inouye, a young ophthalmologist, was assigned to assess visual loss in Japanese soldiers who had suffered brain injuries. The ostensive purpose of these exams was to determine the size of pensions, but Inouye turned his assignment into a research opportunity. The Russians had developed a new high-velocity rifle (Mosin-Nagant Model 91) that fired 7.62 mm hard-jacketed bullets. Unlike most earlier bullets, these pierced the skull without shattering it, leaving tidy entrance and exit wounds. Inouye examined 29 individuals who sustained highly focal damage to the occipital lobe and determined that they experienced blindness in the central part of the visual field when their injuries were to posterior parts of the occipital lobe and blindness in peripheral parts of the visual field when damage targeted anterior regions (see Glickstein, 1988). A similar study by Gordon Holmes (1918; 1919) during World War I generated a more detailed account that supported Minkowski's contention that focal visual areas projected to larger portions of the occipital lobe than peripheral areas. Holmes suggested both that this helped explain the fact that patients often experienced small areas of blindness near the fixation point and that the relatively exposed nature of the occipital poles to which the focal areas project explained the frequency of paracentral scotomata. His diagram (Figure 3.2) maps regions of the occipital lobe in which lesions result in deficits in specific areas of the right visual field of the right eye.

The discovery of topological maps did not itself reveal what the areas in the striate cortex were actually doing. Given that lesions to an area resulted in blindness in a specific part of the visual field, it was possible that the area was somehow responsible for the whole process of seeing in that part of the visual field. To determine what specific function these areas performed required a different research tool, one that could

---

[5] Minkowski also provided an account of when recovery was possible after occipital lobe lesions, maintaining it was due to reliance on preexisting anatomical pathways that could assume new functional significance: "If a portion of the cortical retina is cut out, recovery occurs only inasmuch as such elements of the cortical retina which were earlier in loose connection with the elements of the retina predominantly involved (constituting for these only cortical excitatory side stations), now enter into an especially close relations with these (becoming cortical excitatory main stations). The rapid rate of this recovery and its absence with extensive, partial surgery, demonstrate that it takes place essentially in anatomical paths which already exist, and not in ones newly formed" (pp. 306–7).

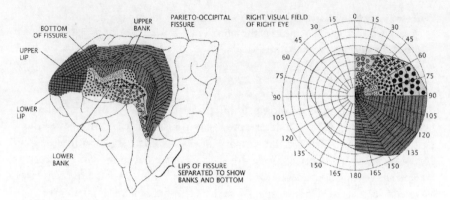

Figure 3.2   Gordon Holmes' (1918) map indicating how different areas of the right visual field (i.e., the right half of the figure on the right) project onto particular regions of the occipital lobe (shown on the left). Note that the right eye sends information about the right visual field to the left visual cortex (and information about the left visual field to the right visual cortex).

determine what a given set of cells was doing in response to the stimulus. In chapter one I described how the efforts of Edgar Adrian and others culminated in techniques for recording from individual neurons in intact brains. The first research recording from intact brain focused on determining how tactile sensory areas mapped onto the post-central gyrus but Talbot and Marshall (1941) soon attempted to generalize this approach to vision. Working with anesthetized monkeys and cats, they mapped what Hartline (1938) had referred to as the receptive fields of cells by finding where in the visual field they could project a stimulus that would result in a response from a given neuron from which they were recording. Talbot and Marshall's map (Figure 3.3) reveals much the same pattern as that discovered earlier by researchers relying on lesions and so did little beyond support the earlier results. To use single-cell recording to identify the information being processed in a given neuron required focusing on the particular characteristics of the stimulus that would cause increased firing of a given neuron.

Hartline (1940) initiated one line of inquiry using frogs and alligators in which he recorded from a single optic nerve fiber in the visual periphery while he varied the location and intensity of a light stimulus. He had previously distinguished three classes of fibers, ones that responded when a light was on in its receptive field (on cells), ones that responded whenever the light changed from off to on or on to off (on–off cells) and ones that responded only when a light was turned off in its receptive field (off-only cells). Moreover, he had found that the receptive fields of individual cells were quite large. He determined that for each type of cell, the intensity of the stimulus determined how far from the center of the receptive field the stimulus could be and still elicit a response. Thus, stimuli further from the center had to be much stronger

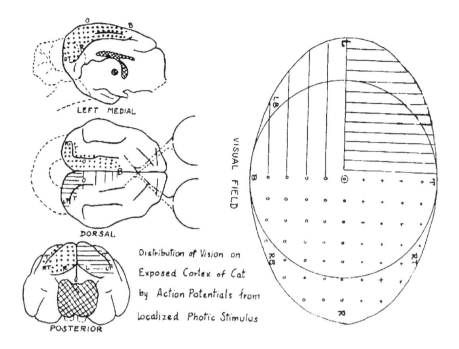

Figure 3.3   Talbot and Marshall's (1941) projection of areas of the visual field onto primary visual cortex in the cat based on recording from cells.

to elicit the same response as would be elicited by a weaker stimulus near the center of the receptive field. Moreover, smaller stimuli had to be more intense to elicit the same response as large stimuli. This suggested that the nerve fiber cells were performing a kind of summation over the different cones that project to them.[6]

---

[6] Hartline also determined that the projections from cones to optic nerve cells was not one-to-one; rather, many cones projected to a given optic nerve cell and the receptive fields of optic nerve cells overlapped extensively: "It is evident that illumination of a given element of area on the retina results in a specific pattern of activity in a specific group of optic nerve fibers. The particular fibers involved, and the distribution of activity among them, are characteristic of the location on the retina of the particular element of area illuminated. Corresponding to different points on the retina are different patterns of nerve activity; even two closely adjacent points do not produce quite the same distribution of activity, although they may excite many fibers in common. The more widely two illuminated spots are separated the fewer fibers will be involved in common, but it is reasonable to suppose that it is only necessary to have two recognizable maxima of activity in order to resolve the separate spots. It is this spatial specificity of groups of optic nerve fibers, and of the distribution of activity among them, that furnishes the basis for distinguishing the form of the retinal image" (p. 698). In these observations Hartline anticipated the idea of distributed representations discussed in chapter five.

Horace Barlow (1953) followed up on the line of experimentation initiated by Hartline. Working with frogs, he confirmed Hartline's claim that ganglion cells performed a nonlinear summation over the cones projecting to them, but also found that with on–off cells when the stimulus exceeded the size of the receptive field, the response diminished. He concluded: "It is immediately obvious from the results ... that 'on–off' units possess an inhibitory, or subtracting, mechanism in addition to the summating mechanism found in 'off' units; there is no other explanation for the fact that adding an annulus to the stimulus spot reduces the sensitivity" (p. 78). By supplying a second stimulus just outside the visual field of a ganglion cell as well as one in the receptive field, it also observed a decline in the responsiveness of the cell. In the final sections of the paper Barlow addressed the functional significance of detecting spots of light, especially moving ones, to the frog's ability to catch insects, anticipating in important respects the influential paper published at the end of the decade by Lettvin, Maturana, McCulloch, & Pitts (1959).

In the same period Steven Kuffler (1953) began recording from ganglion cells in cats, which it turned out had provided a relatively clean preparation as cats did not exhibit the movement responses found both in frogs and other mammalian species such as rabbits. Kuffler employed an optical stimulator that Samuel Talbot had designed by modifying a doctor's ophthalmoscope; it presented to the retina a weak but uniform background light[7] and a highly focused stimulus spot (Talbot & Kuffler, 1952). Kuffler discovered that with either diffuse background lighting or in complete darkness neurons fire from 1 up to 20 spikes per second. Controlling the focused spot, Kuffler found locations that produced either an increase or decrease in this basal firing rate. Although some cells responded with increased activity to a spot of light against a darker surround, an approximately equal number responded to a dark spot on a bright surround. The first came to be known as *on-center* cells, the latter *off-center* cells. Kuffler explored both the size of the spot and the size of the contrasting background area that would elicit maximal responses, and like Barlow, discovered that expanding the size of the focal spot would increase the response of a cell up to a critical point (corresponding to the size of its receptive field), but that further increase resulted in a decrease in the response. He concluded that the center and surround operated in an antagonistic manner such that if a stimulus in the center elicited a response, a stimulus in the surround would defeat the response but the absence of a stimulus in the surround would further increase the response. Moreover, he found that a spot of light of a particular size at a given location would produce a

---

[7] Varying the degree of the background lighting enabled Kuffler to control whether rods, which only operate in dim lighting, or cones, which only operate in bright lighting, were engaged (Hubel, 1995).

high firing rate, but if the spot were moved a small distance, the firing rate of the neuron would drop below its spontaneous firing rate.

As complex as retinal ganglion cells turned out to be, they are only the starting point in the processing of visual stimuli. The research already described made it clear that striate cortex plays a major role in processing visual stimuli and two junior researchers in Kuffler's laboratory at Johns Hopkins University, David Hubel and Thorsten Wiesel, tried to employ the same techniques as Kuffler to analyze the contributions of cells in striate cortex. Initially they were unable to get cells in striate cortex to respond to circular stimuli. But, as Hubel reports, while they were inserting a glass slide into their projecting ophthalmoscope, "over the audiomonitor the cell went off like a machine gun" (Hubel, 1982, p. 438). They eventually figured out that it was not the dot on the slide that was having an effect, but the fact that "as the glass slide was inserted its edge was casting onto the retina a faint but sharp shadow, a straight dark line on a light background" (p. 439). As Hubel later report: "This was unheard of. It is hard, now, to think back and realize just how free we were from any idea of what cortical cells might be doing in an animal's daily life" (Hubel, 1982, p. 439). Nonetheless they shifted their investigations to slits or rectangles of light or darkness, not spots.

The cell from which they elicited this initial response turned out to be of the type that they later identified as complex cells. In their 1959 paper they reported on other cells from which they could elicit a response with a 1° spot of light anywhere in a receptive field was a "long, narrow, vertically oriented region" (in cells responding to peripheral parts of the visual field, the receptive fields were 1° wide by 4° long) (1959, p. 576). But Hubel and Wiesel noted that the strongest responses came from stimuli having the same shape as the receptive field. In a study recording from unanesthetized cats, Hubel (1959) had found that moving a stimulus was often the most effective and sometimes the only way to elicit a response from a cell. Hubel and Wiesel confirmed in their studies with anesthetized cats that moving slits of light back and forth often turned out to be effective stimuli but that some cells responded only when slits moved in one direction, not the other (Hubel & Wiesel, 1959).

After discovering that cortical cells tended to prefer rectangular shaped light, whereas retinal ganglion cells preferred circular shapes, Hubel and Wiesel (Hubel, 1960; Hubel & Wiesel, 1961) confronted the question of whether cells along the pathway to the cortex also responded to such patterns. The pathway from the retinal ganglion cells to the brain proceeds through the optic chiasm, where half of the fibers from a given eye continue on the same side of the head as they project towards the brain and half cross over to the other side. Although some fibers project to other subcortical areas of the brain, many project to the lateral geniculate nucleus (LGN) of the thalamus. The LGN has a relatively complex structure, with interneurons projecting between areas within the LGN and a substantial

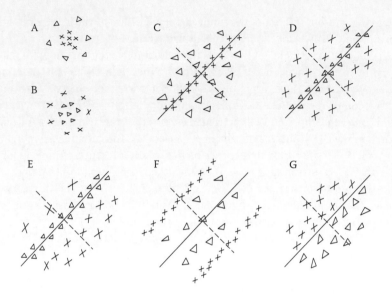

Figure 3.4   Examples of Hubel and Wiesel's mappings of receptive fields of cells in the lateral geniculate (A-B) and of simple cells in primary visual cortex (C-G). X indicates an area producing excitatory responses and Δ an area producing inhibitory responses. Redrawn from Hubel, D. H., & Wiesel, T. N. (1962), *Journal of Physiology*, 160, p. 111, text figure 2, with permission of Blackwell Publishing.

number of neurons projecting back to the LGN from the cortex or subcortical areas such as the reticular formation. Hubel and Wiesel found that LGN cells, like retinal ganglion cells, had concentric on and off regions (see Figure 3.4a,b). When these cells responded to moving stimuli, the response was independent of the direction of movement. They concluded that the properties they had found in recording from striate cortex—responding to rectangular stimuli and motion in only one direction—were "a product of the integrative capacity of the striate cortex, as they are not found in geniculate or retinal units" (Hubel, 1960, p. 102).

Through the 1960s, Hubel and Wiesel probed the striate cortex of both anesthetized and paralyzed cats (Hubel & Wiesel, 1962) and macaque and spider monkeys (Hubel & Wiesel, 1968) while presenting stimuli on a screen 1.5 meters in front of them. From their initial studies with cats, they discovered they were dealing with different types of cells with related but different response patterns. What they termed *simple cells* had receptive fields with spatially distinct *on* and *off* areas along a line at a particular orientation (for example, they had long, narrow *on* areas which they referred to as a *slit* sandwiched between two more extensive *off* areas—see Figure 3.4c–f). Changing the orientation more than 5-10° commonly eliminated the response. Hubel and Wiesel identified some cells that responded when brightness contrasted on two sides of a line, as in Figure 3.4g. They referred to such stimuli as *edges*, although subsequently the label *edge detector* has been applied generally to cells in striate cortex. In addition, they found that striate cortex cells responded both to stationary stimuli and stimuli that moved back and forth across their receptive fields. Whereas simple cells were sensitive to stimuli only at a given retinal location, neurons Hubel and Wiesel termed *complex cells* were responsive to slits of light at a particular orientation anywhere within their receptive fields, but unresponsive when the slits filled their whole receptive fields. Many complex cells were also sensitive to the direction of movement of slits within their receptive field, responding only or considerably more strongly to stimuli moving in the preferred direction. In addition, Hubel and Wiesel discovered that there was a pattern to the distribution of simple and complex cells, with simple cells appearing in large numbers in cortical layers 3 (lower portion), 4 and 6, whereas complex cells were in large numbers in layers 2 and 3 (upper portion) and 5 and 6.[8]

Having established the multiplicity of cell types in striate cortex, Hubel and Wiesel addressed their organization. To do this, they inserted electrodes gradually and recorded from cells at successive depths. In cases where they were able to insert the electrode at an orientation nearly perpendicular to the cortical surface, they found that all cells responded to stimuli oriented the same way (although their receptive fields often varied significantly). In most cases, however, electrodes ended up oblique to the surface, and as they progressed to greater depths, the preferred orientation of cells gradually shifted. From this they

> … concluded that the striate cortex is divided into discrete regions within which the cells have a common receptive-field axis orientation. Some of the regions extend from the surface of the cortex to the white matter; it is difficult to be certain whether they all do. Some idea of their shapes may be obtained by measuring distances between shifts in receptive-field orientation. From these measurements it seems likely that the general shape is columnar, distorted no doubt by any curvature of the gyrus, which would tend to make the end at the surface broader than that at the white matter; deep in a sulcus the effect would be the reverse. The cross-sectional size and shape of the columns at the surface can be estimated only roughly. Most of our information concerns their width in the coronal plane, since it is in this plane that oblique penetrations were made. At the surface this width is probably of the order of 0.5 mm (Hubel & Wiesel, 1962, p. 133).

In their discussion, Hubel and Wiesel related these columns to those Vernon Mountcastle identified in somatosensory cortex in cats (Mountcastle, 1957) and monkeys (Powell & Mountcastle, 1959); they noted, however, that unlike in somatosensory cortex, columns are specific to orientation of stimuli and seem to play a significant role in elaborating the information received at the senses.

---

[8] An important difference between the different layers is that they generally project to different brain areas: layers 2 and 3 project forward to other cortical areas, layer 5 projects backwards to the superior colliculus, pons, and pulvinar, and layer 6 backwards to the LGN.

Hubel and Wiesel further addressed the question of how inputs from the two eyes are processed in striate cortex. Minkowski (1913) had determined that the layers of the LGN that received projections from both eyes degenerated after damage to striate cortex and Talbot and Marshall (1941) had mapped visual inputs from both eyes to the same region of striate cortex. Hubel and Wiesel established that some cells received input from the corresponding receptors in both eyes and that the inputs from the two eyes tended to work in synergy with each other. They varied, however, in that sometimes one eye would have significantly more affect than the other on a particular cell (a phenomenon they referred to as *ocular dominance*). They also found cases in which the cells responded only if they received input from both eyes simultaneously. When they turned to which eye most strongly activated cells, they often found cells within the same column showing different dominance profiles, but commented as follows:

> While these results suggested that cells of different ocular dominance were present within single columns, there were nevertheless indications of some grouping. First, in twenty-three of the thirty-four multiple recordings, simultaneously observed cells fell into the same ocular-dominance group. Secondly, in many penetrations short sequences of cells having the same relative eye dominance were probably more common than would be expected from a random scattering.... If cells of common eye dominance are in fact regionally grouped, the groups would seem to be relatively small. The cells could be arranged in nests, or conceivably in very narrow columns or thin layers (1962, p. 140).

Commenting on the overall pattern of organization, Hubel and Wiesel assert:

> The otherwise puzzling aggregation of cells with common axis orientation now takes on new meaning. We may tentatively look upon each column as a functional unit of cortex, within which simple fields are elaborated and then in turn synthesized into complex fields. The large variety of simple and complex fields to be found in a single column suggests that the connexions between cells in a column are highly specific (1962, p. 144).[9]

The specificity of the processing by different cells, they conclude, explains why striate cortex has so many more neurons than either the retina or the LGN.

Having identified two types of cells in the striate cortex of cats with different response properties, in the discussion section of their 1962 paper Hubel and Wiesel hypothesized a possible processing mechanism whereby one type of cell supplies

---

[9] Hubel and Wiesel (1965a) convinced themselves of the reality of ocular dominance columns in a study of four kittens in which they cut one of the extraocular muscles, creating a divergent strabismus. Their recordings from these animals revealed clearly separated columns dominated by one or the other eye, a pattern they also found in kittens whose earlier visual experience was limited to one eye at a time. They viewed these animals as exhibiting an extreme version of the pattern found in normal animals.

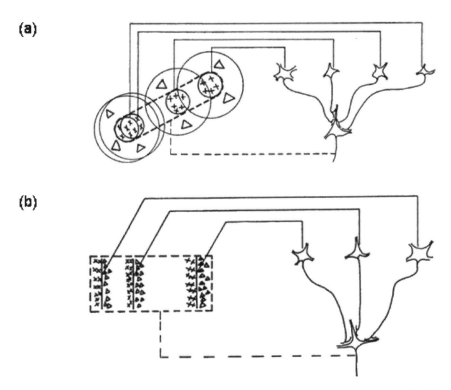

Figure 3.5 Reprinted from Hubel and Wiesel's proposals for wiring diagrams for (a) simple and (b) complex cells. Simple cells receive their inputs from LGN cells with on centers that are aligned so that when a bar of light crosses the receptive fields of all the linked LGN cells, the simple cell fires. Complex cells receive their input from simple cells which are responsive to edges oriented in the appropriate way at any point in their receptive fields. Redrawn from Hubel, D. H., & Wiesel, T. N. (1962), *Journal of Physiology,* 160, p. 142, text figure 19, and p. 143, text figure 20, with permission of Blackwell Publishing.

information to cells later in the pathway and each carries out its own information processing. Thus, they proposed that several LGN cells with center-surround receptive fields might all send excitatory input to a single simple cell, which would sum input from the various LGN cells to which it was connected and fire when the spots of light detected by LGN cells fell along a line (Figure 3.5a). Likewise, they proposed that complex cells received input from several simple cells and would respond when any of these simple cells were active (Figure 3.5b). In terms of logic, the simple cells operated like *and-gates,* whereas the complex cells functioned as *or-gates.*

In their subsequent studies of monkey cortex, Hubel and Wiesel (1968) found support for many of their findings in cats but also some differences. First, Hubel and Wiesel (1968) identified a third type of cell, *hypercomplex cells* (later called

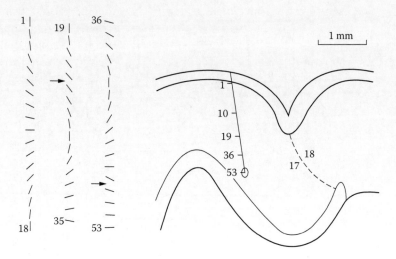

Figure 3.6   Hubel and Wiesel's reconstruction of a penetration by an electrode through striate cortex about 1 mm from the 17-18 border, near the occipital pole of a spider monkey. On the left they show the preferred stimulation orientation of cells at successive depths as the electrode was gradually inserted at an angle of 45°. Redrawn from Hubel, D. H., & Wiesel, T. N. (1968), *Journal of Physiology*, 195, p. 231, text figure 9, with permission of Blackwell Publishing.

end-stopped cells), which responded maximally only to bars extending just the width of their receptive field.[10] (They first found these cells in V2 and V3 in the cat, and I will discuss them further in that context below.) Second, they obtained more detail on the arrangement of cells. In what they described as "by far the most impressive examples of orderly sequences" they gradually inserted an electrode into a part of area 17 near the border to area 18 in a spider monkey at an angle of 30° from perpendicular and recorded at successive locations. Over the first 18 locations (approximately 1 mm.) the preferred orientation of successive cells progressed counterclockwise through a full 180° rotation. As penetration continued, a point was reached (indicated by an arrow in the middle column in Figure 3.6) where the variation in preferred orientation suddenly reversed. The preferred orientations continued to shift in the new direction through most of

---

[10] Hubel and Wiesel (1965b) identified such cells only in areas 18 and 19 of the cat and assumed that these cells received their inputs from complex cells. Later, though, they found them in area 17 in both cat and monkey. After Dreher (1972) found cells in cats that were location specific like simple cells but whose response dropped off as the length of the stimulus exceeded an optimum length, they dropped the assumption that they received their inputs from complex cells.

the rest of the penetration, but shifted again very near the end (second arrow). Third, they found a stronger pattern of ocular dominance in the monkey than in the cat. They proposed that in one direction successive columns (perhaps better characterized as slabs, each judged to be .5 mm wide) were dominated by alternate eyes (ocular dominance columns) while in the other direction successive columns were responsive to different orientations of the stimulus.[11]

On the basis of their investigations with both cats and monkeys, Hubel and Wiesel claimed to have discovered the primary function of striate cortex: "The elaboration of simple cortical fields from geniculate concentric fields, complex from simple, and hypercomplex from complex is probably the prime function of the striate cortex—unless there are still other as yet unidentified cells there" (Hubel & Wiesel, 1968, p. 239). The final phrase represents a prophetic caveat to which I will return. From the perspective of developing a mechanistic account of vision, what Hubel and Wiesel did was discover the structure and operation of the first components of a mechanism. They showed that the cells in striate cortex took in information about dark and light spots of light detected by the retina and LGN and constructed representations of slits or bars of light (edges) that specified both their location in the visual field and their motion. Equally important, the discovery that cells in striate cortex only served to detect edges or rectangles of light revealed that the mechanism of visual processing was not completely located in striate cortex but must involve other brain areas. Accordingly, Hubel and Wiesel conclude their 1968 paper with the comment:

> Specialized as the cells of 17 are, compared with rods and cones, they must, nevertheless, still represent a very elementary stage in the handling of complex forms, occupied as they are with a relatively simple region-by-region analysis of retinal contours. How this information is used at later stages in the visual path is far from clear, and represents one of the most tantalizing problems for the future (Hubel & Wiesel, 1968, p. 242).

3.3   WHERE DOES THE REST OF VISUAL PROCESSING OCCUR AND WHAT OPERATIONS ARE INVOLVED?

By showing that striate cortex carried out only part of the task of seeing, Hubel and Wiesel demonstrated that the initial hypothesis identifying visual processing with operations in striate cortex was incorrect. The mechanism of visual processing minimally had to include operations sufficient to recognize objects. But any efforts to figure out the other parts of the mechanism faced an obstacle.

---

[11] In parts of striate cortex in the monkey Hubel and Wiesel failed to find ocular dominance columns, but attributed this to the possibility that the dominance columns may take the form of slabs that are not straight, but swirling, and the need for ideal conditions to detect them.

At the time Hubel and Wiesel were working, the legacy of early twentieth century holism and antilocalizationism was still prominent. This tradition maintained that, except for primary sensory processing areas, cortical areas did not individually perform specific operations. Rather, the rest of cortex operated in a holistic fashion. This conclusion was in part motivated by the general failure to find loss of specific mental capacities with damage in these cortical regions.[12] On the contrary, what seemed to matter was only how much cortex was destroyed—the severity of the deficit was correlated with the amount of tissue destroyed. Karl Lashley termed this the *principle of mass action* and applied it in particular to the area immediately surrounding striate cortex, an area for which he coined the term *prestriate region*. He denied that prestriate cortex had a specifically visual function, insisting that "visual habits are dependent upon the striate cortex and upon no other part of the cerebral cortex" (Lashley, 1950). To overcome the legacy of Lashley and others required clear evidence that prestriate areas (areas anterior to striate cortex) were in fact dedicated to visual processing.

3.3.1   Prestriate Visual Areas

For many researchers, one sign of the lack of differentiated function beyond striate cortex was the lack of evidence that these areas were topologically organized in the manner of striate cortex. The very lack of a topological organization suggested that these areas operated holistically to integrate sensory information (thus, they were designated *association cortex* by anatomist W. LeGros Clark). One of the first indications of visual processing beyond striate cortex was Alan Cowey's (1964) discovery, using surface electrodes to record evoked responses, of a second topographically organized area in Brodmann's area 18 (which immediately adjoins area 17); this area came to be known as V2 (visual area 2), with striate cortex being designated V1.[13] Using single-cell recording, Hubel and Wiesel (1965b) confirmed the topographical organization of this area and identified yet

---

[12] There had been suggestions of additional processing areas in the late 19th-century. Both Verrey (1888) and MacKay and Dunlop (1899) identified the fusiform gyrus, adjacent to the striate cortex, as the locus of lesions in patients suffering cortical achromatopsia (the inability to see colors). Although this suggested a second visual area, one devoted to color perception, most 19th-century researchers dismissed these claims in favor of the supposition of one cortical center for vision in the striate cortex, which might produce achromatopsia with mild lesions and full blindness with more serious lesions. One finding supporting this interpretation was that most cases of achromatopsia also manifested scotomas or areas of total blindness, suggesting that one lesion produced both effects.

[13] Cowey's findings were anticipated by Talbot and Marshall (1941), who mapped out in each hemisphere two projections of the contralateral visual field. The first they termed *visual area I*; it corresponds anatomically to striate cortex. They failed to link the second, *visual II*, to cytoarchitecture.

a third area, V3, in Brodmann's area 19. They determined that both V2 and V3 received direct projections from V1 and sought to determine the nature of the stimuli that would drive each cell from which they recorded. They found that most of the cells in V2 were complex cells similar to those found in V1 except that they had larger receptive fields. (Habel & Wiesel, 1970, used random dot stereoscopic patterns as stimuli to determine that nearly half of the cells were responsive to binocular depth cues, some cells responding maximally when the input to the two eyes was aligned and others to various degrees of offset.) Complex cells in V3 were also very similar, but Hubel and Wiesel did not assess their receptive fields. Somewhat more than half of the cells they recorded from in V3 fell in the class they labeled as *hypercomplex*, which included several types of cells that deviated from both simplex and complex cells in various ways. Lower-order hypercomplex cells responded to edges as long as they terminated on the requisite end within the receptive field of the cell or by slits or bars that were terminated on both ends within the receptive field. Higher-order hypercomplex cells were a diverse group. Some responded to edges oriented at either of two orientations 90° apart, others responded to bounded regions at a variety of locations within their receptive fields (but not to a stimulus extended over the whole region).

By tracing degeneration of fibers from discrete lesions in striate cortex to areas in surrounding cortex, Semir Zeki (1969) provided collaborative evidence for the existence of these additional areas. Zeki (1971) then extended this approach by creating lesions in V2 and V3 and tracing degeneration forward into areas on the anterior bank of the lunate sulcus in which "the organized topographic projection, as anatomically determined, gradually breaks down" (p. 33).[14] (The gradual breakdown of topographic projection to which Zeki refers reflects the fact that cells in later processing areas have broader receptive fields than those in earlier areas. This results from cells with adjoining receptive fields projecting onto common target cells. The result is that the maps in later processing areas are less finely differentiated.) Zeki labeled the areas into which he traced degeneration as V4 and V4a.

The discovery of topological maps of the visual field in additional brain areas, even if these were less finely delineated, indicated that these too were part of the

---

[14] Zeki ends the paper with the following comment, similar in tone to that with which Hubel and Wiesel ended their 1968 paper, about projections to other brain areas: "How the prestriate cortex is organized in regions beyond (central to) V4 and V4a remains to be seen. It is perhaps sufficient to point out at present that the organisation of the prestriate areas would seem to be far more complicated than previously envisaged and that the simplistic wiring diagram from area 17 to area 18, from area 18 to area 19 and from area 19 to the so-called 'interior temporal' area will have to be abandoned. At any rate, we were not able in this study to find any projections to the 'inferior temporal' areas from areas 18 and 19 (V2 and V3)" (p. 34).

mechanism of visual processing. But the existence of maps did not show directly what operations these areas performed. This required examining just what features of stimuli within the receptive fields of the cells in different areas would produce responses. Zeki (1973) recorded from cells in V4 and found "in every case the units have been colour coded, responding vigorously to one wavelength and grudgingly, or not at all, to other wavelengths or to white light at different intensities" (p. 422). He reported that some neurons only responded to stimuli of a given shape whereas others responded to any shape of the appropriate wavelength. Using a similar procedure to that which Hubel and Wiesel used in studying V1, Zeki recorded from successively encountered cells in a perpendicular penetration and found they responded to stimuli of the same wavelength. Recording from successively encountered cells in an oblique penetration revealed that they responded to stimuli of different wavelengths. Zeki interpreted this as evidence of a columnar organization dedicated to analyzing color:

> ... it would seem that colour coded units are not only grouped together according to colour preferences but that, in addition, such colour coded units are organised into columns, signaling preferred colour, just as the units in striate cortex analysing form are grouped into columns of receptive field axes. The unit of organisation, the column, is the same for both areas; the emphasis on what is grouped into a functional column varies (p. 424).

The next year Zeki (1974) reported on a study recording in rhesus monkeys from cells on the posterior bank of the superior temporal sulcus, an area he would later label V5. This area received projections from V1, V2, and V3. The fact that most of the cells in the area had relatively large receptive fields led Zeki to characterize a "blurring in the detailed topographic representation of the visual field" (p. 550). He found that cells in this area were not selective for wavelength but responded primarily to movement anywhere in their receptive fields. Some fired in response to movements in any direction, but most were sensitive to the particular direction, and sometimes the shape of the moving stimulus. Zeki described many cell types that differed in their specific requirements, including cells that responded to movement in the opposite direction in each eye. He inferred that such cells must be signaling movement towards or away from the animal. Although he could not record the precise speed of movement of stimuli, he reported the impression that cells varied significantly in the speed of motion to which they responded optimally. As with V4, he found evidence of a columnar organization of movement sensitive cells, with adjacent cells exhibiting slight changes in their preferred orientation (see Figure 3.7). About the same time John Allman and Jon Kaas (1971), in the course of a study recording from a number of sites across the cortex of an owl monkey, found a

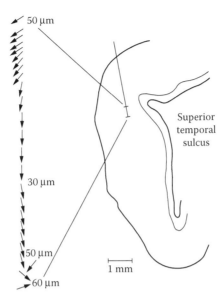

Figure 3.7 Zeki's reconstruction of a penetration into the posterior bank of the superior temporal sulcus (V5 or MT) showing the preferred direction of movement of successive cells from which the recordings were made. Redrawn from Zeki S. M. (1974). *Journal of Physiology*, 236, p. 563, text figure 10, with permission of Blackwell Publishing.

retinotopically organized map in an area in the middle temporal region, which they named MT. This area, in which the cells were highly myelineated, was identified with Zeki's V5, with North American researchers tending to use the name MT15 and British researchers calling it V5.

If areas V4 and V5 performed the specific visual processing operations suggested by Zeki, then damage to there areas ought to result in specific impairments. Indeed, patients were already known in the nineteenth century who experienced a specific deficit in seeing color, a condition known as cortical achromatopsia (see note 12 above). At the time of Zeki's work there were no reports of patients with deficits specifically in motion perception, but in 1983 Zihl, von Cramon, & Mai reported on a patient who, as a result of vascular damage, could not perceive motion. To the patient activities such as the pouring of coffee into a cup appeared as a succession of contiguous shapes, like a glacier. The existence of such deficits provided further support for the hypothesis that color and motion processing are different operations in visual processing performed by different brain areas. In a

---

[15] Van Essen, Maunsell, and Bixby (1981) argue for extending the use of the term MT from the new world monkeys to macaques on the basis of homology despite the fact that in the macaque the area is neither in the middle temporal gyrus nor in the middle of the temporal lobe.

noteworthy study, Anthony Movshon, William Newsome, and their colleagues introduced yet other techniques for identifying the function of MT cells. These researchers presented ambiguous displays to monkeys who were supposed to identify the direction of motion (in the ambiguous displays, approximately half the objects in the display were moving in the same direction). They discovered that the firing of particular cells could predict a monkey's response, and that microstimulation of those cells would bias that response (Britten, Shadlen, Newsome, & Movshon, 1992).

In a study exploring the boundaries of MT in the macaque, van Essen, Maunsell, and Bixby (1981) identified a region at the medial edge of MT where the receptive fields of cells increased in size and shifted in position. The investigators raised the possibility that "this area represents a higher stage in the analysis of moving stimuli than that carried out by MT" but noted "direct evidence on this issue is not yet available" (p. 323). Subsequently Maunsell and van Essen (1983) designated this area medial superior temporal area (MST) and, using retrograde and anterograde radioactive tracers identified connections between it and MT (and between MT and yet another previously unidentified region, the ventral interparietal area, VIP). Differentiation of two movement areas adjacent to each other prompted Keiji Tanaka to investigate what different operations each might perform. Besides noting the wider field of motion to which MST cells were responsive, he also identified their ability to distinguish the motion of a stimulus relative to a background, and drew out the psychological significance of this information for detecting such things as relative depth of objects or assessing the organism's own movement against a background. Subsequently, researchers distinguished two regions within MST, a dorsomedial region MSTd and a lateroventral region MSTl. Cells in MSTl responded most strongly to small movements and lesions to the area generated deficits in maintaining pursuit eye movements (Komatsu & Wurtz, 1989), whereas cells in MSTd responded to movements of large stimuli and to rotating and expanding stimuli. Duffy and Wurtz (1991a; 1991b) linked MSTd to the detection of optic flow, the apparent motion of a visual scene as an organism moves through it, as characterized by Gibson (1950). More specifically, Bradley, Maxwell, Andersen, Banks, & Shenoy (1996) showed the neurons in MSTd adjusted their focus to compensate for eye movements as the animal moved through the scene.

A critical limitation of the approach of presenting stimuli and recording from cells to determine the types of stimuli to which they are responsive is that the results are constrained by the types of stimuli investigators think to test. Without the fortune of a stuck slide creating a bar of light, Hubel and Wiesel might not have explored the responsiveness of V1 cells to such stimuli. Zeki focused on color stimuli in exploring the responses of V4 cells and this suggested that V4 might be a color area. Other researchers tested stimuli with various shapes, and found V4 cells responded differently to shapes. The most natural shapes to test are ones for which we have supplied names, but David van Essen and collaborators decided to explore a variety of concentric, radial, spiral, and hyperbolic gratings (they referred to these as non-Cartesian gratings) and found that many cells in V4 responded more strongly to these shapes than to more traditional Cartesian shapes (Gallant, Braun, & van Essen, 1993; van Essen & Gallant, 1994). Even with these additional findings, the limitation holds—researchers are only able to assess responses of cells to stimuli they decide to test. Other, untested stimuli, might elicit just as strong, or even a stronger response from these cells.

With the identification of these extrastriate areas and proposals as to the operations they performed, the boundaries of the visual processing mechanism had expanded. As Zeki emphasized, the emerging pattern was of different areas selectively responsive to particular aspects of visual stimuli. But these accounts did not yet indicate how or where the information about edges, color, and motion was put to use to recognize objects and events in the world: "The picture that is beginning to emerge, therefore, is one of a mosaic of areas, each with a different functional emphasis. Presumably the visual information analyzed in detail in these areas is then assembled at an even more central cortical area" (Zeki, 1974, p. 569). To determine whether this assumption was correct, researchers had to expand the quest for specialized visual processing areas into yet more anterior parts of the brain in the temporal and parietal lobes.

3.3.2   Temporal Lobe Visual Areas

The first suggestions that areas in the temporal lobe played a specific role in visual processing were provided by a late nineteenth century study by Edward Schäfer (1888a) ostensibly devoted to showing that, contrary to Ferrier's claims, the temporal cortex was not the locus of an auditory center. In monkeys in which either the superior temporal gyrus or nearly all the temporal lobes were removed, Schäfer reported no detectable loss of hearing but a deficit in recognizing visually presented stimuli:

> The condition was marked by loss of intelligence and memory, so that the animals, although they received and responded to impressions from all the senses, appeared to understand very imperfectly the meaning of such impressions. This was not confined to any one sense, and was most evidence with visual impressions. For even objects most familiar to the animals were carefully examined, felt, smelt and tasted exactly as a monkey will examine an entirely strange object, but much more slowly and deliberately. And on again, after only a few minutes, coming across the same object, exactly the same process of examination would be renewed, as if no recollection of it remained (p. 375).

At approximately the same time as Schäfer was conducting his studies with dogs, neurologist Heinrich Lissauer (1890) identified two patterns of deficits in patients who could see but failed to understand what they saw. One group of patients was unable to achieve a coherent percept of the object they saw—they could see features of the object but not the whole. A second group of patients could see the whole object, but still not be able to recognize it. Lissauer distinguished these two deficits as *apperceptive* and *associative* mind-blindness[16]; the following year Freud (1891) introduced the term *agnosia*, and the inability to see form is now referred to as *apperceptive agnosia* and the inability of being able to recognize objects visually is referred to as *associative agnosia*.

These observations drew little attention until Heinrich Klüver and Paul Bucy began their research in the late 1930s. These researchers, in the course of a study of hallucination-producing drugs in animals with cortical lesions,[17] removed the temporal lobe in a rhesus monkey (Klüver & Bucy, 1938). They determined that the monkey's visual reflexes were in tact and that she had no problem picking up objects. Despite her ability to discriminate objects visually, she seemed not to be able to identify them by sight. For example, when food was interspersed with other objects, she picked up all the objects and examined them with her mouth, only then discarding those that were not edible. Moreover, even if she had examined the object shortly before, she would reexamine it with her mouth again when it is represented.[18] Klüver and Bucy followed up this study with one in which they examined seven additional monkeys (rhesus and Cebus) in which the temporal lobe was extirpated bilaterally, six others in which the temporal lobe was only severed from the occipital or frontal lobe or only portions of the temporal lobe were removed, and one in which the left temporal lobe was removed prior to removal of both frontal lobes. Focusing primarily on the animals with bilateral removal of the temporal lobe, they characterized one condition

---

[16] Lissauer invoked these findings in support of a model of visual processing in which visual stimuli from the retina were turned into conscious sensations in striate cortex. The activity in striate cortex then excited cells in the apperceptive center where they were transformed into images of objects. From there activity passed to the center for concepts, where meaning was attached.

[17] This stemmed from Klüver's (1928) interest in mescaline, based partly on personal experience. The resemblance of mescaline hallucinations to the auras that precede temporal lobe seizures led him to remove the temporal lobes in monkeys to determine whether that would impair the mescaline response. It did not (Gross, 2005).

[18] Klüver and Bucy (1939, p. 985) describe the monkey's behavior when left alone: "When in its home cage the animal may examine at random pieces of food, the food pan itself, stones, cigarette stubs and wires lying among the pieces of food, the head of a screw in the wall of the cage and a chain hanging down from the door. If free in a large room the animal may contact and examine more than 100 objects in thirty minutes and may pass the pieces of food lying on the floor many times before picking them up. The examination includes such heterogeneous objects as a steel nut in a motor, an iron pipe, the tail of a monkey, a windowpane, the fingers, shoes and stopwatch of the experimenter and a piece of soap. When free in a room, the monkey again tends to reexamine most objects at intervals, so that a given object, let us say an iron pipe, may be examined a dozen times in the course of half an hour."

they produced as *psychic blindness* or *visual agnosia* in which "the ability to recognize and detect the meaning of objects on visual criteria alone seems to be lost although the animal exhibits no or at least no gross defects in the ability to discriminate visually" (Klüver & Bucy, 1938, p. 984; Klüver, 1948). Finding that these deficits were commonly accompanied by other behavioral changes, including loss of emotional responsiveness and increased sexual behavior, Klüver and Bucy referred to these deficits as constituting a syndrome.

Pribram and Bagshaw (1953) addressed the question of whether the different deficits Klüver and Bucy had found in the monkeys were due to interrupting a single operation performed in one brain area or to different operations in nearby areas. They began by noting that the gross anatomical divisions of the brain into lobes may not pick out working parts of the brain, and maintained that neurological methods provided different divisions (e.g., a frontotemporal region that includes the posterior orbital, anterior insular, temporal polar and periamygdaloid or pyriform cortex and a "lateral temporal" subdivision that includes the cortex of the supratemporal plane and superior temporal gyrus). In their study Pribram and Bagshaw removed the whole frontotemporal region in an adult baboon and five immature macaque monkeys, and more restricted regions in another baboon and two other macaques. Prior to surgery the animals with complete frontotemporal lesions had quickly learned to differentiate and ignore nonfood items and avoid noxious stimuli. After surgery, the animals explored everything they encountered with their mouths and failed to avoid noxious objects. They summarize the results as follows:

> Unaffected by frontotemporal lesions is performance in vision, with respect to acuity, extent of field, and ability to make simultaneous discriminations. Ability to localize tactile stimuli is unimpaired, range of movement unaltered. Performance in the delayed-reaction test is unchanged. On the other hand, altered behavior does occur in the categories of taste, food intake, general activity, and approach to or avoidance of a variety of stimuli including noxious and social ones. This specificity of results takes on added significance in light of the fact that ablations of adjacent regions of the frontal and temporal lobes have produced a different constellation of behavioral changes: *viz,* ablations in the lateral frontal region are associated with selective interference with delayed-response-type functions; ablations in the medial occipitotemporal region result in selective impairment of animal's ability to solve problems involving visual discrimination (p. 368).

The factors they identified in the first sentence as unchanged in these animals had been shown in other studies to be affected by lesions further forward (delayed-response tasks) or further back (discrimination between simultaneously presented objects).

Subsequently, Pribram collaborated with Mortimer Mishkin in localizing damage that resulted in deficits in visual discrimination to the ventral portions of the temporal lobe (often referred to as *inferotemporal cortex*) together with the hippocampal formation (Mishkin & Pribram, 1954). Mishkin (1954) followed up by limiting lesions to either the ventral temporal cortex or the hippocampal formation alone. The monkeys with ventral temporal cortex damage experienced much greater difficulty in relearning shape discriminations after lesion than did those with hippocampal damage. Subsequently, by creating a complex set of lesions involving the striate cortex in one hemisphere and the inferotemporal cortex in the other and then sectioning of the forebrain commissures that linked the hemispheres, Mishkin (1966), succeeded in separating striate and inferotemporal cortex. (The remaining striate and inferotemporal cortices continued to function, but the inferotemporal cortex was now totally cut off from the remaining striate cortex.) He established that the deficits in visual learning and memory result when inferotemporal cortex is cut off from earlier visual processing and thereby ascertained that it was loss of the inferotemporal cortex that resulted in visual agnosia and that it played its normal role in visual learning when it received inputs from striate cortex. Mishkin also demonstrated that TE and TEO, areas within inferotemporal cortex that von Bonin and Bailey (1951) had distinguished on cytoarchitectonic grounds, produced differential deficits, with TEO lesions producing greater deficits in single-pattern discrimination tasks and TE lesions generating greater deficits on learning to perform multiple discriminations in parallel.

These lesion studies were highly suggestive of the existence of pathways from extrastriate cortex to inferotemporal areas. There was also suggestive neuroanatomical data indicating such pathways (Bailey, von Bonin, Garol, & McCulloch, 1943). Gross, Schiller, Wells, and Gerstein (1967) inferred from these findings:

> It is conceivable that inferotemporal cortex might be a site of further processing of visual information received from prestriate and striate cortex. If this were true, its neurons might have receptive fields and highly complex response properties.

But they also consider a competing hypothesis that inferotemporal cortex might primarily send activity back to extrastriate cortex and not itself serve as a visual area, a hypothesis supported by research showing that stimulating inferotemporal cortex resulted in detectable changes in the activity of primary visual cortex (Spinelli & Pribram, 1966). As a result, Gross et al. attempted to record both from inferotemporal cortex and superior temporal cortex, an area thought to be involved in auditory processing. While they succeeded in generating responses in inferotemporal cortex with spots of light, and in superior temporal cortex with sounds, on that occasion they did not find receptive fields in inferotemporal cortex. A couple years later, though, Gross, David Bender, and Carlos Eduardo Rocha-Miranda (1969) succeeded in identifying receptive fields in inferotemporal cortex and concluded that their earlier failure may have been due to the fact that during long recording the brain entered into a highly synchronized, slow-wave state (as indicated by EEG recordings) that was unresponsive to incoming stimuli and required strong acoustic or semantic stimulation to restore normal function. The receptive fields they now found, however, were much larger than those in prestriate cortex, with the center of gaze falling within the receptive field of every neuron. Moreover, the receptive fields often crossed the midline into the ipsilateral hemifield. They emphasized that the responses of inferotemporal cortex neurons were less precise that those in striate or prestriate cortex and put forward two possible explanations, one of which turned out to be particularly telling:

> By largely confining the stimuli to bars, edges, rectangles, and circles we may never have found the "best" stimulus for each unit. There were several units that responded most strongly to more complicated figures. For example, one unit that responded to dark rectangles responded much more strongly to a cutout of a monkey hand, and the more the stimulus looked like a hand, the more strongly the unit responded to it.

As Gross, Rocha-Miranda, and Bender (1972) reported, the discovery of the hand stimulus, like Hubel and Wiesel's discovery of the bar stimulus for V1, resulted from serendipity: "having failed to drive a unit with any light stimulus, we waved a hand at the stimulus screen and elicited a very vigorous response from the previously unresponsive neuron" (p. 103). They then used cutouts of various shapes (several are shown in Figure 3.8) in an attempt to determine what would most strongly drive the cell. A hand shape remained the most effective stimulus, but only when oriented upwards: "Curiously, fingers pointing downward elicited very little response as compared to fingers pointing upward or laterally, the usual orientations in which the animal would see its own hand" (p. 104). They also found cells that responded most vigorously to pictures of faces or of trees and some that responded better to three-dimensional objects in front of the screen than to cutout shapes.

Figure 3.8   Examples of shapes that Gross, Rocha-Miranda, and Bender used to stimulate cells in inferotemporal cortex. The stimuli are arranged from left to right in order of increasing ability to drive the neuron from none (1) or little (2 and 3) to maximum (6). Reprinted from Gross, C. G., Rocha-Miranda, C. E., & Bender, D. B. (1972), *Journal of Neurophysiology*, 35, figure 6, with permission of the American Physiological Society.

As Gross and his colleagues probed inferotemporal cortex, it turned out both to be similar in many respects to earlier processing areas but also to exhibit significant differences. For example, when a cell responded to a shape, the response tended to be the same regardless of its size, contrast, or location as long as the stimulus was within the cell's receptive fields (Desimone, Albright, Gross, & Bruce, 1984). These receptive fields were not laid out retinatopically and tended to emphasize the fovea. When they were able to record from awake, behaving animals, Gross, Bender, and Gerstein (1979) found that cells only responded when monkeys attended to the stimulus appropriate to the cells.

As intriguing as the finding that some neurons in inferotemporal cortex preferred object shapes, including the shapes of faces, nearly a decade passed before further research was published confirming different areas where individual cells were responsive to specific shapes.[19] Bruce, Desimone, and Gross (1981) found cells in the superior temporal sulcus that they termed *superior temporal polysensory area* (STP) that responded especially to faces whereas others were responsive to biological motion. Desimone et al. (1984) identified a variety of different neurons in inferotemporal cortex that responded to faces, with some responding best to a frontal view, others to profile, and yet others to any view. Starting with these findings, they has been an explosion of reports of specific areas in inferotemporal cortex responsive to different specific objects (see Tanaka, 1996, for a review).

3.3.3   Parietal Lobe Visual Areas

A similar pattern of first identification of deficits following lesions, then single-cell recording studies, emerged in research on the role of the parietal cortex in processing visual stimuli. This process began in the late nineteenth century. Both Ferrier and Yeo (1884) and Brown and Schäfer (1888), who were opposing each other on the claim that the angular gyrus was the locus of vision, reported deficits from lesions to the angular gyrus in the posterior parietal cortex which indicated a problem with spatial localization. Ferrier and Yeo report that the lesioned

---

[19] Gross (1998, pp. 199–200) reports on the slowness of response: "for more than a decade there were no published attempts to confirm or deny these and our other early basic results, such as that IT cells have large bilateral fields that include the fovea and are not visuotopically organized. And unlike Panizza, the discoverer of visual cortex in the nineteenth century, we did not publish in obscure journals or from an unknown institution. Perhaps because of the general skepticism, we did not ourselves publish a full account of a face-selective neuron until 1981." Gross (2005) presents a number of reasons why he might have been particularly sensitive to hands and faces as potential stimuli. Two seem particularly salient. He had reviewed Polish neuroscientist Jerzy Konorski's book for *Science* (Gross, 1968) in which he postulated the existence of *gnostic neurons*, which he proposed would be found in IT. In addition, he had worked in the same department at MIT as Hans-Lucas Teuber, who reported on numerous cases of prosopagnosia resulting from temporal lobe lesions.

monkey was "evidently able to see its food, but constantly missed laying hold of it" (p. 494) and Brown and Schäfer report that their monkey "would evidently see and run up to [a raisin], but then often fail to find it… " (both quotations from Gross, 1998, p. 200 and 201). Ferrier (1890) also reported the monkey experienced problems in grasping objects, groping with its whole hand rather than shaping it appropriately to pick up the object.

Rezső (Rudolph) Bálint (1909) described a stroke patient who could not accurately reach with his right hand to visible objects, but would grope in the direction of the object as if blind. Bálint labeled the specific deficit *optic ataxia* but it is commonly grouped with other symptoms, such as the inability to perceive more than one object at a time and the inability to change ocular fixation voluntarily, under the label *Bálint's syndrome*. The deficit seemed to be neither purely sensory, as the patient could accurately guide motion with his other hand, nor purely motor, because the patient could guide motion of his right hand toward parts of his own body when requested to do so orally. Rather, the problem seemed to lie in the coordination between visual processing and motor execution—the patient could not use the visual information to control motor activity.

Based on his studies of brain injuries in World War I veterans, Gordon Holmes (1919; G. M. Holmes & Horrax, 1919) studied eight patients who had suffered missile wounds who could identify objects visually and still not reach for them successfully. Yet, if they were allowed to explore their environment tactually, they performed normally. He described the disorder commonly referred to as *visual disorientation* as "the inability of the patients to determine the position in space, in relation to themselves, of objects which they saw distinctly" (p. 231). Numerous other researchers described patients with similar deficits, or with deficits localized to one part of the visual field (see G. Ratcliff & Davies-Jones, 1972). On the basis of studies they conducted on 40 men with damage to posterior areas of the brain, Ratcliff and Davies-Jones themselves indicated that the locus of damage was in the parietal lobe.

These observations with humans were supported by lesion studies on animals. Ettlinger and Kalsbeck (1962) lesioned the parietal cortex in monkeys and demonstrated much the same behavior as found in human patients. With unilateral lesions, deficits were restricted to reaching with the contralateral arm. Haaxma and Kuypers (1975) determined that small lesions to the inferior parietal cortex rendered a monkey unable to orient its fingers and thumbs so as to secure food with the contralateral hand, but not the ipsilateral hand, suggesting the existence of smaller regions in the parietal lobe involved in particular visual–motor coordination.

Researchers were initially far less successful in recording from neurons in parietal cortex than in recording from the occipital and temporal cortex. The problem was that in anesthetized animals no stimuli would activate the targeted cells in parietal areas. When researchers developed techniques for recording from awake, behaving animals, they found that the cells were responsive to visual stimuli, but only under particular conditions. Juhani Hyvärinen discovered that cells in Brodmann's area 7 responded to a perceptual stimulus only when it was conjoined with a particular behavior of the monkey, such as reaching toward a target or moving its eyes to look at it:

> In many cells a discharge was produced when a sensory stimulus which interested the animal was placed in a specific location in space where it became the target of the monkey's gaze or manual reaching, tracking, or manipulation. Convergence of touch and visual stimuli related to the same body part was also observed. Some cells were clearly related to eye movements whereas others appeared to discharge in response to visual sensory stimuli (Hyvärinen & Poranen, 1974, p. 689).

Hyvärinen interpreted such cells as engaged in visuospatial guidance of movement. This link between activity of parietal cells and eye or body movement pointed to a motor function for these cells. This suggestion was further developed by Vernon Mountcastle and his colleagues, who focused on parietal cells whose responses were linked to different arm and hand manipulation (Mountcastle, Lynch, Georgopoulos, Sakata, & Acuña, 1975; for a more recent study, see Murata, Gallese, Luppino, Kaseda, & Sakata, 2000). Mountcastle interpreted these cells as involving motor commands linked to selective attention. Other research, however, contended that the posterior parietal cortex was primarily involved in visual analysis and only modulated by the significance of the stimulus as some cells are responsive in the absence of any motor activity (Goldberg & Robinson, 1980). Importantly for understanding the differential significance of parietal visual processing, Richard Andersen and his colleagues demonstrated that cells in posterior parietal cortex mapped stimuli in terms of spatial location. This is a feature to which temporal lobe cells are relatively unresponsive (Andersen, Essick, & Siegel, 1985).[20]

Subsequent research has suggested more specific ways in which parietal neurons couple stimulus information with spatial information. In particular, Andersen and his associates determined that for neurons in areas 7a and the lateral interparietal area (LIP; an area known to have reciprocal connections with the frontal eye fields that control eye movements), the position of the eye in the orbit affected the amplitude of the response of the cell to a stimulus in its receptive field. This, they recognized, would facilitate the transformation of locations specified in retinal coordinates into head-based coordinates. Support for

---

[20] Subsequent research, which will be discussed in chapter five, has confirmed a close relation between parietal cells and motor action and has investigated whether these cells are directly involved in planning action or in maintaining attention on visual stimuli (Snyder, Batista, & Andersen, 1997; Batista, Buneo, Snyder, & Andersen, 1999).

this interpretation is provided by the fact that microstimulation of cells within areas 7a and LIP generates saccades to a particular location with respect to the head position (Kurylo & Skavenski, 1991). Duhamel, Colby, & Goldberg (1992) identified another group of cells in the same region that seem to alter their receptive fields just prior to saccades in ways that ensure that the stimulus falls in the receptive field after the eye movement. Yet other researchers have found cells located in the anterior intraparietal area (AIP) that respond to the size and orientation of the object, and are often linked to the hand shape required to grasp the object (Taira, Mine, Georgopoulos, Murata, & Sakata, 1990).

3.4 ORGANIZATION OF THE VISUAL PROCESSING MECHANISM

Research such as that related in the preceding section has revealed a host of brain areas that perform different operations involved in processing visual information. These are critical elements in any account of the visual processing mechanism, but so is their organization, that is, spatial relations between brain areas and temporal ordering of their operations. The organization of a neural system is provided by the patterns of cellular connectivity through which neurons in different brain areas communicate with each other. However, these patterns are extremely complex. On average each neuron is connected to a thousand other neurons. To understand how the neural system is organized, a somewhat coarser view is required. To a degree this was already emerging from the patterns of discovery of brain areas involved in vision. Starting with primary visual cortex, researchers expanded their conception of the visual processing mechanism by moving forward in the brain. Moreover, it became clear that the connections from extrastriate cortex seemed to split into those projecting downwards into the temporal lobe and upwards into the parietal lobe. And as we have seen, evidence began to amass that the areas identified in the temporal lobe were involved in the identification of objects whereas areas in the parietal lobe seemed to process information about the spatial location and orientation of objects.

Focusing on subcortical processing in which lesions seemed to differentially affect location versus object recognition in the hamster, Gerald Schneider (1967; 1969) had proposed a distinction between discrimination and spatial localization, with discrimination involving processing in geniculostriate regions whereas spatial processing involved tectofugal regions. Colin Trevarthen (1968) established a similar division of processing in primates, linking understanding of spatial situatedness to midbrain and object oriented processing to the cortex.[21] Leslie Ungerleider and Mishkin (1982; see also Mishkin, Ungerleider, & Macko, 1983) extended this

---

[21] Trevarthen described his work as emerging from investigations with split brain monkeys and noting that in them some information was limited to one hemisphere after the commissurotomy whereas other information seemed to be available to both. He characterized the difference partly in terms of information from ambient vision focal vision.

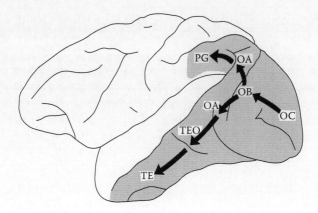

Figure 3.9   Two pathways of visual processing in the rhesus monkey proposed by Mishkin, Ungerleider, and Macko (1983). Each begins in area OC (primary visual cortex or V1) and projects into extrastriate areas OB (V2) and OA (V3, V4, and MT). What they called the *what* pathway then projects ventrally into inferior temporal cortex (areas TEO and TE), whereas the *where* pathway projects dorsally into inferior parietal cortex (area PG).

framework to provide an overall macro-level organizational perspective on visual processing (see Figure 3.9). As a basis for their account they appealed to established neuroanatomy indicating two fiber bundles from the occipital lobe—the superior longitudinal fasciculus follows a dorsal path traversing the posterior parietal region before reaching the frontal lobe whereas the inferior longitudinal fasciculus follows a ventral route into the temporal lobe (Flechsig, 1896; 1920). Ungerleider and Mishkin's strategy was then to dissociate the contributions of these two pathways. In the first study from their laboratory, Pohl (1973) found a dissociation between monkeys with ventral pathway lesions who manifested a deficit on object discrimination tasks, but not on discriminations that required assessing proximity to a landmark, and monkeys with dorsal pathway lesions that exhibited the opposite pattern of deficits. From this and successive studies, Ungerleider and Mishkin arrived at a characterization of the various tasks linked to processing along the ventral pathway as all involved in identifying *what* an object is whereas those linked to processing along the dorsal pathway were involved in identifying *where* an object is: "It has been our working hypothesis that the ventral or occipitotemporal pathway is specialized for object perception (identifying *what* an object is) whereas the dorsal or occipitoparietal pathway is specialized for spatial perception (locating *where* an object is)" (p. 549).[22]

---

[22] Once it became possible to study humans with fMRI, Ungerleider and Mishkin collaborated with James Haxby to establish a similar dissociation of function between pathways in humans (Haxby et al., 1991).

In the case of the ventral pathway, Ungerleider and Mishkin interpret the lesion and single-cell recording evidence described earlier as supporting

> ... a sequential-activation model for object vision in which information that reaches the striate cortex is transmitted for further processing to the prestriate cortex, and from there to the inferior temporal area. This system appears to be important for the analysis and coding of the physical dimensions of visual stimuli needed for their identification and recognition (p. 554).

They propose, though, that "the process of attaching reward value to a stimulus depends on stations beyond the occipitotemporal pathway." In contrast, they viewed the variety of deficits exhibited with dorsal pathway lesions as "different reflections of a single, supramodal spatial disorder" (p. 555), a view they attributed to Semmes (1967).

For Ungerleider and Mishkin, the separation of two pathways began from a common origin in striate cortex. Other researchers soon proposed extending the differentiation of pathways back into V1, LGN, and the retina, generating a model of two processing pathways from the very earliest visual input. An important piece of evidence for projecting the two pathways further back was a distinction between two different cell types in the retina and the LGN. Enroth-Cugell and Robson (1966) had differentiated two types of cells in the cat retina, which they named X and Y cells. X cells had small receptive fields (hence, they were sensitive to high spatial frequencies), medium conductance velocities, and responded as long as the stimulus was present. In contrast, Y cells had large receptive fields, rapid conductance velocities, and responded transiently. A similar distinction of retinal cell-types was advanced for primates. $P\alpha$ (or P ganglion) cells correspond to the X cells in the cat, whereas the $P\beta$ (or M ganglion) cells correspond to the Y cells in the cat. Research on Old World monkeys revealed that this scheme is maintained in the LGN, where the cells in the two inner layers have large cell bodies (the layers are thus known as *magnocellular* or *M-layers*) while the cells in the outer four have small cell bodies (thus called *parvocellular* or *P-layers*). The M-layers of the LGN receive projections from the M ganglion cells, while the P-layers receive input from the P ganglion cells (Dreher, Fukada, & Rodieck, 1976).

The identification of two pathways before and after V1 raised a question of whether they were related. The early studies of Hubel and Wiesel and others had suggested that V1 had a homogenous cytoarchitecture; if this were the case, the two precortical pathways would converge in V1 and then two other pathways would diverge beyond V1. But, in accord with the caveat in the passage quoted above from Hubel and Wiesel, a new technique (developed by Margaret Wong-Riley, 1979), involving the application of cytochrome oxidase stains, revealed additional complexity in V1. Cytochrome oxidase is an enzyme critical to the oxidative metabolism of the cell; staining for it reveals areas of high metabolic activity. In layers 2 and 3 and 5 and 6 of V1 staining produced "blobs"[23] which indicated regions of particularly high metabolic activity. Recording separately from cells in the blob regions and in the interblob regions, Livingstone and Hubel (1984) found orientation selective cells only in the interblob regions, and wavelength sensitive cells in the blobs, indicating a separation of processing within V1. On the basis of this differentiation, Livingstone and Hubel proposed extending Ungerleider and Mishkin's two pathways to account for all visual processing from the retina on.

The integrating scheme of two processing streams receives support from neuroanatomy. The M layers of the LGN project to layer 4B in V1, where there are no blobs, whereas the P layers of the LGN project, via layers 4A and 4Cb, to layers 2 and 3 of V1, where there are both blob and interblob regions. Cytochrome oxidase stain also revealed a differentiation in area V2 of alternating thick and thin stripes with interstripe areas between them. The differentiation in V1 is maintained, with the thick stripe regions receiving their input from layer 4B, the thin stripe regions from the blobs of layers 2 and 3, and the interstripe regions from the interblob regions in V1. From the differentiated areas in V1 and V2, processing largely separates into the ventral and dorsal pathways originally distinguished by Mishkin and Ungerleider.

During the same period as these researchers were pushing the division into two pathways back to V1 and subcortical areas, researchers focusing on cytoarchitecture and relying especially on connectivity between neurons were discovering a more complex set of areas that are involved in visual processing. David van Essen and his colleagues (Felleman & van Essen, 1991) identified 32 different processing areas that seem to be involved in visual processing in the macaque. They also developed a technique for showing these areas in the highly convoluted primate cortex in a flat map which preserves the relative sizes and adjacencies (Figure 3.10). The areas of cortex that are labeled are ones for which, as a result of lesion and single-cell record studies, there are good hypotheses about the type of information they process; the unlabeled areas are ones whose contribution to visual information processing has yet to be ascertained. Having used connectivity as a guide to the individuation of processing areas, Felleman and van Essen were in a position to show how interconnected the visual cortex is. On average, each of the 32 areas is connected to 10 different areas and approximately one-third of the possible interconnections between visual areas are actually realized. Figure 3.11 provides perspective on the resulting pattern of connectivity. Most of the connections shown are actually reciprocal—if there is a projection from one

---

[23] Livingstone and Hubel introduced the term *blobs* to characterize their appearance, citing the *Oxford English Dictionary* for the term. These blobs are "oval, measure roughly 150 × 200 μm, and in the macaque monkey lie centered along ocular dominance columns, to which their long axes are parallel" (p. 310).

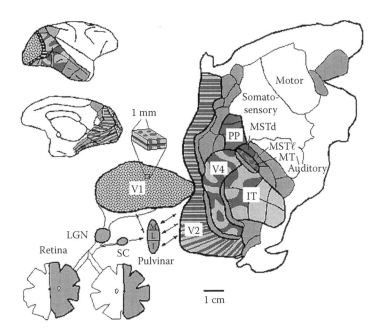

Figure 3.10   Van Essen and Gallant's flat map of the right hemisphere of the macaque identifying major subcortical and cortical visual-processing areas. The blob and inter-blob structure as well as layer 4B are differentiated on the expanded representation of V1, whereas the thin, thick, and interstripe regions of V2 are shown. At the upper left are lateral and medial views of the right hemisphere showing where the respective cortical areas are on the three-dimensional cortex. Reprinted from van Essen, D. C., & Gallant, J. L. (1994), *Neuron,* 13, p. 2, figure 1, with permission of Elsevier Publishing.

area to another, there is also a projection in the reverse direction. The prevalence of reciprocal connections might seem to undercut the presentation of the visual system as a hierarchical system from input areas to higher-processing areas, but anatomically feedforward, collateral, and feedback projections can be distinguished in terms of the layers of cortex from which they originate and the layers to which they project. Forward projections, for example, generally originate in the middle layers whereas recurrent connections project from the lowest and highest layers and lateral connections project from all layers. These clues suffice for arranging brain areas in a processing hierarchy. (Neuroscientists often note the prevalence of feedback or recurrent connections in the brain and sometimes offer suggestions to their significance in, e.g., supporting top-down processing. I will discuss their potential significance further in chapter 6.)

Van Essen and Gallant (1994) use visual icons in Figure 3.12 to indicate the main information processing contributions of different visual areas and lines of

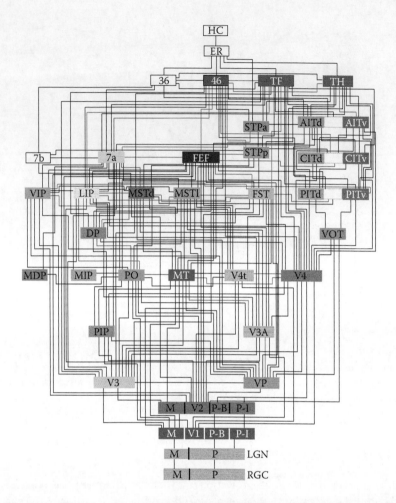

Figure 3.11   Felleman and van Essen's representation of the hierarchy of 32 cortical visual areas and the connections between them. Redrawn from Felleman, D. J., & van Essen, D. C. (1991). *Cerebral Cortex*, 1, p. 30, Figure 4, by permission of Oxford University Press.

varying thicknesses to show the main ways in which information flows through visual cortex. The research of van Essen and his collaborators has not only revealed more areas involved in visual processing than previously anticipated, but also points to some modifications in the portrayal of two pathways by Ungerleider and Mishkin and Livingstone and Hubel. The two pathways are not as clearly delineated as they suggested. There is extensive cross talk between the populations of M and P neurons (as well as the much smaller and poorly understood population of koniocellular (K) neurons) either at the level of the LGN or

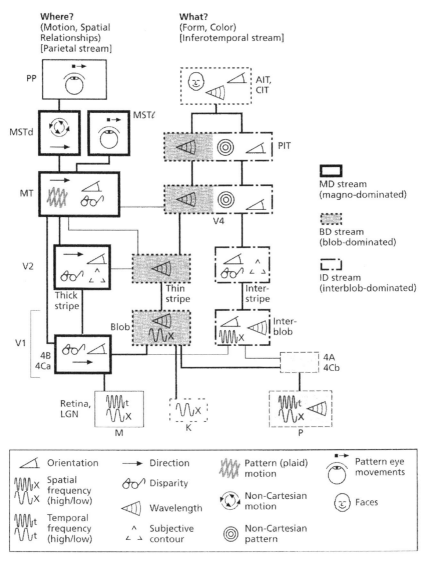

Figure 3.12   Van Essen and Gallant's iconic representation of the organization of multiple processing streams in the macaque, with boxes indicating different processing areas and icons representing the types of information to which cells in each area are responsive. M, P, and K refer to the magnocellular, parvocellular, and K streams identified in the retina and LGN. AIT, CIT, and PIT refer to the anterior, central, and posterior portions of the IT complex. The thickness of lines indicates the relative degree of connectedness of the various areas. Note that there are connections between the What and Where streams at a variety of levels. Reprinted from van Essen, D. C., & Gallant, J. L. (1994), *Neuron*, 13, p. 3, figure 2, with permission of Elsevier Publishing.

the level of V1. One source of evidence for this is that processing in both cortical pathways continues even if the supposedly specific subcortical input is removed. There are also connections at higher levels such as between areas MT and V4, suggesting that the pathways are not parallel but interactive (Merigan & Maunsell, 1993). To capture the idea of interactions between processing areas van Essen and Gallant (1994) refer not to *pathways* but to processing *streams*—information can be drawn into one stream from another or shared with another.

The distinction of processing streams, while still subject to revision, has become a generally accepted feature of the anatomy and physiology of the visual system. Ungerleider and Mishkin's functional characterization of the streams, however, was challenged in the 1990s by David Milner and Melvyn Goodale (1995; Goodale & Milner, 2004). They examined in great detail the deficits suffered by patients with damage to the two streams, and emphasized especially what was preserved. Particularly influential in their account was patient D.F. who, as a result of anoxia due to carbon-monoxide poisoning, seems to have lost much of her higher visual capacities—she cannot report the orientation of objects, match objects by shape, or estimate their size.[24] Nonetheless, she is able to use vision to guide a number of motor activities, including picking up objects and walking around her environment. To assess better the nature of her deficit and what skills D.F. retained, Milner and Goodale adapted a task developed by Marie-Thérèse Perenin and Alain Vighetto (1988) involving "posting" a card into a slot that could be oriented at different angles. A.D. had no problem orienting the card to put it through the slot, but if she was asked merely to match the card with the slot without putting it through, she was at chance. Likewise, A.D. exhibits no difficulty in grasping objects and shows the normal pattern of adjusting her grip as she reaches for an object, but is unable to make judgments about the shape of those very objects. This pattern contrasts sharply with that presented by Bálint's original patient as well as more recent patients who can report the difference in size between objects but not adjust their grip as they reach for them and who can report the orientation of the slot in the posting task, but not actually post something through the slot.

This double-dissociation between patients like A.D. and Bálint's patients suggests a more refined consideration of spatial knowledge. Balint's patients retain a great deal of knowledge about spatial layouts, but are unable to coordinate this knowledge with their bodily movements. A.D., on the other hand, lacks such explicit knowledge but is able to utilize spatial information in her actions. A further step in Milner and Goodale's recharacterization of processing by the dorsal stream was the recognition that the processing by the ventral stream often makes

---

[24]MRI images (Kentridge, Heywood, & Milner, 2004) reveal that her damage is in the lateral occipital area, LO, identified as an object processing area by Malach et al. (1995).

significant use of information about spatial layout. Moreover, the tasks typically used to assess activity in the parietal lobe typically focus on spatial information involving the animal's own body. As a result, Milner and Goodale emphasize that the dorsal stream is primarily vision for action—it is primarily concerned with utilizing information about visual stimuli for carrying out motor behavior. In their view, the ventral stream is principally involved in extracting information about visual stimuli required for higher cognitive processing.

3.5   A COMPREHENSIVE SKETCH OF THE VISUAL PROCESSING MECHANISM

As a result of research over a period of more than a hundred years, investigators have arrived at an account of the mechanism of visual processing that involves identification of a host of brain areas, an understanding of what information processing operations many of them perform, and considerable knowledge of how they are organized into a system that enables organisms to utilize visual information to guide their lives. Research employing neuroanatomical techniques has revealed a hierarchical system of brain areas. Relying on deficit studies as well as single-cell recording and more recently functional imaging, researchers have identified the different types of information processed in many different areas, although, as the grey areas in Figure 3.10 indicate, there remain many areas for which the evidence is still insufficient to determine their function.

This state of affairs in which researchers have a detailed outline of how a mechanism operates, but lack many details, is not uncommon in mechanistic research. Machamer, Darden and Craver (2000) introduced the notions of mechanism schemas and mechanism sketches. A mechanism schema is an abstract account of a mechanism that specifies in general terms the operations in the mechanism that researchers can fill in with accounts of known parts and operations. A schema enables one to understand the general idea of how the mechanism works without getting bogged down in details. A mechanism sketch is an account in which there are gaps in the understanding—researchers recognize that there are parts and operations that they have not yet identified. These become foci for further research. Figure 3.12 should, in this respect, be viewed as a sketch, identifying some of the parts and operations of the mechanism but also revealing points where further research is needed in order to understand in detail how the mechanism operates. (A noteworthy feature of Figure 3.12 is that it does not show how the various brain areas perform the information processing attributed to them. This too needs to be worked out in a more comprehensive account of the mechanism of vision.) Even as a sketch, though, the account of the visual processing mechanism is one of the best worked out accounts of a mental mechanism and a worthy exemplar.

In this chapter I have focused on how the account was developed from an initial identification of visual processing with just one brain area to the discovery that a host of different areas are involved. This initiated research to determine what sorts of information processing are involved in each of these areas and how they are organized into networks. This route to discovery contrasts with that described in chapter two in which researchers began with the phenomenon of memory and attempted to decompose it functionally into component operations. Only after these were identified did researchers try to identify the brain areas in which the operations were localized. As I discussed at the end of that chapter, the determination that the same brain areas are involved in what were thought to be different operations or even different mental phenomena has led researchers to begin to recharacterize the decomposition into operations and even the decomposition into phenomena. In the case of vision, researchers began by identifying one brain area that was involved in visual processing. As they determined that it actually performed operations early in visual processing, they expanded their search to identify other brain areas as serving visual processing and attempted to determine what operations they performed. The specification of operations resulted not from attempts to figure out what operations must be performed in order to see, but from trying to figure out what information processing a given region performed.

In part, this difference resulted from the type of mental phenomena researchers were investigating. Sensory processing enables researchers to start close to the sense organs, find the brain areas to which they project, and work their way inwards to later processing areas. Further, they could vary stimuli presented to the sense organs and record from cells in the target area to determine what features of stimuli seem to be affecting processing. With a phenomenon such as memory there is not a well-defined periphery from which to start moving inwards. Rather, research must start with identification of areas where lesions result in deficits in the phenomena or where activity can be recorded when the phenomenon is elicited. In these cases researchers are more dependent upon first hypotheses about how to decompose the phenomenon and must then rely on subsequent evidence to revise the initial decomposition.

Four

Reduction and Independence of Higher-level Sciences
A Rapprochement

One of the perennial topics in philosophical discussions of psychology is whether psychology can be reduced to neuroscience. If it can be reduced, many philosophers (and psychologists learning of these philosophical debates) assume that psychology loses any claim to be engaging in independent inquiry into psychological phenomena. Psychology becomes, at best, applied neuroscience (and if neuroscience itself is reduced to a more basic science, it is, at best, an application of that more basic science). Mechanistic explanation, in seeking to explain the behavior of a mechanism in terms of the operations of its parts, is committed to a form of reduction. But mechanistic reduction, as I will argue in this chapter, is Janus-faced. As William Wimsatt (1976a) proposes, it is possible to be both a reductionist and an emergentist.

The term *emergence* is used in a variety of senses, sometimes implying the spooky introduction of something radically new into the universe. Emergence, as I use the term here, simply recognizes that whole systems exhibit behaviors that go beyond the behaviors of their parts. It does have some bite against extreme reductionism, though, in that typically the behavior of the whole system must be studied at its own level with appropriate tools for that level. Research at the level of whole systems has a kind of independence—it studies, using its own modes of investigation, phenomena different from those studied at the level of the component parts. Recognizing such independence, however, does not require any spooky metaphysical posits such as vital forces. Moreover, it is not only compatible with, but constrained by the results of mechanistic inquiry into the component parts and operations. (Conversely, the study of the parts and operations is constrained by inquiry into the behavior of the whole mechanism.)

Mechanistic reduction occupies a middle ground between vitalism, which sees no hope of reduction, and the exclusionary account of reduction, which views all explanatory work as performed at the lowest level (a position that Bickle, 2003, calls "ruthlessly reductive" and vigorously defends). To appreciate what is at stake, it will help to begin with the received account of reduction in philosophy, what I term the *theory-reduction* model. One implication of this view, which I describe in section one, is that any defense of the independence of psychology, or other higher-level sciences, requires a rejection of reduction. At the core of the most prominent strand of antireduction arguments on behalf of the independence of psychology is the claim that higher-level phenomena are *multiply realizable*. Although for thirty years a staple in philosophical accounts of mind, the multiple realizability thesis has begun to attract critical attention and no longer looks to be an obvious and undeniable truth. I will present the thesis and develop some of the arguments against it in section two.

Within the mechanistic framework one does not have to reject reduction in order to allow for the independence of the higher-level sciences (section three). The decomposition required by mechanistic explanation is reductionist, but the recognition that parts and operations must be organized into an appropriate whole provides for a robust sense of a higher level of organization. A scientist seeking an account at this higher level will find it essential to undertake independent study of the organization of the mechanism and how it engages its environment. Thus, to understand the mechanistic framework in which scientists work, I first develop an appropriate notion of levels (section four) and then show how mechanistic explanation requires integrating multiple levels of organization (section five). Thinking of higher levels as organized helps to highlight the crucial role organization plays in making functioning mechanisms out of parts, and to emphasize that an adequate scientific account of a mechanism requires more than identifying parts and operations at a single lower level. Accordingly, I will finish this chapter by showing how the independence of inquiry at higher levels of organization can be maintained without appealing to multiple realizability (section six).

4.1   THE TRADITIONAL THEORY-REDUCTION PERSPECTIVE

Philosophical arguments for and against reduction have generally adopted an account of reduction that was developed by the logical positivists as an extension of the deductive-nomological (D-N) account of explanation (see chapter one). Just as on the D-N account phenomena were to be explained by deriving statements of them from statements of laws and initial conditions, on the theory-reduction account laws to be reduced were to be derived from more basic laws (E. Nagel, 1961; see also Woodger, 1952; Quine, 1964; Kuipers,

2001, chapter three).[1] Sometimes the reduction was within a science, as when laws presented in an observation vocabulary (sometimes termed *empirical laws*) were to be reduced to laws stated in a more theoretical vocabulary (*theoretical laws*). But in the cases of interest here, the laws of one discipline (psychology) would be reduced to those of a more fundamental discipline (neuroscience).

For purposes of discussing the theory-reduction model, I will assume that the knowledge achieved within a given discipline can be stated in a set of laws (a view that the mechanistic perspective rejects). In order to carry out deductions between sets of laws, two challenges have to be overcome. First, typically laws in different sciences employ different terminology. Laws in physics, for example, might employ terms such as *mass* and *attractive force*, whereas those in chemistry would involve names of elements and molecules and types of chemical bonds. Neuroscience accounts might refer to increased rates of spiking whereas psychological accounts might refer to retrieving a representation from a working memory buffer. But one cannot logically deduce a conclusion that uses terms that are not in the premises. To address this issue, advocates of the theory-reduction model appealed to *bridge principles* (Nagel called them *rules of correspondence*) that equated vocabulary in the two laws. The second challenge confronting advocates of the theory-reduction model is the fact that the regularity captured in a higher-level law arises only under a particular range of conditions. Chemical bonds, for example, form only within appropriate temperature ranges. To accommodate this, the theory-reduction model also requires statements specifying boundary conditions. With these components in place, a reduction was then conceived to have the form of the following deduction:

Lower-level laws (in the basic, reducing science)
Bridge principles
Boundary conditions

∴ Higher-level laws (in the secondary, reduced science).

---

[1] Kemeny and Oppenheim (1956; see also Oppenheim & Putnam, 1958) advanced an alternative account of reduction that did not derive the reduced theory from the reducing theory but only required generating identical observable predictions from the reducing theory as from the reduced theory. This account of reduction is far more liberal, as it allows for the reduction of what are regarded as false theories (e.g., phlogiston chemistry) from what are taken to be true theories (e.g., Lavoisier's oxygen-based chemistry) as long as the predictions made by the reducing theory include all those made by the reduced theory. Yet another alternative was put forward by Patrick Suppes, who required an isomorphism between any model (in the model-theoretic sense) of the reduced theory and a model of the reducing theory: "To show in a sharp sense that thermodynamics may be reduced to statistical mechanics, we would need to axiomatize both disciplines by defining appropriate set theoretical predicates, and then show that given any model T of thermodynamics we may find a model of statistical mechanics on the basis of which we may construct a model isomorphic to T" (Suppes, 1957, p. 271).

An oft-cited example of such a reduction is the derivation of the Boyle-Charles law from the kinetic theory of gases, as part of an overall reduction of classical thermodynamics to the newer and more basic science of statistical mechanics (E. Nagel, 1961, pp. 338–366). This law states that the temperature (T) of an ideal gas in a container is proportional to the pressure (P) of the gas and volume (V) of the container. Because the term *temperature* does not appear in statistical mechanics, to achieve the reduction it must be related to a term in that science. This is expressed in a bridge principle (rule of correspondence) stating that the temperature of a gas is proportional to the mean kinetic energy (E) of its molecules. A number of boundary conditions also must be specified, such as those limiting the deduction to monotonic gases in a temperature range far from liquefaction. With the appropriate bridge principles and boundary conditions included as premises, the Boyle-Charles law can be derived from laws of statistical mechanics. Here is the key part of the full derivation:

Laws of statistical mechanics (including the theorem $PV = 2E/3$)
Bridge principles ($2E/3 = kT$)
Boundary conditions (monotonic gas; T in specified range)

∴ Boyle-Charles' law ($PV = kT$)

Most of the initial advocates of theory reduction kept their focus on linguistic representations of scientific claims, avoiding ontological issues regarding what such statements refer to. Robert Causey (1977), however, advanced a more ontologically committed account wherein the higher-level theories referred to entities that resulted from the structuring of lower-level entities. On this view, theories at the lower level primarily describe the operation of parts of the structured wholes, whereas those at the higher level focus on the behavior of the structured wholes themselves. For a reduction to be possible, the lower-level theory must itself have the resources to describe the structured wholes and their behavior. (Although this is quite problematic, assume for a moment that it is possible.) We then have two descriptions of the higher-level entity, one as a whole unit in the vocabulary of the higher-level science, and one as an entity structured out of lower-level components. For Causey, reduction then requires bridge principles that relate terms in the higher-level theory referring to the whole entities to those terms in the lower-level theory that characterize them as composed, structured wholes. Assuming that the lower-level theory has laws that describe the behavior of the structured wholes, one can try to derive the upper-level theory from the lower-level one.

Adopting either Causey's account or more linguistic accounts of theory reduction, we can readily appreciate why such accounts seem to threaten the independence of higher-level sciences. In order to derive theories of the higher-level sciences from those of lower-level sciences, the lower-level laws must have the resources from which to derive the higher-level laws. This, however, means that successful reduction obviates any need for laws or theories specific to the higher-level sciences. At least in a hypothetical final picture of science, higher-level sciences would be expendable or redundant: by supplying the appropriate boundary conditions, any higher-level regularity could be derived directly from the lower-level theory and even stated in the language of the lower-level science. In practice, at a given stage in the development of science, appeals to the higher-level sciences may be required because the reduction base may not yet have been developed. Higher-level sciences may even play a heuristic role in the development of the lower-level sciences; for example, they may reveal regularities (laws) in the behavior of the structured wholes that must be accounted for. In this respect, there may even be a coevolution of higher- and lower-level sciences (P. S. Churchland, 1986). In the end, however, the theories of the lower-level science will be complete, and the only reason for invoking the vocabulary and laws of the higher-level science will be that they provide a convenient shorthand for referring to what, in the lower-level theory, may be unmanageably complex statements.

Shortly after it was proposed, the theory-reduction model was criticized as inadequate to account for reduction as pursued in actual sciences. (This is distinct from the challenge to be discussed below that higher-level laws cannot be reduced to those of the more basic sciences.) Many of the early critics challenged the applicability of the theory-reduction model by arguing that it was not possible to formulate the needed bridge principles. Paul Feyerabend (1962; 1970) argued that words in different theories, even if they have the same morphological form, do not mean the same thing and are in fact *incommensurable* with one another. Key to his argument was his characterization of the meanings of the scientific vocabulary of a theory in terms of the theory itself. In classical thermodynamics, for example, *temperature* can be defined in terms of Carnot cycles and its behavior described by the nonstatistical version of the second law of thermodynamics. But in statistical thermodynamics, temperature is characterized in statistical terms. Given the important differences in the surrounding theory and hence the different entailments of the word *temperature*, it would seem impossible to construct bridge principles that would adequately relate *temperature* as used in these two theories.

One specific context in which Feyerabend maintained that reduction would fail was in the attempt to relate psychological theories presented in mentalistic vocabulary to theories of brain function developed in neuroscience. Although Feyerabend later championed the position that incompatible theories ought both to be maintained (Feyerabend, 1975), in his early writing on mind–brain relations he defended a position known as *eliminative materialism* (Feyerabend, 1963). The key claim of Feyerabend and subsequent eliminativists (Rorty, 1970; P. M. Churchland, 1981; P. S. Churchland, 1986) is that instead of reducing a folk or cognitive psychological theory to a neuroscience theory, the psychological theory is *replaced* by the new neuroscience theory and *eliminated* from the corpus of science. As such, folk or cognitive theories would disappear from science just as surely as Ptolemy's astronomy and the caloric theory of heat.

In philosophy of science the incommensurability claim is deployed most frequently in cases of diachronic theory change. For example, Thomas Kuhn (1962/1970) focused on other examples of putative reduction, such as Newtonian to Einsteinian mechanics, and maintained that words like "mass" were used incommensurably in the two theories. On the basis of such examples, Kuhn challenged the account of progress implicitly assumed by the logical empiricists, in which sciences progress towards better theories through a process of continual extension and refinement. He argued instead that the history of science is a history of successive revolutions in which new theories replace, rather than build upon, older theories with which they are incommensurable.

Although Kuhn and Feyerabend presented their arguments as criticisms of reduction, Kenneth Schaffner (1967) advanced a general model of reduction that tried to incorporate their view of replacement of one theory by another together with an account of deductive relations between theories. On his account, a frequent consequence of a new lower-level theory (T_1) is that an old upper-level theory (T_2) gives way to a revised one (T_2^*). T_2^* would be deducible from T_1, just as envisaged in the standard theory-reduction model, but Schaffner thought its relation to T_2 should also be recognized. He suggested that the T_2-T_2^* relation was one of analogy:

> T_2^* corrects T_2 in the sense of providing more accurate experimentally verifiable predictions than T_2 in almost all cases (identical results cannot be ruled out however), and should also indicate why T_2 was incorrect (e.g., crucial variable ignored), and why it worked as well as it did....The relations between T_2 and T_2^* should be one of strong analogy—that is (in current jargon), they possess a large "positive analogy" (p. 144).

Subsequently Schaffner (1969) amended his model to incorporate revision of an existing lower-level theory (T_1) to obtain a corrected lower-level theory (T_1^*) in addition to the revision of the old higher-level T_2 into T_2^* (see Figure 4.1).

Schaffner's model distinguishes two different relations between theories. Shown in the vertical direction are relations between theories at different levels that are contemporaneous with each other (that is, synchronic relations); shown horizontally are diachronic relations. Several authors have drawn out the differences between the two relations (Nickles, 1973; Wimsatt, 1976a; 1976b). One of the most important insights to emerge is Robert McCauley's (1986; 1996) demonstration that, historically, cases of replacement and elimination have always involved succession relations between theories at the same level. He suggests that the same is likely to be true in the case of a psychological theory: elimination would be expected only when it was superseded by a replacement theory that

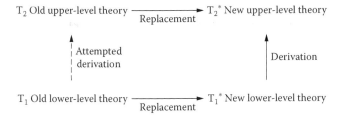

Figure 4.1   A representation of Schaffner's (1969) generalized model of reduction, in which a new upper-level theory (T_2^*) is derived from a new lower-level theory (T_1^*) and each new theory replaces an older theory at the same level.

addressed the same level—i.e., another psychological theory—rather than a neural one. As for interlevel reductions, McCauley also distinguished cases in which there is a tight fit between upper- and lower-level theories and cases in which there is not. Loose fit may result from the very nature of theorizing at the upper and lower level. In some cases, the finer grain of an account at the lower level may enable it to explain what appear to be deviations at the higher level. But the advantage is not always with the lower level. In other cases,

> ... the upper-level theory lays out regularities about a subset of the phenomena that the lower-level theory encompasses but for which it has neither the resources nor the motivation to highlight. That is the price of the lower-level theory's generality and finer grain (McCauley, 1996, p. 31).

McCauley thus advocates a pluralistic approach that would allow theorists a fair degree of independence (see also McCauley & Bechtel, 2001). Theories at higher and lower levels could be developed independently, with no immediate need to force the levels to relate in a reductionist manner. McCauley's call for pluralism is an important step toward defending the independence of psychology, as it suggests that at least epistemically investigators need to pursue psychology without imposing fetters from neuroscience. However, so long as discussion is tied to the theory-reduction model, many philosophers will focus on the questions of whether ultimately psychology will reduce to neuroscience and whether then its accounts will be merely applications of the laws of the more fundamental sciences.

4.2   PHILOSOPHICAL FUNCTIONALISM: INDEPENDENCE THROUGH MULTIPLE REALIZABILITY

The theory-reduction model, either in its classical version or in Schaffner's revisionist version, seems to deny any independence to psychological inquiry. As a result, the advocates of the independence of psychology in philosophy of psychology in the second half of the twentieth century typically made their case by rejecting the possibility of reduction. They did this by advancing a position about the nature of mental or psychological states that has come to be known as *functionalism*.[2] The key idea of functionalism is that mental states are identified not in terms of their intrinsic characteristics, but in terms of their relation to other mental states. Hilary Putnam and Jerry Fodor were two of the chief advocates of such a characterization of mental states. Interestingly, Fodor initially put forward his account of functionalism in terms of mechanisms and characterized what he called *functional analysis* in much the way I characterized functional decomposition as a step in mechanistic explanation:

> In typical cases of functional analysis … one asks about a part of a mechanism *what role it plays* in the activities that are characteristic of the mechanism as a whole: "What does the camshaft do?" "It opens the valves, permitting the entry into the cylinder of fuel, which will then be detonated to drive the piston." … Successful functional analysis … requires an appreciation of the sorts of activity that are characteristic of a mechanism and of the contribution made by the functioning of each part of the mechanism to the economy of the whole (Fodor, 1968, p. 113).

Fodor went on to differentiate the characterization of a component provided in the functional analysis from a physical characterization:

> If I speak of a device as a "camshaft," I am implicitly identifying it by reference to its physical structure, and so I am committed to the view that it exhibits a characteristic and specifiable decomposition into physical parts. But if I speak of the device as a "valve lifter," I am identifying it by reference to its function and I therefore undertake no such commitment (Fodor, 1968, p. 113).

Reliance on functional analysis is not sufficient in itself to support the claim that psychology or any of what Fodor labels *special sciences* is autonomous from more basic sciences. The key step in the claim for independence is to argue not just that functional and structural characterizations are different, but that it is not possible to establish a relation between them of the sort demanded by the theory-reduction account. Fodor (1974) clearly identified theory reduction as characterized by Oppenheim and Putnam (1958) as his target, but construed this version as requiring that bridge principles provide biconditional relations such that a given higher-level functional kind is satisfied just in case the corresponding lower-level structural kind is satisfied.[3] This, Fodor contended, is typically not possible with functional kinds as there will be indefinitely

---

[2] This use of the term *functionalism* is distinct from its use in psychology. Those called *functionalists* in psychology (e.g., James and Dewey) are those who adopted an evolutionary perspective and characterized psychological traits as functional when they benefited the organism. Functionalists in philosophy of mind rather emphasized what a component in the organism did independent of whether it was beneficial to the organism.

[3] As Shapiro (2004) has effectively argued, Fodor has attributed to Oppenheim and Putnam, and theory reductionists generally, a claim they never made or intended.

many structural kinds that fulfill any given functional role, and there may be nothing that they share in common that is not shared with structural kinds that do not share the role. As a result, the bridge principle would have to identify a potentially unbounded set of disjuncts (alternative conditions connected by the logical connective *or*) on the structural side of the bridge principle. Fodor's parade case is one that makes this objection intuitive and very compelling: Consider the structures that could count as one U.S. dollar in an economic exchange. Certain pieces of paper of a specified shape and size qualify, but not others that differ only in that they were made by counterfeiters. But so do certain collections of pieces of paper representing other currencies, pieces of metal, bits in a computer, etc. Fodor's contention is that if one restricted oneself to specifying physical criteria, one would not be able to specify what objects could play the functional role of a U.S. dollar. The same, he claims, is true of psychological functional roles.

The physical object playing the functional role is often referred to as the *realizer*, and Fodor's claim of multiple realizers for the kinds referred to in the special sciences is known as the *multiple realizability thesis*. Claims that psychological states are multiply realizable were advanced already in the 1960s by Hilary Putnam (1967), who motivated his case by considering first the range of terrestrial species capable of satisfying a psychological predicate such as "feels pain." Not just humans but other primates, other mammals, reptiles, and even mollusks seem to experience pain. But given the differences in their brains, he claimed there is not likely to be anything in common in the brain states that realize pain in these various species. Even within humans there already is significant variability in the brain states involved in experiencing pain, and as one ranges across organisms in biological orders who lack neocortex and whose brains consist of a limited number of ganglia, the differences become even more compelling. It thus seems obvious that pain is multiply realized. The case becomes even more compelling if we consider other possible creatures that might feel pain—robots or extraterrestrials. They are not even likely to be made out of the same type of stuff. Instead of biological cells composed of carbon based compounds, they may be made of chips made of silicon.

Until recently, the multiple realizability thesis has generally been viewed as obviously true. Even so, some philosophers resisted the implication that it is incompatible with reductionism.[4] For example, Richardson (1979) argued that

---

[4] A similar argument for multiple realization has been made in the philosophy of biology with respect to the relation between Mendelian and molecular genetics: any one of a number of distinct molecular mechanisms could produce the same phenotypic trait. In making this case, David Hull argues that this counts not against the possibility of reduction but the philosophical conception of reduction: "If the logical empiricist analysis of reduction is correct, then Mendelian genetics cannot be reduced to molecular genetics. The long-awaited reduction of a biological theory to physics and chemistry turns out not to be a case of 'reduction' after all but an example of replacement. But given our pre-analytic intuitions about reduction, it *is* a case of reduction, a paradigm case" (Hull, 1974, p. 44).

classical reduction models did not require type-identities between higher- and lower-level kinds. Defenders of reduction showed that even in classical cases of reduction in physics (e.g., the reduction of temperature to statistical mechanics), properties in the reduced theory were multiply realized, with the result that different reductions would be offered in cases of different realizers (Lewis, 1980; Hooker, 1981; Enç, 1983; P. S. Churchland, 1986; Kim, 1993). The difference between reductionists and their opponents then seems to turn on whether there is a tractable set of alternative realizers for the entities or properties in the reduced theory. Proponents of independence insist that the set of realizers of the entities or states specified in the special science is open-ended.

Although multiple realizability has seemed obviously true to many philosophers, it flies in the face of neurobiological practice (and physiological practice more generally) in which researchers investigate one species to draw inferences about another (Kim, 1993, chapter 16; Bickle, 1998, chapter 4). Together with Jennifer Mundale (Bechtel & Mundale, 1999), I raised the question of how neurobiological states are typed. Noting that neuroscientists generally do not talk in terms of *brain states* but refer to activity in a brain area or conglomerate of areas, we focused in particular on how brain areas are delineated in neuroscience. Korbinian Brodmann (1909/1994) created his map of areas in the human cortex (Figure 1.2) by pursuing a comparative study of the brains of a number of different species. By using the same numbering system across species, he was clearly identifying brain areas in different species while remaining cognizant of their differences. Brain mapping is primarily a neuroanatomical project, but in the hands of Brodmann and subsequent researchers it clearly relies on identifying types across species. Mundale and I found a similar situation when we turned to functional considerations. In identifying motor areas in the brain by use of mild electrical stimulation, David Ferrier (1876), for example, conducted comparative studies on macaque monkeys, dogs, jackals, cats, rabbits, guinea pigs, rats, pigeons, frogs, and fishes. He was not able to elicit many motor responses in pigeons, frogs, and fishes, but he found numerous brain areas in mammals for which stimulation would produce some type of movement. He tried to render them comparable by relying on such indicators as gyri and sulci. Ethical considerations prevented Ferrier from doing similar studies on humans, but they were clearly the target of his investigation as he projected his results onto the human brain, relying on gyri and sulci to determine homologues. Similar ethical considerations constrained the investigators working on mammalian vision discussed in chapter three, who likewise proceeded using comparative data (especially from cat and monkey). Recently PET and fMRI have provided researchers a means of studying these and other functions directly in humans, but to ground these investigations in neuroanatomy, which is better studied in other species, researchers still use a comparative strategy.

Underlying this practice in neuroscience is a willingness to identify a brain area as the same across species despite substantial differences. In making their case for multiple realizability, philosophers have insisted on noting the differences in the brain processes involved, whereas neuroscientists emphasize the commonalities. On the other hand, philosophers have emphasized the commonalities in identifying psychological states across species despite often massive differences (to use Putnam's example of the octopus, its responses to pain or hunger are fundamentally different than those of humans). Mundale and I diagnosed the plausibility of the case for multiple realizability in terms of what we referred to as *grains of analysis*:

> What has made the multiple realizability claim as plausible as it has been is that researchers have employed different grains of analysis in identifying psychological states and brain states, using a coarse grain to identify psychological states and a fine grain to differentiate brain states. Having invoked different grains, it is relatively easy to make a case for multiple realization. But if the grain size is kept constant, then the claim that psychological states are in fact multiply realized looks far less plausible. One can adopt either a coarse or a fine grain, but as long as one uses a comparable grain on both the brain and mind side, the mapping between them will be correspondingly systematic. For example, one can adopt a relatively coarse grain, equating psychological states over different individuals or across species. If one employs the same grain, though, one will equate activity in brain areas across species, and one-to-one mapping is preserved (though perhaps further taxonomic refinement and/or delineation may be required). Conversely, one can adopt a very fine grain, and differentiate psychological states between individuals, or even in the same individual over time. If one similarly adopts a fine grain in analyzing the brain, then one is likely to map the psychological differences onto brain differences, and brain differences onto psychological differences (Bechtel & Mundale, 1999, p. 202).

On a fine-grained analysis, there are reasons to be dubious of multiple realizability claims based on engineered systems. Although different designs for a mechanism may produce coarse-grained similarities in behavior, investigating the behavior of alternative engineering designs in fine detail usually yields differences. This is quite compatible with different mechanisms producing qualitatively similar behavior and corresponds to cases in biology of convergent evolution in which different lineages each develop different mechanisms to deal with a problem (e.g., flight). In these biological cases, the behavior that is realized is not exactly the same (e.g., bird and insect wings support different amounts of weight and allow for different speeds of flight).

In a more recent critique of the multiple realizability thesis, Lawrence Shapiro advances a promising proposal as to when two realizers should count as the same or different. In this he appeals to what Cummins' (1975) characterized as a functional analysis, which closely approximates my notion of a functional decomposition of a mechanism. Shapiro adopts the designation R-properties for the properties specified in such an analysis. Invoking an example he develops extensively, Shapiro construes a waiter's corkscrew and a double-lever corkscrew as different realizations of the type of corkscrew because they have different functional analyses: "the functional analysis of each reveals that each employs different mechanisms in the production of cork removal, that is, different R-properties" (Shapiro, 2004, p. 54). On the other hand, two waiter's corkscrews in different colors do not count as different realizations since they have the same functional analysis.

Applying the framework of mechanistic explanation to Shapiro's proposal, two realizations should count as different realizations of the same phenomenon only if they involve different operations (i.e., different mechanisms). From this perspective, we can address an objection that has been raised against Shapiro's account. Aizawa (2007) argues that any difference in realizer, not just one that involves different operations, should count as a different realizer. Let's consider two ways in which a realizer might be different and not involve a different set of operations. The first would be differences involving features of realizers that do not contribute in any way to the production of the phenomenon. If two waiter's corkscrews differed only in the color of the material of which they were made, then the realizations do not seem to be significant alternatives. From a theory-reduction point of view, such properties would not enter into the reduction. If there are biological examples of such differences, they are simply of no interest to the practice of science. The second would be differences that involve features of realizers that affect how the operations within the mechanism are realized. For example, the arms of a waiter's corkscrew might be made of metals of different molecules or the enzymes of a cell might involve different amino acid sequences. In such cases, it would be the operations within the mechanism that are multiply realized, not the mechanism itself. As most empirical investigations of mechanisms only engage in one or two rounds of decomposition of the mechanism, any realizability below the level of focus will not affect the science focused on the mechanism itself.

The sort of analysis Shapiro advances restricts what would count as multiple realization, but does not show there are no cases that meet his restricted conditions. However, he then goes on to argue that there are not likely to be many, if any, alternative realizations in the requisite sense of having different functional analyses. He does this by focusing on constraints on possible realizers and claiming that in many cases the realizer is so constrained that its structural characteristics can be predicted from the initial functional characterization. His strategy, using vision as his example, is to show that the ways of producing the relevant psychological capacity are quite limited. For example, to achieve the resolution that we enjoy in vision requires closely packed receptors with finely tuned receptive fields. Increase or decrease the density of receptors and you change the resolution. Moreover, distinguishing two nearby objects from one contiguous object requires receptors with overlapping receptive fields and lateral inhibition between adjacent receptors. Perhaps more surprisingly, the cortical area processing features of these visual stimuli must be organized into topological maps in which cells processing stimuli from adjacent parts of the visual field are located adjacent to each other (Allman, 1999). This follows from the need for cells processing nearby areas of the visual field to communicate with each other plus the fact that there is a serious constraint on cables between cells—their conductivity is proportional to their diameter and inversely proportional to their distance. To transmit information over longer distances requires bigger cables, which has a cascade of effects including increased brain volume and metabolic requirements. Shapiro identifies two further requirements on brains that realize the properties of human minds, both of which follow from the demands on communication through cables. First, they must be organized in modules (Ringo, 1991), albeit not encapsulated modules *a la* Fodor. Second, the cables must be myelenated (Morell & Norton, 1980).

Although considerations such as those Shapiro advances do leave open the potential for alternative realizations of a cognitive function such as vision, they dramatically reduce the range of viable realizations (which is all he sought to demonstrate). As research proceeds, new constraints will almost certainly be discovered that further limit the range of viable realizations. That poses an interesting question—why is it that there seem to be so many possible realizers in the case of humanly designed machines and so few in the case of biological mechanisms? In answering this question, we need first to make sure we are not trying to explain an artifact. Although numerous alternative designs may be possible for relatively simple machines, such as a corkscrew, when the machines get more complicated and the demands on how they function grow, the number of alternative designs seems to drop quickly. For example, a large number of highly inventive designs for manual typewriters were developed before settling on the one that became common by the first decades of the twentieth century. Even though some of these designs went into commercial production, most exhibited performance shortcomings that led them to be discarded. There may simply not be as many workable designs as philosophers envisage from their armchairs. Designing mechanisms is a challenging activity, and there are good reasons why there are significant rewards for those who do it well. The demands on biological mechanisms are even greater. As I will discuss in chapter six, they must be viable parts of systems that build and repair themselves, extracting and channeling free energy and raw materials from their environment and deploying them to perform all the operations needed to maintain themselves (Ruiz-Mirazo & Moreno, 2004). When these constraints are taken into account as well as the specific function the mechanism is supposed to serve, the number of realizers may be vanishingly small.

The strategy of defending the independence of psychology by appeal to multiple realizability seems far less plausible than it did during the heyday of functionalism. This does not itself undermine functionalism and the attempts to identify mental states in terms of their interactions. As I have noted, that is precisely what functional decomposition does. But it does open up the possibility that functionalism is in fact compatible with the identity of functionally characterized entities with structurally characterized entities. The heuristic identity theory that I introduced as a tool for discovering how mechanisms work in chapter two, and appealed to in chapter three, makes good use of just such an identity between functionally and structurally characterized entities. Having rejected multiple realizability as the basis for maintaining the independence of higher levels, I turn now to the issue of whether independence can be maintained in the face of claims identifying psychologically characterized operations with the operations performed in brain areas as identified by neuroscientists.

4.3   REFOCUSING THE REDUCTION–INDEPENDENCE DEBATE IN MECHANIST TERMS

When confronted with opposing positions, as in the debate between advocates of reducing psychology to neuroscience and those defending its independence, the natural tendency is to assume that one of the positions is right and to try to adjudicate the argument. But sometimes the assumptions underlying the debate are flawed. Such is the case in the present controversy. At the heart of the theory-reduction account is the D-N model of explanation, which treats laws as the engine of explanation. The contention of this book, however, is that the explanatory projects in the mind–brain sciences fit mechanistic accounts of explanation far better than they fit the D-N model. We saw in chapter one that laws that are explanatory are relatively scarce in psychology; more numerous are laws, usually called *effects* as noted by Cummins (2000), that simply describe phenomena that remain to be explained. An explanation is provided by specifying the parts and operations that comprise a mechanism and how they are organized so as to produce the phenomenon of interest. If the D-N account of explanation does not fit the mind–brain sciences, it should not be surprising that the theory-reduction account based on it fares little better.

Turning now to mechanistic explanations, there is a clear sense in which they are reductionist. This sense, however, is importantly different from the sense involved in the theory-reduction model. It focuses not on the derivability of one theory from another but on decomposing a mechanism into parts and operations that explain why the mechanism behaves in a particular way. Recharacterizing reduction in mechanistic terms, though, radically reconfigures the debate between reduction and independence. In the sections below, I will show how they are in fact compatible when reduction is construed mechanistically and independence is divorced of its links to multiple realizability. Before I can do so, though, I need to introduce a vexed notion that figures in debates over reduction and independence, that of levels. Reduction is often presented as appealing to lower levels for explanation while independence maintains the importance of independently investigating higher levels. But what are levels?

4.4   LEVELS OF ORGANIZATION IN MECHANISMS

The notion of *levels* is ubiquitous in discussions of science. Yet, it is used in such a variety of ways that when it is invoked in discussions of reduction without explication, it is unclear what is to be reduced to what. After surveying some of the most common ways of construing levels and their limitations, I will develop a notion of levels appropriate for mechanistic explanation.

In the introduction to this chapter I brought attention to the question of whether the discipline of psychology might be reduced to the discipline of neuroscience. This was a common way of putting the question in the heyday of the theory-reduction account, for a prominent feature of that account was the idea that different sciences address phenomena at different levels. Physics addresses the most basic level, chemistry a level above that, and biology, psychology, and sociology each address successively higher levels. There are a variety of problems with such an account. One is that physics itself deals with a broad range of entities, from the very small (subatomic particles) to the extremely large (galaxies). There doesn't seem to be a clear sense in which these reside at the same level, other than that they are all dealt with by scientists who are called *physicists*. Nor is there an obvious sense in which all of the entities of physics lie at a lower level than those of biology, which also vary considerably in size (e.g., genes, cell organelles, organisms, ecosystems).

The attempt to sort out levels in terms of disciplines seems to be fraught with problems (for further discussion, see Craver, 2007, chapter five). A very different approach is to start not with the categorization provided by disciplines, but with the phenomena of nature. An initially plausible view is to demarcate levels in terms of the size of the entities involved—small things are at a lower level than big things. This is the picture Churchland and Sejnowski adopted when they used structure at different scales to illustrate levels of organization in the nervous system. Thus, they populated successive levels with molecules (1Å), synapses (1μm), neurons (100μm), networks (1mm), maps (1cm), and systems (10cm) (P. S. Churchland & Sejnowski, 1988). Wimsatt likewise proposed size as a way to differentiate levels, though he further elaborated his suggestion by proposing that entities of the same size tend to "interact most strongly and frequently" (Wimsatt, 1976a). Thus, levels are "*local maxima of regularity and predictability in the phase space of alternative modes of organization of matter"* (Wimsatt, 1994, p. 238). Accordingly, he develops a stratified account according to which entities tend to fall into discrete clusters based on size: levels *"are constituted by families of entities usually of comparable size and dynamical properties, which characteristically interact primarily with one another, and which, taken together, give an apparent rough closure over a range of phenomena and regularities"* (Wimsatt, 1994, p. 225).

If it were true that entities of a given size range interacted primarily with other entities of similar size, then using size to demarcate levels would be a principled approach. There are, however, numerous examples of things of different sizes interacting causally. There are gravitational forces between very large objects (the Earth) and small objects (a ball rolling down an inclined plane). Storms can sweep seeds from one location to another. On the other hand, small things can radically affect big things—a bullet can kill an elephant. Absent a quantitative analysis, it is not obvious that causally interacting objects tend to be of the same size and that this will serve to delineate levels.

Wimsatt proposed that, at least among organisms, evolutionary forces will support such a congregation of entities into levels. In order to operate efficiently, an organism needs to be able to predict reliably how things in its environment will behave, and accordingly it will evolve so as to interact with entities at a given level. For example, organisms typically interact most frequently with other organisms, cooperating or competing, acting as a predator or serving as prey, and so forth. Organs, on the other hand, interact mostly with other organs within the body. Organisms may interact with the organs of another organism's body (e.g., a surgeon operating on a person's heart, or a predator selectively consuming specific organs of the prey), but these interactions, according to Wimsatt, are less frequent, and we can differentiate the two sets of more frequent interactions as demarcating different levels.

Although there is an intuitive attractiveness to this argument, it is not clear that it holds up any better than the raw claim that objects tend to interact with things of the same size. Predators can be of very different sizes than their prey and each needs to be aware of the other. Moreover, small entities in the environment can be very important for large organisms (small molecules that can be detected by smell play a large role in animal behavior, and large-scale events in the environment such as forest fires can be critically important for the behavior of small organisms, e.g., seeds that open only under such heat).[5]

---

[5] Wimsatt acknowledges a number of ways in which this framework is complicated. Especially with higher levels of organization, cross-level interactions increase in frequency and at these stages, he advocates alternative conceptions such as what he terms perspectives and causal thickets (Wimsatt, 1974). Perspectives, as Wimsatt characterizes them, cross levels, relating, for example, the parts to a whole system. The problem for Wimsatt's account is that the frequency of what Wimsatt would construe as cross-level interactions may in fact be so great as to vitiate the use of such interactions to identify levels.

Wimsatt often combines his analysis of levels by sizes with a compositional or mereological treatment of levels:

> By level of organization, I will mean here compositional levels—hierarchical divisions of stuff (paradigmatically but not necessarily material stuff) organized by part-whole relations, in which wholes at one level function as parts at the next (and at all higher) levels (Wimsatt, 1994, p. 222).

The first thing to note is that, although a consequence of this compositional analysis is that parts, which will be at lower levels than the wholes composed of them, are smaller than the whole, this analysis is quite different than the size analysis. For one thing, there is no constraint that the parts of an entity must be of the same size—they may vary radically as long as each is smaller than the whole. Second, it is local: parts will be at different levels than the wholes to which they belong, but the compositional analysis does not tell us how to relate the parts to things outside the whole. Third, unlike the size criterion, the part–whole analysis has natural affinities with mechanistic explanations and helps capture the sense in which mechanistic explanations are reductive in appealing to lower levels.

Another proposal involves bringing together two different notions of level in construing phenomena, and considering how this maps onto disciplinary divisions (Abrahamsen, 1987). The mereological notion of level is subordinated to a different notion of levels in which phenomena are grouped in a way that generally corresponds to common academic divisions: ordinary physical phenomena (physical sciences), phenomena of life (biological sciences), behavioral/mental phenomena (behavioral sciences), and phenomena involving products of human behavior/thought (humanities and social sciences). Only within each of these four levels do mereological levels come into play: each has its own part–whole hierarchy that is unlike those at other levels. What is most interesting about the primary levels, though, is that if one focuses on the actual entities whose functioning instantiates the phenomena, the levels are hierarchically structured. That is, they involve different levels of analysis of the same sets of entities (ontological domains). "What produces the nesting is that each higher domain is generated from the lower one; entities and processes in the lower domain tend towards increasing complexity, and organized systems emerge for which specialized concepts and explanations appear necessary. Disciplinary divisions mirror this nested structure, with each division in turn telescoping away from its parent division towards a more specialized account" (pp. 262–263). One consequence of this nesting is that domains at a higher level (e.g., physiological systems) are regarded as specialized subdomains at a lower level (e.g., physiological systems as a special case of physical systems), creating opportunities for interdisciplinary inquiry. Relating this to the mereological levels, the same entity may be viewed as a membrane within a cell by a biologist and as an osmotic barrier in a chemical system by a physical scientist. Mereological levels are often related, at least loosely, to different disciplines within a division; e.g., they distinguish particle physicists, chemists, and astronomers within the physical sciences and molecular biologists, physiologists, and ecologists within the biological sciences.

One problem with the mereological notion of levels is that it allows for arbitrary differentiation of the parts of a whole (see Craver, 2007, for a discussion of this and many other problems with the formal treatments of mereology). One way to resolve this problem is to wed the mereological account not with another type of level, as in Abrahamsen's account, but rather to the mechanistic framework. Within a mechanism, the relevant parts are, as discussed in chapter one, working parts—the parts that perform the operations that enable the mechanism to realize the phenomenon of interest. These may be of different sizes, but they are distinguished by the fact that they figure in the functioning of the mechanism. It is the set of working parts that are organized and whose operations are coordinated to realize the phenomenon of interest that constitute a level.

There are several features of levels of organization in a mechanism that merit comment. First is an obvious but critically important feature to bear in mind when thinking about different levels in a mechanism: the working parts of a mechanism do different things than does the whole mechanism. A given cellular mechanism might transfer the energy in foodstuff to ATP, but none of the individual enzymes do this. An enzyme such as oxidase succinate, instead, catalyzes a component reaction. Hence, individual lower-level components do not explain the overall performance of the mechanism. Only the mechanism as a whole is capable of generating the phenomenon, and then only under appropriate conditions. (I will return to this point.)

An important consequence of the differences in what the mechanism does and what its parts do is that different vocabulary is required to describe the operations of the parts of the mechanism from that used to describe the activity of the whole mechanism. Thus, the respiratory system *catabolizes* glucose to carbon dioxide and water, whereas a given enzyme *catalyzes* a reaction. There are contexts in which scientists use the same term to describe what the mechanism does and what a part of it does (e.g., both cells and sets of chromosomes divide). Even in such cases, the term is used differently (chromosomes pair up and are pulled to separate spindles, whereas cell division involves a process of segregating the new cells, including their chromosomes, within membranes). When we look at levels as levels of organization in mechanisms, we can better appreciate why bridge principles were needed in theory-reduction accounts. The difference in vocabulary between lower-level and higher-level accounts is not accidental but reflects the fact that parts of a mechanism do different things than the mechanism as a whole. So, some means of relating the vocabularies is required. But the relevant connections are not just a matter of translation—they characterize the compositional relations between parts and wholes in a mechanism.

The account of levels in mechanisms fails to capture some of the characteristics of levels found in other accounts. In one alternative, levels are strata spanning the natural world, with each entity determinately either at the same level or at a higher or lower level than some other entity. Such a picture confronts difficulties in its own right: Are glaciers at the same level or a higher or lower level than elephants? Is an enzyme inside the oxidative phosphorylation system at a higher level, a lower level, or the same level as a chip in a computer? The mechanistic account of levels provides no answer to such questions, as neither glaciers and elephants nor enzymes and chips are working parts of a common mechanism or in componential relation with each other within a mechanism. The account offers no way to evaluate whether the components of a mechanism are at the same level as entities outside the mechanism. For those seeking a global account of levels, this may seem to be a serious limitation. Yet, as I just noted, that view of levels is problematic. Local identification of levels is sufficient for understanding levels in a mechanism and for capturing how mechanistic explanation is reductionist.

A further consequence of the mechanistic construal of levels is that even entities of the same physical type may not be at the same level if they are employed in different ways in a mechanism. For example, a critical part of the mechanism of oxidative phosphorylation, through which cells transform the energy of foodstuffs into ATP, involves the pumping of hydrogen ions across a membrane to create a gradient that can then drive the process of ATP synthesis. Hydrogen ions, however, are also constituents of the molecules comprising the membrane. The membrane and the hydrogen ions being pumped across it are at a higher level within the mechanism than the hydrogen ions that comprise the molecules of the membrane. Although locating hydrogen ions at different levels seems problematic from the point of view of levels as strata across nature, it is what one should expect on a mechanistic construal of levels.

The account of levels within a mechanism can be generalized to multiple levels of organization in a natural way, once we recognize that a working part of a mechanism may itself be a mechanism. To explain how a working part performs its operation, investigators decompose it into its own working parts. These parts are at a lower level than the working part they comprise, and hence two levels below the mechanism as a whole. This kind of decomposition clearly can be iterated. Yet, the problems noted above with identifying levels as strata soon reemerge as we move down two levels. Because of the lack of a compositional relation between the subparts of two different working parts of the mechanism, the question of whether these are at the same level is not well defined.

Although it cannot provide a global account of levels, the mechanistic account is sufficient for understanding mechanisms and the respects in which mechanistic explanation is inherently reductionist; parts are at lower levels, and mechanistic explanation appeals to parts and their operations to explain the behavior of a mechanism. Yet, the local character of the treatment of levels has a rather surprising consequence that distinguishes mechanistic reduction from traditional views of reduction. Traditional views tend to assume that higher-level explanations can be reduced level by level until we hit some fundamental level. On a theory-reduction account, the theories at this fundamental level provide the foundation on which all higher-level theories are grounded. Even those who forego a theory reduction perspective find it plausible that at some fundamental level we can identify the parts and operations out of which all higher-level mechanisms are built. Theorists such as Kim (1998) then maintain that if we had a complete account of causal processes at this level, we would at least in principle be able to determine all that happens in the universe. We would simply supply the initial conditions and make deductions from the laws governing the most basic level. Higher-level causal relations would overdetermine outcomes as they were already determined at the lower level. But if we adopt the mechanistic account, in which the notion of levels is defined only locally, then we are not confronted with the prospect of a comprehensive lower level that is causally complete and closed. Such a picture of complete causal determination at a lower level is further brought into question when we consider why mechanistic explanations are inherently interlevel.

4.5   MECHANISTIC EXPLANATIONS AS INHERENTLY INTERLEVEL

As I have characterized levels, a mechanism as a whole and its working parts are at different levels. When dealing with a mechanism, investigators are dealing with two different levels of entities (the mechanism itself and its parts). Entities at each level engage in causal interactions with other entities (the mechanism with other entities in its environment and the parts with each other). In offering a mechanistic explanation, researchers often focus on the working parts which causally engage each other. Yet, the mechanism as a whole also engages entities in its environment, and this is the level at which the phenomenon to be explained is characterized. While this level is sometimes taken for granted in the quest to develop mechanistic explanations, it is critically important. Mechanisms behave in a particular way only under specific environmental conditions. People are operantly conditioned only when the environment provides appropriate reinforcers. Cells in MT increase their firing rate only when there is movement in their receptive fields. Accordingly, often the explanation for why a phenomenon was instantiated on a given occasion involves establishing that the relevant environmental conditions were satisfied. Both the level of the parts and the level of the mechanism engaging its environment play roles in mechanistic analyses. A mechanistic explanation therefore inherently spans at least these two levels.

Before turning to the question of how levels are bridged in mechanistic explanations, it is worth attending to the inquiries scientists perform on the mechanism as a whole. Often a great deal can be learned about a mechanism without decomposing it. During an era when it seemed dubious that investigators would ever be able to identify the chemical reactions occurring within yeast as they fermented sugars, Pasteur (1860) ascertained that they only performed fermentation when oxygen was not available in their environment, a regularity that came to be known as the *Pasteur effect*. Very often scientists use equations to describe the relation between various factors in the mechanism's environment and aspects of its behavior. In many instances, these equations will take the form of laws as characterized in nomological accounts of explanation. In section three above I cited approvingly Cummins' (2000) characterization of such laws (effects) as not providing explanations; rather, they describe phenomena. While invoking the law does not explain how the mechanism brings the phenomenon about, identifying that the antecedent conditions are met on a given occasion can be explanatory. Thus, learning that a person developed serious nausea several hours after eating mahi mahi for the first time will explain (in accord with the Garcia effect) why they cannot face eating it on subsequent occasions. An investigation that focuses on the engagement of the mechanism with its environment identifies the environmental factors that affect the operation of the mechanism and describes the relationship in as much detail as possible—often, though not necessarily, in a lawlike equation.

From what I have said so far, with mechanisms we have descriptions of causal relations at two levels, one focusing on what the whole mechanism is doing and the other on what the parts are doing. What relates these? A central idea of mechanistic explanation is that the operation of the parts enables the mechanism as a whole to behave in a specific way. But often it appears mysterious why this should be the case. Fodor captured this sense of mystery:

> Damn near everything we know about the world suggests that unimaginably complicated to-ings and fro-ings of bits and pieces at the extreme microlevel manage somehow to converge on stable macrolevel properties. On the other hand, the "somehow" really is entirely mysterious ... (Fodor, 1997, pp. 160–161).

This mystery is what often leads theorists to talk of *emergence*. But that is simply to give a label to the mysterious relation between what the parts of a mechanism do and what the whole does. Not everyone, however, shares the sense of mystery. Shapiro, for example, responded to Fodor as follows:

> The bigger mystery is why this seems at all mysterious. Task analysis of two significantly different realizations of the kind corkscrew will reveal how it is that each realization is able to remove corks. Once one understands the principles by which waiter's corkscrews remove corks, and the principles by which double-level corkscrews remove corks, what is so puzzling about how two causally distinct devices can "do the same thing"? (Shapiro, 2004, pp. 161–162)

To understand Shapiro's response, we need to consider carefully what a *task analysis* involves. It involves knowing not just the operations involved in performing the task, but also how they and the parts are organized. In order to get parts, which individually do not perform the task in question, to do so, the right collection of parts needs to be put together in a way that enables the whole to perform the task. That performance will involve operations that also are organized (temporally). One way to capture what seems to be driving Fodor is the idea that if reduction were correct, we ought to be able to discover from what we know of the parts and operations how they are organized so as together to realize the phenomenon of interest. Knowing how things are put together, though, requires knowing more than knowing the "to-ings and fro-ings of bits and pieces at the extreme microlevel." Knowledge of organization is not information at that level.[6]

It is helpful to look at the process from the point of view of a designer—either an engineer or Mother Nature. The challenge is to make something that exhibits a phenomenon not already realized by other things. To do this, entities which do other things are put together in the mechanism, organized such that by all of them doing their thing, the mechanism performs the new activity.[7] The simplest way of organizing multiple parts performing different operations is to locate them spatially such that operations will occur serially there, with each successive operation taking as input the output of the preceding operation. Already here we have systems that, as a whole, carry out an operation that none of the components alone could do. Assembly lines, for example, make whole cars, whereas an individual worker may only attach the engine. One might counter that the worker could indeed make a whole car. Perhaps—but not without a great deal of additional

---

6 This extra knowledge is brought into the theory-reduction model through the invocation of boundary conditions. Typically there is little discussion among defenders of the theory-reduction model as to where information about such boundary conditions comes from. But it is clearly additional to the lower-level theory and by noting that we can see how, even if one insisted on the theory-reduction account, a kind of independence arises for higher-level sciences—they are needed to spell out the boundary conditions. However, by just characterizing such information as specifying boundary conditions and not considering what that information is about, namely, the organization involved in constituting a higher-level system out of lower-level constituents, the theory-reduction account camouflages the contribution of higher-level inquiries.

7 A useful reference point in thinking about organization is the null case in which organization is lacking. Wimsatt (1986) provides a characterization of such a state as purely aggregative—components are put together but no order is imposed. He identifies four features of aggregations: the parts are intersubstitutable, adding or deleting parts does not yield a qualitative change, reaggregating the parts does not produce a change, and there is minimal interaction between parts. Sand in a sandbox closely approximates such an aggregative system—grains of sand can be substituted for each other, a bucket more or less of sand makes no qualitative difference, moving sand from one part of the box to another generally has no effect, and the grains of sand do not interact significantly with each other.

training through which he or she would master the skills of all the workers on the assembly line. And he or she would still have to carry out all the operations in the right order. It is the coordination of those operations that enables either the assembly line as a whole, or the individual craftsperson, to produce a product.

In the previous chapter I presented the visual system as comparable to an assembly line: each brain area received input from the previous brain region and performed a computation on it, then passed its results to the next area. In chapter six I will focus more explicitly on biological mechanisms, and will argue that such linear modes of organization are inadequate to capture the active nature of biological mechanisms. Where biological mechanisms depart from simpler ones is with respect to how they are organized. The products of the operation of one part often alter the operations of parts earlier in the processing pathway. The organization in biological mechanisms is often rich in reliance on modes of organization such as negative feedback and cyclic pathways. The result is typically a highly integrated system in which any given operation is dependent upon and in turn influences many others within the whole mechanism. Such complex couplings of operations yield systems in which the operation of each component is highly constrained and regulated by activity occurring elsewhere. What is important for current purposes is simply to note the critical role played by organization in giving rise to a mechanism whose overall behavior far exceeds the operations of its component parts (Boogerd, Bruggeman, Richardson, Stephan, & Westerhoff, 2005).

We have now reached a point at which we can recognize how the mechanistic perspective provides for a rapprochement between reductionism and the independence of investigations focused on higher levels of organization. The mechanistic perspective is reductionist in that when investigators seek to explain how a mechanism performs an activity in its particular context, they decompose the mechanism into its parts and the operations those perform. And this is, at least in principle, an iterative process—when investigators want to explain how a component part of a mechanism performs its operation in the context of the mechanism, they can decompose it into its parts and their operations.[8] But an understanding of the parts alone is not sufficient to understand why the mechanism behaves as it does. In addition, the scientists need to consider how the parts and operations are organized so

---

[8] As I noted earlier, typically a given set of investigators will only decompose a mechanism in one or two steps. Knowing how the components behave and understanding how they are organized is sufficient for the purposes of explaining how the mechanism as a whole behaves. Moreover, the research techniques required to carry out another round of decomposition typically are very different than those required for the first round and a further round of decomposition would require recruiting other researchers with mastery of different research tools and techniques. Unless the parts of a mechanism are behaving in a puzzling or unusual way, there is no incentive for performing further decompositions.

as to produce the activity of the mechanism as a whole. Often unheralded, organization is key to bridging between the operations of parts and the activity of the mechanism. But even this is not sufficient. Scientists need to know what factors are operative in the mechanism's environment, for these affect how it will behave on a given occasion. No matter how much they investigate the parts, their operations, and their organization, investigators will not identify the variables in the environment that are impinging on the mechanism. Discovering these variables and their effects requires inquiry directed at the environmental variables using appropriate investigatory techniques.

To appreciate this multilevel character of mechanistic inquiry, consider hypothetically that we are in possession of a fully worked out account of the internal processes within a particular cell. We know the parts, we know what they do, and we understand, to some degree of detail, the spatial and temporal organization. Thus, we understand the internal processes by which the cell incorporates materials from the environment into its structure, how it metabolizes them to secure energy and building blocks for its own structure, how it disposes of waste, and so forth. We also understand the regulatory systems that alter its behavior—that allow it, for example, to switch from oxidative respiration to fermentation when oxygen is not available. The reductionist inquiry will not tell us about the conditions in the environment which determine the availability of oxygen. To determine that requires investigation of what is happening in the cell's environment.

The same is true of mental mechanisms. Again, assume we are in possession of a full account of the mechanism(s) involved in encoding and retrieval of episodic memories. Moreover, assume we know all the brain regions involved, what operations each performs, and how they are orchestrated in the service of encoding and retrieving memories. With such information we might hope to understand why some events are better encoded than others, how different kinds of memory cues will succeed in eliciting recall of the events, and even why subjects develop false memories and confabulate in recalling events. But this information will not tell us what events the individual was exposed to in the first place, what sorts of experiences they had between encoding and recall, or what demands for retrieval the individual encounters. This requires not investigations into the internal operations of the responsible mental mechanism but accounts of such things as the person's experiences, the opportunities they had for rehearsing the experience, the renditions of the event they heard from others, and the situations in which they are trying to recall it.

Having shown that entities at two levels (at least) are involved in mechanistic explanation, and that organization is the bridge that relates levels, the question arises of how to describe the relations between levels. A common strategy has been to characterize the relation between a mechanism and its parts causally. This reflects the fact that when something causally affects a mechanism, there are changes to parts within the mechanism. When a bowl of food is put before a laboratory animal and it begins to eat it, chemical changes in its brain and digestive system ensue. Likewise, when people volunteer for memory experiments and are asked to remember words on a list, there are changes in their brains. To describe how actions on a mechanism result in changes in its components, theorists will often speak, following the lead of Donald Campbell (1974), of *downward* or *top-down causation*. The motivation for talking of top–down causation is clear—the mechanism as a whole is at a higher level than its components, and it is causal processes acting on the mechanism that result in changes to the constituents of the mechanism. One can in a similar manner motivate appeal to *upward* or *bottom–up causation*. If the parts of a mechanism perform their operations, the mechanism as a whole will perform its activity. Mechanisms, after all, behave as they do because of the operations of their parts, and it is natural to construe this relation as causal.

Certainly there are relations between levels within a mechanism. This is the reason researchers investigating mechanisms need to bridge between levels. But there are good reasons not to characterize the relation between a mechanism and its parts causally. The notion of *causation* commonly entails a number of associations that do not comport well with interlevel relations. For example, causes are often assumed to precede and be independent of their effects in the sense of being separate events. As Lewis presents the independence requirement, it rules out effects being part of causes and vice versa: "C and E must be distinct events—and distinct not only in the sense of nonidentity but also in the sense of nonoverlap and nonimplication" (Lewis, 2000). Perhaps the most problematic aspect of invoking causal vocabulary in interlevel cases is that we seem to encounter problems of overdetermination—if the change in the behavior of a component of a mechanism was caused both by events internal to the mechanism and by factors impinging on the mechanism as a whole, we seem to end up with two causal accounts of the same event. Moreover, there is a tendency to view the lower-level account as primary and the higher-level account as superfluous. (These and other reasons for not invoking causation in interlevel contexts are developed further in Craver & Bechtel, in press.)

To avoid these problems, it is better to limit the concept of causation to relations at a given level. We can do this, and still make all the points for which concepts such as top–down and bottom–up causation were proposed, by referring to *mechanistically mediated effects*. Such effects are a hybrid of constitutive and causal relations. On such a view, causal relations are exclusively intralevel whereas constitutive relations bridge between levels. In the top–down case, environmental forces causally affect the mechanism which is constituted of parts. Thus, the effect on the mechanism is also an effect on one or more of its parts or on the organizational relations among the parts. If nothing that constituted the mechanism changed, the mechanism as a whole would not have been affected. In the bottom–up case, once a part of a mechanism is altered, that causally results in other changes in the mechanism. The mechanism as a whole is thereby altered, and the altered mechanism may then cause changes in other things in the mechanism's environment. This provides a general strategy for explaining what happens in putative cases of top–down or bottom–up causation without requiring appeal to causal relations between mechanisms and their parts.

To show how this schema can be applied, I will develop a couple of examples. You add some memory chips to your computer. Afterwards you take your computer with you to a lecture to take notes. Even though you made no special efforts to bring the computer's memory with you, you would be very surprised to find when you got there that your computer lacked the memory. Once installed within the computer, the memory goes with the computer wherever it goes. The memory is constrained by the structure of the computer. When you apply the causal forces to the computer in carrying it with you, the constitutive relations between the computer and the memory ensure that the memory comes along. In such a case, nothing very interesting happens to the memory as a result of being physically contained within the computer and transported with it. But the case provides a clear example of how we can avoid talking about top–down causation—the computer did not cause its memory to be transported with it. The memory is part of what constitutes it, and so moved with the computer.

For a more psychological case, consider what happens to you as a result of listening to a lecture and taking notes. At some later point you tell a friend about something you heard in the lecture. How are you able to do that? It seems natural to say that hearing the lecture caused chemical changes in your brain, and that these chemical changes were part of the cause of your later report of the lecture. We can capture all the causality in this scenario in terms of mechanistically mediated effects. The utterances of the lecturer did impinge causally on you. This impingement on you involved changes in the conditions under which your cognitive mechanisms operated. One of the consequences of these changes is the generation of electrical signals (action potentials) that are transmitted through your brain, including through your hippocampus. The effect on your hippocampus consists in changes in the concentrations of various chemicals at the synapses between cells, which then caused the chemical changes known as long-term potentiation, which in turn rendered these cells more likely to produce action potentials in response to release of neurotransmitters at these synapses in the future. This change in capacity to produce action potentials constitutes a change in the electrochemical activity of the hippocampus, which in turn causes different electrical activity elsewhere in the brain, including those processes involved in generating speech. This new state constitutes remembering the content of the lecture. In this sketch of events involved in remembering a lecture, I twice stepped down levels by appealing to an identity between the effect on a system and a change in constituents of the system. At the lower level the causal story was an ordinary causal one. Then I stepped up a level by appealing to an identity between the new operations within the mechanism and the way it behaved as a whole. At the level of the whole the story was again an ordinary causal one.

In this section I have shown how mechanisms inherently are interlevel in nature. A mechanism consists of an organized set of parts, each of which performs its own operation. These parts and operations are at a lower level than the mechanism as a whole. The orchestrated operation of the parts explains how the mechanism as a whole behaves in a specific manner when it is in particular conditions. To present such an account an investigator must both identify the relevant intralevel causal relations and determine the constitutive relations between parts and the whole mechanism. There is no additional need to posit interlevel causes, and good reasons to avoid introducing them.

4.6   HIGHER LEVELS IN MECHANISMS: INDEPENDENCE WITHOUT MULTIPLE REALIZABILITY

The account of levels in mechanisms that I have developed here explicates in a very natural way the independence of inquiries at different levels. Inquiry at each level targets the causal processes occurring at that level. The causal processes at different levels are of different types and, as I emphasized above, are properly described in different vocabularies. People operate in the environment around them via appropriate orientation of their bodies. The dorsal stream of the visual system processes information from the visual scene required to coordinate such movements. MT, an area in the dorsal stream, extracts information about movement of objects in the visual scene, and individual cells in MT exhibit specific patterns of spiking under specific conditions. Moreover, the experimental strategies used to investigate each of these processes are different. Behavioral experiments are required to determine how a given organism moves in response to a visual scene, whereas electrodes are inserted to determine how cells in MT respond to a moving stimulus. To understand the spiking patterns of neurons, researchers must investigate such phenomena as fluxes of ions across membranes. Through employing different types of experimental apparatus, particular investigators track different sets of causal processes.

Such a defense of the independence of levels does not require appeal to the multiple realizability of higher levels. There may only be one kind of mechanism that is fully appropriate for engagement in a particular causal process. Any changes in the components of the mechanism or their organization may produce detectable changes in the way the mechanism as a whole behaves. Even so, different inquiries are needed to determine the variables that affect the behavior of the mechanism as a whole and to understand how the organized set of parts and operations enables the mechanism to behave in that way.

In arguing for a kind of independence for inquiry conducted at different levels, I am not proposing that researchers conduct their investigations in isolation from one another or that they do not benefit from knowing the results of inquiry at other levels or from collaborating with investigators focused on other levels. These may provide clues that help constrain the possible mechanisms that produce a phenomenon. An independent inquiry is not one conducted in isolation, but one that takes a particular phenomenon as focal and identifies the causal processes involved in generating that phenomenon.

To fully understand a mechanism, inquiries are needed that look down to the parts and sideways to the causal factors impinging on the mechanism. Looking sideways is required since mechanisms do not always behave in the same way; they function differently when in interaction with different entities. Inquiry is required to identify what factors outside the mechanism affect its behavior and specify how they do so. Such inquiry is often required to pin down the phenomenon. Researchers look down when they seek to understand how the mechanism produced the behavior it does in a given context. This requires discovering what the parts and operations are within the mechanism and how they are organized.

Sometimes, in addition to looking down and around, it is necessary to look up from a given mechanism to yet a higher level of organization to understand its behavior. This is necessary when the targeted mechanism is incorporated within a larger system (another mechanism) and the behavior of this system determines the causal factors impinging on it in a systematic manner. Consider the conditions affecting a single-celled animal seeking a glucose-rich environment. The locations of glucose concentrations may be close to random. Contrast that with the conditions confronting a cardiac muscle cell, which is regularly receiving a stimulus prompting its contraction. To understand the behavior of the latter it is important to appeal not just to the way the cell responds to particular inputs, but to the regular pattern of inputs that it is receiving due to the overall organization of the relevant parts of the nervous system. Moreover, the nervous system not only provides regular input, but plays a regulative role, keeping critical parameters in the range needed to maintain the system. The same is true for many of our cognitive processes. Some of the sensory inputs we receive are relatively random, but others are highly structured, often in ways that are coordinated with our own behavior. For example, by being members of social groups such as families, individual humans receive systematic inputs. These also can impose regulative control over individuals and their cognitive mechanisms. In general, whenever a mechanism is itself a part of a larger system in which components are organized in ways that produce regularities, mechanistic inquiry may need to look up to that higher level to fully explain the mechanism's behavior.

The rapprochement between reductionism and independence results from the fact that within a mechanistic perspective neither claims to reduction nor claims to independence are absolute. Mechanistic reduction only proposes to explain the response of an entity to the causal factors impinging on it in terms of its lower-level constituents. It does not try to explain the causal factors impinging on the mechanism. Understanding these requires inquiry focused on the mechanism as a whole, and often on yet higher-level systems in which the mechanism is embedded. Independence stems from the fact that inquiry at each level provides information additional to that which can be secured at other levels, and generally does so using different tools of inquiry. Thus, when studying the cognitive system as a whole and detecting the regularities in its behavior, researchers use behavioral tasks. To study the operations in it that enable it to realize those regularities, researchers instead choose such techniques as lesioning, stimulating, or recording the activity of components. Whereas in a theory-reduction account the lower level was, in principle, capable of providing a complete account of nature, in a mechanistic account no given level provides a complete account but each provides some relevant information. Thus, from within a mechanistic framework one can embrace both reductionism and the independence of each level of inquiry.

Five

Representations and Mental Mechanisms

Representation is one of the most widely invoked terms in both cognitive science and neuroscience and is much discussed in philosophical accounts of these fields. One of the clearest ways of differentiating the cognitive tradition from its behaviorist predecessor in psychology is to note that cognitive theories invoke representations whereas behaviorists (as well as Gibsonians) eschew them. The motivation for introducing representations into accounts of mental processing follows from viewing the mind/brain as a set of mechanisms for controlling behavior and, in the case of more complex organisms, performing a variety of *off-line* cognitive tasks that relate them to objects and events in the world around them. As discussed in chapter one, this requires conceiving of the mind/brain as a set of information-processing mechanisms. Central to the idea of an information-processing mechanism is that states within the mechanism serve to carry information about objects or events external to it. The term *represent* characterizes the relation between states within the information processing system, which in chapter one I referred to as the *vehicle* of representation, and external objects or events, referred to as the *content* of the representation. The term *representation* refers to both the vehicle and its content.

In the simplest nervous systems, representations figure in the immediate coordination of motor systems in response to information secured through the senses (e.g., swimming, so as to move upwards through a sucrose gradient). More complex nervous systems can do much more, ranging from the ordinary (planning and controlling a sequence of behaviors to achieve the goal of procuring milk for breakfast) to the sublime (thinking about human freedom). In both the simpler cases and the more complex cases, part of the challenge for the organism is to coordinate its mental activity with things external to it. Often the relevant external phenomena are immediately available to the organism through its senses. Other times they are removed in space and time. In either case, in order to coordinate the organism's responses, the brain must acquire information about the external phenomena. As the proximal causal processes that determine the mechanism's responses are the operations of the components of the mechanism, these must represent the external phenomena in order to be coordinated with them.

We understand how representations work reasonably well from our use of language and other symbols to communicate with others or to facilitate our own activities. This book, for example, contains words and diagrams that I have used as tools to convey ideas to you. To give someone directions to a store, you might describe the route in words or draw a map. To remember someone's phone number you might write it on a sticky note. To compare your appearance before and after a haircut, you might take photographs. All of these activities involve representational vehicles—spoken or written words, diagrams, maps, and pictures, which can be characterized in terms of their intrinsic physical properties. They are used to designate something else—the mechanisms by which the mind works, the route through space that you can take to reach the store, your appearance before and after the haircut—which constitute the content of the representations. Recent empirical study of our use of representations in social practices has revealed some surprising aspects. Gesture, for example, turns out to play a much more significant role in face-to-face verbal communication than often assumed (Goldin-Meadow & Wagner, 2005; McNeill, 1992; 2005). But as experienced participants in the social practices using these representations, cognitive and neuroscientists have felt they have a sufficient understanding of them to invoke them as models in understanding representation as it occurs within mental mechanisms.

It is important to note that using external representations with which we are already familiar to characterize internal representations within our mind/brain involves advancing a theoretical hypothesis as to how these mental mechanisms operate. Cognitive scientists and neuroscientists are not simply reporting on internal representations they have observed. Rather, they are proposing that there are such things as internal representations and that these work much like the external representations which we, as humans engaged in social practice, use in our daily lives. This is not, in itself, a reason to reject characterizations of mental mechanisms as relying on representations. Rather, by noting the theoretical character of the appeal to representations, we are alerted to the potential for controversy when various types of representations are introduced into accounts of mental mechanisms. Theorists are called upon to defend appeals to one or another characterization of these representations.

In introducing the sorts of external representations we use in our social practices, I included both linguistic and nonlinguistic representations. But there are crucial differences between these. Diagrams, pictures, and maps are all considered iconic, in that the structure of the vehicle in some manner corresponds to the structure of the content. The spatial layout of a map is intended to correspond to the spatial layout of the location being represented. The colors used in a picture are intended to correspond to the colors of the objects pictured. Linguistic representations, for the most part, are not iconic. Words do not typically share features with what they represent, and the way in which words are combined does not correspond to the way the objects are related to one another. As I will develop in the following section, cognitive scientists have tended to find linguistic representations most appealing as models for the representations in mental mechanisms, whereas neuroscientists have been more inclined towards iconic representations. This constitutes a major difference in the way representations are understood in these approaches to mental mechanisms.

Regardless of how one characterizes the vehicle of representations, there is a need to account for the relation between vehicle and content. Both cognitive and neuroscientists have attempted to develop causal accounts of this relation, but again, there is a striking difference in their approaches. Much cognitive theorizing, especially modeling efforts in classical artificial intelligence (AI), has not substantively addressed the relationship, and the accounts that are offered (mostly by philosophers) have tended to treat the vehicle's relation to the content as relatively unconnected to the role of the vehicle within the mental mechanism. This has been the focus of well-known critiques. In contrast, neuroscientists have tended to make the relation to the content central to the identification of vehicles and so have not faced the challenge of reconnecting the content to the vehicle. But they have faced the opposite challenge of showing how the vehicle can become sufficiently detached from the content to represent phenomena not immediately present to the organism and to be deployed in such activities as planning, decision making, and contemplation.

After describing the different treatments of vehicles and relations to content that are found in cognitive science and neuroscience, I will introduce the dynamical systems perspective that has recently emerged in cognitive science. In its more radical moments, this approach attempts to do away with representations. In responding to this challenge, I will advance an account of representations as general features of control systems. This account, like the one employed in neuroscience, emphasizes the relation of vehicles to contents, leaving it unclear how such vehicles can figure in higher cognitive tasks that seem to require structured representations. I finish by discussing a perspective recently articulated by Lawrence Barsalou that suggests how one can bootstrap from sensory–motor representations of the sort identified in neuroscience approaches to representations adequate for performing higher cognitive activities.

5.1   REPRESENTATIONAL VEHICLES

In this first section I focus on the different sorts of vehicles that have been advanced as representations in cognitive science and neuroscience. These differences follow in large part from the sorts of inquiry in which practitioners in the different disciplines have been engaged when they found it advantageous to posit representations. Cognitive scientists have largely focused on cognitive performance and have been divided over whether or not representations must be syntactically structured in the manner of representations in natural language. Neuroscientists have focused more on processing within the nervous system and have been impressed by the map-like layout of many processing areas in the brain.

5.1.1   Cognitive Science Accounts of Vehicles

Much of the pioneering research in AI during the 1970s and 1980s adopted the symbol processing framework, according to which information is represented in symbol strings and operated on according to formal rules. To say that the rules are formal is to say that they apply to strings simply by virtue of their form (not their meaning). Systems of natural deduction in logic provide an exemplar of a system involving formal operations on symbols. In propositional logic individual letters represent simple sentences which are then composed using connectives such as *and* and *if, then*. The rules of deduction allow for the generation of new statements when premises or previous statements in the deduction have the requisite structure. For example, the rule and-elimination allows that if an existing line has the structure

$$X \text{ and } Y$$

where X and Y are any statements, simple or compound, a new line having the structure

$$X$$

can be added to the derivation. This formalizes the intuition that if you know both X and Y are true, you know X is true. To perform a deduction, a person does not need to know what any of the simple statements mean. The statements can be in a language the person does not know. All a person needs to be able to do is identify the logical connectives and be able to determine that the statements are composed in the appropriate way for the rules to apply.

Although most AI researchers do not employ principles of natural deduction, their programs are similarly formal. Consider the nature of a production system such as Newell and Simon (1972; Newell, 1973) pioneered in their modeling endeavors. A production system has (a) a working memory in which a number of symbolic structures can be stored temporarily and (b) conditional rules (rules of the form *if X, then Y*), where X is a symbol structure that could appear in the working memory, and Y is an action such as adding or deleting symbols from working memory or generating an output from the system. Thus, if the content of working memory is

$$A, C, E, G, H, J, L, M$$

and the system has the rule

IF C AND E, THEN DELETE C AND WRITE D

the system would remove C from the working memory and add D to it, yielding

A, D, E, G, H, J, L, M

As is true of rules of natural deduction, the rules in a production system can be applied without knowing the meaning of any of the symbols in working memory.

Early in the development of the symbolic approach to cognitive modeling, philosopher Jerry Fodor (1975) drew attention to the similarity between the representations used in cognitive models and linguistic representations, and argued that cognitive theories are committed to a *language of thought*. He also drew out implications of this commitment that were not always obvious in the work of the cognitive scientists themselves. One such consequence was that the language of thought had to be different from a natural language such as Hungarian or Korean that a person might learn. He argued that learning the meanings of words, even in one's native language, requires formulating and testing hypotheses. For example, in learning English a child has to formulate the hypothesis that *dog* refers to any dog (as opposed to cats or spiders). Only after the hypothesis is formulated could the child test it (e.g., by noting whether adults ever used *dog* to refer to things other than a dog or refused to use *dog* to refer to a dog). As the hypothesis had to be already constructed before a child had learned that part of the natural language, the language of thought could not be a natural language. A second consequence follows immediately from this: the language of thought itself cannot be learned but must be innate. Fodor often refers to the innate language of thought as *mentalese*. Mentalese must have the expressive power to state any hypothesis, no matter how bizarre, that we might ever test. For example, the language of thought must have the resources to formulate the hypothesis that mentalese is not innate.

Although he recognized that not all artificial intelligence researchers or cognitive psychologists would readily embrace these entailments, especially the nativist claim, Fodor took himself to be simply spelling out the consequences of taking a cognitivist approach to the mind. AI models explicitly proposed operations over representations in formal languages, and these languages were built into the models. Although much cognitive psychology research was less explicit in its commitments to representations, those who did articulate theories or models tended to incorporate representations that were at least somewhat similar to those in natural language. (Not uncommonly, they made use of those already proposed in AI.) Fodor, like his colleague Chomsky in linguistics, recognized that he was advancing a rationalist account of the mind and celebrated this feature of his account. He viewed associationism and its descendant, behaviorism, as the primary alternatives and he contended that they offered demonstrably inadequate accounts of mental abilities as they lacked the necessary representational resources to explain human cognitive performance.

A decade later, however, the neural network tradition was reenergized by cognitive scientists who designed *connectionist networks* and ran them as computer simulations

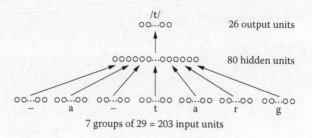

Figure 5.1   Sejnowski and Rosenberg's (1986) NETtalk network. Each group of 29 input units codes for a single letter of text. The network is supposed to pronounce the middle letter. The 80 hidden units recode the input into a form from which the last layer of units can generate the appropriate phoneme.

to be tested against human data. This was initially regarded as a resuscitation of the associationist tradition, but more nuanced interpretations emerged later (e.g., Elman et al., 1996). Connectionism's success can be attributed in part to the development of a learning algorithm that made it possible to train multilayer feedforward networks.[1] In the simplest version of this network architecture, a pattern of activation imposed on input units is sent across weighted connections (and thereby transformed) to units in an intervening *hidden layer*, then again from the hidden layer to the output layer.

Sometimes individual units on the input and output layers are construed as representational vehicles having content. For example, in Sejnowski and Rosenberg's (1986) NETtalk network (Figure 5.1), individual input units represented seven successive letters (the target letter to be pronounced and the three letters before and after it) and each of the twenty-six output units represented a feature relevant to pronunciation (i.e., articulatory, stress, and syllable boundary features). The representations produced on the hidden units, in contrast, were distributed over all eighty units; as a result, every hidden unit contributed to the generation of every output pattern. As all of the hidden layer units were taken to be activated simultaneously, distributing the transformed content across them, some connectionists preferred to call their approach *parallel distributed processing* (Rumelhart & McClelland, 1986b). Distributed representations are not structured in a way that can be operated on by rules like those of logic or classical AI

---

[1] In the eyes of many researchers, the earlier generation of neural network research developed by McCulloch and Pitts, Hebb, and Rosenblatt (discussed in chapter two) had been discredited by Minsky and Papert's (1969) argument that the two-layer networks for which a learning rule existed could not perform a variety of cognitively important tasks. These tasks could be performed by three-layer networks, and a learning rule for such networks was developed by Rumelhart, Hinton, and Williams (1986).

programs (van Gelder, 1990b), and they emerge during training; hence, they do not constitute an innate language of thought. The appearance of a competitor to the symbolic tradition prompted Fodor, in collaboration with computer scientist Zenon Pylyshyn, to mount a vigorous critique of connectionism (Fodor & Pylyshyn, 1988). They maintained that the representations in connectionist networks were insufficient for modeling cognitive activity.[2] In particular, they contended that connectionist systems failed to exhibit two features that they insisted were characteristic of thought: productivity and systematicity.

Productivity and systematicity are properties commonly associated with natural languages, and the first step in Fodor and Pylyshyn's argument is to maintain that they are characteristic of thought as well. Productivity with respect to language refers to the capacity to indefinitely extend the corpus of sentences in a language by creating new sentences. For example, the sentence "San Diego is closer to the sun than is Pluto, and thankfully a good deal warmer" has, in all likelihood, never been produced until I inserted it into this text. Applied to thought, productivity refers to the possibility of thinking a thought that no one has thought previously; the set of possible thoughts, like the set of possible English sentences, is not bounded. Systematicity with respect to language refers to the claim that there are relations between the sentences of a language such that if one string is a well-formed sentence, so is another that results from appropriate manipulations of it. For example, if "the florist loves Mary" is a sentence in English, so is "Mary loves the florist." If people can understand one of these English sentences, they can also understand the other. Applied to thought, systematicity denotes that a cognitive system that can think one thought necessarily has the capacity to think variants of it.

The second step in Fodor and Pylyshyn's argument is to maintain that productivity and systematicity are expected properties of systems using representations generated by compositional syntactic rules, but would not be expected otherwise. A compositional syntax builds complex structures from component structures while preserving the structure in the components. Thus, the phrase "the turtle" still appears in and makes its own contribution to the semantics of the whole sentence when it is embedded in the sentence "Andy was looking for

---

[2] Fodor and Pylyshyn treated connectionist representations as involving activations of individual units in a network—for example, one node might represent the color red, another the color blue, a third being a square, and a fourth being a circle. They contended that in such a system there is no way to represent the fact that the square is red and the circle is blue. In fact, most connectionists view representations as distributed across units. Although Fodor and Pylyshyn maintain that this complication does not matter, in fact, distributed patterns of activation can encode complex information so that a different pattern would result when the square is blue and the circle red than when the square is red and the circle blue.

the turtle that had been trudging through the grass." In a linguistic system in which sentences are composed employing recursively applicable syntactic rules, productivity and systematicity arise automatically. For example, applying the relative clause rule again (one recursion) produces such sentences as "Andy was looking for the turtle that had been trudging through the grass that was turning brown." As well, swapping the animate subject and direct object of a sentence will yield a grammatically well-formed sentence.[3] Productivity and systematicity would accrue equally to a cognitive system if it employed representations that are composed according to syntactic rules. Without positing such syntactically structured representations, Fodor and Pylyshyn maintain that it is not possible to provide an account of these properties of thought.

Connectionists have responded to Fodor and Pylyshyn's challenge in a variety of ways. One is to explicitly implement syntactically structured representations in connectionist networks (Touretzky & Hinton, 1988; Shastri & Ajjanagadde, 1993). Fodor and Pylyshyn acknowledged that this is possible, but argued that connectionism then *merely* provides an implementation of symbolic processing, and that it is the syntactically structured symbols that do the important cognitive work, not the connectionist implementation. (Fodor & McLaughlin, 1990, maintain that even if networks can be made to exhibit systematicity, they don't explain it because it is not a necessary feature of connectionist systems.) Connectionists maintain, in opposition, that the implementation is more than *mere* since it contributes in important ways to the performance of the cognitive system, such as the tendency of cognitive systems to degrade gracefully when overloaded or damaged rather than crash. For example, even if a sentence is too complex to remember every word, most people will be able to report the gist. Graceful degradation is also a feature commonly exhibited by connectionist systems using distributed representations.

A second connectionist response is to argue that connectionist models can achieve the functionality of syntactically structured representations without employing such representations explicitly (van Gelder, 1990a). In Jordan Pollack's (1990) recursive autoassociative memory (RAAM) models, networks are trained to recover the structured symbolic representations presented on the input layer from compressed representations on hidden layers that do not exhibit explicit syntactic structure. Chalmers (1990) demonstrated that other networks could operate on these compressed representations in ways that respected the syntactic structure from which they were generated even though it was not explicitly present in the compressed representations. This suggests that the information processing system need not employ the same structure internally as is found in its inputs or generated on its outputs (cf. Smolensky, 1990; 1994).

---

[3] However, see Johnson (2004) for an argument that it is quite difficult to state the claim of systematicity in a manner that does not confront counterexamples.

These first two responses concede to the symbolic approach the claim that internal processing must in some way capture the formal syntactic organization that a language of thought would exhibit, even if the compositional structure is not explicit in the representational vehicles. A third avenue of response is more radical. It acknowledges that natural language representations are syntactically structured but denies that this is a feature of mental representations. Whereas Fodor and Pylyshyn maintain that one must be able to represent something to learn it, this does not seem to apply to skill knowledge. A person can learn how to do something without developing an explicit representation of the skill (Ryle, 1949). Arthur Reber (1967) showed that such implicit learning was possible with artificial grammars—a person could perform better than chance at detecting which strings were grammatical without figuring out the grammar that generated them. It is possible that the same applies to the ability to learn a natural language. One might not need to represent the language in a syntactically structured language of thought to be able to learn it. In this spirit, when Jeffrey Elman (1993) provided sentences from a miniature grammar to a recurrent network word by word, it could learn to predict the possible grammatical categories of the next word—a task that requires sensitivity to the grammatical structure implicit in the input. Whereas a symbolic account would invoke a representation of the grammatical structure (e.g., in a tree diagram), the network masters the task without employing syntactically structured internal representations. Elman and others have developed techniques for analyzing the structure implicit in the weights of a trained network that enables it to perform the task, but this structure does not involve symbolic representations. (See Bechtel & Abrahamsen, 2002, chapter seven, for a detailed discussion of the three strategies for answering Fodor and Pylyshyn presented in the last three paragraphs.)

I will not try to adjudicate whether these or other connectionist accounts are adequate to account for the productivity and systematicity of thought claimed by Fodor and Pylyshyn, but will assume that the third approach holds sufficient promise to be taken seriously. One can capture the import of this approach by returning to the characterization of a mechanism advanced in the first chapter and the distinction between the phenomenon to be explained and the mechanism that is proposed to explain it. Systematicity is construed as a feature of mental phenomena; human language use, and arguably human thought more generally, exhibit systematicity. Symbolic computational models of the kind favored by Fodor and Pylyshyn assume that the structure of the mechanism will closely correspond to the structure found in the phenomenon, whereas connectionist models maintain that the phenomenon can be generated by a mechanism operating according to rather different principles.

One strategy for thinking about how human cognizers might generate systematic phenomena from a nonsymbolic or statistical learning procedure is found in work by Elissa Newport and her colleagues. They have offered provocative evidence that even infants are highly sensitive to distributional statistics in an artificial language (Saffran, Aslin, & Newport, 1996). In this respect language learners resemble connectionist networks. But Newport and her colleagues have also maintained that the product of learning involves the sort of syntactically structured representations advanced in linguistic theory. That is, they propose that the language acquisition system, while sensitive to the statistics in input, exhibits tendencies to sharpen or regularize so as to produce a nonstatistical mental grammar. In support of this possibility, Newport and Aslin (2000) cited the finding that children acquiring a signed language like ASL from nonnative signers get past the inconsistent input to achieve a more native-like morphological system. On their interpretation "the strongest consistencies are sharpened and systematized: statistics are turned into 'rules'" (p. 13). They and their collaborators have also contributed a growing body of ingenious studies of artificial language learning by infants, adults, and primates, from which they argue that the statistical learning mechanism has selectivities in its computations that bias it towards the phenomena of natural language (see Newport & Aslin, 2000; Singleton & Newport, 2004).

So far in assessing Fodor and Pylyshyn's claims about the systematicity of thought, I have focused on cognitive activities that are commonly characterized in terms of thoughts. In our folk idioms we often characterize people's thoughts in terms of what Russell called *propositional attitudes*—specifications of attitudes such as believing, doubting, and wishing, towards propositions. Thus, we might characterize a person as believing that it is not too late for governmental action to change the course of global warming, doubting that governments will take actions sufficient to change the course of global warming, and hoping that the arctic ice cap will not melt. Sometimes this folk idiom is treated as describing processes operating within an agent, as when believing is characterized as storing a proposition in one's "belief box" (Schiffer, 1981). Although such a literal view of beliefs and other mental states could be accommodated in an account of symbolic representations, it does not fit well with a connectionist conception.[4] Connectionist processing might explain how a person would behave in ways characterized as having particular beliefs, hopes, desires, etc., and how they

---

[4] It is noteworthy that for Fodor a major criterion for a successful psychology is the ability to ground folk psychology. He maintains that it would be an unmitigated disaster if cognitive science were to show that folk psychology were not true. But finding processes in the head that correspond to propositional attitudes is not the only way of vindicating these folk psychological characterizations of people. It could turn out that people are well-characterized in terms of beliefs, desires, etc., without there being beliefs and desires in their head. The states in their heads only need to explain how it is that people act as agents in ways described by folk psychology (Bechtel & Abrahamsen, 1993).

might report them in natural language, but it would not treat these as involving literal storage of propositional representations.

Although propositional attitudes figure centrally in many philosophical accounts of mental life, it is noteworthy that they do not figure nearly as prominently in psychological accounts. Psychologists most often focus on phenomena that are describable in terms of relations between variables, preferably quantitative relations. Psychophysics provides some familiar examples, such as Weber's law which holds that the minimum noticable difference between successive stimuli is a constant percentage of the intensity of the first stimulus. In the mid-twentieth century a tradition of mathematical psychology developed in which phenomena involving learning, choice, and other key behavioral domains were characterized mathematically. Examples include the Markov models proposed by William Estes (1950) and Robert R. Bush and Frederick Mosteller (1951) and the multidimensional scaling analysis of human similarity judgments (Shepard, 1980). Even in what is regarded as core cognitive psychology, much research focuses on finding important relations between behavioral variables. For example, Ebbinghaus (1885) established that spaced learning trials produce better learning than massed learning trials; Craik and Lockhart (1972) established that different levels of processing produce differential patterns in recall, and Morris, Bransford, and Franks (1977) showed that recall was better when learning and retrieval contexts were similar. In none of these cases are we dealing with mental states that are naturally characterized in propositional attitude terms, and claims about the systematicity of thinking do not seem to have much traction here. Thus, even in the cognitive domain, systematicity may be far more restricted than Fodor and Pylyshyn have suggested. (See Waskan & Bechtel, 1997, for further discussion.) These phenomena, which are the focus of many of the investigations conducted in the cognitive sciences, do rely on representations—internal vehicles which carry information about contents. But since they do not exhibit productivity and systematicity, they do not seem to require the sorts of compositionally structured representations for which Fodor argued. Moreover, as I argued earlier, it is plausible that even the phenomena that do seem to involve productivity and systematicity, such as use of natural languages, might be explained in terms of the acquisition of representations which themselves are not compositionally constructed.

5.1.2   Neuroscience Accounts of Vehicles

Whereas cognitive scientists posit the existence of vehicles with specific properties and typically do not address what materially realizes those properties, neuroscientists take the opposite approach. They reach issues of representation from a starting point that emphasizes particular material processes, such as the spiking of neurons. There is a substantial question of how to characterize the activity of neurons so as to appreciate their role as representational vehicles.

Different theorists have focused on the average spiking rate of neurons or population of neurons, on the particular spiking pattern produced, and on the synchrony in spiking within or among populations of neurons. Crucially, however the vehicle is described, there is nothing that transparently plays a role equivalent to that of syntax in symbolic cognitive models. It is most interesting that the focus on neurons has resulted instead in discovery of a common kind of structure in representational vehicles—a map-like organization in which spatial relations between units correspond to spatial or other relations within the contents being represented.

The exploration of representation in neuroscience originated from the attempts to link activity in the brain to an organism's sensory and motor activities. In chapter one I noted the investigations of Fritsch and Hitzig (1870) and Ferrier (1876) that employed mild electrical stimulation to localize motor centers in the brain. Both Hitzig (1900) and Ferrier (1873)[5] presented their contributions as confirming conclusions arrived at by John Hughlings Jackson on the basis of his clinical studies of neurological patients. It was Jackson who developed the framework of referring to brain regions as *representing* the muscles that they controlled. Although focusing on motor activity, Jackson's account fits within the tradition of British associationism, according to which mental states arose from sensory states, rather than the tradition of faculty psychology embraced by Gall and Broca.

Jackson's clinical observations were of patients experiencing paralysis (inability to move) and epileptic seizures (excessive and uncontrolled movement). The latter proved particularly important in developing his theoretical framework. Whereas most neurologists concentrated on full-blown seizures, Jackson (1863; 1870) concentrated on patients with incomplete unilateral seizures. This enabled him to seek, in subsequent autopsies of his patients, brain regions that could be linked specifically to seizures in particular parts of their bodies.[6] Contrary to the

---

[5] Ferrier says: "I regard them as an experimental confirmation of the views expressed by Dr. Hughlings Jackson. They are, as it were, an artificial reproduction of the clinical experiments performed by disease, and the clinical conclusions which Dr. Jackson has arrived at from his observations of disease are in all essential particulars confirmed by the above experiments (1873, p. 85)."

[6] Jackson himself explains his reason for focusing on these cases, which subsequently were known as Jacksonian epilepsy: "If we take for first investigation cases of general convulsions (such as are sometimes called 'idiopathic epilepsy'), we shall, I believe, make little out. The paroxysms are too sudden, too quickly universal, and of too short duration for precise investigation. But if we take simple cases we shall, I think, accomplish a great deal. Most unquestionably the simplest cases of convulsion are those in which the spasm begins deliberately on one side of the body and affects that side only, or affects it more than the other. Such fits are often very limited in range, and then the patient is not unconscious, and can describe the seizure. As they begin deliberately, and as they may last many minutes, we are able, if we are present at a paroxysm, to note the place of onset and the order of spreading of the spasm" (J. H. Jackson, 1875, p. 163).

received views of the time, according to which epileptic seizures originated in the lower brain stem, he linked them to the corpus striatum and cortical regions:

> In very many cases of epilepsy, and especially in syphilitic epilepsy, the convulsions are limited to one side of the body; and, as autopsies of patients who have died after syphilitic epilepsy appear to show, the cause is obvious organic disease on the side of the brain, opposite to the side of the body convulsed, frequently on the surface of the hemisphere (J. H. Jackson, 1863, p. 110).

Jackson connected his observations on unilateral seizures with cases of unilateral paralysis by noting that the muscles that were affected first and most severely in hemiplegia (paralysis) were the same as those that were affected first in seizures. He attributed these symptoms to different types of lesions affecting the same neural tissue: paralysis as due to what he termed *destroying lesions* and convulsions to *discharging lesions*: "Palsy depends on destruction of fibres, and convulsion on instability of the grey matter" (J. H. Jackson, 1870, p. 163). In the case of seizures he was particularly interested in how they spread and he subsequently characterized convulsions as the "mobile counterpart of hemiplegia" (J. H. Jackson, 1873, p. 163).

In describing the relation between brain tissue and motor activity, Jackson adopted the language of *representation*, and he drew the consequence that different moveable parts of the body (arms, legs, fingers) were represented differently in the brain. Moreover, to account for the pattern of muscular movement in both normal activity and seizures, he developed an account according to which the same muscles were represented multiple times in the brain, with higher areas representing what was represented in the more basic areas. Thus, he maintained that the centers that directly represented various muscle groups were located in the corpus striatum, but re-represented in nearby areas of cortex:

> I suppose that these convolutions represent over again, but in new and more complex combinations, the very same movements which are represented in the corpus striatum. They are, I believe, the corpus striatum "raised to a higher power." *Discharge* of the grey matter of those convolutions *develops* the same groups of movements which are *lost* when the corpus striatum is destroyed (J. H. Jackson, 1875, p. 163).

Jackson viewed the cortical re-representation as providing the basis for voluntary movement, whereas the representation in the corpus striatum was responsible for automated movements. In addition, he proposed yet a third tier of representations, located in more frontal areas of the brain, which figured in more complex, coordinated voluntary actions:

> The lowest motor centres are the anterior horns of the spinal cord, and also the homologous nuclei for the motor cranial nerves higher up. … The lowest centres are

the most simple and most organized centres; each *represents* some limited region of the body indirectly, but yet most nearly directly; they are *representative*. The middle motor centres are the convolutions making up Ferrier's motor region [just anterior to the central sulcus] and the ganglia of the corpus striatum. These are more complex and less organized, and *represent* wider regions of the body doubly indirectly; they are *re-representative*. The highest motor centres are convolutions in front of the so-called motor region. . . . [They] are the most complex and least organized centres, and *represent* widest regions (movements of all parts of the body), triply indirectly; they are *re-re-representative* (J. H. Jackson, 1884, p. 649, emphasis added).

Jackson invoked this model of multiple representations to explain the sequence of motor areas affected in seizures. He noted that in some patients the motor areas were engaged in different orders, and attributed this to different higher-level representations being affected in each case.

An important aspect of Jackson's talk of representations and re-representations was that for him, representation did not create a gap between a physiological and a mental process. A representation simply provided a means of control, with higher-level control systems modulating the behavior of lower-level ones. He thus explicitly rejected the understanding of mental faculties that had figured in both phrenology and in Broca's research. With respect to Broca's conception of a locus for articulate speech he contended it was "incredible that 'speech' can 'reside' in any limited spot" (J. H. Jackson, 1868-1869/1931, p. 234).[7] The basis of his opposition to

---

[7] In general, Jackson rejected a distinction between mental capacities and motor control, insisting instead that the brain operated via control over sensorimotor processes: "It is asserted by some that the cerebrum is the organ of mind, and that it is not a motor organ. Some think the cerebrum is to be likened to an instrumentalist, and the motor centres to the instrument; one part is for ideas, and the other for movements. It may then be asked, How can discharge of part of a *mental* organ produce *motor* symptoms only? I say motor symptoms only, because, to give sharpness to the argument, I will suppose a case in which there is unilateral spasm without loss of consciousness. But of what 'substance' can the organ of mind be composed, unless of processes representing movements and impressions; and how can the convolutions differ from the inferior centres, except as parts representing *more* intricate co-ordinations of impressions and movements in time and space than they do? Are we to believe that the hemisphere is built on a plan *fundamentally* different from that of the motor tract? What can an 'idea', say of a ball, be, except a process representing certain impressions of surface and particular muscular adjustments? What is recollection, but a revivification of such processes which, in the past, have become part of the organism itself? What is delirium, except the disorderly revival of sensori-motor processes received in the past: What is a mistake in a word, but a wrong movement, a chorea? Giddiness can be but the temporary loss or disorder of certain relations in space, chiefly made up of muscular feelings. Surely the conclusion is irresistible, that 'mental' symptoms from disease of the hemisphere are fundamentally like hemiplegia, chorea and convulsions, however specially different. They must all be due to lack, or to *disorderly* development, of sensori-motor processes" (J. H. Jackson, 1870/1931, p. 26 fn.).

Broca was straightforward: complex abilities such as speech involved, for him, a coordination of more fundamental abilities. One source of evidence Jackson presented for the re-representation account was that it provided a natural explanation of the character of the deficits found in various pathological conditions. Patients would retain the ability to perform simple movements, often without voluntary control, but no longer be able to integrate these movements in a coordinated fashion. The ability of Broca's patient Leborgne to utter *Tan* and a couple other simple expressions reflected, for him, the loss of higher-level coordination of more basic responses controlled at lower levels in the motor control system.

Inspired by Darwin, and especially Herbert Spencer, Jackson developed an evolutionary perspective in which higher-level representations evolved relatively late through the selection for higher-level control mechanisms that operated on more primitive representations of muscles. These, however, did not displace the earlier evolved mechanisms, whose activities would be manifest whenever the higher-level representations were disrupted. Jackson (1884) thus spoke of the evolution and dissolution of higher mental capacities (the term *dissolution* he adopted from Spencer), and viewed brain injuries, alcoholic intoxication, epileptic seizures, and insanity as all serving to release lower-level representations from control by higher-level representations.

Jackson, Fritsch and Hitzig, and Ferrier all focused on identifying the locations where different motor systems are represented in the brain. Although they began to identify systematicity in the organization of these sites, it would not be until much later that others made a major breakthrough in understanding the brain as representing sensory and motor systems. This was the discovery of a topological arrangement among the representations that allowed them to be understood as constituting a map of body areas. Maps are a prototypical form of representation with which, like language, we are quite familiar in our cultural lives, and hence offered a natural framework for describing the relation between the topology of brain areas and the layout of the body or sensory world. In chapter three I described the initial proposal advanced by Henschen for a map in primary visual cortex and the revised maps of Inouye and Holmes. These were based on establishing correlations between areas of damage to primary visual cortex and areas of the visual field to which a subject was blind.

Topographical maps are not unique to the visual system. In the early years of the twentieth century Charles Scott Sherrington continued the project of Fritsch and Hitzig and Ferrier, applying electrical stimulation to the brains of great apes. As a result he was able to generate maps of the motor cortex of the chimpanzee, gorilla (see Figure 5.2), and orangutan (Grünbaum & Sherrington, 1903; Leyton & Sherrington, 1917). Electrical stimulation also provided a tool for discovering somatosensory maps in the cortex of humans. Robert Bartholow (1874) found

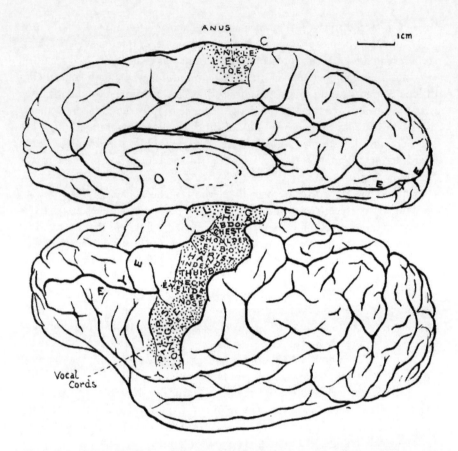

Figure 5.2   Map of the motor cortex of the gorilla from Leyton and Sherrington, 1917, Figure 10. C designates the area on the medial surface corresponding to the central sulcus.

that mild electrical stimulation to the dura and cortex of a dying girl, posterior to the central fissure, produced tingling sensations on the opposite side of her body. Working with two epileptic men, Harvey Cushing (1909) determined that electrical stimulation to various areas in the post-central gyrus elicited sensations in different parts of the body that were similar to the auras that preceded epileptic seizures. Some years later Wilder Penfield confirmed and further articulated the map of sensory areas in the post-central gyrus (Penfield & Boldrey, 1937). These are illustrated with great effectiveness by means of motor and sensory homunculi in Penfield and Rasmussen's (1950) famous figures (Figure 5.3).

A different and very powerful strategy for identifying maps resulted from the development of techniques for recording electrical impulses in neurons. As I noted in chapter one, Edgar Adrian played a pivotal role in developing these techniques.

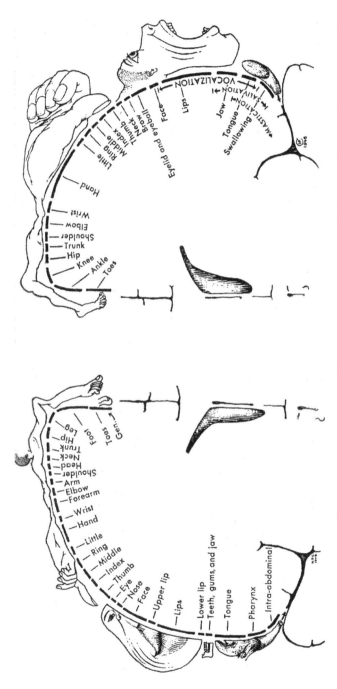

Figure 5.3 Representations of the primary sensory cortex (left) and primary motor cortex (right), using homunculi to show the relative amounts of brain tissue devoted to different portions of the body. Redrawn from Penfield and Rasmussen (1950).

He and Detlev Bronk identified a causal relation between the intensity of the stimulus and the frequency of spiking and spoke of the neurons as carrying a message: "The frequency of the discharge controls the intensity of the effect which the message produces and is itself controlled by the intensity of excitation" (Adrian & Bronk, 1929). In his 1928 book *The Basis of Sensation: The Action of the Sense Organs*, Adrian explicitly talks of the nerve fiber as transmitting information. Referring to the work of Francis Gotch and his mentor Keith Lucas that identified the refractory period after an action potential, he says it "gave us for the first time a clear idea of what may be called the functional value of the nervous impulse. They showed what the nerve fibre can do as a means of communication and what it cannot.… It is of the first importance in the problems of sensation, for it shows what sort of information a sense organ can transmit to the brain and in what form the message must be sent" (Adrian, 1928).

These efforts by Adrian offered investigators a powerful new way to determine sensory maps. They could now present different sensory stimuli to the organism and record from cells to determine which cells increased their firing rate in response. Adrian (1940) himself put the technique to use in mapping somatosensory areas in the parietal lobe of the cerebral cortex in cats. This involved presenting stimuli to the cat's paws and recording neural activity from cells just above the Sylvian fissure. In addition to confirming the results that Penfield had obtained with electrical stimulation in human patients, Adrian found to his surprise that there were two representations of the forepaw, one slightly below the other. Shortly thereafter Clinton Woolsey found similar evidence for a second map in monkeys and dogs (Woolsey & Fairman, 1946; Woolsey, 1943).[8] As Finger (2000, p. 255) reports, "Scientists were soon talking about a large parietal lobe region depicting the body upside-down and facing forward, and a smaller area below it showing the animal lying on its back with its head toward the front." In chapter three I discussed comparable developments in research on vision, when Talbot and Marshall (1941) confirmed by recording with electrodes the maps advanced by Inouye and Holmes based on lesions. Hubel and Wiesel then applied the approach to discover a more intricate pattern of columns responsive to particular orientations of stimuli within a cell's receptive field. They and others then used the finding of maps in other areas of extrastriate cortex to characterize them as additional visual processing areas.

Woolsey was also a leader in the exploration of auditory projection areas in cortex and there, too, he found maps, but this time they were organized tonotopically, that is, cells tuned to one frequency were adjacent to those tuned to an adjacent frequency. Woolsey and Walzl (1942) took advantage of the fact that it

---

[8] Woolsey may have been the first to identify the second map and in any case developed the second map in far more detail (see Thompson, 1999).

had already been established that regions in the cochlea responded selectively to tones of different frequencies. By stimulating areas of the cochlea while recording from the auditory cortex they were able to demonstrate tonotopic maps in cats and monkeys. Subsequently several different tonotopic maps have been identified in a variety of mammals (Merzenich & Brugge, 1973; Kalatsky, Polley, Merzenich, Schreiner, & Stryker, 2005). Bats are particularly dependent on auditory processing, as it is required for echolocation, and they have been found to have multiple maps sensitive not just to tones but to complex relations between auditory signals such as Doppler shifts (Suga, 1990).

The reliance on map-like representations is often thought to be limited to early sensory-processing areas and motor-control areas. But using fMRI, Martin Sereno found maps in what he took to be the lateral interparietal area (LIP) in humans when engaged in attentional and working memory tasks (Sereno, 2001). More recently he and a colleague investigated areas in frontal and prefrontal cortex that had been shown by Patricia Goldman-Rakic (1987; Goldman-Rakic, Funahashi, & Bruce, 1990) and others to play a role in working memory, and found evidence of two areas that employ spatial maps (Hagler & Sereno, 2006).

Although it certainly is not the case that all areas of neocortex are laid out in a map-like way, it seems to be a fairly common arrangement. One of the best known examples of spatial representation in behavior, however, seems to be an exception to the reliance on topographical maps in the brain. In his experiments with rats navigating mazes, Edward Tolman (1948) concluded that they operated with internal representations of the mazes, which he called *cognitive maps*.[9] When John O'Keefe and Lynn Nadel (1978) determined that lesions to the hippocampus impaired the ability of rats to reason spatially (e.g., losing the ability to navigate to a known platform in the Morris water maze from a novel starting location), they attributed the deficit to the loss of the cognitive map realized in the hippocampus. O'Keefe and Dostrovsky (1971) had already identified cells in the hippocampus that seemed to register the rat's location in a space, which they named *place cells*. These were assumed to constitute the cognitive map. Place cells, however, are not laid out topographically, a curious result given the utility we find in having maps laid out topographically. Subsequent research, however, has revealed that one of the areas projecting to the hippocampus, the

---

[9] Tolman presented his account of rat behavior as contrasting with stimulus–response behaviorists: "We assert that the central office itself is far more like a map control room than it is like an old-fashioned telephone exchange. The stimuli, which are allowed in, are not connected by just simple one-to-one switches to the outgoing responses. Rather, the incoming impulses are usually worked over and elaborated in the central control room into a tentative, cognitive-like map of the environment. And it is this tentative map, indicating routes and paths and environmental relationships, which finally determines what responses, if any, the animal will finally release" (p. 193).

dorsocaudal medial entorhinal cortex, does map spatial location topographically (Hafting, Fyhn, Molden, Moser, & Moser, 2005). It may be that the hippocampal cells serve an ancillary function in forming temporary memory representations rather than representing space itself, for which it would rely on the topographical representations in entorhinal cortex.

5.2   RELATING VEHICLES TO CONTENT

So far I have focused on the differing conceptions of vehicles that have been advanced in cognitive science and neuroscience and have not emphasized the relation between vehicles and their content—what they represent. Again, there are fundamental differences in the accounts offered by cognitive scientists and neuroscientists reflecting the manner in which they introduce representations into their accounts. Both typically appeal to causal relations. Cognitive science accounts begin by positing vehicles that figure in information processing operations and then attempt to relate these causally to their contents. In contrast, neuroscientists identify vehicles as a result of the causal processes linking neural processes to sensory and motor systems. Their causal link to content is therefore already assured.

5.2.1   Cognitive Accounts of Intentionality

Within cognitive science the question of how representational vehicles are linked to their content has largely been a preoccupation of philosophers. Cognitive theorists have tended to focus on how representational vehicles are employed in a system so as to generate behavior. Fodor, again acting as the major formulator and advocate of a major theoretical position, argued that yet another consequence of cognitive science's implicit commitment to a language of thought was that cognitive operations involve only formal operations on representations. Whatever exists beyond the representations themselves and the procedures for operating on them is irrelevant for understanding cognition. With respect to the cognitive activities in which a person engages, it does not matter whether what she represents using her mentalese word *dog* is really a dog, a wolf, or a robot. The inferences she draws will be determined by her mental representation, not the entity in the world. Fodor (1980) contended that cognitive science is committed to this position and, following Putnam (1975), labeled it *methodological solipsism*.[10]

For Fodor, while it is a significant feature of cognitive processing that it relies only on the vehicles, not what they represent, it is nonetheless an important fact

---

[10] This renders Fodor's account incompatible with more recent views of embodied and situated cognition, which emphasize how cognitive agents perform intelligently as a result of coordinated action with features of the world, included external symbols. (For a clear introduction and exposition of such views, see Clark, 1997; Clark & Chalmers, 1998).

about representations that they do have content. He views it as an important challenge to provide a fully naturalized account (i.e., an account in terms of ordinary physical processes) of how they have this content. The challenge to developing such an account was presented by Franz Brentano (1874), who recognized that the things or events represented need not be real. We can represent what is not real and in fact link such representations to a host of others. We can, for example, represent Santa Claus and represent him as having a white beard, wearing a red suit, and bringing gifts on Christmas. As Brentano characterized mental states, they involve an object or objects being presented to or appearing to the subject even if the objects themselves do not exist. He characterized this feature as the *intentionality* of mental states and viewed it as distinguishing such states from purely physical states:

> Every mental phenomenon is characterized by what the scholastics of the Middle Ages called the intentional (or mental) of an object, and what we might call, though not wholly unambiguously, reference to a content, direction towards an object (which is not to be understood here as meaning a thing) or immanent objectivity. Every mental phenomenon includes something as object within itself, although they do not all do so in the same way. In presentation, something is presented, in judgment something is affirmed or denied, in love loved, in hate hated, in desire desired and so on. This intentional in-existence is characteristic exclusively of mental phenomena. No physical phenomenon exhibits anything like it. We can, therefore, define mental phenomena by saying that they are those phenomena which contain an object intentionally within themselves (p. 88).

Brentano viewed intentionality as distinguishing mental phenomena from purely physical phenomena, and accordingly denied that it was possible to naturalize them.

The challenge Brentano presented is a serious obstacle to characterizing the relation between vehicles and their content in straightforward causal terms according to which contents cause their vehicles. We can clearly represent what does not exist, but what does not exist cannot cause the occurrence of a representation. Nonetheless, some sort of causal linkage seems to be required if we are to link vehicles to their contents. Some theorists have been tempted to avoid the problem by claiming that representations themselves serve as the content of our thoughts, but although this provides a solution in the case of thoughts about nonexistent entities (as our representation exists even if the objects do not), it has as an untoward consequence the idea that our thoughts are always about representations, never about real things (Richardson, 1981).

Fred Dretske (1981) has been one of the leading theorists in formulating a causal account of intentionality while still allowing that we can represent things that do not exist. He employs the term *information* to characterize the appropriate causal dependence.[11] His starting point is the idea that the effect in a causal process carries information about its cause. As causality is ubiquitous, this implies that information is ubiquitous. Moreover, a given effect may be the effect of a whole cluster of causes, and so carries information about all those causal variables. Dretske's proposal is that the cognitive system develops representations with specific content by stripping away information (a process he calls *digitalization*):

> In passing from the sensory to the cognitive representation (from seeing the apple to realizing that it is an apple), there is a systematic stripping away of components of information (relating to size, color, orientation, surroundings), which makes the experience of the apple the phenomenally rich thing we know it to be, in order to feature *one* component of this information—the information that it is an apple. Digitalization (of, for example, the information that *s* is an apple) is a process whereby a piece of information is taken from a richer matrix of information in the sensory representation (where it is held in what I call "analog" form) and featured to the exclusion of all else) (p. 6).

Provided it is possible to identify the mechanism of digitalization, Dretske's account seems to succeed in linking vehicles to their contents. Yet, it does not explain how representations can ever misrepresent things or represent things that do not exist. One strategy that Dretske employs is to allow that the connection between content and vehicle can sometimes be distorted and it is only in the undistorted cases that the content causes the vehicle. In particular, he proposes to distinguish and privilege the situation in which a person learns the representation from situations in which the person uses (possibly incorrectly) an already-learned representation:

> In the learning situation special care is taken to see that incoming signals have an intensity, a strength, sufficient unto delivering the required piece of information *to* the learning subject. ... But once we have meaning, once the subject has articulated a structure that is selectively sensitive to [the information that p] ... , instances of this structure, tokens of this type, can be triggered by signals that *lack* the appropriate piece of information (194–195).

Theorists inclined to invoke a causal link to characterize the relation between content and vehicle have adopted a number of strategies for identifying when causal connections are appropriate. In other writings, for example, Dretske (1983; see also Fodor, 1990a) proposes that the connection exists under optimal conditions, a move that presents the challenge of identifying optimal conditions.

---

[11] Dennis Stampe (1977) had slightly earlier advanced an information-based account of linguistic meaning.

Still later, Dretske (1988) adopted a teleological/evolutionary perspective that was proposed and defended by Ruth Millikan (1984), according to which a vehicle has a particular content because earlier instances of the vehicle were selected because of their connection with the content. Recall that Lettvin et al. (1959) determined that cells in the frog's retina are particularly responsive to small black objects moving across their visual field and, considering what would typically cause such states in the frog, came to characterize such cells as bug detectors. Millikan's account provides a justification for claiming that bugs constitute the content of the cell's response as that is presumably why such cells were selected for in the evolution of the frog.

Although Fodor was at various times attracted to both the optimal conditions account and the teleological account, he ended up rejecting both. One reason was that neither seemed to provide an answer to what he identified as the disjunction problem—the fact that adding disjuncts to the specification of the content does not have causal or evolutionary consequences. In the environment in which the frog evolved, there were no bee-bees, so one cannot tell whether the frog developed the response to flies or to the disjunction flies or bee-bees:

> ... it's equally OK with Darwin which[ever] way you describe the intentional objects of fly snaps, so long as it's reliable (say, nomologically necessary; anyhow, counterfactual supporting) that all the local flies-or-bee-bees are flies. The point is, of course, that if all the local flies-or-bee-bees are flies, then it is reliable that the frog that snaps at one does neither better nor worse selection-wise than the frog that snaps at the other (Fodor, 1990b, p. 73).

To avoid this difficulty, Fodor developed an asymmetrical dependence account designed to privilege only the appropriate causal relation between content and vehicle. The idea is that c is the content of vehicle v if there is a law that cs cause vs, that some vs are caused by cs, and that for anything else that causes vs, its doing so is asymmetrically dependent on cs doing so. To use the fly detector example, flies do cause the activation in the frog's retina and the ability of flies or bee-bees to produce the same response depends on flies doing so.

Fodor's proposal, like those of Dretske and Millikan, has been the focus of extensive critical discussion as to whether it picks out the proper content for particular vehicles (see Adams, 2000; J. Cohen, 2004 for reviews and critical discussion). Whether or not Fodor's account or some other variant on a causal hypothesis is correct, there is a problem inherent in the causal approach to linking content to vehicles: the connection is entirely external to the cognitive system. Treating it as external was of course the intention behind Fodor's characterization of cognitivist accounts as committed to methodological solipsism: mental activity was to be accounted for entirely in terms of operations on representational vehicles. From within the system of representational vehicles, if there were to be an account of meaning, it would be achieved by specifying relations between vehicles. In *conceptual role semantics*, for example, the meaning of a vehicle is provided by its relations to other vehicles in the inferences a subject makes (Harman, 1987; Block, 1986). Fodor and Lepore (1992) have raised a number of objections to conceptual role semantics, but the main flaw is that without addition or amendment, it gives up the connection to the vehicle that we were trying to capture.[12]

Neither causal accounts nor conceptual role accounts capture the relation between vehicle and content in the way that they seem to be connected in our thoughts: just as Brentano insisted, when we think about something, the object or event seems to be presented to us. More is going on than that the object or event is causally related to our thought, or that we can make additional inferences about it. John Searle (1980) captured the heart of this objection in criticizing what he terms *strong AI*, the view that a properly programmed computer really thinks (as opposed to providing a tool for studying mental processes). Searle presented his "Chinese room" argument in the form of a *Gendankenexperiment* (thought experiment) in which he plays the role of a computer programmed to execute a version of an AI program described in Schank and Abelson (1977). The original program was designed to answer questions about stories in English using what Schank called *scripts*. (Scripts model people's knowledge of common situations—for example, the usual sequence of events when going to a restaurant.) In Searle's version, he is sitting in the room with two large batches of Chinese writing characters that, could he read Chinese, he would realize were a story and the relevant script. Someone gives him a third, smaller batch of Chinese writing (in fact, a question about the story) and expects him to respond. The only resource Searle has for doing this is sets of rules for correlating the batches (i.e., the program that he as the computer is to run). So, when one batch (a question) comes in, he finds and applies the rules that enable him to send back out an appropriate batch of Chinese writing, which constitute an answer. (In one version of the experiment Searle executes the program by manipulating written pieces of paper and applying rules to the symbols on them, but he later proposes that he could simply memorize all the rules and carry out the operations in his head.) Chinese speakers who put questions to Searle believe they are speaking with another Chinese speaker who understands the story. But Searle fails to understand it. His conclusion is that programs operating on formal structures do not produce understanding:

> In the Chinese case I have everything that artificial intelligence can put into me by way of a program, and I understand nothing; in the English case I understand everything, and there is so far no reason at all to suppose that my understanding

---

[12] Defenders of conceptual role semantics have deployed two basic strategies. One is to offer a two factor account, supplementing conceptual role with a causal relation (H. H. Field, 1977) whereas the other is to allow conceptual linkages to extend out into the world (Harman, 1987).

has anything to do with computer programs, that is, with computational operations on purely formally specified elements. As long as the program is defined in terms of computational operations on purely formally defined elements, what the example suggests is that these by themselves have no interesting connection with understanding. They are certainly not sufficient conditions, and not the slightest reason has been given to suppose that they are necessary conditions or even that they make a significant contribution to understanding (p. 418).

Searle's argument has given rise to quite a cottage industry of critical responses, but for the case at hand it offers a compelling perspective on why the different strategies I have discussed for linking contents with vehicles fail to provide the sort of linkage exhibited in cognitive agents. External causal connections to contents do not provide any understanding of those contents within the system. Formal linkages of a vehicle to other vehicles fails to link them in any way to the contents. The resulting representations do not represent anything for the system using them. Contents were not central to the use of representational vehicles in cognitive science and it is challenging to figure out how to bring them into the analysis in a way that is compelling.

5.2.2   Neuroscience Accounts of Content

Cognitive theorizing, especially in the symbolic tradition, focuses principally on representational vehicles for which the investigators stipulate a content; the task of saying how the vehicles are related to their contents is left to philosophers. In contrast, neuroscientists identify vehicles via their content. The inability of individuals to detect sensory stimuli after lesions provided the first suggestions that brain areas served to represent those stimuli. Likewise, the response of muscles to stimulation of particular parts of the brain indicated that those brain regions represented the affected muscles. When single-cell recording became available researchers were able to identify more precisely the part of the sensory field that was represented, leading Hartline (1938) to introduce the phrase *receptive field* for the particular area in the visual field in which a stimulus would produce a response. As investigators discovered that particular cells responded to specific stimuli in their receptive fields, it became common to think of each cell as a *feature detector* (Barlow, 1972; 1999).

The strategy neuroscientists adopted in identifying representations of sensory stimuli fits quite naturally with Dretske's (1981) account of content as discussed above, which focuses on the notion that an effect carries information about its cause. Moreover, the manner in which multiple visual areas can each represent the same portion of the visual field but extract different pieces of information about the stimulus in that field seems to fit with his original account of digitalization. At first Dretske's account seems incompatible with claims that motor areas of the brain represent the muscles that are controlled by those areas, but Pete Mandik (1999) showed how an information-based account can be adapted to allow representations to have as content the effects they will cause. I also discussed how, in an attempt to isolate the appropriate content for a representation, Millikan appealed to the evolutionary context in which the vehicle was selected as a result of its relation to the content. But there is more to her account, and it becomes relevant to how neuroscientists characterize representations. To see how representations might make a difference that selection can operate on, Millikan (1993) focused on the *consumers* of representations—the downstream processes that are differentially affected by what is represented. She maintains that in order for a vehicle to be selected it is not enough that it be an effect of its content; it must be used by the organism by virtue of its relation to its content. Millikan thus draws upon Charles Saunders Peirce, who viewed representation as a three-place relation involving the vehicle, the content, and an *interpretant* that interprets the vehicle. Millikan (1996) developed as her model what she calls *pushmi-pullyu* representations, representations that both describe the content and direct activity in response to it—as the dance of honeybees says both where the nectar is and directs other bees to it.

Typically, the role of the consumer is left implicit in neuroscience discussions of representation. It is simply assumed that information that is represented in neural activity will be used by subsequent neural processes. But there are contexts in which neuroscientists have appealed to the ability of the organism to use information in ascertaining its content. For example, Newsome and Movshon's research on perceived motion (Britten, Shadlen, Newsome, & Movshon, 1992), which I introduced in chapter three, relied on the correlation between activity in MT and the monkey's behavioral response in indicating the direction in which it perceived motion. By showing both that the monkey responded to ambiguous stimuli in accord with the activity in MT and that microstimulation of particular MT cells could bias the monkey's response. These researchers employed knowledge about how the representations were used to assess the representations themselves.

Focusing on the user of a representation can be particularly informative when there is uncertainty about what is actually represented. For example, there are areas in parietal cortex that are involved in processing information about location. But in a task in which the organism is presented a stimulus to which it responds by either saccading or moving its arm to the location, it is not clear whether the activation of particular cells indicates attention to the location or the intention to make a delayed movement to the location. Differentiating these possibilities is difficult, since attention is usually directed towards the target location of a motion. Nonetheless, Larry Snyder and colleagues devised a strategy that worked. They presented a stimulus at a specific location to which the animal had to make a delayed response, with the color of the stimulus specifying whether the monkey was to saccade to the location or reach to it. The investigators reasoned that if the activation represented attention to the location, then the specific response the animal was planning should make no difference. If it was sensitive to the particular response, then it would represent intention. They found cells in area LIP in which there was increased activity when the animal was instructed to saccade to a location in its response field. Cells were also found in area PRR (parietal reach region) in which there was increased activity when it was to move its arm to the location, indicating that both areas encoded intention to act (Snyder, Batista, & Andersen, 2000; 1997).

A word of caution is needed. As neuroscientists are engaged in reverse engineering the brain and do not have independent access to its design, hypotheses about what is represented by specific neural activities must be treated as extremely tentative. As I noted in chapter three, the project of single-cell recording has been limited by the stimuli investigators think to test. It was serendipitous that Hubel and Wiesel discovered that light or dark bars elicited responses from cells in a cat's primary visual cortex and that Gross tested hand-shaped stimuli when recording from an area in the inferior temporal cortex. It would be easy for a researcher simply to fail to test the most relevant stimulus, and therefore fail to find that it would drive a target cell. In this light, it is important to note that Tanaka and Saito (1989) found that expanding stimuli or rotating stimuli would cause specific MSTd cells, which fired weakly in response to straight line movements, to fire vigorously, thereby discovering that the its representational function of MSTd was different from that of MT.

Moreover, it should not be assumed that the cell is carrying information only about the stimulus that causes it to fire most vigorously, as is implicit in speaking of cells as feature detectors. As van Essen and Gallant (1994) stressed, less than full responses may still carry important information that can be used by downstream consumers. Thus, cells may not be feature detectors, but may better be construed as filters with a representational profile.

Another complexity encountered in understanding neural representations is that, as emphasized by Kathleen Akins (1996), neurons may not respond to absolute properties of stimuli, such as temperature, but rather to changes from the current state of the organism (e.g., a given response may indicate that the stimulus is warmer or colder than the prevailing condition). Akins takes this as a reason to reject a representational analysis, but it seems rather to be a reason to reject a particular account of the content of neural representations and as suggesting an alternative. As several critics have noted, organisms are not trying to build up complete pictures of the world they inhabit, but are acquiring information that is useful in guiding their action. Changes in conditions are the sort of information an organism needs in order to evaluate actions. To figure out what about the world an organism represents, then, we need to move beyond looking at the external world through the lens of our how we or scientists would describe the world objectively and instead focus on the needs of the organism (a perspective long advocated in perception by Gibson, although he, too, opposed a representationalist account of the organism's inner activity).

With these qualifications incorporated, the neuroscientific strategy for identifying representations in the brain is relatively straightforward. Researchers seek to determine what sensory stimulus or motor response is causally linked with the activity of particular neurons. It is usually simply assumed that other areas in the nervous system utilize the responses induced by sensory stimuli, and in some cases investigators have established such use experimentally. The connection between content and vehicle is fundamental to how representations are characterized in neuroscience; consequently, neuroscience representations are more clearly grounded in the causal nexus relating organisms to their environments than are those advanced in cognitive science. But there is a cost to that grounding—it seems more difficult to invoke such representations in the sorts of planning and problem-solving activities that have been the focus of cognitive science. As I noted above, neuroscientists often focus on how vehicles figure in map-like structures, but that is still far removed from the way in which words in a language and potentially vehicles in a language of thought can be recombined in diverse cognitive processes. I will return below to this contrast between neuroscience and cognitive science with respect the kinds of representations on which they focus, and will suggest how one might bridge from the neuroscience representations to those adequate for higher cognitive processes.

5.3   DYNAMICISTS: ELIMINATING OR RETHINKING REPRESENTATIONS?

As ubiquitous as appeals to representations have been in both cognitive science and neuroscience, a group of investigators emerged in the 1990s that rejects the invocation of representations. For these researchers, who have adopted the perspective of dynamical systems theory (DST), the appeal to representations distracts and misleads cognitive science from the proper path it needs to follow if it is to develop as a science. The principal targets of the dynamicists' critique are the language-like representations used in symbolic models. But often they direct their critique at a larger target, objecting to representations of all sorts. Thus, philosopher Timothy van Gelder presents his challenge as addressed to "pretty much any reasonable characterization, based around a core idea of some state of a system which, by virtue of some general representational scheme, stands in for some further state of affairs, thereby enabling the system to behave appropriately with respect to that state of affairs" (van Gelder, 1995, p. 351; he adapted this characterization of representation from Haugeland, 1991). This characterization applies equally to the syntactically structured or distributed connectionist representations of cognitive science and the map-like representations of neuroscience.

The rhetoric against representations is found as well among computational modelers and neuroscientists who have embraced a dynamical perspective. Thus, Randall Beer, who employs connectionist style networks as controllers for insect legs, maintained that "there need be no clean decomposition of an agent's dynamics into distinct functional modules, and no aspect of the agent's state need be interpretable as a representation" (Beer, 1995, p. 144). Freeman and Skarda described how the concept of representation impeded their neuroscience research on the olfactory bulb:

> For more than 10 years we tried to say that … each burst served to represent the odorant with which we correlated it…. This was a mistake. After years of sifting through our data, we identified the problem: it was the concept of representation. … [They explain that the pattern for a given odor occurs only under conditioning and changes if the reinforcement contingency is altered or a new odor is added.] Our findings indicate that patterned neural activity correlates best with reliable forms of interaction in a context that is behaviorally and environmentally co-defined by what Steven Rose (1976) calls a dialectic. There is nothing intrinsically representational about this dynamic process until the observer intrudes. It is the experimenter who infers what the observed activity patterns represent to or in a subject, in order to explain his results to himself (Werner, 1988a; 1988b) (Freeman & Skarda, 1990, p. 376).

Behind the dynamicists' challenge to representations is a very different way of thinking about cognition, an approach that has its roots in Newtonian physics. Characterizing complex interactions in Newtonian terms presented a challenge for physicists that was not adequately addressed until Poincaré developed new geometrical ways to represent changes in systems in the late nineteenth century. What came to be called *dynamical systems theory* (DST) enables investigators to visualize the change in the state of a system over time. The simplest case is a plot of the states traversed by a system through time, that is, the system's *trajectory* through *state space*. Each dimension of state space corresponds to one variable of the system, and each point in the space corresponds to one of the possible states of the system. For systems described by one continuous variable, the state space is a range of values on one dimension (e.g., the frequency of a tone, the height of a person, the firing rate of a neuron, and the population size of a species in its habitat). Additional variables result in additional dimensions for the state space.

Certain further concepts are extremely useful for describing the trajectories of systems through state spaces. A system might simply cycle through a number of locations in the state space, or follow a trajectory to what is termed an *attractor*. This may be a specific point in the space, in which case it is called a *point*

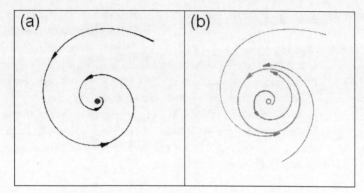

Figure 5.4   Attractors in a two-dimensional state space. (a) A point attractor with a spiraling transient. (b) A cyclic attractor with spiraling transients beginning at points inside and outside of it.

attractor, or it may be a cycle, in which case it is called a *cyclic attractor* (see Figure 5.4). More exotic attractors are also possible, such as *chaotic attractors,* in which the system moves through a variety of points that roughly approximate a geometrical shape but never returns to exactly the same point. For some systems the state space may contain multiple attractors such that, from different starting points, the system ends up in different attractors (the region from which the system approaches a given attractor is then referred to as a *basin of attraction*). For a highly accessible introduction to these and other key concepts of DST see Abraham and Shaw (1992).

DST was initially applied to physical systems such as eddies in a stream (Landau, 1944), but by the 1980s it was extended to motor coordination problems by Michael Turvey, Peter Kugler, and Scott Kelso (see Kelso, 1995) and by the 1990s to the development not only of coordinated activity but also more cognitive capacities (see Thelen & Smith, 1994; Port & van Gelder, 1995). Many of the researchers in psychology who were first attracted to DST viewed it as providing a radical departure from other approaches. Van Gelder and Port (1995, p. 10), for example, claimed that "dynamical and computational systems are fundamentally different *kinds* of systems, and hence the dynamical and computational approaches to cognition are fundamentally different in their deepest foundations." They further characterized the advent of the DST approach as a Kuhnian revolution that was meant to supplant the computational approach:

> The computational approach is nothing less than a research paradigm in Kuhn's classic sense. It defines a range of questions and the form of answers to those questions (i.e., computational models). It provides an array of exemplars—classic pieces of research which define how cognition is to be thought about and what counts as a successful model.... [T]he dynamical approach is more than just powerful tools; like the computational approach, it is a worldview. The cognitive system is not a

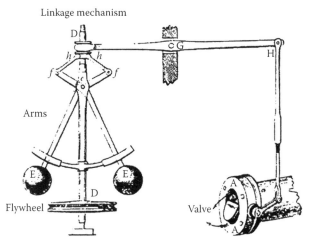

Figure 5.5   Watt's centrifugal governor for a steam engine. Redrawn from J. Farley, *A Treatise on the Steam Engine: Historical, Practical, and Descriptive* (London: Longman, Rees, Orme, Brown, and Green, 1827).

computer, it is a dynamical system. It is not the brain, inner and encapsulated; rather, it is the whole system comprised of nervous system, body, and environment. The cognitive system is not a discrete sequential manipulator of static representational structures; rather, it is a structure of mutually and simultaneously influencing *change*. Its processes do not take place in the arbitrary, discrete time of computer steps; rather, they unfold in the *real* time of ongoing change.... The cognitive system does not interact with other aspects of the world by passing messages or commands; rather, it continuously coevolves with them.... [T]o see that there is a dynamical approach is to see a new way of conceptually reorganizing cognitive science as it is currently practiced (pp. 2–4).

In the passage just cited, van Gelder and Port limited their attack to "static representational structures," but as I noted above, van Gelder elsewhere broadens the attack to "pretty much any reasonable characterization" of representation. To show how one could approach cognition without appeal to representations, van Gelder describes the centrifugal governor James Watt devised for the steam engine, which he maintains is "preferable to the Turing machine as a landmark for models of cognition" (van Gelder, 1995, p. 381). The task facing Watt was to regulate the output of steam from a steam engine so that the flywheel would rotate at a constant speed regardless of the resistance being generated by the appliances connected to it (e.g., sewing machines). Watt's governor was ingeniously simple (see Figure 5.5). He attached a spindle on a flywheel driven by the steam generated by the steam engine, and attached arms to the spindle, which would, as a result of centrifugal force, open out in proportion to the speed at which the flywheel turned. Thus, whenever the flywheel would slow down, the arms would drop, and as it speeded up, they would move outwards. A mechanical linkage connected the arms to the steam valve so that, when the wheel turned too fast, the valve would close, releasing less steam, thereby slowing the flywheel; but when the flywheel turned too slowly, the valve would open, releasing more steam and speeding up the flywheel.

Van Gelder contended that the Watt governor operates without representations. He labeled "misleading" : "a common and initially quite attractive intuition to the effect that the angle at which the arms are swinging is a representation of the current speed of the engine, and it is because the arms are related in this way to engine speed that the governor is able to control that speed" (p. 351). Here I will focus on just the first of van Gelder's arguments against construing the angle of the arms as representations, as it helps elucidate why, in fact, it is appropriate to view the angle of the angle arms as a representation (I have responded to his other arguments in Bechtel, 1998). Van Gelder contends that there is no explanatory utility in describing the angle of the arms in representational terms (that is, the dynamical analysis is sufficient). To establish explanatory utility, I must argue that (a) a mechanistic analysis is informative and (b) mechanistic analysis requires employing a particular representational story about the arm angles: they *stand in for* the speed of the flywheel and can regulate the valve opening *because* they carry this information.

Let us begin by providing a brief mechanistic analysis of the Watt governor. The governor has several different parts, including the flywheel, the spindle and arms, and a linkage mechanism connected to a valve. As Figure 5.6 makes clear, each component operates on a different engineering principle and hence performs a specific operation; each operation contributes to the ability of the governor to keep the flywheel rotating at a constant speed. That is, the opening of the valve gets transformed (via a piston) into the rotation of the flywheel, which gets transformed into the angle of the spindle arms, which gets transformed into the opening of the valve. In this way, we have shifted vocabularies from one describing the overall behavior of the Watt governor to one describing what its parts do. Then there is an extra step back up to the system level by connecting the task of each component to the needs of the whole system. Here, it becomes clear why Watt inserted the spindle arms. It is *because* the spindle arms rise and fall in response to the speed of the flywheel that their angle can be used by the linkage mechanism to open and shut the valve in the appropriate way. Without the spindle arms and their linkage mechanism, the valve has no access to information about the flywheel's speed. They were inserted in order to encode that information in a format that could be used by the valve-opening mechanism.

This account of the function of the spindle arm angle illustrates a more general point about representation: typically, someone (a designer or evolution) has gone to the trouble of representing a state of affairs in another medium because that

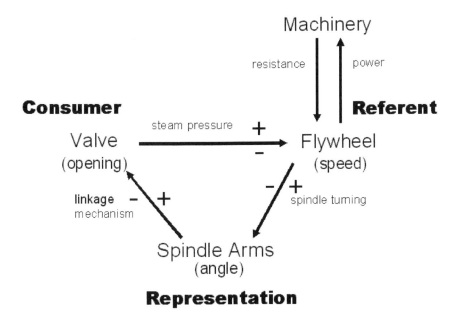

Figure 5.6   A schematic representation showing that the angle of the spindle arms carries information about the speed of the flywheel for the valve, which uses the angle to determine the opening, thereby regulating the speed of the flywheel.

medium is more suitable for use by the consumer. This can be due to its format, its accessibility (e.g., words are generally more accessible to our cognitive system than are their referents), the efficiency with which it can be manipulated (e.g., computer-aided design), economy (e.g., industrial prototypes), and so forth. It is important to emphasize that in Figure 5.6 the representation is not just one vertex of the triangle, a part like any other part of the dynamic loop; it was inserted to play a particular (representational) role and the system functions because it was designed appropriately for that role.

Contrary to van Gelder, it is not misleading but informative to characterize the angle of the arms as representing the speed of the flywheel to the valve linkage mechanism. The governor works precisely because Watt discovered a way to represent the speed in a way that allowed the system to use the information. This response to van Gelder also exhibits a general strategy for addressing the repudiation of representations by some advocates of DST. As I will develop in the next section, representations play a critical role in systems that control other systems—they can achieve appropriate control only by representing relevant information.

Interestingly, advocates of DST, including Port and van Gelder, are not always critical of representations. At times they emphasize how DST opens the possibility for very different styles of representation than those found in traditional cognitive accounts. Van Gelder at one point proposed that dynamicists might "find their representations among the kinds of entities that figure in DST, including parameter settings, system states, attractors, trajectories, or even aspects of bifurcation structures" and eventually "even more exotic forms" (van Gelder, 1998, p. 622; see also van Gelder & Port, 1995, p. 12). There is, in fact, good reason to look to DST for guidance as to the representations cognitive systems employ because minds are dynamical systems constantly changing their state in response to a wide variety of factors. For example, once one takes into account the lateral and recurrent projections in the visual system, it becomes clear that it is a complex dynamical system. By employing tools of DST, researchers may find a way to characterize its representational capacities that is superior to those advanced to date.

5.4   REPRESENTATIONS AS A GENERAL FEATURE OF CONTROL SYSTEMS

A variety of critics of van Gelder have treated his arguments as compelling against representations in the Watt governor and have accepted the example as showing that representations may not be needed in simple cognitive tasks in which the mind/brain is directly engaged with the relevant features of the environment (Clark, 1997; Kirsh, 1991; Eliasmith, 1996; 1997). These critics base their objections to van Gelder on the fact that there are a host of cognitive tasks, such as making long-term plans, in which cognitive systems must deal with items not present in the immediate environment and that these contexts are, in the words of Clark and Toribio (1994), *representation hungry*. In their view, governing the speed of a steam engine or engaging in purely sensory-motor activities are not representation hungry tasks. The reason is that only ordinary causal linkages are required in these circumstances. The fact that putative representations are causally produced by what they represent, however, ought not to count against their being representations, as that is a frequent part of accounts of the semantics of representations (Dretske, 1981; Fodor, 1987; see Prinz & Barsalou, 2000, for a similar argument). Rather, the objection seems to be that if the causal linkages are as simple as they are in the Watt governor or in a sensory–motor response system engaged with an environment, nothing is added by speaking of representations. In particular, in the case of the Watt governor, once one has described the causal response of the flywheel, spindle, angle arms, mechanical linkage, and valve, one has given a complete account. What does talk of representations add to the story?

If we were dealing with a simple linear causal scenario, there would be little point in talking about various stages in the causal sequence as carrying information. As I discussed above, Millikan emphasizes the role of the consumer in her account of representation and frequently what the consumer does is use information to coordinate its actions with what is represented. The consumer in the case of the Watt governor is the valve control mechanism, which is able to adjust the valve in the manner appropriate to the load on the engine because it is provided with the information about the flywheel. To appreciate this point, it is important to recognize that Watt designed the governor as a component mechanism within a larger mechanism and its specific task was to *control* parts of the larger mechanism.

The Watt governor is an example of what we now recognize as one of the simplest forms of control systems: closed loop control using negative feedback. In control theory, what is being controlled is commonly spoken of as the *plant*. In negative feedback control, information about the effects of the operation of the plant is fed back so as to alter in appropriate ways the operation of the plant. The representation directly determines the operation performed on that which is represented. As I will describe in the next chapter, over 2000 years passed from the time negative feedback was first discovered and deployed in regulation of water clocks until, with the rise of the cybernetics movement in the 1940s, it was recognized as a general means for achieving control in both mechanical and biological systems. As many in the cybernetics movement conceptualized it, the brain is a governor for controlling the behavior of an organism (Ashby, 1952). For example, one function of sensory systems is to provide feedback so as to redirect and fine-tune activities of motor systems.

In feedback control, it is information directly about the effects of an activity that is fed back through the system to regulate its behavior. But in many cases the information the organism needs does not concern the effects of already initiated activities but what Gibson (1979) called the affordances an environment offers. These are possibilities for action by the organism. In some cases, the organism needs information about something in its environment not in order to approach it, but to avoid it (e.g., a predator, or even just an obstacle in its path). Although the relations become more complex than provided in the simple loop in Figure 5.6, the general framework of control theory still applies. In order for the mind–brain control system to control behavior, it requires information about various things in its environment. Moreover, animals often need to coordinate their action with things that are not immediately present, such as a food source that is out of sight. In this case there are no direct causal connections from the thing represented to the representation. The representation must be maintained in the absence of occurrent causal input. The challenges are still greater when the control system has to take into account changes occurring in what is represented during periods in which it is out of causal contact with the thing represented. This requires the system to represent the dynamic activity of something remote and out of causal contact.

In an illuminating example, Rick Grush (1997) considered the case of an Earth-based controller for a heating plant on a remote space station. The prospects of regulating such a plant by negative feedback from Earth are dim. By the time feedback information is received by the controller that the temperature has dropped too low and it sends back a command to increase the heat, the temperature has dropped even further, perhaps damaging the space station. Eventually the feedback system will begin to restore the system to the proper temperature, but by the time that information is received by the controller and it can issue a command to stop increasing the heat, the temperature has risen far beyond the target range, further damaging the space station. To deal with such systems, engineers have devised control systems that maintain a model of the plant—an emulator. Grush envisions, for example, that before the space station was launched, a neural network was trained to emulate the heating plant. Its outputs specify the temperature produced by a certain degree of activation of the heating or cooling system on the space station. After the space station is launched, the emulator stays behind and is used by the local control system to determine what is happening remotely. The local control system then responds to the emulator's predictions of what is happening remotely rather than waiting for the signal from the space station, and so avoids the disastrous oscillations that would result from utilizing only feedback control.

Grush's main objective was to point out the virtues of relying on such emulator systems and to argue that they constitute the point at which we are properly led to appeal to representations. He construed the sort of internal processes within the Watt governor or the human visual system as *presentations* and differentiated them from representations. Although granting that there is a significant evolutionary advance from internal states that are generated from the environment relatively directly to those that are maintained and employed when this connection is broken, and that the latter provide the organism with opportunities which the former do not, I nonetheless maintain that there is a point to examining the continuity between the two sorts of processes. The essential step, that of having something stand in for something else and using the stand-in to coordinate behavior with that which is distal, is already realized in the Watt governor and in organisms with simple sensory–motor systems. The key elements in establishing the relation between vehicle and content are already secured in these simpler cases. Were it not for having invoked an appropriate causal relation between content and vehicle and having a consumer who utilized the vehicle because of the information it carried about the content, Grush's emulator would lack the appropriate semantics.

Two worries that have been raised with respect to accounts such as mine that extend representations to simple devices such as the Watt governor are that they make representations ubiquitous and observer dependent (Haselager, de Groot, & van Rappard, 2003). Neither worry, however, constitutes a serious objection. Representations will be found wherever control systems secure information about external phenomena, but this is entirely appropriate. In order to understand such systems we need to be able to identify how information about a distal object or event is made available for the control system to use. The vocabulary of representation, of re-presenting what is not immediately present, accurately captures what is happening. Moreover, appeal to representations is not simply a means for us to interpret such systems. The systems themselves (as we saw in the instance of the Watt governor) would not work if information about the distal circumstances were not being made available within the control system. So representations are a central feature of the systems themselves.

5.5   FROM SENSORY–MOTOR REPRESENTATIONS
TO HIGHER COGNITION

In this chapter I have distinguished the appeal to syntactically structured representations that has been a focus of much cognitive science modeling, especially in the symbolic tradition, from the emphasis on map-like representations in neuroscience. I emphasized how the map-like representations of neuroscience are grounded in the causal nexus of sensory and motor processes and thereby closely linked to their contents, whereas those advanced in cognitive models are much less tightly linked to contents. One consequence of neuroscience representations being tightly linked to sensory–motor processes is that they seem less suitable for the sorts of off-line cognitive activities such as reasoning and planning that Clark and Toribio (1994) characterize as *representation hungry* and that have been the focus of much cognitive theorizing. This gives rise to the question of whether there is a way to bridge from the map-like representations that are highly embedded in sensory–motor activity to the more flexibly employed representations required for higher-level cognitive activities.

Recent research by Laurence Barsalou (1999) on concepts suggests how we might go about closing the gap between sensory–motor representations and higher cognitive activities. Concepts are often presented as the flexibly deployable atomic units we use in thinking; we use concepts to represent objects and events and compose concepts to form thoughts. Words of natural languages have typically provided the starting point for characterizing concepts, and sentences of natural languages have been the basis for characterizing the content of thoughts. Fodor's *language of thought* provided a vivid portrayal of this perspective. Within philosophy, concepts themselves have been assumed to be definable by specifying the necessary and sufficient conditions for satisfying the concept. Socrates' quest for definitions of concepts such as piety, justice, and knowledge set the agenda that has been pursued in philosophy for nearly 2,500 years. Wittgenstein (1953) was one of the first to question whether ordinary concepts such as *game* could in fact be defined and, as I noted in chapter one, in the 1970s psychologists began to develop alternative accounts of concepts that emphasized things like prototypes, exemplars, and theoretical knowledge.

Even as they broke from the classical view of concepts, psychologists tended to remain close to the linguistic perspective as they attempted to characterize concepts in terms of sets of nameable features and the like. In particular, concepts were generally taken to be the atoms of thought, available to be summoned and combined with others when required, but not altered in the process. Research in the 1980s led Barsalou to question this common assumption about concepts. First, he established that many of the features of ordinary concepts applied equally to concepts describing ad-hoc categories (e.g., things to take to the beach on a rainy day) with which subjects had no previous experience (Barsalou, 1983). These could not plausibly be thought to be stored atoms of thought but had to be constructed. He also established unexpected variability in how his subjects represented ordinary taxonomic concepts on different occasions (Barsalou, 1987). This led him to begin to question whether concepts exist in the mind as static, amodal, language-like symbols (symbols not tied to a particular sensory modality). In the late 1990s Barsalou proposed that instead of amodal concepts, people rely on perceptual representations and that they "can play *all* of the critical symbolic functions that amodal symbols play in traditional systems, such that amodal symbols become redundant" (Barsalou, 1999). Barsalou makes it clear here that the perceptual representations he is considering are neural; he describes perceptual symbols as "records of the neural states that underlie perception." (Although much of his discussion focuses on visual perception, he intends his account to include perception in other modalities, including perception of emotion and introspection.)

The attempt to ground cognition in perception goes back at least to the seventeenth century empiricists in philosophy such as Locke. Their program has been much ridiculed, but the target in most attacks is the view that perception gives rise to static pictures or images (images of which we are consciously aware) that are holistic recordings of the input. Perceptual representations for Barsalou, however, are not (despite his reference to them as "records of neural states") pictures or images—they are not recordings. In particular, they are interpreted in that "specific tokens in perception (i.e., individuals) [are bound] to knowledge for general types of things in memory (i.e., concepts)." The key to this move is a proper understanding of neural processing in vision. The brain is not constructing a picture of the world (if it did, it would then need another perceiver to view the picture) but, rather, an analysis of the visual input geared to action. This is already suggested by the way the brain decomposes visual processing, with different brain areas analyzing distinct features of a scene such as color, shape, or location. Neural activity in different brain areas serves to categorize and conceptualize visual input: the stimulus has *this* shape, *this* color, or occurs at *this* location.

Barsalou refers to perceptual representations as schematic representations in that only certain features of the perceptual input are represented. He appeals to psychological research on attention to show how a schematic representation is constructed—selective attention isolates and emphasizes pieces of information that are given in perception and facilitates storage of these features in long-term memory. Neuroscience research on attention supports such an analysis. Relying on the evidence that different features of stimuli are analyzed in different brain areas, Corbetta, Miezin, Shulman, & Petersen (1993) have shown that when subjects are required to attend differentially to different features of stimuli, brain areas responsible for processing those features show increased activity. The fact that perceptual symbols are schematic in this manner allows them to be indeterminate in ways that pictures cannot—representing a tiger, for example, as having stripes, but not a determinate number of stripes.

The challenge is to show how representations that arise in the course of on-line visual processing and motor control can be useful in the sort of off-line cognitive activities in which humans engage: activities of contemplating and remembering what we have seen, conceiving of possibilities that we have not experienced, and so forth. Barsalou's proposal is that the very same representations that arise in on-line visual and motor activities can be activated in the absence of their usual visual stimulus or without the actual motor activity. Evidence that this is possible is provided by research into visual imagery, which indicates that when people are asked to imagine an object or a scene, the same areas in their brains are activated as when they actually see the object or scene (Kosslyn, 1994; Farah, 1995; Zatorre, Halpern, Perry, Meyer, & Evans, 1996). This ability to reactivate brain areas normally activated as a result of sensory stimuli is enabled by the extensive recurrent connections back to these areas from more anterior areas of the brain. Turning to motor activity, an experience familiar to anyone who has tried to learn new motor routines, is the attempt to rehearse those routines *in one's mind*. A variety of evidence (Jeannerod, 1994) points to the fact that the same neural processes are involved when a person mentally plans a motor activity and actually executes it. This explains the surprising result that imagining a motor activity is constrained in the same manner as actually executing it so that, for example, Fitts' law describing speed–accuracy trade-offs applies equally to imagined and executed motor activities (Crammond, 1997). One of the surprising results is that imagining movement leads to subsequent improvements in much the same manner as actual practice of the movement (Yue & Cole, 1992).

This now-rich body of literature suggests that one of the major capacities provided by the brains of humans and a range of other species is to activate the operations involved in sensory and motor processing in the absence of sensory stimuli or motor action. These processes provide a plausible basis for the off-line mental activities of planning and reasoning on which cognitive scientists have focused. A natural way to characterize motor imagery is that an individual is *mentally simulating* the performance of the activity in that they are going through the same brain activity as they would if they were to perform it. Barsalou extends this characterization to visual imagery—an individual's brain is executing (many of) the same operations as would be involved in actually seeing or otherwise experiencing the object in a sensory manner. By emphasizing mental simulation, Barsalou draws attention to the dynamic nature of these processes—the neural processes are related temporarily and the person's experience accordingly has a temporal character. Thus, a person may attend to different parts of an object as they conceptualize it. Moreover, they are not confined to just repeating previous sensory experiences, but can put the components of the experience together in different ways on different occasions. Barsalou refers to the organizing systems specifying how different perceptual representations can be related as *frames*, thereby invoking earlier cognitive science research on the type of complex information structures that seem to figure in cognition. For Barsalou, frames allow individual perceptual representations to be integrated into what he terms "simulation competences."

Linguistic representations, on Barsalou's account, are also processed as perceptual symbols resulting from hearing or reading words. They, however, extend the capacities of the conceptual system to operate with other perceptual representations. He proposes that:

> As people hear or read a text, they use productively formulated sentences to construct a productively formulated representation that constitutes a semantic interpretation. Conversely, during language production, the construction of a simulation activates associated words and syntactic patterns, which become candidates for spoken sentences designed to produce a similar simulation in a listener.

But it is clear that while linguistic indexing supplements the cognitive capacities provided by perceptual symbols, it is the perceptual symbols themselves that do the cognitive work for Barsalou. Linguistic symbols serve, for him, to coordinate our use of other perceptual symbols. Thus, it is important for him to show that perceptual symbols themselves can have the sorts of properties Fodor argued were needed for cognition—productivity and systematicity—without appealing to language-like representations underlying their use. Barsalou maintains that the very features of perceptual symbols that I have already reviewed provide him the resources to do this.[13] The key is that perceptual symbols and simulations

---

[13] In his own discussion, Barsalou uses the term *productivity* somewhat differently, referring to the ability of subjects to supply instantiations by filling in schemas that were created by filtering out features of the initial perceptual situation. In his treatment of this filling-in, Barsalou allows for supplying features that were not part of the initial perception, thus allowing for novelty, including novel representations that violate physical principles. Thus, what he terms productivity is one way of generating new representations, but it is not the only one operative in his account of perceptual symbols.

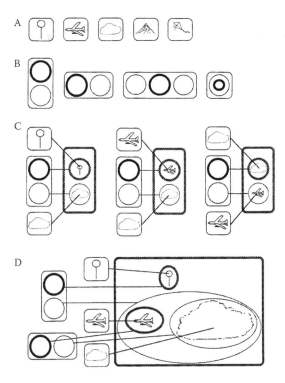

Figure 5.7   Barsalou's representation of how perceptual symbols for object categories (A) and spatial relations (B) implement productivity through combinatorial (C) and recursive (D) processing. Boxes with thin solid lines represent simulation competences; boxes with thick lines represent simulations. Redrawn from Barsalou, L.W. (1999). *Behavioral and Brain Sciences, 22*, p. 593, figure 4. With permission of Cambridge University Press.

are built up componentially. Thus, just as linguistic representations, they can be continually put together in new ways, thereby accounting for productivity. They also permit substitutions of different component representations, thereby accounting for systematicity. Barsalou illustrates this potential by employing diagrams much like those used by cognitive linguists (Langacker, 1987). Figure 5.7 is an example. It illustrates how perceptual symbols for object categories (A) and spatial relations (B) can be combined (C), even recursively (D), to productively generate new representations. The symbols in this diagram, e.g., the balloon and airplane in (A) are not intended as pictures, but to stand for perceptual representations, that is, neural activity as would arise from seeing these objects. The boxes with thin solid lines are intended to represent simulation competences that have developed over many experiences with the object or relation. The boxes with thick lines then represent particular simulations that might be generated from the simulation competences by combining them, sometimes recursively.

I have offered only a partial sketch of Barsalou's account of perceptual symbols (he goes on to suggest how even abstract concepts such as *truth* can be constructed from perceptual representations), but what I have described is sufficient to indicate the potential to build up from the sorts of representations found in the brain to those that can support higher cognitive activity. The key ingredient in his construction is to construe the kind of analysis the visual system performs (by having different neurons represent such things as shape and color of stimuli) as involving categorization and conceptualization. The separately analyzed features afford composition, thereby providing a resource similar in some respects to that which Fodor identified for language-like representations. Perceptual symbols, however, do not thereby become implementations for Fodorian language-like symbols; perceptual symbols are modality-specific, and the particular features of the symbols themselves generally specify definite features in what they represent. Unlike amodal language-like symbols, the particular embodiment of the symbols as patterns of neural firing in particular brain regions is important to the information that they carry. One consequence of this, which Barsalou happily endorses, is that different individuals, with different learning histories, are likely to have somewhat different representations.

Barsalou's conception of a perceptual symbol system provides the basis for a bridge from neural representations to cognitive representations. On such an account, the same neural processing that underlies perception also figures in conceptual reasoning. The virtue of the neural accounts of representation is that the representations introduced are naturally embedded in perceptual processing and motor planning, and so there is much less of a challenge of relating these representations to contents. Insofar as Barsalou's strategy for showing how perceptual representations exhibit a structure that provides for a form of productivity and systematicity, they may also be the basis for higher-level conceptual thought. Moreover, to the extent that his strategy succeeds—treating linguistic representations as additional perceptual symbols that index other perceptual symbols and enable them to be elicited in mental simulations—he provides a means to link internal mental activities to linguistic activities in communities. Although the account requires much elaboration, it offers perhaps the most promising strategy for extending the representational capacities of the brain to account for human cognitive performance.

Six

From Responsive to Active Mechanisms

The account of mechanisms I have presented so far in this book has focused on mechanisms that respond to a condition presented to them. They are not ones that are intrinsically active. Indeed, the idea of an intrinsically active mechanism seems on first appearance to be misguided since it apparently involves a kind of perpetual motion machine. As we will see, this is not the case. Active mechanisms are dependent on external sources of matter and energy; thus, they do not violate thermodynamic principles. The key is that they are, or are parts of, systems that are organized so as to control the flow of matter and energy in ways that serve to maintain themselves. It is the constant risk of dissipating that requires such systems to remain active.

As I will show below, thinking in terms of active mechanisms is necessary if we are to account for fundamental features of living organisms. Accordingly, I will start to build a framework for thinking about active mechanisms in biology by introducing the notion of autonomous adaptive agents. My goal, though, is to understand mental mechanisms in particular as active. Thus, after developing the basic notion that organisms are autonomous adaptive agents, I will address how mental mechanisms are situated in such autonomous adaptive agents, and the impact this should have on our understanding of mental mechanisms. In a separate chapter I will then show how this provides an avenue for addressing more popular concerns about whether the mechanical framework is compatible with human freedom and dignity.

6.1   THE TENDENCY TO VIEW MECHANISMS AS RESPONSIVE

In thinking of a mechanism, it is common to think of it as receiving input and generating an output. This is, after all, how we conceive of machines that we employ; certain things are put into the machine, and when it is working normally, it generates what it was intended to produce. Thus, we put water and coffee grounds into the appropriate reservoirs in a coffeepot, turn on the switch, and it outputs freshly brewed coffee. We supply inputs to a programmed computer (e.g., the data about our income and deductible expenses for the past year) and it produces an output (a properly completed tax form indicating the taxes we owe or the refund we shall receive). Sometimes lots of operations intervene in the functioning of the machine, but it is still a machine that takes an input and generates an output.

We tend to think similarly about biological mechanisms. For example, we conceptualize the fermentation mechanism in yeast as taking in sugar and outputting alcohol. Typically, the reactions are diagrammed linearly: sugar is shown at one end and arrows (reactions) lead the eye through a sequence of intermediate products to alcohol at the other end (see Figure 6.1a.). Additional chemical substances, such as inorganic phosphate (P_i), oxidized and reduced nicotinamide adenine dinucleotide (NAD^+, NADH), and adenosine diphosphate and triphosphate (ADP, ATP) enter and leave the main linear pathway in what are typically appended as "side reactions." The focus is on the main pathway: fermentation as a way to turn grapes and grains into alcohol that we can enjoy drinking.

If we think of fermentation from the yeast's perspective, we would conceptualize it rather differently. In any work a yeast cell performs, ATP is broken down to ADP and P_i to release energy. To be able to perform additional work in the future, ADP and P_i must be resynthesized into ATP. This requires energy, which is obtained by the oxidation of certain of the intermediates on the main pathway (triosephosphates) at the expense of the reduction of NAD^+ to NADH. The energy released in the oxidation is temporarily stored in the phosphate bonds of the triosephosphates, from which it can be transferred back to ATP. To provide a renewed supply of NAD^+ that can be reduced in the future, NADH must again be oxidized, this time reducing the pyruvic acid formed after the phosphates have been removed from the triosephosphates to create alcohol. From the yeast's perspective, the process focuses on the regeneration of ATP; alcohol is simply a waste product. Figure 6.1b, obtained by closing the side loops in Figure 6.1a, provides a better characterization of the process as it affects the organism in which it is situated—the yeast cell.

In Figure 6.1b the overall process of fermentation is seen to involve cyclic processes. This is of considerable significance, and I will discuss cycles in more detail shortly. For now, though, the most salient point is that the overall mechanism of fermentation is still represented here as involving the input of glucose and ending with the production of alcohol. Fermentation is hardly unique among biological processes in this regard. We think in a similar way about processes such as protein synthesis—it starts with the instructions specified in the genetic code and proceeds to the synthesis of polypeptide chains, which subsequently fold into proteins. Likewise, we think of cell division as beginning with a single cell that divides into two cells through a sequence of operations in which paired chromosomes condense, are aligned by spindle fibers in the middle of the nucleus,

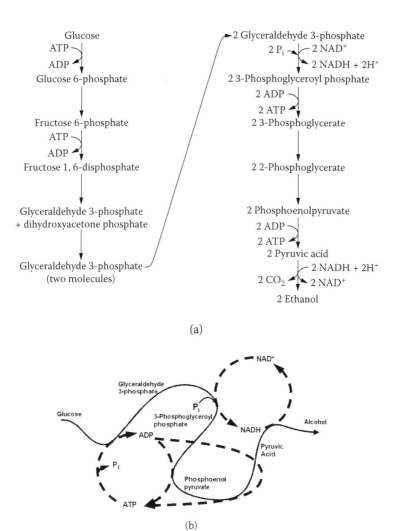

Figure 6.1 (a) A standard representation of the fermentation pathway, starting with glucose and ending up with alcohol. (b) An alternative portrayal created by closing the loops involving the side-chains in (A).

then are pulled to the spindle poles, after which nuclear membranes separate the daughter nuclei, and the cell membrane pinches the cytoplasm into two daughter cells. Moving up to physiological processes, we characterize the kidney as initiating its activity when it receives blood carrying waste products from other organs.

In the nephrons of the kidney a capillary carrying the blood intertwines with a tubule to which waste products are transferred through filtration. The chemicals in the filtrate are then sorted: some, such as water and ions, are reabsorbed into the blood, whereas others are excreted in the form of urine. In all of these cases, we view the input as a starting point and the mechanism's functioning as a response to the input.

The same tendency to think in terms of responsive mechanisms dominates the sciences of the mind/brain. The various mechanisms of the mind are construed as activated by stimuli in the environment to which the mechanisms respond. Moreover, this responsivity presumption is manifest in the research strategies employed. As diagrammed in Table 1.2, in behavioral experiments investigators alter the input to the mechanism and record the resulting behavior. In lesion or stimulation experiments, they intervene in the operation of one or more components and evaluate the effects of the intervention on the mechanism's behavior under various conditions. Finally, in recording experiments, investigators record the response of internal components to particular inputs supplied to the system. In all of these cases, the causal stream is viewed as running from the input through a sequence of intervening steps within the mechanism to the mechanism's output. (For tractability, a given investigation will target only a part of the full causal stream; e.g., sensory and perceptual mechanisms are assumed to be involved in receiving the stimulus in a memory experiment, but the stimulus is treated as coming directly into the memory mechanism.)

Consider just a few examples from the research on mechanisms of memory and visual perception that were the focus of chapters two and three. The overall framework in which memory is conceptualized is one in which a stimulus or skill is encoded (sometimes over repeated trials), the memory is stored for some time, and then the memory is retrieved. Researchers traditionally treated storage as a rather passive process in which memory traces were either stable (akin to books sitting on a shelf) or subject to decay or loss. (More recently there has been greater appreciation of Bartlett's emphasis on constructive processes during storage: false memory and related tasks have provided a way to study how mental operations occurring between encoding and retrieval can change what is stored. However, this has had little direct impact on the design of memory research using other experimental tasks.) Typically, the encoding process is construed as initiated by the event to be remembered (e.g., the presentation of a word or picture in a memory experiment, or the experiencing of an event in ordinary life) and ending with the fixing of the item in memory. The challenge has been to figure out the operations in the encoding mechanism that occur over time. Retrieval is then construed as a process that elicits the stored memory with a prompting event. Different sorts of prompting events (e.g., requesting that a subject recall all the items she can, or asking a subject to identify whether a cued item was on the list previously studied) are then construed as calling into play different operations that, if successful, have the effect that the mechanism outputs the target item.

The idea that memory processes are ones that transpire as the organism first reacts to an event to be encoded and later reacts to a cue to remember is reflected in the ways in which memory is studied in the laboratory. In studying recall, researchers present the cue and then measure a variable such as how many items are recalled, how accurately they are recalled, or the time it takes subjects to perform the recall task. Until recently investigators could study encoding only by including a recall task to determine what was encoded. For example, regularities in the phenomena such as the *depth of processing* effect (F. I. M. Craik & Lockhart, 1972; F. I. M. Craik & Tulving, 1975) were discovered by altering the conditions in the encoding phase and identifying the effects on a retrieval task. Since the 1990s, though, neuroimaging has made it possible to observe the effect on the brain immediately after presentation of a stimulus. In all of these cases, the strategy is one of presenting the stimulus and determining how the mind/brain, or some part of it, responds.

This perspective is even clearer when we turn to vision. The classic approach has been to present a visual stimulus to a subject and obtain a measure of the subject's response. In a psychophysics experiment of the sort pioneered by Weber, for example, a subject is presented with two stimuli and must verbally respond whether they are the same or different. Since Helmholtz (1867), the working assumption has been that between the arrival of light at the retina and a subject's perception of objects there are intervening processes that involve the transformation of information (what Helmholtz called *unconscious inferences*). Neuroscientists investigating the visual system have tried to figure out where and how the information processing occurs in the brain. Lesion studies are interpreted as showing what kinds of operations on the visual input are omitted when particular neural areas are removed. The effects differ depending on where in the pathway the lesioned area is located. Single-cell recording studies attempt to relate the activity in a given neuron to properties of stimuli presented in the neuron's receptive field. The visual mechanisms are viewed as functioning in response to such stimuli.

The same perspective can be found in many other domains of the mind/brain sciences. Problem solving begins with presentation of a problem and ends with the production of a solution. Language comprehension begins when people hear or read linguistic utterances and ends when they comprehend them; language production begins with intentions to communicate and ends with the generation of sentences. Imagery tasks begin with a directive and end with some behavior that depends upon forming an image.

This perspective is not only pervasive, but it is initially hard to conceive how things could be otherwise. Perception, it seems, must begin with encountering something to perceive and end with perceiving it. Memory must begin with something to remember and end with remembering it. This perspective, however, is one that researchers impose. They construe the mind/brain they are studying as a passive responder, simply waiting for their input and producing outputs they can measure. It does not reflect the mind/brain as it functions naturally. As an informal illustration, consider the difficulty that experimenters face in securing cooperation from their subjects. Developmental psychologists have to work hard to maintain children's attention and get them to perform the desired task. Researchers with adult subjects know they often do not follow directions and many times seem to disregard directions intentionally. Other times they try to figure out the task and skew their behavior so as to produce the results they think the researcher is looking for. Their minds/brains are not passive, waiting to respond to the experimental challenge, but active. The experimental task is an intrusion into the ongoing activity of the mind/brain. (See Bickhard & Terveen, 1995, who offer a much broader and systematic diagnosis of what they call "encodingism" and propose to replace it with "interactivism.")

My contention in this chapter and the next is that if mechanistic explanation is to prove adequate for understanding the mind and brain, mental mechanisms must be construed as active. At the end of the chapter I will draw out what this might involve in the case of vision and memory. First, though, I turn to recent threads in thinking about biological systems. These go some way towards building a framework that focuses on active mechanisms. Moreover, they can be taken as providing answers to the objections to explaining biological organisms mechanistically.

6.2   THE VITALIST CHALLENGE TO MECHANISM IN BIOLOGY

Mechanists in biology long confronted a challenge from theorists, often called *vitalists*, who objected that mechanistic accounts were inadequate to account for the distinctive features of living organisms. Mechanistic approaches to physiology proved so successful that by the early-twentieth century vitalism was remembered only for its misbegotten appeals to vital forces or vital spirits. Although some vitalists did posit special powers or forces that they construed as nonphysical, others downplayed the radical nature of their position. They compared their approach to Newton's: just as Newton had deviated from the Cartesian mechanists in appealing to gravitational forces to explain the behavior of ordinary physical objects, the vitalists maintained the need to appeal to vital forces to characterize what happened in living organisms. Just as Newton packaged his account in terms of laws of motion, the vitalists sought the distinctive laws of biology that described the operation of forces in living systems. They insisted they were no more obliged than Newton was to explain these laws in more fundamental terms.

The main significance of the vitalists' challenge was not their alternative explanations, but their focusing attention on features of living organisms that mechanists tended to ignore. Vitalists thus provided an honesty check on mechanists, drawing attention to phenomena of life that were recalcitrant to existing mechanist explanatory strategies. A particularly instructive vitalist in this regard is the French anatomist working at the turn of the nineteenth century, Xavier Bichat. He began his project of explaining the properties of biological organs in the fashion of a mechanist: He proposed a decomposition of living systems into twenty-one different types of tissues that were distinguishable in terms of their sensibility and contractility. These properties, he thought, sufficed to explain why different organs exhibit different behavior. But here, he contended, the explanatory project reached its limit. Bichat highlighted two features of living tissues that he thought thwarted mechanists' attempts to explain organisms purely in terms of their material constitution. First, whereas physical phenomena behave in a deterministic fashion, living systems respond nondeterministically: "The instability of vital forces marks all vital phenomena with an irregularity which distinguishes them from physical phenomena [which are] remarkable for their uniformity" (Bichat, 1805, p. 81). Second, he contended that living tissues engage in activities that oppose the physical forces exerted against them; accordingly, he characterized life as the "sum of all those forces which resist death." This last characterization is particularly potent as it points to the importance of self-initiated action that is directed at maintaining the living organism as a distinct system. The more general feature of living systems is that they maintain themselves as living systems far longer than would be expected of nonliving systems. (Note: this is a relative assessment. Living systems do not maintain themselves forever, but do so longer than comparable nonliving physical systems that do not resist the physical forces exerted against them.)

One way of responding to these objections is to do what the vitalists did: reject mechanism and invoke something else, such as vital forces, to explain living organisms. A second route was taken by most mechanists. They simply ignored vitalists and persevered in the effort to identify the mechanisms responsible for various phenomena in living organisms. This has been an enormously successful strategy, yielding detailed accounts of the component parts and operations of numerous biological mechanisms, their organization, and increasingly, how their functioning is orchestrated in real time. Yet, the challenges of the vitalists have not fully been answered. One way to see this is to focus on the differences between human-made mechanisms and biological organisms. A key difference is that organisms are continuously active. An individual cell is a busy biochemistry laboratory, hosting a multitude of reactions that often impact the size, shape, and components of the cell itself. Cells under a microscope do not remain stationary until something happens; they are in constant motion. The same applies to multicelled organisms—all the way up to the prototypical bird moving through air, fish through water, and mammal over the ground. These not only move, but sense and interpret their environment and coordinate these sensory activities with motoric ones. Human-designed mechanisms, in contrast, are responsive. Compare, for a moment, a computer mouse and a biological mouse. A computer mouse remains stationary until a human moves it or presses its buttons. But a biological mouse is typically moving. Even while asleep, its lungs are moving, metabolism is occurring, and neurons are spiking. When it is awake, it is always looking around, often darting from one place to another. It does not wait for a stimulus before it responds; rather, it is already acting when a stimulus inserts itself into the mouse's ongoing dynamic. Such action is not always in the mouse's best interest; it may encounter a cat as it scampers around a corner. But that cannot be helped; activity is a fundamental feature of mice and other living organisms, us included.

One does not have to be a vitalist to emphasize such features. Tibor Gánti, whose proposal for a minimal mechanism exhibiting the features of life I will describe below, begins by noting points of contrast between biological organisms and extant humanly engineered machines:

> First, living beings are soft systems, in contrast with the artificial hard dynamic systems. Furthermore, machines must always be constructed and manufactured, whereas living beings construct and prepare themselves. Living beings are growing systems, in contrast with technical devices which never grow after their completion; rather, they wear away. Living beings are multiplying systems and automata (at least at present) are not capable of multiplication. Finally, evolution—the adaptive improvement of living organisms—is a spontaneous process occurring of its own accord through innumerable generations, whereas machines, which in some sense may also go through a process of evolution, can only evolve with the aid of active human contribution (Gánti, 2003, pp. 120–121).

Many of these features, such as multiplication and adaptive change through evolution, are salient differences between extant machines and living systems, but the most fundamental of the features Gánti lists is the engagement of living beings in self-construction and growth so that they do not merely wear away or dissipate in the fashion of ordinary physical objects. These capacities must be exhibited by any system that is to be a candidate for reproduction and evolution and are not found in extant machines. Hence, they are critical phenomena for which any viable mechanistic account must offer an explanation. The point of noting these contrasts is not to argue that we will not be able to make mechanisms that share many of the features that now seem distinctive of biological systems. Rather, it is to keep the focus on the features of biological systems, especially those that might be challenging to explain without expanding beyond the construal of mechanism inspired by human-made machines.

Thus, we can do better than the approaches, rooted in the nineteenth century, of rejecting mechanistic science in favor of vitalism or, alternatively, pursuing a basic mechanist program while ignoring what it cannot explain. A third approach to accounting for the seemingly intractable features of living systems is to realize that the initial conception of mechanism is inadequate and develop one that is more capable of explaining living systems. Given the widespread acceptance of mechanistic explanation in the life sciences, this strategy is likely to be more successful than simply rejecting mechanism. Moreover, it is one that has already been pursued by several recent theorists who have explicitly addressed the distinctive features of living organisms. What it requires, though, is that we build into the conception of mechanism at the outset an account of the conditions that must be met by even the simplest biological organisms and link proposed biological mechanisms closely to the satisfaction of these conditions. To assess what these conditions might be, let us return to the objections of Bichat and how they have been addressed by various theorists in the past 150 years.

6.3   FIRST STEPS: THE INTERNAL ENVIRONMENT
AND NEGATIVE FEEDBACK MECHANISMS

The indeterminacy to which Bichat and other vitalists pointed is the easier of the objections for mechanists to answer, as demonstrated by Claude Bernard (1865) half a century after Bichat. Fundamental to Bernard's conception of science was explanation in terms of deterministic causal relations; accordingly, it was critical for his attempt to develop a science of experimental medicine to counter the apparent indeterminism in the activities of living organisms that Bichat had highlighted. The key element in Bernard's response was a focus on the internal *organization* of living systems. He proposed that each internal part of a living organism resides in an *internal environment* that is distinct from the external environment in which the organism as a whole dwells. With this move he could contend that whereas the response of a part of an organism to changes in the external environment might not be regular, strict determinism could be observed in the response by a component to conditions of the internal environment. For example, decreased glucose levels in the blood would regularly produce lowered metabolic activity in somatic tissue. Reduced glucose in the food, on the other hand, would not necessarily show up in reduced metabolic activity as the organism might convert energy stored in other forms, such as fat, into glucose. These other internal activities compensated for or obscured the causal link between external factors and physiological responses of the organism.

The focus on the internal environment also provided Bernard the beginnings of a response to the claim that organisms are not mechanistic insofar as they operate to resist death. The way in which the internal environment provided a buffer between conditions in the external environment and the reactive components of the mechanism, according to Bernard, was by having individual parts of the organism each perform specific operations that served to *maintain the constancy of the internal environment*. They thereby ensured that other component parts of the organism encounter the conditions they need in order to perform their own operations. Thus, he says "all the vital mechanisms, however varied they may be, have only one object, that of preserving constant the conditions of life in the internal environment" (Bernard, 1878, p. 121, translated in Cannon, 1929, p. 400). Insofar as some of its mechanisms are designed to maintain a constant internal environment despite changes in the external environment, a living system can appear as an active system doing things that resist its own demise.

Bernard's insights were built upon in the early-twentieth century by physiologist Walter Cannon (1929). One of his conceptual contributions was to introduce the term *homeostasis* (from the Greek words for *same* and *state*) for the capacity of living systems to maintain a relatively constant internal environment. He also described a number of modes of organization through which animals are capable of maintaining homeostasis. The simplest involves storing surplus supplies in time of plenty, either by simple accumulation in selected tissues (e.g., water in muscle or skin) or by conversion to a different form (e.g., glucose into glycogen) that can be reconverted in time of need. A second means for achieving homeostasis involves altering the rate of continuous processes (e.g., changing the rate of blood flow by modifying the size of capillaries to maintain uniform temperature). Cannon determined that such control mechanisms are regulated by the autonomic nervous system.

Negative feedback is an organizational principle that is crucial to understanding how biological systems are organized to maintain themselves in the face of external challenges. It perhaps was first discovered by Ktesibios of Alexandria around 270 BCE. Ktesibios faced the challenge of ensuring a constant flow of water into a water clock so that he could measure the passage of time by the accumulation of water. To do this he used a supply tank in which he maintained water at a constant level by means of a float that rose into the supply line and cut off the flow into the tank whenever it reached the target level. As water drained out of the supply tank into the collecting tank, the float dropped, allowing more water to enter the supply tank. This was an ingenious solution to a specific problem but it was not recognized as a general design strategy that could be utilized for other problems. As a result, negative feedback had to be repeatedly rediscovered in different engineering contexts in which this form of control was ideal. For example, around 1624 Cornelis Drebbel developed a temperature regulator for furnaces, and in 1745 British blacksmith Edmund Lee developed the fantail as a feedback system to keep the windmill properly oriented (Mayr, 1970).

Famously, James Watt in 1788 rediscovered the idea of negative feedback when he designed the governor, as discussed in the previous chapter, to ensure that the steam supply in his steam engine would be appropriate to keep the various sewing machines attached to it working at a constant speed even as individual machines went on- and off-line. Watt's governor became the focus of a mathematical analysis by James Clerk Maxwell (1868) that helped to establish negative feedback as a general principle for regulating complex systems. The recognition that it could regulate biological as well as engineered systems inspired the cybernetics movement of the 1940s and 1950s. With support from the Macy Foundation, mathematician Norbert Wiener and his collaborators launched a series of twice-yearly conferences known as the Conference for Circular Causal and Feedback Mechanisms in Biological and Social Systems. After Wiener (1948) coined the term *cybernetics* (from the Greek word for "steersman"), it was renamed the *Conference on Cybernetics* and galvanized a broader movement that was interdisciplinary and bold. Early on, for example, Mexican physiologist Arturo Rosenblueth, MIT electrical engineer Julian Bigelow, and Wiener argued that negative feedback provided a means of resuscitating such notions as *purpose* and *teleology* without invoking vitalism (Rosenblueth, Wiener, & Bigelow, 1943). Their idea was straightforward and powerful: If negative feedback enabled the system to maintain a given temperature, then one could view maintaining that temperature as the system's goal or telos.

With the development of the cybernetics movement and of control theory as a central topic in engineering, negative feedback finally came to be viewed as a general design principle. Although enriched by a variety of tools, such as the use of off-line emulators and filtering techniques (Grush, 2004), negative feedback remains at the center of the modern field of control theory. It is also recognized as a general principle in the organization of biological systems that need to regulate themselves. A wide range of chemical reactions occur in even the simplest cells. If these were allowed to run unchecked, the cell would rapidly exhaust its supply of resources. Feedback loops provide a way of ensuring that critical processes, such as the consumption of nutrients to generate ATP, occur only when they are required. Figure 6.2 illustrates negative feedback at the junction between glycolysis and the citric acid cycle (shown in Figure 6.3), which is the chief pathway for oxidizing foodstuffs to produce ATP in most cells. There are pathways leading from nearly every metabolite found in the cell to the citric acid cycle; if these pathways functioned unchecked, all available metabolites would soon be oxidized. The negative feedback loop slows the generation of pyruvate from phosphoenolpyruvate (coupled with the synthesis of ATP) when there is already a plentiful supply of acetyl-CoA waiting to enter the citric acid cycle. When this happens the glycolysis pathway shown in Figure 6.1 above also slows due to the lack of available NAD^+, and glucose is preserved until it is needed.

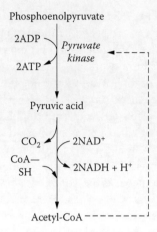

Phosphoenolpyruvate

Figure 6.2   Feedback loop in the linkage between glycolysis and the citric acid cycle. In the final reaction of glycolysis, phosphoenolpyruvate produces pyruvic acid. Pyruvic acid then produces acetyl-CoA, some amount of which is needed to continuously replenish the citric acid cycle (shown in Figure 6.3). If more acetyl-CoA is produced than can be used in the citric acid cycle, it accumulates and feeds back (dotted arrow) to inhibit pyruvate kinase, the enzyme responsible for the first step in the reaction. This in turn will stop glucose from entering the glycolytic pathway (Figure 6.1).

6.4   FURTHER STEPS: POSITIVE FEEDBACK AND AUTONOMOUS SYSTEMS

Especially when it was used to enable thermostats to maintain the temperature in a room or missiles to pursue their targets, negative feedback seemed to enable systems to achieve goals. But in such engineered systems, the goals are imposed on the system by the designer rather than arising out of the system itself. Biological systems appear to set goals for themselves, and setting one's own goals is an important aspect of human mental life in particular. To arrive at systems that set their goals internally, we need to take another conceptual step and consider mechanisms that are intrinsically active. This idea is somewhat strange in a post-Newtonian world in which causation is viewed as efficient causation and in which an efficient cause for each change is sought.[1] A key component for understanding how self-initiating activity is possible in a system of efficient causation

---

[1] In Aristotle, efficient causes were prior events that brought about a given change. The major contrast was with final causes, which were the goals or ends to be achieved by such an event.

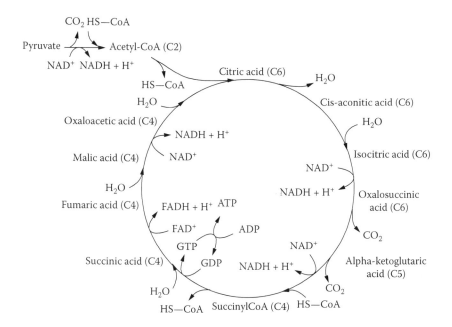

Figure 6.3   The main reactions in the citric acid cycle (also known as the tricarboxylic acid cycle or the Krebs cycle). Acetyl-CoA enters the cycle by combining with oxaloacetic acid to form citric acid, which undergoes a number of reactions, including oxidative ones, until another molecule of oxaloacetic acid is generated, which can then combine with more acetyl-CoA. Shown on the inside of the circle are the reactions in which the oxidation of a citric acid cycle intermediate serves directly to support capture of energy in ATP or the reduction of NAD or FAD, which are then oxidized at the beginning of the electron transport chain, in which ATP is formed.

is once again the idea of feedback, but now *positive feedback* rather than negative. Positive feedback is often viewed as problematic, as it can lead to runaway systems. But in the twentieth century several theorists began to realize that positive feedback loops provide a vehicle for a system to self-organize and perform new activities as a whole system.

A potent example of a positive feedback system that excited much thinking was initially developed by Soviet chemist and biophysicist Boris P. Belousov. He was attempting to develop an inorganic analogue of a central metabolic pathway in all living cells: the citric acid cycle (shown in Figure 6.3; also called the tricarboxylic acid cycle or Krebs cycle). It is cyclic in that a molecule of citric acid undergoes a series of oxidations and other biochemical reactions to produce oxaloacetic acid, which then combines with a molecule of acetyl-CoA to synthesize a new molecule of citric acid. In the course of his research Belousov discovered that when he combined citric acid, acidified bromate (BrO_3^-), and a ceric salt, he created a solution that oscillated between appearing yellow and appearing clear. The idea of a system that continued to oscillate between states violated the general conceptual framework of equilibrium thermodynamics, according to which chemical reactions proceed until a stable configuration is obtained and then stop. Belousov's paper was initially rejected for publication in a journal on the grounds that what he reported was impossible, and appeared only in a relatively obscure volume of proceedings from a conference. Subsequently, biophysicist Anatol M. Zhabotinsky developed a variant on Belousov's reaction, using malonic acid rather than citric acid, and showed that when a thin layer of reactants is left undisturbed, varying geometric patterns such as concentric circles and spirals propagate across the medium, producing a variety of new patterns over a period of time.

Inherently oscillatory phenomena, such as the Belousov-Zhabotinsky (B-Z) reaction, were primarily a curiosity until they were subjected to serious examination by Richard Field, Endre Koros, and Richard Noyes (1972), who articulated a detailed model of the kinetics of such reactions. The key idea is that of coupled autocatalytic reactions, which can be illustrated in the following set of hypothetical reactions (the following account is adapted from Ball, 1994). Assume that you start with a supply of substance A, some of which spontaneously converts to B, which then acts as a catalyst to convert more A to B (a reaction called *autocatalytic* because the reaction creates its own catalyst):

$$A \rightarrow B \qquad\qquad (1)$$

$$A + B \rightarrow 2B \qquad\qquad (2)$$

Assume further that the rate of the reaction is proportional to the concentration of the reactants entering the reaction. In this case, reaction (2) will lead to an ever quicker conversion of A to B as B begins to accumulate, and continue to do so until A is totally consumed. But assume that reactant C is also available and that it figures in the following two reactions, the first of which is also autocatalytic:

$$B + C \rightarrow 2C \qquad\qquad (3)$$

$$C \rightarrow D \qquad\qquad (4)$$

The second pair of reactions serves to reduce the amount of B, and hence the rate at which A is converted to B. In fact, the more C accumulates, the faster these reactions will generate D.

The coupling of these two sets of reactions creates an unstable dynamic which will appear as a visible oscillation if we add an indicator that is red in the presence of B and blue in the presence of C. Initially the concentration of B will rise and the solution will turn red. As the concentration of B increases, more B will be converted to C, which will then catalyze the conversion of even more B to C. As the concentration of C grows and B declines, the solution turns blue. But as C accumulates, it is turned ever faster into D, leading the concentration of C to drop. Now B will not be consumed as rapidly and autocatalytic reaction (2) will lead the quantity of B to increase ever faster. The solution now turns red again. This oscillation between red and blue will continue until the supply of A is exhausted.

Examples of autocatalytic chemical systems, such as the Belousov-Zhabotinsky reaction, produce impressively complex patterns but exhaust themselves as soon as the initial supply of reactants is consumed. Living systems, on the other hand, maintain themselves for extended periods of time. Moreover, successful positive feedback systems seem to require just the right bringing together of needed materials and an energy source. Although such circumstances might arise fortuitously in the natural world, this would be very infrequent. For the idea of autocatalytic systems of reactions to provide insight into how living systems can endure, we need an account of how a system of autocatalytic reactions could maintain itself. The challenge stems from thermodynamics, in which the only stable state is an equilibrium state with all matter and energy equally and randomly distributed. As organized systems of component parts, organisms are not at equilibrium with their environments but will, according to the Second Law of Thermodynamics, move towards an equilibrium state. The only way to avoid this fate is to have a source of free energy. This means that organized systems must be situated between an energy source and an energy sink in order to maintain themselves. But having a source of free energy is not alone sufficient. In order to maintain itself, a system must be able to utilize the energy available in the source so as to keep itself in a nonequilibrium state. This requires some means of transforming the energy available at the source into a form that can facilitate its use in performing the work required to maintain its organization. In a fundamental sense, this is what an organism does: It transforms free energy into a form in which it can perform the work needed to maintain itself.

This reliance on energy to perform work is a point of commonality between human-made machines and living organisms. We build machines to perform work we seek to have done and ensure they have the necessary energy. But the first target of work for a living organism, unlike a machine, is to maintain itself. In accord with the tendency to approach equilibrium, both machines and organisms will tend to break down over time. (One way in which humans have mitigated this problem in their manufactured products is to make them out of solid, rigid components such as steel. Although such machines do experience "wear and tear" and so need repair, the bonds that render them into solids make them less subject to dissipation than structures that arise in a fluid milieu. Nonetheless, over time all human-designed machines do tend to deteriorate.) When human-built machines break down, if we do not simply discard them (symptomatic of an increasingly throwaway society), we summon repair people to restore them. But this is not an option available to organisms; there is generally no external repair person to bring in (doctor and veterinarians are excepted). The organism must repair itself (Collier and Hooker, 1999).[2] A similar line of reasoning applies to development. Except for single-cell organisms that arise from division of existing cells, organisms must execute the processes needed to develop on their own. They must grow their own parts and organize them so as to perform the activities needed to survive.

Francesco Varela (1979), in advancing his notion of *autopoiesis*, emphasized the need of organisms to construct themselves. He arrived at this concept by starting with Cannon's notion of homeostasis and proposing two critical extensions: first, "by making every reference for homeostasis internal to the system itself through mutual interconnections of processes, and secondly, by positing this interdependence as the very source of the system's identity as a concrete unity which we can distinguish" (p. 12–13). In other words, he proposed that all homeostatic operations in organisms are efficiently caused from within the system itself, and it is the continued existence of the set of causally dependent processes that constitutes the continued existence of the system. Varela then offered his canonical characterization of autopoiesis:

> An autopoietic system is organized (defined as a unity) as a network of processes of production (transformation and destruction) of components that produces the components that: (1) through their interactions and transformations continuously regenerate and realize the network of processes (relations) that produce them; and (2) constitute it (the machine) as a concrete unity in the space in which they exist by specifying the topological domain of its realization as such a network (Varela, 1979, p. 13; see also Maturana & Varela, 1980).

---

[2] From considering the requirements on organisms to repair themselves, biologist Robert Rosen (1991) argued that biology needed to reject the broadly Newtonian, mechanistic perspective. The key element in Rosen's argument is that living systems must be "closed to efficient causation." As Rosen conceives of a mechanism, there is always some operation in it which is not caused by other operations within the mechanism but by something external. As Rosen develops the theme of developing causal loops so as to keep all efficient causation within the system, it is clear that what is crucial is the mode of organization within the system. This provides the strategy for a mechanist account to incorporate Rosen's insight; such an account must rely on modes of organization that close the loops of efficient causation. (For discussion, see Bechtel, 2007)

Autopoiesis is important for Varela because autopoietic systems can be *autonomous*, where an autonomous system is one that performs the necessary operations to maintain its own identity:

> Autonomous systems are mechanistic (dynamical) systems defined as a unity by their organization. We shall say that autonomous systems are organizationally closed. That is, their organization is characterized by processes such that (1) the processes are related as a network, so that they recursively depend on each other in the generation and realization of the processes themselves, and (2) they constitute the system as a unity recognizable in the space (domain) in which the processes exist (p. 55).

This notion of autonomy provides a powerful way to conceptualize what is special about living systems. The mechanisms within an autonomous system operate in part so as to maintain the system of mechanisms, and that self-maintaining system of mechanisms has an identity that endures over a stretch of time. But this claim must be qualified in a couple of ways. An autonomous system will not be totally encapsulated but, in important ways, must be open to its environment. What is critical is what the system does in response to impingements from its environment. If the system itself initiates and regulates its responses, then autonomy is maintained. If, on the other hand, an external cause simply imposes an alteration on the system (e.g., a falling rock smashes an organism or wind transports it to a new location), the resulting effects are not due to the system's autonomous action.[3]

Although focusing on the importance of an interrelated network of processes that serve to maintain the system itself in existence, Varela's discussion of autonomy fails to bring to the fore the energetic considerations that apply to such systems. Even if we look at only the basic physical principles of thermodynamics, the tendency of all systems toward higher states of entropy alone requires a living organism to repair itself (restore itself to a lower entropy state) to maintain itself in existence. As I have already noted, such repair imposes thermodynamic demands—the system must procure energy to perform the work needed to maintain itself. Kepa Ruiz-Mirazo and Alvaro Moreno (2004) have made these energetic considerations the focus of their account of autonomy. They begin with the recognition that as organized systems, living systems are far from thermodynamic equilibrium and, in order to maintain that organization, must maintain themselves far from equilibrium (cf. Schrödinger, 1944). Many of

---

[3] In Varela's treatment of autonomy he also seeks to dissociate the system from it material basis by focusing only on relational properties as constituting the system itself: "We are thus saying that what defines a machine organization is relations, and hence that the organization of a machine has no connection with materiality, that is, with the properties of the components that define them as physical entities. In the organization of a machine, materiality is implied but does not enter *per se*" (p. 9). Varela advances this argument by appealing to multiple realizability. I argued against such invocations of multiple realizability in chapter 4. The aspect of Varela's discussion of autonomy I embrace is simply the claim that in an autonomous system the system itself is in control of the operations within it.

the chemical reactions required to develop and repair such a system are endergonic (require Gibbs free energy) and so must be coupled with exergonic reactions that liberate energy from another source. Ruiz-Mirazo and Moreno focus on how the system *manages* the flow of energy so as to provide for its own construction and reconstruction. The boundary between the system and its environment (a membrane in the case of cells) presents one point of management, determining what gets in and out of the system. The metabolic pathways that extract energy and raw materials and then synthesize constituents of the organism's own structure are another. Focusing on these management processes, Ruiz-Mirazo and Moreno characterize *basic autonomy* as:

> The capacity of a system to *manage* the flow of matter and energy through it so that it can, at the same time, regulate, modify, and control: (i) internal self-constructive processes and (ii) processes of exchange with the environment. Thus, the system must be able to generate and regenerate all the constraints—including part of its boundary conditions—that define it as such, together with its own particular way of interacting with the environment (Ruiz-Mirazo & Moreno, 2004, p. 240; see also Ruiz-Mirazo, Peretó, & Moreno, 2004, p. 330).

In what follows, I will adopt Ruiz-Mirazo and Moreno's conception of autonomy. Neither Ruiz-Mirazo and Moreno nor Varela discuss in detail how a system comprised of chemicals might be organized so as to exhibit basic autonomy. Here, the theoretical proposals of the Hungarian chemist Tibor Gánti (1975; 2003) provide a useful complement. Gánti's project is to characterize the simplest system exhibiting key features of living organisms (above I quoted his characterization of what are the distinctive features of living organisms), one he calls a *chemoton*. In developing his account of the chemoton, Gánti takes his lead from actual cells, but simplifies to three fundamental sets of operations (shown in Figure 6.4).

The first of these sets of operations is a mechanism for extracting material and energy from food sources. His attention is especially drawn to the cyclic organization of the citric acid or Krebs cycle (Figure 6.3) that he takes as his model. He initially deemphasizes the importance of new inputs of acetyl-CoA and instead emphasizes that oxaloacetic acid, and all other intermediates, are regenerated by the cycle. That is, the mechanism is one that repeatedly traverses the same states. He represents this by the following notation:[4]

---

[4] This notation, as James Griesemer & Eörs Szathmáry (2007) discuss, was introduced by Gánti so as to draw attention to the stoichiometric requirements of catalyzed reactions. This attention to the flow of matter through the system by balancing eaa need, when dealing with reactions occurring in a fluid milieu, to keep reaction components together in sufficient reaction is an important feature of Gánti's approach.

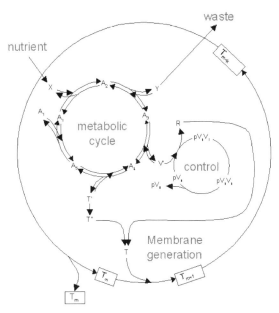

Figure 6.4 Gánti's chemoton—a model of the simplest chemical system exhibiting properties of living organisms.

To show that nutrient material is entering the cycle and waste products are leaving, he expands the notation:

$$\text{Oxaloacetic acid} + CH_3\text{—}CO + 3H_2O \xrightarrow{\text{Krebs}} \boxed{1} \text{Oxaloacetic acid} + 2CO_2 + 9H$$

More abstractly, Gánti uses **A** for the chemical intermediates in the cycle, **X** for the reactants entering the cycle, and **Y** for the reaction products:

$$A + X \xrightarrow{\text{Krebs}} \boxed{1} A + Y$$

For Gánti the citric acid cycle is only the starting point. He views living systems as fundamentally systems that grow; he therefore introduces autocatalytic cycles which, on each iteration, create more of the intermediates than they began with. Gánti claims the malate cycle is an example of such a cycle:

$$A + X \xrightarrow{\text{Malate}} \boxed{1} 2A + Y$$

As the intermediates that figure in this mechanism are soluble, they can easily diffuse through any liquid medium and fail to be present in sufficient concentrations to allow such autocatalytic reactions to sustain themselves. This is one factor that leads Gánti to introduce a second component to the chemoton, a semipermeable membrane.[5] The membrane both isolates the autocatalytic system (ensuring, for example, that the concentration of intermediates is sufficient that ordinary diffusion will bring reactants together) and also helps control the admission and expulsion of materials from the system. (Insofar as it is a selective semipermeable barrier, the membrane itself is a sophisticated and complex mechanism—a nontrivial component for the system to build and maintain.)

It is critical for Gánti's account that the chemoton creates its own membrane. To explain how it might do this, Gánti further amends his account of the metabolic cycle so that it generates not only more molecules of the intermediates on each cycle but also components of the membrane, which Gánti designates as T (as Gánti has now moved into the realm of a purely theoretical cycle, he designates it simply as A):

$$A + X \longrightarrow \boxed{1}^{A} \longrightarrow 2A + T + Y$$

Assuming that the membrane-bound system naturally takes the shape of a sphere, Gánti notes that the stoichiometric relation he proposed would lead to the membrane increasing more rapidly than the volume of metabolites enclosed. He hypotheses that the system will divide into new spheres when the membrane grows sufficiently to close in on itself and bud. Growth and reproduction are for him just the expected consequences of the existence of a metabolic system that makes its own membrane.[6]

The membrane (including membrane generation) and metabolic systems together give rise to a *supersystem* that Gánti claims exhibits biological features:

> We have combined two systems of a strictly chemical character into a "supersystem" (or, to put it another way, we have combined two chemical subsystems),

---

[5] The membrane was not part of Gánti's initial account (see Griesemer & Szathmáry, 2007) and was introduced only as he recognized a need, when dealing with reactions in a fluid milieu, to keep components together in sufficiently high concentrations. Moreover, Gánti's account underplays the role membranes play in actual living cells—he not only provides a way to create distinct environments, but a potent tool for energy storage. In oxidative metabolism, for example, a differential concentration of protons across a membrane, as a result of the oxidations along the electron-transport system, results in a proton-motive force that then drives the synthesis of ATP.

[6] Gánti's account of the membrane is overly simplistic. In order to deal with the osmotic crisis that results from concentration differences inside and outside the enclosure and the tendency of water to spontaneously enter the enclosure, resulting in its swelling and bursting, the membrane must from the outset be active in pumping materials in and out (Ruiz-Mirazo & Moreno, 2004, p. 244).

and we have obtained a system with a surprising new property of expressly bio-logical character. What can this system do? It is separable from the external world and its internal composition differs from that of the environment. It continuously consumes substances that it needs from the environment, which are transformed in a regulated chemical manner into its own body constituents. This process leads to the growth of spherule; as a result of this growth, at a critical size the spherule divides into two equal spherules, both of which continue the process (p. 105).

The supersystem is a system that extracts resources, including energy, from its environment and builds itself, thereby constituting a basic autonomous system in Ruiz-Mirazo and Moreno's sense.

But, according to Gánti, this system is still not living because it lacks an information-storing or control subsystem.[7] Gánti proposes to provide this third capacity by having the metabolic system also add a monomer to a polymer that is built along an existing polymer template. The length of the polymer is thereby able to carry information about the number of cycles completed.[8] Gánti seems to have been led to insist on this third subsystem only because such an information storage system, in the form of DNA, has been found in extant organisms: "This property is not one of the classical life criteria, but on the basis of knowledge gained from molecular biology, it has been selected as an absolute life criterion" (p. 106). Gánti, in fact, says little about what the information system is to be employed for, and one might ask why such an information system is required in a living system. An appreciation of its significance is provided by Gánti's own cou-pling of the notions of *information* and *control*. In the two-component supersys-tem, the metabolic and membrane systems were strictly linked with each other such that as the metabolic system generated products it also produced membrane. This will work as long as the environment of the system continues to provide the system exactly what it needs, regularly removes its waste, and does nothing to interfere with either the membrane or the metabolic process.

Even slight variations in the environment may disrupt such a system. Imagine the environment changed so that a new substance enters the system and reacts with exist-ing metabolites, either breaking down structure or building new additional structure.

---

[7] Griesemer and Szathmáry include marginal notes accompanying Gánti's text, and Gries-emer notes at this point that had Gánti not been focused on a template-based information system, he could have included an information encoding structure within the membrane system by allowing, for example, the incorporation of a variant molecule into the membrane that will be replicated as the membrane is replicated, resulting in what Jablonka and Lamb (1995) describe as a "structural inheritance system."

[8] Griesemer provides some suggestions as to how polymer length carries information. For example, if one molecule is added to the polymer at each turn of the metabolic cycle, it can provide a more reliable indicator of the growth that has already occurred and specify when the next division should occur.

This would disrupt the delicate balance between metabolism and membrane generation that Gánti relies on to enable chemotons to reproduce. What this points to is the desirability of procedures for controlling operations within the system that are not directly tied to the stoichiometry of the metabolic reactions themselves. Although stoichiometric linkages between reactions are effective for ensuring linkages between operations, they do not provide a means for varying the reactions independently. Such independent control can only be achieved by a property not directly linked into the critical stoichiometry of the system.

Griesemer and Szathmáry (forthcoming) provide an account of the stoichiometric freedom that is made possible in the information subsystem Gánti proposes. If, instead of just one type of molecule being combined into the polymer, two or more constitute the building blocks, then the polymer will exhibit both a composition of monomers in specific concentrations and a sequence. The concentrations, like other features of the chemoton, will depend on specific stoichiometric relations. The sequential order, however, will not; it is a "free" property which can then be linked to component operations in the chemoton in other ways so as to control them.[9] Moreover, by providing the chemoton with structures that can be varied and selectively retained, the information subsystem renders the chemoton capable of evolution by natural selection.[10]

Gánti's proposed chemoton is highly speculative. But it does suggest how a system of chemical components might be organized to constitute a basic autonomous system, a system that recruits matter and energy as needed to maintain itself in existence for a sustained period of time. At the core of the model are cyclic processes, ones that repeat themselves indefinitely provided they are supplied with the requisite matter and energy. What cycles do is ensure that materials are directed in appropriate ways within an overall system so that the system remains capable of performing more such operations in the future. Thus, a cyclic system maintains identity while performing work, a basic requirement of any autonomous system.

One of the important features that arises with a basic autonomous system is a naturalized sense of teleology—operations are functional for an autonomous

---

[9] This points to a general consideration regarding control systems: If control is to involve more than strict linkage between components, what is required is a property in the system that varies independently of the basic operations. Particular values of this variable property can then be coordinated with responses by other components so that the property can exert control over the operation of the other component.

[10] Unlike some accounts of evolution (Dawkins, 1976), which treat genes as independent structures whose evolution is essentially independent of the organism, Gánti's approach, as extended by Griesemer and Szathmáry, establishes the critical linkage between the information storage and control system and the basic metabolic processes of the organism or chemoton.

system if they contribute to the system's maintaining itself (Christiansen & Bickhard, 2002). As I noted in discussing cybernetics above, Rosenblueth, Wiener, and Bigelow (1943) had proposed viewing systems that were controlled by negative feedback as goal-directed. Their basic idea was that the endpoint at which a system (usually) arrives via negative feedback is what it is directed towards. In the case of humanly engineered systems, though, the goal seems to be imposed on the system by the designer—the system does not have goals of its own. Subsequently a number of philosophers have suggested appealing to natural selection as a way to ground teleology (L. Wright, 1972; Wimsatt, 1972). The idea is that if a current entity with a specific trait exists because an ancestor was selected to reproduce as a result of having that trait, then the function of the trait is set by the selection forces operative on the ancestor. Just as in the case of engineered negative feedback systems, the teleology is external. The trait does not have the goal or purpose itself, but only in light of its history. The sense of function in an autonomous system, though, is directly linked to the continued existence of the system. As Barandiaran and Moreno (2006) maintain, these "functional descriptions are not merely observer dependent … but intrinsically causal since the very system will not exist otherwise." If the metabolic system in the chemoton, for example, ceases to operate properly, the chemoton itself will cease to maintain itself. And when it dissipates, so will the metabolic system's components. Hence, securing matter and energy is functional for the autonomous system itself, not simply a goal imposed on the system from outside.

6.5   AUTONOMOUS ADAPTIVE AGENTS

In characterizing basic autonomous systems, Moreno and his collaborators focus on what the systems do with the energy and materials presented to them by their environment—they selectively admit matter and energy and use it to maintain their own existence. If the system itself takes no action to procure matter and energy, it must rely on an environment that brings these to it. Sulfur bacteria living near vents in the ocean floor provide examples of systems that rely on their environment to bring them matter and energy as well as to remove their waste products. Such organisms are vulnerable to any changes in the environment that interrupt that supply. Organisms can make their existence more robust if they are able to act so as to secure the resources they need. Accordingly, Barandiaran and Moreno (2006; see also Christiansen and Hooker, 2000) consider several additions to basic autonomous systems to arrive at *adaptive agents*; the account I offer here is inspired by theirs but differs in details. Adding adaptivity and agency involves adding new mechanisms to the basic system, mechanisms that must be built and maintained by the system itself but that, in turn, support the ability of the system to continue maintaining itself. As a result, these mechanisms become part of the identity of the organism, not simply additions on to it. In the sense introduced at the end of the previous section, by helping to secure the continued existence of the autonomous system, such mechanisms perform functions for it.

First, consider adaptivity. While basic autonomous systems are homeostatic, they do not function in fundamentally different ways when their environment changes. But if an organism encounters a variety of environments in which different nutrients are available, it may function better if it produced different enzymes when in these different environments. Producing enzymes that are not used, after all, is costly, and matter and energy are usually in short supply. Environment-sensitive enzyme production may be accomplished by an internal switching system. The lac-operon model, originally put forward by François Jacob and Jacques Monod (1961), provides a means by which bacteria can switch from glucose metabolism to lactose metabolism in low glucose environments. As Barandiaran and Moreno elaborate, such switching systems not only have a goal implicit in their operation (the bacteria switches to lactose metabolism to take advantage of its presence in the environment), but serve to select functions based on how they help realize that goal.

Second, consider agency. Although basic autonomous systems may affect their environment (for example, they may excrete waste products into the environment), they do not alter the environment in ways that promote their own autonomy. But there is no reason that the operations the system performs in order to maintain itself have to occur entirely within its boundaries; the system could, for example, excrete enzymes into its environment to alter substances found there, rendering them more suitable to bring inside itself. Such agency might be possible without adaptivity, but in many environments there are advantages to performing different operations in the environment, depending upon conditions either internal or external to the organism. For example, an organism that has an ability to detect conditions in the environment and to navigate about that environment may well benefit from executing different movements under different conditions. Bacteria, for example, use their flagella to move, and many can execute either a swimming or a tumbling movement. When such a bacterium detects a sucrose gradient through reactions of proteins on its membrane, it uses its flagella to swim up the gradient toward the source of sucrose. At other times it tumbles, thereby sampling a broader range of environments where sucrose might be available. Such a bacterium is thus an *autonomous adaptive agent*; it functions in the environment in an adaptive fashion to promote its own existence.

Autonomous adaptive agents are comprised of mechanisms—mechanisms to capture and transform energy, mechanisms to synthesize new components, mechanisms to locomote, etc. But they also answer the objections of vitalists such as Bichat. Because the various mechanisms are each causally affected most immediately by the other mechanisms within the complex system, their behavior in response to events impacting on the system from without may seem indeterminate. For example, whether or not it metabolizes a compound present in its local environment may depend as much on the current energetic needs of the system as on the availability of the compound in the environment. Moreover, insofar as it is an autonomous system, it is recruiting matter and energy to maintain itself in existence and hence to oppose death. When it is equipped with adaptive capacities, its behavior will be even more successful in extending its lifespan. Finally, recruiting matter and energy and utilizing them to repair and maintain itself are ongoing activities. At a foundational, metabolic level, such a system is always active.

Someone who grants these considerations may still question how important they are for understanding biological mechanisms. The reason they are important is that all biological mechanisms are operative in the highly specialized context of an autonomous organism. An organism is an *organized* system. Organization imposes constraints on the functioning of the component mechanisms. Biological mechanisms are not just organized parts and operations that are responsible for a phenomenon, but are constituents of organisms and are regulated by the organisms in which they exist. Moreover, the continued existence of these mechanisms depends upon the organism; as an autonomous system it must build and maintain all mechanisms comprising it. In thinking about biological mechanisms, we need to look not only inwards at each mechanism's parts, operations, and organization, but also outside each mechanism to consider how it interacts with other mechanisms and how the various mechanisms together enable the organism to operate in its environment in a way that maintains its own existence.

6.6 ADDING MENTAL MECHANISMS
TO AUTONOMOUS ADAPTIVE AGENTS

The autonomous adaptive agents I described in the previous section are far simpler than the sorts of agents investigated by neuroscientists, cognitive scientists, and cognitive neuroscientists. They are mere single-celled organisms without neurons, brains, or minds. Yet, they already exhibit some of the fundamental features that are important to cognitive agents. They act for themselves—for goals of their own. They are adaptive; they select courses of action appropriate for their goals. These are some of the key features of cognitive agents such as ourselves; we make decisions in light of goals that are our own. Moreover, like us, these simple autonomous adaptive agents must secure information about their internal states or their environment to select actions appropriately.

Although lacking minds, such organisms provide the context in which cognition evolved. This has often been ignored in the sciences of the mind/brain, which have taken up the various cognitive phenomena of interest (perception, memory, decision making, etc.) as if they were produced by independent mechanisms not grounded in living organisms. This tendency is most clearly exemplified in traditional artificial intelligence research, which set out to realize such phenomena in computers. But the same tendency characterizes cognitive science and cognitive neuroscience more generally: they attempt to explain each cognitive capacity in terms of how a mechanism could perform in the appropriate way (e.g., encode memories, perceive the world) without considering that these capacities evolved within systems that were already autonomous adaptive agents.

In this section, I will sketch how mental mechanisms might have emerged over the course of evolution in autonomous adaptive agents that initially lacked them. A full account of how mental mechanisms evolved would require an analysis of the phylogeny of the mind/brain, a topic too complex to be addressed here in any detail (for a much more developed discussion, see Allman, 1999). I will, however, focus on a few highlights of that phylogenetic path with the objective of providing context for our thinking about the mind/brain. My contention is that viewing the mind/brain in this context provides a potent corrective to the tendency to think about it as a responsive system—instead, it helps to resituate our thinking about mental mechanisms towards viewing them as constituents of active systems. Each neural or mental mechanism that developed in evolution arose in creatures that were already autonomous adaptive agents.[11] Moreover, the mechanisms manifest themselves behaviorally only as they become integrated into the extant organism and influence its behavior. Each mental mechanism, accordingly, is highly intertwined with the organism's operation as an autonomous adaptive system.

A common pattern of evolutionary change is the creation of multiple copies of an existing mechanism with each then varying so as to operate in a more specialized manner. The result is a division of labor between specialized components. When single-celled organisms such as bacteria arose there already was such division of labor between different parts of the cell. When such cells divide and go their own way as new organisms, each daughter cell retains all the parts and performs all the operations of the parent. But at some point cells divided but remained together. This created new potential for further specialization and division of labor. It also created a new challenge of coordinating the operation of the parts that were now spatially separate. One way to surmount the challenge was for some cells to assume the task of communicating between other cells and ultimately of regulating their operation. A feature already present in each cell

---

[11] It should be noted that this appeal to evolution, unlike that in evolutionary psychology, does not require that mental mechanisms be adaptations in the strict sense. They could well be spandrels (Gould & Lewontin, 1979) as long as they do not seriously undermine the autonomy of the organisms that have them. What I am emphasizing is the context in which new mechanisms develop and the constraints that imposes on them.

provided a starting point for such specialization. The membrane that maintains the environment within cells necessary for such operations as metabolism and synthesis of new parts also segregates ions on different sides of the membrane. This creates a small electrical potential between the interior and exterior of the cell. The establishment of the electrical potential may well have begun as a side effect of producing a membrane, not as a trait serving a function. Even so, it was available to become coopted to serve a function subsequently. If the membrane is breached at a given location, it becomes depolarized first at that location and depolarization can spread along the membrane. In most cells, such depolarization does not spread far, but with modifications such as the development of extended processes (axons), there arises the possibility of long-range electrical transmission that can provide a means for coordinating the activity of other cells. Jellyfish provide an example of an organism in which a network of neurons serves to coordinate the behavior of muscle cells comprising the lower rims of their bodies so that they contract together, forcing out water and propelling the jellyfish forward. By supporting the ability of the jellyfish to swim, it supports the jellyfish's recruitment of new food, which is employed in part in maintaining the neurons themselves.

A point to note about neurons is that they are living cells. As such they are active entities, maintaining themselves in the conditions required for life. That is, like single-celled animals, they recruit matter and energy from their environment (now an environment interior to the organism) and deploy these resources so as to maintain themselves. One of the consequences of this is the maintenance of the electrical potential difference that is required to generate action potentials. A further factor of note is that neurons produce occasional action potentials even in the absence of input from neurotransmitters released by other neurons that synapse on them. This maintains the whole system in a tonic state ready for activity when called upon.

Neurons in jellyfish comprise a diffuse network; there are no chords or ganglia such as found in worms. In worms the most anterior ganglion begins to take on functions we associate with a brain, controlling the movements of other parts of the worm. But, interestingly, such control is often inhibitory and when removed, the worm retains the capacity to move and often will do so continuously. Moreover, flatworms have ocelli or eyespots that send impulses to the brain when exposed to light; the response of the flatworm is to avoid light. In its earliest appearances, the central nervous system seems to involve mechanisms that regulate other components of the body by imposing constraints on their spontaneous activity. Like negative feedback systems, they suppress the operation of parts at times they are not needed or when their operation might interfere with other operations. The control these neural mechanisms provide is in the service of the autonomous adaptive agent, and the ability of specific mechanisms to function depends upon the whole organism securing resources to maintain its own existence. In addition, the brain mechanisms are themselves active as a result of intrinsic activity in individual neurons as they operate to maintain themselves. The first evolved brain mechanisms are thus active components whose functioning is intertwined with the self-maintenance of an autonomous system.

As brains continued to evolve, the same scenario was iterated—new components were fashioned out of existing components which then took on new functions within the autonomous adaptive system constituting the organism. For example, with insects the brain becomes yet more complex, typically consisting of the optic lobes and three specialized segments: the protocerebrum, the deutocerebrum, and the tritocerebrum (Butler, 2000). There is increased division of labor, and each segment is involved in different types of information processing. The optic lobes, and in some cases the protocerebrum, process visual information. The mushroom bodies of the protocerebrum are active in learning and memory, especially for smells, which are initially processed by the antennal lobe in the deutocerebrum. The differentiation of processing centers corresponds to an increasingly rich repertoire of behaviors. The point to be emphasized is that this differentiation of brain structures is coupled with a differentiation of body parts capable of performing different kinds of activities or securing information required for effective performance of those activities. Each brain mechanism is coupled with bodily mechanisms that figure in the life of the agent. The frog's visual system provides a useful illustration. As I discussed in chapter 3, in the 1950s Barlow (1953) and Lettvin, Maturana, McCulloch, and Pitts (1959) focused on one visual mechanism in the frog that enabled it to catch flies. But, as David Ingle (1973) subsequently established, frogs employ a separate visual mechanism when navigating their environment. Each responds to information taken in through the eyes and couples it with the motor components needed to execute the relevant activity. The result is a collection of mechanisms built of active parts that are employed in the activities of an autonomous adaptive agent.

The pattern of three distinct regions in insect brains was preserved in the evolution of vertebrates, where they are commonly characterized as the hindbrain, midbrain, and forebrain. In the hindbrain, the cerebellum developed as a distinctive structure, serving a role particularly in coordinating motor behavior (and, as found more recently, a plethora of more cognitive roles as well). In the mammalian order the neocortex developed out of the front portion of the forebrain. In most mammals, the neocortex is relatively small compared with the remaining parts of the brain, and many of the mechanisms on which mammals rely are housed in these subcortical regions. These mechanisms are often overlooked as the neocortex is sometimes treated as "the brain." But cortical areas are often highly connected with a variety of subcortical areas and are highly dependent upon them. Cortical mechanisms, like subcortical ones, serve regulative and control functions in autonomous adaptive agents and are integrated into the lives of such agents.

As I discussed in the previous chapter, in the nineteenth century John Hughlings Jackson (1884) offered a very suggestive way of viewing the evolution of new brain structures according to which they serve primarily to coordinate the operation of already extant brain mechanisms. The point to emphasize now is that these more recently evolved mechanisms perform their functions just as the earliest evolved neurons did—as active mechanisms, maintaining themselves and executing their operations within the context of the rest of the organism. The active nature of these mechanisms, moreover, is not incidental to the functions they perform. Their internal activity provides the building blocks which evolution could employ in crafting mechanisms that enable the organisms possessing them to maintain themselves in existence.

6.7   MODELING THE MIND/BRAIN WITH ACTIVE MECHANISMS

Adopting the perspective that the mind/brain consists of active mechanisms, not merely responsive mechanisms, has the potential to change how researchers in the sciences of the mind/brain approach their explanatory endeavors. To illustrate, in this section I offer an example of how some researchers have approached the project of understanding visual processing differently as a result of viewing the components in the system as active mechanisms.

Most connectionist or neural network accounts of how systems of neurons can perform mental activities take individual neurons as inactive unless they receive input. But as we have seen, neurons in living organisms are not quiescent. They maintain a basal or intrinsic firing rate in the absence of stimulation, a rate which may be modulated up or down given inputs. Accordingly, they can be viewed as oscillators, as systems that alternate between different states (one can also view a network of neurons as an oscillator). Recall that when Belousov identified a set of chemical reactions as oscillating, editors to whom he submitted the paper responded that such oscillating reactions are impossible. Subsequent investigation showed that such reactions are possible, but they rely on positive feedback cycles. This suggests a way to model neurons as oscillators: Assume a positive feedback of a neuron on itself so that its future behavior depends at least in part upon its past activity. This might result in a neuron that continues to spike once per second unless it receives a stimulus that increases or decreases its spiking rate. However, such a regular oscillation turns out to be far less useful for information processing than one that is more irregular. An activation function that has been used effectively in modeling neural behavior is the logistic map function. A map is a type of function in which values are iteratively determined in discrete time based on the previous value of the function. In its simplest version,

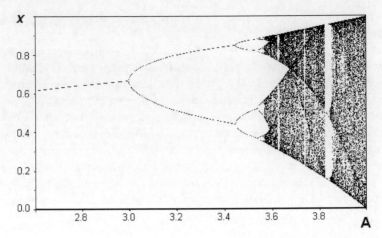

Figure 6.5 Plot of the logistic function for values of A between 2.6 and 4.0. For values of A less than 3.0, the function settles into a point attractor. Above 3.0 the attractor bifurcates into two attractors, with successive values of the function falling into different attractors. It then bifurcates into four attractors, then eight, and so forth. Beyond 3.6 it enters a chaotic regime in which each successive value is distinct. The region beyond 3.6 is punctuated by narrow ranges in which there are again periodic attractors.

the logistic map simply updates the activation of a unit (a) based on its previous activation using the following equation:

$$a_{t+1} = A \, a_t \, (1 - a_t)$$

As shown in Figure 6.5, depending on the value of the parameter A, this function results either in the unit settling to a fixed activation (values of A < 3.0), generating a periodic oscillation through a limited number of values (most values of A between 3.0 and 3.6), or exhibiting chaotic behavior (most values of A > 3.6).

The spiking of an individual neuron has efficacy only insofar as it synapses on other neurons and contributes to the generation of action potentials in these other neurons. One way to model the interactions of neurons viewed as oscillators is to couple them. Kunihiko Kaneko (1990) explored the behavior of networks of oscillators that he termed a *coupled map lattice*. A lattice is a sparsely connected network in which the couplings (connections) can be viewed as topologically arranged such that neighbors are coupled and other units are not. Kaneko used the logistic map function as the activation function and determined that such networks could exhibit a variety of types of behavior depending on the values assigned to various control parameters, including synchrony across units (i.e., all units in a cluster go through the same sequence of activation values, even if that sequence is chaotic) and chaotic behavior across chaotic units (chaoto-chaotic emergence).

Kaneko's focus was not specifically on modeling the mind/brain, but Cees van Leeuwen and his colleagues have adapted Kaneko's coupled map lattices to model perceptual processes (van Leeuwen, Steyvers, & Nooter, 1997; Raffone & van Leeuwen, 2001). Critically, the networks they employ exhibit complex dynamical behavior involving synchronized and desynchronized activity prior to being connected to sensory stimuli. The activation of a unit at a given processing cycle is determined by the total input (*netinput*) to the unit, which is a function of the previous activation of the unit (a_x) and of the other units to which it is connected (a_y):

$$netinput_x = \sum Ca_y + (1 - C)a_x$$

In this equation, C is a coupling parameter that determines how much the activation of a unit is affected by its own previous state and how much by the states of other units. The activation of a unit is then computed by the equation:

$$a_{x,t+1} = A\ netinput_{x,t}\ (1 - netinput_{x,t})$$

As before, the value of A determines whether the units behave chaotically. Even with values of A that generate chaotic behavior, the units can still synchronize, but when they do, they will also have a tendency to decouple.

The basic behavior of such a system can be illustrated in a network with just two units. The units are synchronized when the difference between their activation values at each time-step is zero. Even if the units start out unsynchronized, the difference between their activations will decrease monotonically to zero when C falls into a range defined in terms of A:

$$\tfrac{1}{2}(1 - 1/A) < C < \tfrac{1}{2}(1 + 1/A)$$

Outside this range, the difference may be a constant or vary periodically, quasiperiodically, or chaotically. Of particular interest are values for which the difference varies *intermittently*, alternating between zero (a semistable state of synchronization) and a chaotic sequence of values (wandering through state space until the difference temporarily becomes zero again). The same phenomenon arises in larger networks in which there are couplings between units in a local neighborhood. With appropriate values of A and C, small groups of units will synchronize their behavior for periods of time before again desynchronizing. Note that this activity is completely intrinsic to the network—it is not being driven by external inputs but by the activation function governing the individual units.

To employ such a coupled map lattice to model perceptual tasks, units must be responsive to external inputs. Van Leeuwen and his colleagues viewed each

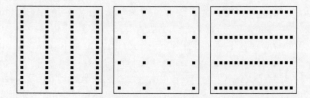

Figure 6.6   Stimuli used in van Leeuwen, Steyvers, and Nooter (1997). If the gestalt principle of symmetry is used to group items, the black squares in the left display will be grouped vertically and those in the right display horizontally. Those in the center display, however, will be ambiguous and subjects may alternate between grouping them vertically and grouping them horizontally.

unit as having a receptive field and treated A not as a fixed parameter but as a variable that is reduced by the presence of an input in its receptive field. Having input reduce the value of a variable seems counterintuitive at first, but lower values of A tend to push a unit into a less chaotic regime where it is more likely to synchronize with other units. This causes connected units that receive external input to synchronize their behavior. To further increase synchronization, the parameter C was replaced by variables representing adaptive weights for each connection. When the activation sequences of two units begin to synchronize, the weight between them is increased; this favors greater synchronization in the succeeding time-steps. As a result, synchronization that initially just happens to occur between two chaotic sequences gets grabbed and used by the system to move it towards more structured activity. In a sense, the weights serve as a short-term memory of recent synchronization that helps to reinstate that synchronization. With this occurring across multiple pairs of units simultaneously, the system can advance towards larger clusters within which all units are synchronized.

Van Leeuwen and his collaborators have employed such networks to interpret visual input patterns such as those shown in the panels of Figure 6.6, interpreting the black squares on the left as forming vertical lines and those on the right as forming horizontal lines. In these cases van Leeuwen's network exhibited behavior that would be desired in any pattern recognizing network. It reveals its distinctive characteristics when presented with stimuli such as that in the middle panel. With such stimuli the inputs plus the internal dynamics of the network prevent it from settling into synchronous firing representing just one interpretation—rather, after beginning to settle, it escapes and begins to settle into a competing pattern of synchronous firing. In this behavior, van Leeuwen et al.'s network captures a well-documented phenomenon involving the perception of ambiguous figures. When humans examine figures such as the Necker cube they experience spontaneous shifts between the alternative interpretations. Such shifts are not triggered by any change in the stimulus, and so must be manifestations of the visual system's processing.

Van Leeuwen et al.'s network illustrates a very different way of thinking about mental mechanisms. Coupled map lattices such as he employs are active systems in that they exhibit behavior even in the absence of external stimulation. External stimuli serve only to modulate the ongoing behavior of the system. This is not to deny that the function for the organism of visual processing is to provide it with information about its environment. But it secures that information in the process of executing its own activities. One consequence of adopting this view is that the information from the senses is not simply processed and stored, but modulates the operation of the visual system. The visual system adapts its operation as a result of visual input. That entails that the information itself is being actively incorporated into the activities the system produces; it is not just being absorbed by the system.

6.8 ACTIVE VISION AND ACTIVE MEMORY

The proposal advanced in this chapter to reorient the way mental mechanisms are conceptualized from responsive to active coheres well with developments in research on vision and memory. In this final section I will identify some of these connections so as to illustrate more fully what the view of active mechanisms entails.

The traditional approach in vision research, illustrated by the program of David Marr but also exemplified in much of the neuroscience inquiry into vision described in chapter three, regards vision as constructing a full representation of the visual scene before the viewer. This representation would then be the basis of further reasoning and ultimately of action, activities carried out by different mechanisms. Churchland, Ramachandran, and Sejnowski (1994) characterized this as the approach of *pure vision*, capturing the idea that visual processes were independent and prior to other activities, especially motor activities.[12]

---

[12] Churchland, Ramachandran, and Sejnowski present their account of pure vision as a caricature, but offer the following two quotations as illustrative of the way visual processing came to influence research in artificial intelligence: John K. Tsotsos (1987) says, "The goal of an image-understanding system is to transform two-dimensional data into a description of the three-dimensional spatio-temporal world" (p. 389). In a review of computer vision in *Science*, Yiannis Aloimonos and Azriel Rosenfeld (1991) quote this characterization and add, "Regarding the central goal of vision as scene recovery makes sense. If we are able to create, using vision, an accurate representation of the three-dimensional world and its properties, then using this information we can perform any visual task" (p. 1250).

They advocated instead a perspective that they called *interactive vision,*[13] according to which other mental mechanisms, especially those involved in motor action, figure in vision. On this view, vision only samples information from a small part of the visual scene at a given time, is constantly predicting what its input will be on subsequent samples, and relies on constant movement of the eyes to secure new perspectives.

The themes underlying the interactive perspective on vision have been developed by a variety of researchers. It has long been recognized that the fovea, a small portion of the retina which occupies one to two degrees of the visual field, contains very densely packed cones but no rods, and as a result we have an order of magnitude greater acuity there than in the rest of the visual field. If we and other organisms can secure high-resolution information only for a small portion of our visual field, how do we get information about different locations? The eye moves to focus on those locations in what are known as *saccades.* Although saccades have been extensively studied using tools such as eye trackers to determine how the eye samples various parts of visual sciences, until recently they have not figured in the analysis of how the visual system processes information from the scene. In the early 1990s Dana Ballard (1991) introduced an alternative conception of vision he called *animate vision,* which emphasized the value of the ability of organisms to shift their gaze to sample information acquired by the fovea. He maintained that, contrary to what might be assumed, computational demands are significantly less for an animate vision system that controls and directs its gaze than for a system that builds a complete representation of the scene and employs it in its actions.

Not only are the eyes of a perceiver moving and sampling a scene, but in most situations the perceiver itself is moving. This is a feature that James Gibson (1979) emphasized in developing his ecological approach to perception. He investigated the sorts of information a perceiver could procure by moving in its environment. *Optic flow* refers to the manner in which the perceived image changes as a result of the relative movement of the objects and the perceiver. Such relative movement sometimes arises from the movement of the perceived objects. For example, as an object rotates, the increasing and decreasing size of features of the object in the resulting retinal image enable perceivers to identify its three-dimensional structure (a phenomenon named the *kinetic depth effect* by Wallach & O'Connell, 1953). Optic flow, though, also results when the perceiver moves and

---

[13] Related views have appeared in the literature employing similar terms. For example, Alva Noë (2004) refers to his view as *enactive perception,* a name he borrows from Varela, Thompson, and Rosch (1991). In Noë's usage, the emphasis is on the role of action and on the ability to act on what we see: "*What we perceive* is determined by *what we do* (or what we know how to do); it is determined by what we are *ready* to do. In ways I try to make precise, we *enact* our perceptual experience; we act it out" (Noë, 2006).

the object stays stationary. For example, as a perceiver approaches a point, the points around it will appear to spread out in the visual field (an effect known as looming; the reverse happens if the perceiver is retreating from a point). Perhaps more interesting, if an observer is moving orthogonal to the object she is observing (e.g., looking at a haystack while driving down a country road), everything closer than the object will move opposite the direction of motion while everything further will move in the direction of motion. The speed of movement in the visual field corresponds to the relative distance to the observed object. More complex patterns result from less regular movement, such as the up-and-down motion obtained from walking, or walking on a curved path. Gibson himself developed these principles in application to the navigation of flying and swimming organisms, including humans engaged in flying airplanes (Gibson, Olum, & Rosenblatt, 1955), an approach pursued further by many subsequent researchers (Loomis & Beall, 1998). Gibson also emphasized how objects in real-world scenes commonly occlude each other, but that by moving about, a perceiver can determine how the objects are positioned vis à vis each other.

In these various ways, an active perspective on the process of perception explains how perceivers are able to secure rich information about the world. But I should emphasize that moving in space is not initiated just so as to secure information; moving is something perceivers are already doing as autonomous adaptive agents. Information received through the eyes as well as other senses helps to modulate these ongoing activities. One aspect of an organism performing ongoing activities, noted in Churchland et al.'s characterization of interactive vision, is that it forms expectations of what it will see in the future. These predictions serve not only to facilitate selection between possible movements but also provide a powerful basis for learning. A standard approach in neural network modeling has been to have a network generate a response and then alter the weights on connections within the network to reduce the difference between the actual response and a target response. A challenge to such error-correction approaches is to account for the network's access to the correct target response. An alternative that is very powerful is to have the network learn to predict its next input; when that input arrives, it is in position to execute error correction. Assuming that there is some order to the inputs, as there would be if they originate from a structured environment which the network was sampling (e.g., by being incorporated in a robot-body that was moving through the environment), the network has the capacity to learn on its own (Nolfi & Parisi, 1993).

Adopting the perspective that vision relies on active mechanisms within autonomous adaptive systems that maintain themselves through engagement with their environments allows us to understand some features of vision that have often been noted, but seem mysterious, especially when vision is viewed as a process that responds to visual input by building up a visual representation.

Some things, for instance, are hard to see even if they are presented right in front of us and are not much different from ordinary objects that we have no difficulty seeing. For example, if a person flashes playing cards in front of you, and one of them is a four of spades, but the spades on the card have been colored red, you will likely not see it for what it is but rather as a four of hearts (Bruner & Postman, 1949). If presented for a slightly longer period of time, you might register that something seems wrong but still identify it as a four of hearts. At longer presentation intervals, you are more likely to recognize the card, but sometimes you may never recognize it for what it is unless someone points out that it is unusual. If seeing were purely a reaction to the stimulus presented, there should be no more difficulty in seeing a red four of spades than a black one. But vision, as this example suggests, seems to be driven in part by expectations of the perceiver. In another telling example, Irving Biederman (1981; Biederman, Mezzanotte, & Rabinowitz, 1982) showed subjects pictures with ordinary objects, such as a sofa floating in the air or a fire hydrant on top of a mailbox, and found that subjects took longer to identify and sometimes misidentified the objects in positions where they were not expected. This finding is challenging to explain when vision is construed as a passive response system but is expected if it is a process guided by expectations.

Another puzzling visual phenomenon that makes sense once we regard perception as involving active mechanisms in perceivers that are actively engaging their environments is change blindness.[14] In a pioneering study, Ulric Neisser (1979) presented subjects a video in which two groups of players, one dressed in white and one in black, each tossed a basketball among themselves. The groups were intermixed in the focal area of the video, and the subjects were instructed to keep track of the players in white and count the number of times the ball changed hands between them. While subjects watched the video, a person dressed in a dark-colored gorilla outfit walks into the scene, turns and does a quick dance for the audience, and then exits. Most of those attending to the players in white fail to notice the gorilla. More recently other studies have shown that we often fail to note changes even in prominent features of scenes. For years filmmakers have been able to get away with editing errors in scenes shown in sequence without the audience noticing changes, and in the 1990s Daniel Simons and his colleagues subjected this to experimental study. In one particularly striking example the only actor in a video is replaced during a scene change (while exiting a room to answer a phone in the hall) by another who looks distinctly

---

[14] The name *change blindness* is due to Ronald Resnick, who pioneered the technique of showing two variations of a scene in alternation with a short exposure of a blank scene separating the two views. Subjects find it very difficult to notice the change (Resnick, O'Regan, & Clark, 1997).

different (Levin & Simons, 1997). The phenomenon is not restricted to video. Simons also showed that people often failed to note a change in the person from whom they are asking directions (Simons & Levin, 1998). There are now several competing theories as to what makes some changes very difficult to detect, with some theorists maintaining that the phenomenon demonstrates the absence of visual representations (O'Regan & Noe, 2001), others that the representations are sparse (Simons & Levin, 1998), and still others focusing on the processes involved in making comparison between representations (Mitroff, Simons, & Levin, 2004). Whatever the correct explanation of change blindness, it suggests that the passive view of perception as simply registering what is presented is incorrect. Seeing, including seeing changes, is an activity, one that sometimes occurs automatically as the visual system operates and sometimes requires conscious effort. The visual system is driven by its internal dynamics and determines which external inputs are responded to and how.

I turn briefly to memory, which has often been construed as involving the passive recording of material to be remembered, the storage of the recording, and recovery of it when cued. But, as I noted in chapter two, the discovery of the many ways in which people produce false memories suggests a much more active process. First, the strategy for inducing false memories of hearing words by presenting their closest associates indicates that subjects are actively processing stimuli as they are recording them. Second, the fact that queries in the interval between encoding and retrieval can alter what people later remember about a scene they witnessed indicates that memories are stored in a volatile manner in which they are still subject to cognitive processing. Finally, mismatches between content on the Watergate tapes and the rich details that John Dean reported in all sincerity regarding his encounters with President Nixon suggest that memory recall involves active construction of plausible accounts of events. All of these phenomena fit more readily into an account in which experiences modulate active mental processes in ways that affect later behavior than one in which items are placed in storage and later retrieved.

The examples I have cited from research on visual processing and memory provide further support for the perspective on mechanisms I have advanced in this chapter, according to which mechanisms are not responsive systems waiting to be activated by a stimulus, but active systems. I motivated this perspective by turning to biology, and in particular to an objection vitalists advanced to mechanistic accounts of life according to which living organisms operate to oppose physical phenomena that would otherwise destroy them and hence are themselves not physical. Rather than showing the error in the mechanist perspective, such phenomena point to the need to focus on the modes of organization found in biological systems. The organization must be such as to enable the system to recruit matter and energy from the environment and utilize it to make and repair itself. In order to maintain themselves in the face of variable environments, such biological systems usually incorporate mechanisms that enable them to be agents altering their environment and adapting to the requirements of different environments. A critical feature of autonomous adaptive agents is that they are active systems, continuously engaging in the activities requisite to maintaining themselves in far from equilibrium states.

Autonomous adaptive agents provide the biological foundations for mental mechanisms, which are further accoutrements that enable such systems to better maintain themselves. Such mechanisms are built using neurons, cells that are themselves autonomous adaptive systems that operate in the context of larger autonomous adaptive systems. As parts of larger autonomous systems, they function to regulate other mechanisms, inhibiting or down-regulating certain mechanisms when they are incompatible with the operation of other mechanisms. When functioning as control systems, they do not need to initiate activity; the mechanisms in the organism are already active. The neurons comprising mental mechanisms are active components, ensuring that the mental mechanisms are themselves active mechanisms. I provided an example of recent modeling that employs such active units and drew attention to psychological phenomena highly congenial to a focus on active mechanisms. Active mechanisms, though, exhibit yet another attractive feature: They provide a basis for addressing the objection that understanding humans in terms of mental mechanisms deprives them of their freedom and dignity as moral agents. I develop this feature in the next chapter.

Seven

Confronting Mechanism's Critics

Accounting for Freedom and Dignity via Mental Mechanisms

The prospect that our mind/brain consists of an organized collection of mechanisms and that our behavior is determined by the causal operation of these mechanisms is, to many people—scientists, philosphers, and lay people alike—threatening to their sense of dignity and personal worth. This is true even when it is acknowledged that the mechanisms in question are unimaginably complex, the most complex yet dealt with by any science. Conceiving of ourselves as constituted of mechanisms may seem to deny too many things we hold dear about human life—that we are free agents, that we have values and direct our lives according to them, and that we enjoy a special sort of dignity as human beings. Theorists otherwise committed to treating the human mind/brain as an object of scientific inquiry, such as Kant and James, have contended that when it comes to living our lives as human beings we must reject the causal mechanical perspective and adopt a different framework. For those purposes, they contended, we must view ourselves as free, autonomous, responsible agents and deny (or overlook) that we are made up of mechanisms. Being an organized set of mechanisms, it seems, is incompatible with being free and dignified agents in the world.

Skinner (1971) notoriously maintained that we need to abandon the false ideals of freedom and dignity, ideals originating in the Enlightenment and perpetuated by a misguided mentalistic conception of people. Instead we should focus on how to shape contingencies in the environment such that people live the most harmonious and productive lives possible. Many critics see Skinner's conception of the ideal life as a reductio of the causal mechanical framework. My contention is the opposite of Skinner's—rather than reject freedom and dignity as false ideals to be jettisoned once we have a proper understanding of the causal processes operative in human behavior, I maintain that a proper understanding of these causal processes enables us to affirm a conception of humans as agents with the appropriate freedom to act responsibly and to possess personal dignity. In defending this view I will argue that, although naïve or simplistic accounts of mechanism are incompatible with freedom and dignity, the mechanistic framework, especially as I have enriched it in the last chapter, has the resources to account for these characteristics of human life. When we understand mechanisms as parts of active systems, we can show how these systems can exhibit the sort of freedom human agents actually possess and can act based on their own values and enjoy the dignity associated with agency. My contention is stronger than merely showing the compatibility of mechanism and a conception of human life as involving freedom and dignity. Our capacity to be free, autonomous, responsible agents arises not in spite of but in virtue of the kind of mechanisms that constitute us. It is our mental mechanisms in particular that make us autonomous adaptive agents who can enjoy freedom and dignity.

The discussion in chapter four developed an important feature of the analysis of mechanisms for purposes of understanding how being constituted of mechanisms can enable us to be free, autonomous, responsible agents. There, I developed the idea that due to their organization and the environment in which they operate, mechanisms as wholes are capable of things their parts are not. In the particular case of us as agents, we are not identical to the parts or operations of any of the mechanisms that constitute us. We are, rather, the whole that is comprised of such mechanisms. And what we do as a whole is engage with our environment, including other people, and from such engagement we develop in particular ways, acquire memories, and embed ourselves in specific social networks.[1] This last sentence highlights a further feature of mental mechanisms: They are plastic mechanisms that develop and change as a result of experience. Every waking moment of our lives sensations impinge on us that alter conditions in our brain. But we are not just being passively sculpted by our environment. Brains are active systems that reorganize themselves, so that the results of impingements from outside are the substrate for further internal operations, and often actions that alter the environment. The mind/brain is an active, dynamically changing system.

Accordingly, when we want to understand how it is that we are able to operate as free and responsible agents, we need to consider not just the components that constitute our mental mechanisms, but how as an integrated system we engage our environment and the consequences of those engagements for the mechanisms that constitute us. Some of our engagements are with various social networks which

---

[1] The relationship is comparable to that between a component mechanism and a larger mechanism—the component mechanism comes to be, in important respects, governed by the incorporating mechanism. Just how appropriate and fruitful it is to view social systems as mechanisms is a topic beyond the focus of this book. But clearly some social systems have characteristics of mechanisms; they are coordinated systems constituted of individuals that perform a variety of operations. Of special importance is the fact that they are organized and, as a result, feed back upon their constituents and constrain their behavior.

embody a culture. We both affect that culture through our own activities and are affected by it. In part, our values are shaped by the culture in which we develop and live. But this shaping is not merely passive. We as active agents select from what our culture offers and modify pieces of it. Moreover, we routinely employ features of our environment in our activities, allowing us to accomplish more than we might on our own. To take just one example, in preparing this text I made use of the resources, especially linguistic, that my culture provided. Moreover, writing is not just a process of outputting already structured thoughts. It involves putting new sentences and paragraphs together, reading them back, revising them, and so forth. This process is interactive. I construct sentences on the computer screen, but then interact with those external representations I have constructed. I am engaged in an ongoing, dynamical interaction with these representations.

The fears about mechanism, however, are deeply entrenched and not easily conquered. If I am to overcome the resistance to conceiving of ourselves as constituted of mental mechanisms, I need to identify and address those factors that make threatening such a conception of ourselves. At the core of many of these objections are traditional philosophical concerns about determinism. If we are constituted of mechanisms, and mechanisms are causal systems that behave as they do because of their constitution, their history, and their current sensory stimulation, then it seems that we cannot do anything other than what these causal factors determine that we will do. Indeed, as I have presented them, mechanisms are causal systems, and there seems to be no possibility of a mechanism doing something other than what it is determined to do. But for us to be free, autonomous, responsible agents, many think it must be possible for us to do something other than what we are determined to do. We must make free judgments as to what is appropriate and then be able to act on these judgments. Otherwise, we are mere automata, not free agents who can be held responsible for our actions.

Relaxing the principle of causal determinism and envisaging that the responsible mechanisms operate probabilistically will do nothing to answer this concern. If anything, it makes things worse. If we are constituted of mechanisms that behave probabilistically and the probabilities are conceived of as purely chance-like, then our behavior is due to chance events. It is still not the result of free and responsible choices. Introducing chance in the operation of a mechanism does nothing to secure what is needed to provide for autonomous and responsible agency. To do that, I must confront head-on the main objection and show how deterministic mechanisms are compatible with personal autonomy and responsibility.

7.1   DETERMINISM AND AGENCY

A common conception of what is required for personal autonomy and responsibility is that agents must be free in the sense that their actions are not caused. The challenge for the advocate of this position is to make clear what it would be for an action (or a decision to act) to be uncaused and to show that such uncaused activity has the right features to account for responsible action. Let's begin by trying to conceive of something happening that has no causal ancestry but does not seem to involve mental activity. Perhaps a red balloon just pops into existence in front of you as you read this book. Such an occurrence would appear problematic as it does not just involve a change happening with no cause, but something coming into existence *de novo*. Not only would this seem to violate the conservation of mass and energy, it also would not seem to give us any grip on understanding free action.

Free actions must be the actions of agents. Moreover, these actions must, in some way, depend on the agent and his or her values and beliefs. Consider another example: your coffee cup, which was on the table beside you, begins to move away. It is not just sliding on a slippery surface, but seemingly moving from its own initiative. You retrieve it, but when you turn your attention elsewhere, it starts to move away again. This seems a more likely candidate to illustrate free action. But if a coffee cup just moved spontaneously, and try as we might we could not explain its activity, we would probably regard it as simply mysterious. To begin to see it as engaged in free action we need more than uncaused action. We need an explanation of why it moved away, an explanation we would typically couch in terms of beliefs and desires. Try to take seriously for a minute the phenomenon of your coffee cup doing things that you cannot explain. The tendency in such a situation is to begin to suspect that it is really animate, or enchanted, and to begin to attribute a mind to it. The coffee cup might, for example, be expressing its profound disgust that you are sitting at a table rather than doing your usual 5K run. Notice, though, that in attributing to it beliefs and desires, we are providing a reason for the coffee cup to be moving away. On many standard interpretations, reasons are causes—conditions which increase the likelihood of certain consequences. If we pursue this strategy, we are no longer thinking of the cup's behavior as uncaused. Rather, we are thinking of it as having a certain kind of cause—a reason.

What this seems to indicate is that if someone does something for no reason, but just does it without any causal processes involved, we are not presented with an exemplar of free, autonomous, responsible agency. Note further that before we treat something as an agent performing its own actions, the causal processes must be appropriately linked to the agent itself. If, on further investigation of the mysteriously moving coffee cup, you discovered that someone else had engineered things to move the coffee cup—perhaps they had set up a sophisticated magnetic system which they controlled so as to start the cup in motion when your attention was diverted—you would no longer think of the coffee cup as the agent. The action must start from causes within the agent; otherwise they are not actions for which the agent is responsible. As Hume noted, "Where [actions] proceed not from some cause in the characters and dispositions of the person, who perform'd them, they infix not themselves upon him, and can neither redound to his honor if good, nor infamy, if evil" (Hume, 1739; Selby-Briggs, p. 411).

Reflections such as these suggest that to understand free agency we should not reject causation, but rather focus on the type of causation that is involved. But what has led so many people—philosophers and others—to see causality as incompatible with free, autonomous, responsible agency? Presumably it is the assumption that if behavior was caused, it was not due to the agent. A common way of characterizing what it is for an agent to be morally responsible for her actions is to maintain that whatever action the agent actually performed, she *could have done otherwise*. In many respects, this is a very reasonable demand. If the agent was, for example, pushed into another, tripping that person, then it seems unfair to hold the agent responsible for tripping the other person. But it is not straightforward to explicate the notions of *being forced* and *could have done otherwise*. When one rejects an action as not being a reflection of free, autonomous, responsible agency on the grounds of being forced, one typically has in mind something like externally applied force. If someone else makes you give your money to charity, either by forcing your hand to take hold of your wallet and to give it to someone or by threatening you, you do not get moral credit for giving to charity. Likewise, if someone directly controls your mind/brain, either through mind-control techniques or through direct chemical or electrical stimulation of your brain, the resulting behavior is not an expression of free, autonomous, responsible agency.

Such cases seem unproblematic defeaters of free agency. But what about a case where a person could not have done otherwise than to give to charity because that is just the kind of person she is? Let's not envisage an obsessive giver but one who gives in moderation, as a result of her deepest values. We might imagine that this person will justify her actions, if asked, in terms of the importance of insuring the welfare of the less fortunate and, if further pressed, will develop a detailed and coherent moral and political philosophy. She is able to understand and even articulate reasons for not giving to charity, but rejects them with cogent counter-arguments of her own. On the basis of such reflections, she cultivated in herself the habit of giving to charity and typically now does not engage in serious deliberation when opportunities to give to charity arise. She simply gives. Such a person might not have been able to do otherwise than to give to charity on a given occasion, at least without fundamentally changing the person she is. But even though she could not have done otherwise in this sense, this person seems to be an exemplar of a free, autonomous, responsible agent, not of an agent who is being forced to do something.

The requirement of being able to do otherwise, therefore, must be appropriately articulated. One might try the following: one would have done otherwise if, after appropriate deliberation, one had chosen to do otherwise. Not all acts of free, autonomous, responsible agents are the products of deliberation. We have neither the time nor resources to deliberate in all cases where action is possible and, as James noted, must rely on developed habits. A person might have developed the habit of giving a certain amount of her resources to charity. But such a person is still capable of deliberating—of considering whether the need to pay her upcoming tuition bill justifies her in not giving to charity on this occasion. She might reason that she could do more in the long term if she completed her education in a timely manner and so withhold her contribution. When actions are responsive to such deliberation, then perhaps it makes sense to construe them as an expression of our free, autonomous, responsible agency.

To avoid counterexamples, this requirement must be explicated far more carefully than I have done here. But this discussion is sufficient to establish the conclusion that free, autonomous, responsible agency does not depend upon decisions being uncaused. What matters is the kind of causation. But now things get complex. External causes such as being pushed seem to be sufficient for not treating a person as a responsible agent. But there are internal causes that would also seem sufficient to exonerate a person from responsibility. Behaviorist conditioning, whether classical or operation, works by creating changes within the organism, strengthening neural connections so that when appropriate conditions arise in the future, the organism is more likely to respond. In cases where conditioning accounts for behavior, we seem to have removed agency. After one has conditioned an animal to behave in a certain way (to bark at the sound of a bell), it hardly seems appropriate to hold it responsible for behaving in that way on a given occasion. We, as humans, are not immune from conditioning, either classical or operant. The Garcia effect is perhaps the best known exemplar of classical conditioning that operates in us. If a person develops nausea in the hours after eating an unusual food, the person will develop an aversion to that food (Garcia, McGowan, Ervin, & Koelling, 1968). The mechanism underlying this effect is robust and it hardly seems right to hold someone responsible for developing such an aversion. Likewise, appropriate schedules of reinforcement can be powerful determinants of human behavior and if someone behaves in a certain way after being subjected to such reinforcement, his or her behavior does not seem to be an expression of his or her own free, autonomous, responsible agency.

In cases such as these, the causal processes do seem to bring agency into question. What challenges attribution of agency in these cases, however, is not the mere fact of causal processes operating inside the organism since, as we noted above, causal processes operating inside an organism are necessary for it to exhibit responsible agency. The challenge is to spell out what makes these mechanisms problematic for purposes of responsible agency. One idea that has sometimes been appealed to in addressing this question is that in cases such as conditioning, the organism's behavior has been rendered predictable by an external agent. It might seem that if actions are free, they should not be possible for someone else to reliably predict them. To see what is wrong with this line of reasoning, I turn briefly to a traditional theological issue—predestination.

7.2   CAUSAL MECHANISMS AND PREDESTINATION

In religious monotheisms it is not uncommon to view God as an all powerful creator and as omniscient. This seems to entail predestination: Our actions were all predetermined by God when he made the universe, and we are powerless to do anything other than what he knew that we would do. Although the notion of mechanism is not invoked in these contexts, something very like it is lurking in the thought that God made us a certain way and what we do is dependent on the way we were made. From there it seems an easy step to the conclusion that God determined whether we would do good or evil, and since God knew what we would do at the outset and made us accordingly, then it seems most unfair to hold us responsible. Instead, God would seem to be the responsible agent. A common conclusion to draw from such arguments is that if we are to be held responsible for our actions, our actions must not be predetermined such that what we do could be foreknown.

On first blush, it may seem just obvious that if our brains consist of mechanisms then, if someone knew the inputs to them, that person could predict our behavior. Perhaps the computations might be difficult and the person might need to rely on very powerful computers to carry them out, but prediction, at least in principle, seems guaranteed. Laplace famously presented this view:

> We ought then to regard the present state of the universe as the effect of its anterior state and as the cause of the one which is to follow. Given for one instant an intelligence which could comprehend all the forces by which nature is animated and the respective situation of the beings who compose it—an intelligence sufficiently vast to submit these data to analysis—it would embrace in the same formula the movements of the greatest bodies of the universe and those of the lightest atom; for it, nothing would be uncertain and the future, as the past, would be present to its eyes (Laplace, 1812/1951).

My goal in this section is to defuse the worry that determinism entails fatalism and predestination when the mechanisms in question are as complex as those found in our brains. Complexity alone, as we will see below, is not sufficient to provide for the requisite notions of freedom and dignity, but it does diffuse some of the most obvious worries about the mechanistic perspective.

To see why, let's begin by considering the magnitude of the computation that would be required to predict behavior in advance. At least in part, the brain is an electrical switching system. The production of action potentials in individual neurons is one fundamental activity of the brain. Whether an action potential develops in a particular neuron is determined by action potentials in neurons that synapse on it. The simplest assumption is that an action potential will develop in a particular neuron if there are enough action potentials in the neurons that synapse on the neuron in question in a requisite time frame. If this is the case, we can in principle write the equation describing the response of any given neuron. (The Hodgkin–Huxley model of the neuron describes the depolarization of the neuron, whereas the algorithms used to determine netinput in neural network modeling characterize the summation of inputs to a given neuron.) Now all we need to do is calculate on a moment-by-moment basis the propagation of electrical activity through the system. Mathematical modeling of artificial neural networks has very much this character. The activity of each unit in the network is calculated from the activity of the units providing inputs to the unit (generally by applying a nonlinear activation function), and this is determined successively for each unit in the system.

For simple artificial networks of a few dozen, hundreds, or thousands of units, these calculations are routinely performed on current digital computers. But as the number of units and the number of connections grows, these calculations become ever more complex and time consuming. The real brain is vastly more complex than any artificial network yet simulated; it is estimated to have approximately 10^{12} neurons, with each neuron having (on average) 10^3 connections to other neurons. The behavior of individual neurons, moreover, is nonlinear, making it impossible to simply sum the behavior of multiple components for modeling purposes. Even if real neurons operate in accord with the simple assumptions of artificial neural networks, calculating the behavior of the system for a single time interval on the most powerful digital computers yet built will take enormous processing time. But these assumptions are almost certainly false and the operation of real neurons is far more complex. For one thing, the processes determining whether an action potential will be generated in any given neuron involves more than just summing activity in neurons that synapse onto it—it depends upon where on the dendrites the incoming action potential is received and how multiple inputs are integrated in time. For another, the behavior of synapses is constantly changing as a result of chemical alterations accompanying synaptic discharges, requiring continual updating of the equations governing neural responses. To make things worse, there is no common clock determining the update process for each neuron. When this is combined with the fact that many of the actual processes in the brain are recurrent, the envisioned computation becomes dauntingly complex.

Calculations require time. As the system includes more parts, the time to perform the calculation grows substantially and if there are complex interactions between the parts, the computations required to determine how the system will behave become even more numerous, increasing at more than a linear rate. What do human engineers do when the equations describing a system they are contemplating become too complex? Consider the task of developing a wing for an airplane, where it is crucial to know how it will behave under a variety of aerodynamic conditions. Typically engineers begin with computer simulations using approximations to get a sense of the type of behavior a wing with a particular design will likely exhibit under a variety of expected conditions. But when greater precision is required, they leave off calculating and build the wing itself, or a scale-model of it, and conduct experiments on it in a wind tunnel. Even if we assume that the equations we employ are accurate and that the measurements we make are precise, it is often far more efficient to build a complex system and observe its behavior than to calculate how it will behave.

In traditional mathematics, it was assumed that even if detailed calculations were laborious, one could make simplifications and still calculate the neighborhood in which the result would lie. Likewise, one could ignore certain interactions which would alter the outcome only minimally and still make a sufficiently accurate prediction of the effect. The discovery of deterministic chaos, however, undercut that assumption. In systems exhibiting chaos, subsequent states of the system are determined by the present state of the system. But the nonlinear nature of the equations has the effect that sometimes very small changes in the state of the system at a given time result in very different states some time later. This sensitivity to initial conditions was found in the equations Edward Lorenz developed for modeling weather phenomena and is informally known as the *butterfly effect*, although in Edward Lorenz's initial example the animal was a sea gull:

> When the instability of uniform flow with respect to infinitesimal perturbations was first suggested as an explanation for the presence of cyclones and anticyclones in the atmosphere, the idea was not universally accepted. One meteorologist remarked that if the theory were correct, one flap of a sea gull's wings would be enough to alter the course of the weather forever. The controversy has not yet been settled, but the most recent evidence seems to favor the gulls (Lorenz, 1963, p. 431).[2]

---

[2] Robert Hilborn (2004) traced the path from seagulls to butterflies in illustrating sensitivity to initial conditions as well as identifying a very similar example in a review of Duhem written in 1898 by W.S. Franklin which featured grasshoppers: "Franklin wrote that 'Long range detailed weather prediction is therefore impossible, and the only detailed prediction which is possible is the inference of the ultimate trend and character of a storm from observations of its early stages; and the accuracy of this prediction is subject to the condition that the flight of a grasshopper in Montana may turn a storm aside from Philadelphia to New York!'" (p. 426).

Given the nonlinearities found in the brain, sensitivity to initial conditions is likely to be a serious obstacle to predicting the resulting behavior of a person even if we consist of deterministic machines. If it can be done at all, it would require exact calculations, not shortcuts, and thus require enormous amounts of time. Although we cannot conceive how an omniscient intelligence reasons, it may turn out that even God would operate in the same way as human engineers if he sought to know how a mechanism such as the human brain would behave—he would build it and observe its operation. This would not be due to limits on his cognitive capacities but the selection of the most efficient reasoning strategy— calculating how a complex interactive dynamical system will behave is more difficult than building the system and observing its behavior. This is even more true when those doing the predicting are not omniscient but fallible calculators like us or the machines we build. Even if neuroscientists figured out all the details of the neural mechanism operating in a human being and all the sensory inputs it was receiving, the simplest and most reliable way to predict how it would behave would be to let it process the inputs and behave. Given the nonlinear nature of the equations describing us, even small errors of measurement or small errors in calculation could lead to radically incorrect predictions.

7.3   CAUSAL MECHANISMS AND VALUES

These considerations about the problems in predicting serve to moderate worries about predestination; determinism does not necessarily entail foreknowledge of the behavior. But there is a more important point underlying it. What calculations of behavior based on equations do is specify how a mechanism of a particular kind will behave. Even if its behavior is accurately predicted in advance, it is still the mechanism itself that produces the behavior. When we perform actions, it is still our brains that perform the information processing so that we can behave. The central question is whether, as organized systems of mechanisms, our brains can enable us to act on the basis of reasons, especially reasons concerning values of our own choosing. If they can, then we will have taken a major step in showing how we can be free, autonomous, responsible agents.

To see how values should enter into a mechanistic account of agency, let's consider what it takes to get a mechanical system to make decisions. This is a problem that was confronted early in the development of artificial intelligence (AI). Although one factor influencing the development of AI was simple curiosity about whether computers could perform cognitive operations, another was practical: would it be possible to improve on human cognition, especially in the domain of decision making. In domains such as expert systems research this became a central issue as it was increasingly recognized that there are contexts in which humans make normatively bad decisions, failing to take into account important considerations such as base rates (Tversky & Kahneman, 1974; Kahneman, Slovic, & Tversky, 1982; Hastie & Dawes, 2001). Researchers who developed the field known as *expert systems* often found that they could improve on human decision making in fields like medical diagnosis and evaluation of credit worthiness by employing relatively simple rules—rules which human decision makers tend to ignore (Bishop & Trout, 2005).

My objective here is not to enter into a discussion of AI and expert systems, but to note a simple feature of such systems. For an AI system to make decisions, it must represent the goals to be accomplished. For example, in order for a computer system to play a credible game of chess, it must represent the goal of checkmate and evaluate possible strategies in terms of their likelihood of achieving that goal. The representation of a goal becomes a causal factor determining the system's behavior. Observing such a system in operation, one might be inclined to say that the system itself values achieving the goal. When restrictions are placed on the ways in which such a system will achieve its goals, the resulting behavior seems to respect other values specified in those restrictions, thereby modeling a person reasoning in light of goals.

The manner in which goals are typically built into AI systems, by setting parameters or specifying rules, strike many as showing that the operations in an AI system are profoundly different from our activities of valuing. Part of what is different is that the operation of these representations of goals does not seem to engage the system in the way normative principles engage us. Values for us do not seem to be just another set of states governing our operation. Values engage us as agents in a far more immediate manner than descriptions of goals engage the computer. One way to appreciate how values are more than rules governing a decision is to recognize that values are not always realized in behavior. Not infrequently values are violated. Sometimes this is due to value conflicts in which, to promote one value, a person must violate another. Even though a person values winning a game, the person may choose to lose in order to retain a friendship, something she values even more. Although an individual generally respects private property, she may destroy another's property as a form of protest. Other times an individual may fail to act in accord with his values for less noble reasons, seeking an immediate reward while sacrificing the possibility of realizing a longer term goal. Often when queried the individual cannot explain why he did so. The phenomenon of weakness of will is all too familiar in human behavior.

It may be possible to build AI systems whose behavior more accurately reflects the fact that espoused values are often violated. Yet, many will still judge such systems as not really engaged in valuing and acting for things they value. What lies behind this powerful intuition? A factor to which I have already alluded is that AI systems do not seem to *care* about their values. They lack passion. Achieving a valued objective does not result in any happiness, and failure does not generate disappointment. Such systems do not regret sacrificing one value so as to satisfy another. Part of engagement with values for humans is affective. We *care* about our values. Witness the fact that when we disagree about values, we often become animated and angry. We can be threatened when we encounter other people who do not share them. Valuing is not just a matter of representing abstract principles or rules. What more is involved in caring about values and feeling passion?

Many theorists, including many philosophers, have drawn a sharp contrast between reason and emotion and have construed reason as itself able to direct behavior and indeed as the proper guide to behavior. Plato, for example, treated emotions as disruptive and in need of control. But Plato did not deny them a role. The appetitive part of the soul, properly directed by reason, was necessary to achieve ends. In the domain of morality Kant went further, denying any role for the emotions in moral reasoning. An action is right when it is done simply because it accords with the moral law—the categorical imperative. If other considerations, such as the good outcomes that will result or how the action makes one feel, influenced the person's thinking, then for Kant the action is not a moral one. This rejection of interest and affect as relevant for value discussions, however, makes Kantian ethics seem unnatural to many.

Recent neuroscience research has demonstrated that emotions play a critical role in human decision making, including moral decision making. As is often the case, important insights came for the study of patients with specific deficits which had surprising consequences. Perhaps the most famous such person is the nineteenth-century railroad worker Phineas Gage. In an accidental explosion, a tamping pole thrust through the orbital regions of his frontal cortex. At first it appeared that Gage survived his injury unscathed. Not only did he live, but his reasoning ability appeared to be normal. But in other respects he was anything but normal. Previously a very responsible individual, Gage became irresponsible; he could not hold his job, maintain his marriage, etc. (Macmillan, 2000). Something about the damage to his frontal cortex seemed to have produced dramatic changes in his character.

The contribution of the orbitofrontal areas damaged in Gage's brain remained a mystery for over a century after his accident. Since no clear cognitive function was attributable to this region, it was an area surgeons would remove if tumors occurred there. E.V.R. was one such patient who had a tumor removed from the ventromedial part of his frontal lobes that resulted in bilateral lesions. Prior to surgery, E.V.R. had an IQ of about 140, which was not diminished as a result of the surgery. Like Gage, he seemed to emerge from surgery unharmed in terms of his general cognitive abilities. But outside the laboratory his life was severely impacted. His performance at work suffered as he showed up late, failed to complete tasks, etc. E.V.R. became the focus of a long-term investigation by Antonio and Hannah Damasio. As the Damasios investigated him, they discovered that although he often knew what would be the rational choice, he would act otherwise.

Working with the Damasios, Antoine Bechara developed an experimental procedure that helped reveal the nature of E.V.R.'s deficit (Bechara, Damasio, Damasio, & Anderson, 1994). In what has come to be known as the Iowa Gambling Task, a subject is presented with four decks of cards and is free to choose cards to turn over on each round from any of the four decks. As the subject turns over the cards, he or she receives or loses the amount of money specified on the card. The penalty cards that result in loss of money are dispersed through the decks so that the subject cannot anticipate when they will show up. Two of the decks have cards with relatively low payouts and low penalties, with the total payouts exceeding the total penalties. Thus, over the long term a subject will make money by choosing cards from those decks. The other two decks have cards with higher payouts, but even higher penalties, so that over the long-term a subject will lose money by choosing cards from those decks. Normal subjects learn after 15–20 trials to choose cards primarily from the low payout/low penalty decks. In contrast, E.V.R., and other patients with lesions in the ventromedial frontal areas continue to choose cards from the higher-payout/even-higher-penalty decks. It is not, however, that E.V.R. cannot figure out which decks would produce the better outcome. He can report which is the more rational strategy. Nonetheless, he acts otherwise.

Further research revealed that the difference between patients such as E.V.R. and other subjects has to do with the connection between reason and emotion. When skin conductance was measured with normal subjects, they started to exhibit a skin conductance response when they reached for the decks of bad cards on trials even before they learned to reliably reject the bad cards. As noted, around trial 15–20 they started to avoid the bad cards, and reported a feeling that something was "funny" about the bad decks. Only after about 50 trials could they articulate why avoiding these cards was the winning strategy. E.V.R. and other ventromedial patients, however, never showed the skin conductance response. Although they did figure out what was the winning strategy, they did not adhere to it. These findings suggest that something linked to the skin conductance response was responsible for the difference in behavior between E.V.R. and normal subjects.

The skin conductance response is assumed to be an indication of emotional responses such as fear, anger, etc. The ventromedial areas of frontal cortex are known to be areas with projections both to limbic areas, thought to be involved in emotional responses, and cortical areas thought to be critical for higher-level reasoning. Lacking these connections, E.V.R. does not exhibit the normal emotional responses and, on the Damasios' interpretation, it is this failure that accounts for his abnormal responses. Without the appropriate emotions and links to them, he is not able to put his knowledge into action.

It is important to note that for normal subjects, the skin conductance response preceded the reasoned analysis of the situation. This suggests that emotion is not just a handmaiden of reason, but itself potentially an important independent guide to action. Many of the areas of the limbic system that are involved in neural processing of emotions are evolutionarily very early. They began to develop in organisms whose nervous systems were primarily directed at monitoring and regulating internal organs, including those in the alimentary canal. Even in more complex organisms, in which much brain activity, including emotional responses, is directed outwards towards the environment, there is still a close connection between limbic processes and internal organs. One traditional theory of the emotions, due to James and Lange, proposed that emotions first involve changes in the body and only subsequently registration in the mind/brain (for a contemporary defense, see Prinz, 2004a). Without taking a stance on this hypothesis, it is nonetheless noteworthy that emotional responses are highly integrated with other physiological processing in our bodies, including digestive activity in particular. The colloquial expression "gut reaction" seems to have a foundation in our neuroanatomy (Prinz, 2004b). Minus such somatic responses, our cognitive systems seem unable to execute what our reason dictates.

The disorders exhibited by patients such as Gage and E.V.R. provide a first clue as to what is required for our brain mechanisms to possess values in the appropriate sense. The system must be affective as well as reasoning. From an evolutionary perspective, this is unsurprising for, as I noted, a primary function in the earliest evolved brains was to regulate internal organs associated with the alimentary canal, and the parts of the brain that are most directly involved in such regulation are components of the limbic system. The more cognitive components of the brain, the neocortex generally and the frontal areas more specifically, are later phylogenetic developments added to parts of the brain already developed to utilize affect in guiding behavior. As I discussed in the previous chapter, typically when new traits develop in organisms, they do not replace existing structures, but operate in coordination with them. Although philosophy and AI have been tempted down the path of segregating reason and treating it as if it is a self-contained faculty that is alone sufficient to determine action, brains do not work that way.

There is a great deal we do not yet know about how valuing is realized in the brain. What we do have, though, is a suggestion as to why our values are so central to our identity (and why talk of values with current computers seems misconceived). Valuing involves not just reasoning, but affective processes. As a result, it is not detached from us in the way theoretical reasoning, including philosophical theorizing about morality, often seems to be. Noting a link between affect and agency only takes us a small distance to understanding what sort of mechanisms might constitute an agent. The relevant system of mechanisms must experience emotion, but acting from emotion does not make one a free, autonomous, responsible agent. For one thing, emotions often seem to be states induced involuntarily within us by external stimuli. Although the emotions we feel on a given occasion are distinctive expressions of the persons we are, they often are not under our control at the time they arise.[3] In the language I employed in the previous chapter, they seem to be responsive mechanisms, not active ones.

7.4   VALUING AND ACTING: REVISITING AUTONOMOUS ADAPTIVE AGENTS

One thing consideration of emotion does do is begin to refocus attention away from abstract reasoning to processes more associated with our existence as biological creatures. But like the introduction of goals or purposes into models of decision making, they are frequently presented as states induced in an agent, not an expression of the agent in the sense that would account for freedom and dignity. In this section I will show how, by adopting the framework of autonomous adaptive agents we can understand both emotions and goals and purposes more generally not as responsive mechanisms but as an active set of mechanisms operating in autonomous adaptive agents. In such a framework, they represent the system's own valuing of alternatives and constitute the basis for understanding valuing as an activity that contributes to the freedom and dignity of moral agents.

At the core of the account of what is distinctive of living organisms that I offered in the previous chapter was the characterization of living organisms as autonomous systems that recruited matter and energy from their environments and utilized it so as to maintain themselves as identifiable entities in a far from an equilibrium state. Through evolution, additional mechanisms can be incorporated into organisms (autonomous systems) that better enable them to maintain themselves, and these often served to make the system both adaptive and an agent operating in its environment. These accoutrements often serve the fundamental need of the organism (maintaining itself far from equilibrium) and hence constitute functions in a teleological sense that understand goals and purposes as intrinsic to an organism. While the simplest autonomous agents are far from the sorts of free, responsible agents that we take ourselves to be, they provide a foundation upon which evolution could build. Mental mechanisms, I argued, should be construed as additional mechanisms, constructed out of living components and performing functions, typically regulatory, for living organisms.

---

[3] Changing one's emotional responses to stimuli is often a long-term project. For example, highly irascible people who lash out violently when they are provoked may not be able to change their behavior at the moment when they are provoked. Rather, they must work over a period to change their propensities to anger and learn strategies for dissociating themselves from provoking situations before their anger develops.

These mental mechanisms operate in the context of the organism and depend for their own continued existence upon the organism maintaining itself far from equilibrium. Thus to the degree they facilitate the maintenance of the organism, they maintain themselves and to the degree they harm the ability of the organism to function, they undercut their own continued existence. Following that thread yet further will provide us a better entrée to understanding how mental mechanisms can enable us to be the sorts of agents we take ourselves to be—free agents responsible for our actions—by showing how valuing and values secure a place in autonomous adaptive agents.

In much philosophical and lay thinking about values, valuing precedes doing—an agent values something, considers courses of action that might yield what is valued, and then acts. The process of deliberating about possible actions is classified as practical reasoning. For such accounts of practical reasoning it is mysterious how the conclusions of reasoning translate into action. Such a question only arises, however, by taking up the issue of reasoning in a reified intellectual framework. For biological organisms, in contrast, activity is fundamental. The requirements of staying alive are such that organisms must continually engage in basic metabolic processes. The other mechanisms that develop in them, including those supporting motor activity, are also routinely engaged. Mental mechanisms evolved not to initiate the activity of basic metabolic and motor mechanisms, but to regulate their ongoing activity, often by suppressing it. There is no need to translate the operation of the mental mechanisms in order for the organism to act. (The challenge is rather to explain how the effects of such mechanisms can be suppressed by taking the mechanisms off-line.)

This at first seems counterintuitive: Why would evolution create mechanisms only subsequently to have to suppress their operation? When engineers devise new components to add to existing systems, they typically design the new component to operate only when it is needed. Engineers, however, are able to use foresight. They often begin with a design problem of enhancing their device to perform a new function and design a component that could perform that function. They control the component to operate at the time the function is needed, and not otherwise.[4] Evolution does not have the luxury of trying out new components off-line in thought and then adding them to a system. The variant performing the new activity or operation must be generated. If the organisms in which it develops are nonetheless able to maintain themselves and are competitive in the quest for reproduction (whether due in part to the new component or not), then

---

[4] In the engineer's own thinking, however, something more like the evolutionary process occurs. The engineer figures out a way a mechanism might perform a desired task without focusing on the fact that the task may only need to be performed in special circumstances. After developing a mechanism that could perform the task, he or she considers the question of how to insure that it performs the task when, and only when, it is needed.

the new component or mechanism may be retained in a lineage of organisms. Once a new mechanism has developed, then it is possible for control mechanisms to develop that would serve to regulate its operation, thereby fine-tuning its operation in the context of the functioning of the overall autonomous system.

The prime reason to regulate a mechanism is that its operation in some cases interferes with the operation of another mechanism whose contributions to the overall system are more valuable. If the second operation were always of greater value to the system, then simply shutting down the first operation would make sense. But in many cases there will be contexts in which the first operation is actually useful to the system. Then regulating it so that it does not operate except in those conditions makes sense. This is how one of the basic metabolic regulatory mechanisms, the lac-operon discovered by Jacob and Monod (1961), operates. E. coli has evolved the capacity to extract energy from either glucose or lactose. Glucose enters the metabolic pathway directly, but lactose requires preprocessing, making it less desirable as a food source since energy must be expended before it can be extracted from lactose. The critical genes for making the enzymes involved in lactose metabolism are located adjacent to one another in the genome, and ahead of them is a region involved in regulating these genes. One part of this regulatory system serves to block the synthesis of the enzymes required to metabolize lactose whenever lactose is absent. When glucose is in low concentrations, cyclic AMP accumulates and binds to catabolite activator protein, which serves then to promote the transcription leading to the synthesis of the enzymes responsible for lactose metabolism. The design of the lac-operon is such as to synthesize the additional enzymes required for lactose metabolism only when glucose is in low supply but lactose is available.

Similar regulation can be achieved in the brain using inhibitory connections such that when one system is operating, another is suppressed, but remains able to operate when the suppression is removed. When a regulatory mechanism operates in an autonomous adaptive system to suppress one mechanism in favor of another, it is natural to speak of the system as valuing the later operation to the former, at least in that context. In the case of the lac-operon and similar biological regulatory systems, including many in the brain, there is no sense in which the individual organism chose one mechanism over the other; the organism came equipped with the regulatory mechanism that exhibited such preferences. In adaptive systems, however, regulatory mechanisms develop through the lifetime of the system. Acquiring effective means of regulating the operation of sensory and motor mechanisms is a major part of what occurs during the developmental process of behaving organisms.

Starting from the framework of autonomous adaptive agents, valuing appears as a fundamental activity any time there are competing mechanisms and mechanisms regulating their operation. It emerges naturally and is not something that must be imposed upon such systems from without. The values that arise are intrinsic to such systems as they are part of what the system can rely upon in order to maintain itself in operation. Moreover, they provide a foundation such that when mechanisms providing for self-awareness arise, the organism in which they arise already is engaged in valuing.

7.5   THE SELF AND MENTAL MECHANISMS

Having tried to address some of the reasons why one may think that conceiving of the mind as comprised of mental mechanisms is incompatible with free, autonomous, responsible agency, let me turn now to a feature that seems to be necessary to the sort of human agency we have in mind when we think of ourselves as free and responsible agents. Unlike basic autonomous adaptive agents who act for themselves but are not self-aware as they do so, we seem, at least in our most deliberative states, to act as *selves*, as individuals with identities who contemplate themselves as they act. We assess our situation, evaluate and decide on possible objectives for ourselves, choose courses of action to achieve the goals we have set, and bear responsibility for these decisions.

At first glance, the prospects for developing a mechanistic account of the self seem daunting. The central nervous system and the brain, as I have presented them, evolved as a set of control systems to coordinate the operation of different mechanisms within the organism's body. The brain itself is not a single mechanism but a motley collection of mechanisms each serving a specific range of tasks, often narrowly identified. Moreover, the control that many of these mechanisms exert is not that which we associate with a free, responsible agent. For example, mechanisms within the autonomic nervous system operate so as to maintain such things as the internal temperature of the organism even at the expense, in humans, of potentially embarrassing sweat. Emotional responses in the limbic system often operate outside the control of the responsible agent by, for example, creating food aversions that are difficult to override. Even the cortical mechanisms that we associate with higher cognition comprise a diverse group, with different visual processing and memory mechanisms serving diverse needs of the organism. How, from such a collection of mechanisms, might something resembling the self that we take to be central to free agency and human dignity emerge and have a role in our decision making and action?

An unpromising approach is to seek the self as a special component of the organism, as either another mechanism or perhaps a nonmechanical part of the organism. A number of theories of human cognition introduce the idea of a *central executive* which carries out the highest level processing and exercises executive control over other parts of the brain. If it makes sense to treat a certain part of the brain as such an executive, then one might be tempted to construe it as the self. But this has all the negative features traditionally associated with homuncular theories, especially the challenge of explaining how the homunculus can itself perform all the operations attributed to it. The point of identifying mental mechanisms and decomposing them into their parts is to explain our mental lives, whereas attributing the characteristic in question to a homunculus offers no explanation. Moreover, as I have argued above, it is far more plausible that higher-level control systems modulate the behavior of lower-level systems rather than directing all of their activity. The self is not likely to be a micromanaging executive that sends out commands scripting the operation of component mechanisms.

A far more promising approach is not to localize the self as a specific mechanism, but identify the self, the agent, with the brain as a whole, or even better with the person as a whole. There is much to motivate such an approach. It is whole persons that we hold responsible for actions. The vocabulary for describing agents, so-called folk psychology, is pitched at the level of persons (Bechtel & Abrahamsen, 1993). It is persons who have beliefs, desires, values, etc. Mechanistic explanation is directed toward explaining how agents are able to carry out the activity of responsible agents. The goal is not to identify agency as a part of the system. Moreover, as I have developed the account of autonomous adaptive agents, these were whole systems comprised of mechanisms. It is they who have identities over time and operate so as to maintain themselves in existence. They do so by relying on a host of mechanisms that comprise them, but they are not identical to any one of those mechanisms.

To gain some traction on the issue of the self, it will be helpful to focus in more detail on what we take a self to be. In this pursuit, I follow Ulric Neisser's (1988) attempt to differentiate distinct aspects of the self. Neisser distinguishes five aspects of self, which he labels different selves: ecological, interpersonal, extended, private, and conceptual. Referring to distinct selves can be misleading, as each is not a separate entity within a person, but an aspect of a person. As I will discuss, some of these aspects of self are so basic that they will be found in any animal that perceives its environment and exists in a social context. Others rely on more specialized abilities made possible by mechanisms that may exist only in humans.

In developing different aspects of self, it is important to keep in mind that they are developed within what I have characterized as autonomous adaptive agents, autonomous systems that maintain themselves in part though being adaptive and acting in their environment. In recognition of this, I propose adding a level beneath that at which Neisser begins—the *autonomic self*. The autonomic self highlights the fact that foundational to any more elaborated abilities, the self maintains itself in an organized state (i.e., far from equilibrium) by recruiting and controlling the utilization of resources from its environment.

The foundational level for Neisser is what he terms the *ecological self*. In this he follows James J. Gibson in focusing on how perceptual processes in animals are linked to their capacities for action. On Gibson's (1966; 1979) ecological account, perceptual processes specify where one is in one's environment and what are the possibilities (affordances) for action in that environment. It is crucial for understanding this conception of self that perception for Gibson and Neisser is not directed at providing an objective, organism-independent portrayal of the environment, but at acting in the environment. This requires a decidedly egocentric perspective, specifying where things are related relative to the organism and what the organism might do with them, given its particular motor capacities. Such a perspective contrasts with the allocentric perspective provided by tools such as maps. A map does not specify where a given individual is relative to the locations shown in the map, but in an egocentric representation our location vis-à-vis the stimulus is automatically specified (Mandik, 2005). As Neisser (1989) has further developed his conception of the ecological self in humans, it is closely tied to the dorsal visual stream (see chapter three), which enables us to analyze the environment in ways directly tied to action. Although the dorsal stream perceptual–motor mechanisms are the crucial mechanisms for possessing an ecological self, it is the whole organism that is situated and is capable of acting in various ways.

Animals, including humans, live in interrelation with other organisms and, to a significant degree, the identity of an individual is determined by its relations to other organisms. Especially important in this respect are predators and prey and familial relations that link an organism to parents, siblings, and offspring. An organism is dependent on some organisms and has particular responsibilities to others. This nexus of relations determines a set of roles for the individual. Neisser characterizes these as constituting the *interpersonal* self. Like the ecological self, the interpersonal self is inherently relational and egocentric. Other organisms are identified in relation to oneself. Some are prey, some are predators. Some are possible mates, others are rivals. Individuals at the outset are identified by the relationships in which they stand relative to the organism in question. Recognizing this is important, for at the foundational stage of possessing an ecological and interpersonal self, an organism is positioned in relation to things outside itself, not characterized by internal or intrinsic features. What is internal at this stage is only those mechanisms required in order to operate as a situated organism.

The aspects of self I have identified so far are ones we share with many other animals. They are critically important, however, as they lay an important foundation for an account of human life as one of freedom and dignity. They provide an understanding of how an organism composed of mechanisms can engage its world as an autonomous system open to a variety of actions in the world and nested into an ecological context, including relations with conspecifics. The mechanisms incorporated into such an agent are not appropriately viewed as passive entities controlled from outside. Accordingly, agents initiate action from within and manage their own relations with their environment.

An organism with these foundational elements of the self has an identity in relation to what is external to it. For a human agent who is accustomed to engaging the world with self awareness, cognizant of his or her past and planning for a future, and continually thinking and reasoning not only about feature states of the world but about aspects of his or her own mental life, such an account of agency will seem to miss too much. To see how these can be accommodated, we need to consider the other features of self that Neisser identified, ones that may well be uniquely human.

As far as we can tell, few or no nonhuman animals have an understanding of themselves existing through time. Although many learn from events in their lives, they do not remember these events in the sense of being able to relive them. Their cognitive activities seem to be directed at the environment that presents itself to them in the moment. But when humans attempt to describe themselves, they frequently allude to their history—what they have experienced and what they have done. Our self identity as humans extends through time from the past we have experienced to the future we have planned. Neisser refers to this aspect of one's self as the *extended* self. It relies on what Endel Tulving dubbed *episodic memory*, a form of memory which I discussed in chapter two. Tulving emphasized that such memory enables one to revisit episodes in one's life—to engage in mental time travel. It is not just that we know things happened to us, but we are able to relive the experience. (The relived experience may not, in fact, correspond to the originally lived experience. The active mechanisms that enable us to relive the experience may also be constructing that experience, as suggested at the end of chapter two.) Episodic memory enables each of us to define ourselves in terms of what we have done in the past. As numerous tragic cases of amnesics who have lost their episodic memories or who cannot acquire new ones make clear, such memories are critical to our self construal. Jerome Bruner (1991), among others, has shown how narratives about our lives as well as group narratives that place us in a broader social context are central in giving substance to ourselves. An important aspect of Neisser's characterization is that it shows that just as one's identity extends to the past, it also extends to the future and to projects we can envisage pursuing in the future.

Neisser's fourth self, the *private* self, captures an important feature of conscious mental life to which William James drew attention—that our conscious awareness is uniquely ours and is private. Part of what is private is our phenomenal experience of our sensations. Sensory stimulation such as that produced by a paper cut does not simply cause us to respond in particular ways (as we can imagine the sensing of a sucrose gradient simply causes a bacterium to swim up it). It also generates an experience, a feeling of a certain kind of pain, which is difficult to describe and is available exclusively to the person experiencing the sensation.

These private experiences have seemed philosophically mysterious. They led behaviorist U. T. Place (1956), who could not see how to explain them in terms of behavior, to maintain that they were simply brain processes. A host of philosophers have, however, viewed such experiences as inexplicable in material terms, and have instead defended some form of dualism at least about what are termed *qualia*—the qualitative character of experiences (D. Chalmers, 1996; F. Jackson, 1982; T. Nagel, 1974). Qualia in such debates are construed as private, ineffable, and monadic features of experience. The reification of qualitative experience in terms of qualia has been challenged by other philosophers (Dennett, 1988). One strategy adopted by critics of qualia-dualism has been to reject the assumption that such experiences are monadic and to contend that they have a complex structure (van Gulick, 1993). Doing so enables theorists to make headway in relating such processing to the brain (for a highly suggestive account, see Prinz, 2000). Whether or not cognitive neuroscientists succeed in explaining why qualia have the features they do, it will remain the case that our sensory experience is fundamentally private; the qualitative character of the experience is appreciated only by the persons themselves.

So far I have not introduced language into the discussion of self. But as I noted in chapter five, language is a powerful representational tool. It is highly likely that language was first developed to coordinate interactions between individuals (and thus as enriching the capacities of the interpersonal self). But the ability to imagine speaking as well as actually speaking brought additional powers for the private self (Vygotsky, 1962). With such capacities, people could draw upon the representational power of language in their own private cognitive activities, representing things in the world, events remembered, or things that they imagined happening. As practiced language users, such internal monologues are a ubiquitous feature of our mental life. We can relate this internal monologue to others, but it occurs inside our skulls. Moreover, it can enhance our mental resources as we, in private soliloquies, recall things that are not present, evaluate them, and plan actions with respect to them. For those creatures able to represent the world, past, present, and future, in language, the domain of the private self becomes incredibly rich.

An organism equipped with the mental mechanisms that enable it to move through time and to have private experiences on top of the more basic capacities to be autonomous, adaptive agents that are situated in space and presented with affordances to act and to relate to other individuals is something far beyond what the critics of mechanism might have imagined. It is not a simple stimulus-response mechanism, but an agent that places value on outcomes, has a history and a future that it can represent and in the moment has an internal, private set of experiences. In its monologues in covert speech it can consider off-line scenarios of what might have happened or what it might do. But, one might object, there is still one thing lacking—a self-identity. This brings us to the last aspect of the self Neisser considers, what he terms the *conceptual* self.

With the capacity to represent and think about things in the world comes the capacity to represent and think about one's own being as an agent operative in a world of other objects and agents. We can call this concept the concept of ourself—our representation of the autonomous adaptive agent that we find ourselves to be. (It seems plausible that only linguistic creatures could create such a concept.) Neisser's conceptual self is clearly linked to the selves he already introduced. It draws upon our being ecologically situated as the subject of experiences and actions. As a subject that experiences the world from a specific perspective and acts on things situated in the world, we can also conceptualize ourselves as distinct from the other things that we see and act on. By having episodic memory, we are able to consider that self not just at its current location, but at others where it has been or might be. Once we have conceptualized ourselves as distinct entities, though, we can also think about ourselves as agents (as distinct from just being an agent) and represent ourselves in narratives. We can consider what we value, what we are doing and why, how we are related to other things and other people, etc.

With such representations in hand, we can detach ourselves from what we find ourselves to be and consider how we might change ourselves. One might worry that such a self concept would be purely epiphenomenal. Epiphenomenal theories of mind construe the mind as something caused by one's physical body but having no causal effects on the body. But there is no reason for the conceptual self to be epiphenomenal. Mental mechanisms, including those that enable us to conceptualize the world, arise as regulatory mechanisms in autonomous adaptive agents, agents engaged in their environment. Concepts in general, as discussed in chapter five, are tools some of these mechanisms use in exercising their regulatory function. They are operative parts of cognitive mechanisms, and the self concept is no different. People can invoke their concepts of themselves in making choices about action. If, for example, part of a person's concept of herself is being a person who does not inflict needless pain on other sentient creatures, then she may check herself when she is about to do something that would inflict such pain. Another person, who conceives of himself as aesthetically sophisticated, may not suppress himself when he has the opportunity to make an aesthetic comment.

Where does the content of our self concept come from? A common perspective on our concept of ourself is that we are simply reporting on our inner life in much the manner we report on other things we experience. We *introspect*—that is, we look into ourselves and report what is there. But what is this self we think we are reporting on and by what means do we access it? Adopting the view that our talk about ourselves involves reporting on a secret, hidden entity—one's self—that is the recipient of our experiences and the author of our actions, is a route into a mysterious dualism. Nonetheless, our self-concept does seem to have content. We report on our reasons for action, on what we value, and how we intend to achieve our aspirations.

In the "myth of Jones" Wilfred Sellars (1956) provides an instructive perspective on how such capacities might come about. Sellars imagines a situation in which people have a rich language for talking about public phenomena but no language for talking about inner experiences. Among the public phenomena they can talk about are the actions of agents, including themselves (treated purely as autonomous adaptive systems among others that they encounter). Moreover, these individuals have a language for talking about public phenomena that enables them to construct theories to explain the phenomena they experience. One of them might, accordingly, have developed the kinetic theory of gases that proposes processes occurring within the public observed gases that accounts for their behavior. Moreover, on Sellars' account, these individuals have developed semantic theories that explain their own and other people's linguistic utterances:

> Let it be granted, then, that these mythical ancestors of ours are able to characterize each other's verbal behavior in semantic terms; that, in other words, they not only can talk about each other's predictions as causes and effects, and as indicators (with greater or less reliability) of other verbal and nonverbal states of affairs, but can also say of these verbal productions that they *mean* thus and so, that they say *that* such and such, that they are true, false, etc.

What these mythical people have not done, until the arrival of Jones, is construct theories about inner mental lives of people—theories of the events within people that explain their behavior. Jones advances such a theory by proposing that covert speech occurs within the heads of people, names these covert speech events *thoughts,* and develops explanations of other people's behavior in terms of their thoughts. The evidence for the thought-theory is the same as the evidence for any theory—its ability to explain behavior. Of course, Jones can also offer the same kind of theory with respect to his behavior. Such a theory will be anchored in Jones' overt behavior. Now Sellars proposes one final twist: Jones might teach another person, Dick, to give such reports without consulting his overt behavior:

> ... it now turns out—need it have?—that Dick can be trained to give reasonably reliable self-descriptions, using the language of the theory, without having to observe his overt behavior. Jones brings this about, roughly by applauding utterances by Dick of "I am thinking that p" when the behavioral evidence strongly supports the theoretical statement "Dick is thinking that p"; and by frowning on utterances of "I am thinking that p," when the evidence does not support this theoretical statement. Our ancestors begin to speak of the privileged access each of us has to his own thoughts. *What began as a language with a purely theoretical use has gained a reporting role.*

Dick provides a model of someone who, in the context of concern to us, can report on his own self reasonably accurately. Although there must be some explanation of how he is able to do so, Sellars' point is that it need not involve mysterious introspection of some private self. However he does it, Dick is now in a position to do something new. He can include in his private monologues references to his own self, his plans, his responses to how current situations impinge on those plans, etc. (Dick can, of course, speak aloud about these aspects of his self.) Dick may have no more idea why he is inclined to say certain things about himself than he is about why he responds to visual stimuli as he does. He reports that a banana is on the table because that is what he sees, and he reports that he wants ice cream because that is what he desires.

Dick's self reports about himself need not fully agree with those advanced by external observers. Social psychologists construct experimental protocols in which they control the variables that determine a person's response without a person's being aware of those variables. When asked why they acted as they did, subjects offer reasons, but almost never identify the variables that are demonstrably producing the behavior. Since their reports are erroneous, but they are not intentionally lying, such subjects are said to *confabulate* (Nisbett & Wilson, 1977). From the perspective of Sellars' myth of Jones, we can understand such confabulations. Having arrived at a theory that their own behavior is due to thoughts, subjects expect to have reasons for their behavior. Because their access to their own reasons consists simply in having a tendency to report on themselves in terms of thoughts, they have no problem constructing plausible reasons for their actions and then accepting these as self reports.

Recalling that on Sellars' analysis, mental reports are really theoretical explanations of behavior, we should not be surprised that in some cases they are erroneous. The conceptual self is in this respect constructed. It is the product of our attempt to make sense of who we are and why we behave as we do. This is not to say that it lacks a basis in objective experience any more than our scientific theories, correct and incorrect, are grounded in experience. Where it differs from the theoretical concepts we develop to characterize the physical world is in the use to which we put it. We employ our self-concept not just descriptively but normatively insofar as it is produced and used in mechanisms that figure in self regulation. Understanding ourselves as pursuing a goal can lead to overriding desires to do things inconsistent with that goal, thereby increasingly the likelihood of realizing the goal.

The account I have offered of self-concept provides a basis for understanding why we think of ourselves as valuing and responsible agents. An important part of our self-concept involves characterizing what we value. Such valuing does emerge as a natural part of who we are. As we acquire our self-concept developmentally, we characterize ourselves as we exist in the world, already autonomous adaptive agents doing things. Typically, however, there are many opportunities for action, and we cannot pursue them all if we are going to be successful in any action. Accordingly, we choose. Often, as in nonhuman animals, the mechanisms that execute the choice are not conscious ones. But as we develop our self-concept, it becomes a regulative system that directs choices. Insofar as we formulate a coherent self-concept that regulates our behavior in choice situations, we act according to our values—the values represented in our self-concept. Moreover, insofar as these are our values (who else are we to attribute them to?), we are responsible for the actions that follow from them. If we had not settled on these values, we would not have so acted.

7.6   CONSTRUCTING A UNIFIED SELF

In the previous section I followed Neisser's characterization of different aspects of our knowledge of the self that builds from the foundational level of an organism as an autonomous adaptive agent to a self-concept that guides action. I have emphasized the multiplicity of mental mechanisms that have evolved and serve to control our behavior. Nonetheless, the self-concept we develop characterizes ourselves as unities. But what insures that we are unified? In fact, nothing does since we are often not unified. The mechanisms that comprise us operate on their own and often without any awareness on our part. Wherever we look at a scene, our eyes saccade to different parts of it, typically without any awareness on our part. When we walk, we walk with a distinctive gait and follow a particular path. When we are required to choose items from a display, our choice may be influenced by factors such as relative location of which we have no awareness. These are all actions we perform, but they do not reflect choices made on the basis of our unified self-concept.

Cases such as these are relatively unproblematic unless we are under the mistaken impression that everything we do is determined by a unified central self that is aware of what it is doing. Sometimes we are aware of a divided self. Weakness of will is a ubiquitous phenomenon in which we behave in ways opposed to what we claim to want. We go to a lecture desirous of attending closely to the whole presentation, but find ourselves struggling to stay awake. We set out to eat right and exercise regularly, but find ourselves enjoying ice cream and missing workouts. As disturbing and frustrating as these cases are, we are generally not helpless in the face of them. We can take action to reduce the chance that we will succumb to the choice we, in our reflective moments, don't want to make. We can, for example, always take notes or draw sketches during lectures so as to maintain ourselves in an active state where we are less likely to feel sleepy. We can keep ice cream out of the house and arrange to meet others for workouts. In these and other ways we can shape ourselves to be more the sorts of persons we desire to be.

Creating one's is, in part, an activity in which we are constantly engaged. But it is not something we undertake from a position outside ourselves and our engagement with the world. Rather, we are autonomous adaptive agents situated in the world and behaving in the world. As a result of a host of mental mechanisms, we have an ecological and social point of view of the world, engage in mental time travel, have personal experiences, and construct personal narratives. As humans, these mechanisms enable us to create a concept of one's self, a concept that may be both descriptive and prescriptive insofar as we use it to regulate our lives. Like other mental mechanisms, regulating our lives in accord with a self-concept often involves suppressing the operation of other more basic mental mechanisms. In some cases, the operation of those more basic mechanisms can be recognized even as we work to counter them.

Tricky reasoning problems provide a good example of this. Psychologists such as Peter Wason, Amos Tversky, and Daniel Kahneman have identified numerous ways in which human judgments in reasoning problems are mistaken (see Piattelli-Palmarini, 1994, for a very instructive overview). Most of these problems are ones in which a response that seems highly plausible turns out to be incorrect when proper methods are applied. Yet the temptation to make the response remains compelling. Consider the following problem:

> You visit your doctor with an unusual symptom. Your doctor tells you that it might well be due to a rare condition that affects one percent of your age group and requires very painful treatment. There is a test she can do which has been shown to identify seventy-nine percent of those with the condition, but in ten percent of cases produces a false positive. You decide to have the test and it comes back positive. Should you check in for the painful therapy?

Most people think in this situation that they are likely to have the condition. Yet, this is a probabilistic reasoning problem for which a theorem developed by Thomas Bayes provides the normatively correct result, and the result is that we are very unlikely to have the condition. Let $p(A/B)$ be the probability of having the condition given a positive test, $p(B/A)$ be the probability of a positive test given the condition, $p(A)$ be the probability of the condition itself, etc., then:

$$p(A/B) = \frac{p(B/A) \times p(A)}{p(B/A) \times p(A) + p(B/notA) \times p(notA)}$$

If you supplied the information stated in the problem above, the probability that you have the disease given the positive test is .0739, a very low probability.

A more intuitive way to arrive at the same result is to construct the following table using the same information:

	Has condition	Lacks condition	Total
Test is positive	790	9,900	10,690
Test is negative	210	89,100	89,310
Total	1,000	99,000	100,000

From the table one can recognize the overriding importance of the fact that only one percent of the total population has the condition. A test which correctly picks out seventy-nine percent of the positive cases among those with the condition and misdiagnoses just ten percent of those without the condition yields a situation in which, of those who test positive, very few actually have the condition. You can also see that if you assume even a much lower rate of false positives and a much higher rate of correct detection, the test still offers little guidance as to whether you have the condition.

The proper inference to draw from this example is that it is necessary to pay close attention to the base rate, and if the base rate is extremely low, no test will provide useful information unless it is extraordinarily accurate. Nonetheless, it is extremely hard for us humans when faced with such a problem not to assume that the test will give highly reliable information about our condition, and to be greatly alarmed when it comes back positive. We readily ignore the crucial information about base rates. A theoretical understanding of the importance of base rates, moreover, typically does not generate a better intuitive feel for such problems. We still feel as if the test must be highly informative. The remedy is to recognize problems that rely in such a way on base rate information, put our intuitive judgments aside, and perform the normatively correct calculations. We must then suppress our intuitive judgments and abide by what we have established as the correct response.

This strategy for dealing with tricky reasoning problems is simply an example of how, by developing our explicit knowledge, including knowledge about ourselves and our tendencies to make certain kinds of errors, we are in a position to exert control over our actions. Developing the capacity to reason in normatively correct ways on problems such as these is not easy. Many people resist efforts to be taught such modes of reasoning, preferring to rely on their own instincts. In gambling situations they can easily be taken advantage of in what is referred to as a *Dutch Book*, a gambling situation in which the odds are such so as to insure that the bettor will lose money. One form of Dutch Book arises as a result of inconsistent preferences—for example, different preferences for the same circumstances described differently. For example, people tend to prefer an action when it is described as possibly saving three hundred out of four hundred who would otherwise die than when it is described as resulting in one hundred out of four hundred dying, but in fact the outcomes are the same. We have the ability to develop ourselves in ways that protect ourselves from such situations, but only through effort.

The strategies for developing into reasoners who maintain consistent preferences, attend to base rates, etc., are just examples of a broader class of strategies for deploying mental mechanisms in ourselves so as to better promote ourselves as autonomous adaptive agents. A major factor in developing such mechanisms to the level that they can best serve our functioning as such agents is our representation of the self. By developing a concept of one's self as striving to be a cohesive rational and emotional agent and employing that to regulate our various mental mechanisms, we are able to act as responsible agents. This capacity, importantly, arises because of our being constituted of various mechanisms which function in our composite organized being to maintain ourselves as autonomous adaptive agents. As autonomous adaptive agents, we are engaged in acting in the world, but as a result of our mental mechanisms, especially those involved in creating a self-concept, we are able to regulate those activities to subserve focused ends.

7.7   ACCOUNTING FOR FREEDOM AND DIGNITY

My contention in this chapter has been twofold. First, I have argued that there is no threat to our freedom and dignity as a result of our mind/brain being constituted of mental mechanisms. Causality is not inimical to the sort of freedom that is involved in responsible action. Rather, what is needed is the right kind of causation—causation in which the agent itself controls the response to external factors that impinge on it. The regulative capacities of mental mechanisms, especially the high-level ones that enable persons to regulate their behavior in accord with their self-concepts, allow that people can be responsible agents. Second, this sort of causation is possible, and perhaps only possible, with the sort of active mechanisms that arise in autonomous adaptive agents. Such systems are engaged in maintaining themselves in existence through their engagement with the world, from which they draw the resources necessary to maintain themselves. Mental mechanisms are, as I discussed in the previous chapter, accoutrements to the basic autonomous system that are both active and provide resources for further engagements with the environment.

The temptation is to think of values as the beginning point of the process leading to action. But I have suggested that the reverse perspective may be more productive. The more promising approach is to view an autonomous system as already engaged with its environment and to construe mental mechanisms as supplements that enable the system to regulate and control its activity. Such regulatory mechanisms do not start out de novo to direct the organism along a path. Rather, they serve to resolve conflicts, allowing the system as a whole to pursue one activity when it is thought to conflict with another by suppressing the mechanism responsible for the later activity. Such a system would thereby value the first activity more than the second. As a result, it does not create values for the system out of nothing, but out of propensities to act already in the system.

In some cases, even when we have highly developed self-concepts that serve to regulate behavior, we still struggle and deliberate in a choice situation. This reflects the fact that our self-concept is continually in development. It does not have a ready resolution to the choice situation. Sometimes people can resolve conflicts by realizing that one of the choices coheres better with their already developed self-concept than the other. Sometimes, however, there is a need for decision without any obviously compelling reasons to decide one way rather than another, and one decides. In such cases, the choice that is made can establish a new precedent—the agent comes to value what she has chosen, and makes further choices in that light. Agency, however, does not typically manifest itself in such active deliberation and decision making. More commonly, as adults, our self-concept is already settled with respect to most decisions that confront us, and we act according to that concept. This is often not deliberate. Recall the example, which I offered early in the chapter, of the woman who has cultivated in herself the habit of giving, in moderation, to charity. She is no less a responsible moral agent for acting in accord with such habits, for the actions that result are the product of her self concept, now expressed in routinized ways.

What the high-level mental mechanisms that have developed in us allow us to do is direct our lives along pathways that we have chosen. The *we* in this case are the autonomous adaptive systems that constitute our whole existence. We are not merely pushed here and there by the causal factors in our environment, but respond to them using our developed mental mechanisms. When these mechanisms include the capacity to develop a concept of self, to modify and refine that concept through the course of experience, and to engage the world on the basis of that concept, I maintain that we have a robust basis for freedom and dignity.

References

Abraham, R.H., & Shaw, C.D. (1992). *Dynamics: The geometry of behavior*. Redwood City, CA: Addison-Wesley.

Abrahamsen, A.A. (1987). Bridging boundaries versus breaking boundaries: Psycholinguistics in perspective. *Synthese, 72*(3), 355–388.

Adams, F. (2000). Fodor's asymmetrical causal dependency theory of meaning. In M. Nani & M. Marraffa (Eds.), *A field guide to the philosophy of mind*. http://www.uniroma3.it/kant/field/asd.htm.

Adrian, E.D. (1928). *The basis of sensation: The action of the sense organs*. New York: W. W. Norton & Company.

Adrian, E.D. (1940). Double representation of the feet in the sensory cortex of the cat. *Journal of Physiology, 98*, 16P–18P.

Adrian, E.D., & Bronk, D.W. (1929). The discharge of impulses in motor nerve fibres. Part II. The frequency of discharge in reflex and voluntary contractions. *Journal of Physiology, 66*, 119–151.

Aizawa, K. (2007). The biochemistry of memory consolidation: A model system for the philosophy of mind. *Synthese, 155*, 65–98.

Akins, K. (1996). On sensory systems and the 'aboutness' of mental states. *The Journal of Philosophy, 93*(7), 337–372.

Allman, J.M. (1999). *Evolving brains*. New York: W. H. Freeman.

Allman, J.M., & Kaas, J.H. (1971). A representation of the visual field in the caudal third of the middle temporal gyrus of the owl monkey (*Aotus Trivirgatus*). *Brain Research, 31*(1971), 85–105.

Andersen, R.A., Essick, G.K., & Siegel, R.M. (1985). Encoding of spatial location by posterior parietal neurons. *Science, 230*, 456–458.

Anderson, J.R. (1990). *Cognitive psychology and its implications* (3rd ed.). New York: Freeman.

Armstrong, D.M. (1968). *A materialist theory of mind*. London: Routledge and Kegan Paul.

Ashby, W.R. (1952). *Design for a brain*. London: Chapman and Hall.

Atkinson, R.C., & Shiffrin, R.M. (1968). Human memory: A proposed system and its control processes. In K.W. Spence & J.T. Spence (Eds.), *The psychology of learning and motivation: Advances in research and theory* (Vol. 2, pp. 89–195). New York: Academic.

Baddeley, A.D. (1986). *Working memory*. Oxford: Clarendon Press.

Baddeley, A.D., & Hitch, G.J. (1974). Working memory. In G. Bower (Ed.), *The psychology of learning and motivation: Advances in research and theory* (Vol. 8, pp. 47–90). New York: Academic Press.

Bailey, P., von Bonin, G., Garol, H.W., & McCulloch, W.S. (1943). Long association fibers in cerebral hemispheres of monkey and chimpanzee. *Journal of Neurophysiology, 6*, 129–134.

Bálint, R. (1909). Seelenlähmung des Schauens, optische Ataxie, räumliche Störung der Aufmerksamkeit. *Monatschrift für Psychiatrie und Neurologie, 25,* 5–81.

Ball, P. (1994). *Designing the molecular world: Chemistry at the frontier.* Princeton, NJ: Princeton University Press.

Ballard, D.H. (1991). Animate vision. *Artificial Intelligence, 48,* 57–86.

Barandiaran, X., & Moreno, A. (2006). On what makes certain dynamical systems cognitive: A minimally cognitive organization program. *Adaptive Behavior, 14,* 171–185.

Barlow, H.B. (1953). Summation and inhibition in the frog's retina. *Journal of Physiology, 119,* 69–88.

Barlow, H.B. (1969). Pattern recognition and the responses of sensory neurons. *Annals of the New York Academy of Sciences, 156,* 872–881.

Barlow, H.B. (1972). Single units and sensation: A neuron doctrine for perceptual psychology? *Perception, 1,* 371–394.

Barlow, H.B. (1999). Feature detectors. In R.A. Wilson & F. Keil (Eds.), *The MIT encyclopedia of the cognitive sciences* (pp. 310–312). Cambridge: MIT Press.

Barsalou, L.W. (1983). Ad hoc categories. *Memory and Cognition, 11,* 221–227.

Barsalou, L.W. (1987). The instability of graded structure: Implications for the nature of concepts. In U. Neisser (Ed.), *Concepts reconsidered: The ecological intellectual bases of categories.* Cambridge: Cambridge University Press.

Barsalou, L.W. (1999). Perceptual symbol systems. *Behavioral and Brain Sciences, 22,* 577–660.

Bartholow, R. (1874). Experimental investigations into the functions of the human brain. *American Journal of Medical Science, 67,* 305–313.

Bartlett, F.C. (1932). *Remembering.* Cambridge: Cambridge University Press.

Batista, A.P., Buneo, C.A., Snyder, L.H., & Andersen, R.A. (1999). Reach plans in eye-centered coordinates. *Science, 285,* 257–260.

Beatty, J. (1995). The evolutionary contingency thesis. In G. Wolters & J. Lennox (Eds.), *Theories and rationality in the biological sciences, The second annual Pittsburgh/ Konstanz colloquium in the philosophy of science* (pp. 45–81). Pittsburgh, PA: University of Pittsburgh Press.

Bechara, A., Damasio, A.R., Damasio, H., & Anderson, S.W. (1994). Insensitivity to future consequences following damage to human prefrontal cortex. *Cognition, 50,* 7–15.

Bechtel, W. (1995). Biological and social constraints on cognitive processes: The need for dynamical interactions between levels of inquiry. *Canadian Journal of Philosophy, Suppl. 20,* 133–164.

Bechtel, W. (1998). Representations and cognitive explanations: Assessing the dynamicist's challenge in cognitive science. *Cognitive Science, 22,* 295–318.

Bechtel, W. (2000). From imaging to believing: Epistemic issues in generating biological data. In R. Creath & J. Maienschein (Eds.), *Biology and epistemology* (pp. 138–163). Cambridge: Cambridge University Press.

Bechtel, W. (2002). Aligning multiple research techniques in cognitive neuroscience: Why is it important? *Philosophy of Science, 69,* S48–S58.

Bechtel, W. (2006). *Discovering cell mechanisms: The creation of modern cell biology.* Cambridge: Cambridge University Press.

Bechtel, W. (in press). The epistemology of evidence in cognitive neuroscience. In R. Skipper, C. Allen, R.A. Ankeny, C.F. Craver, L. Darden, G. Mikkelson, & R.C. Richardson (Eds.), *Philosophy and the life sciences: A reader.* Cambridge, MA: MIT Press.

Bechtel, W. (2007). Organization and biological mechanisms: Organized to maintain autonomy. In F.C. Boogerd, F.J. Bruggeman, J.-H. Hofmeyr, & H.V. Westerhoff (Eds.), *Systems biology: Philosophical Foundations* (pp. 269–302) New York: Elsevier.

Bechtel, W., & Abrahamsen, A. (1993). Connectionism and the future of folk psychology. In R. Burton (Ed.), *Minds: Natural and artificial* (pp. 69–100). Albany, NY: SUNY University Press.

Bechtel, W., & Abrahamsen, A. (2002). *Connectionism and the mind: Parallel processing, dynamics, and evolution in networks* (2nd ed.). Oxford: Blackwell.

Bechtel, W., & Abrahamsen, A. (2005). Explanation: A mechanist alternative. *Studies in History and Philosophy of Biological and Biomedical Sciences, 36,* 421–441.

Bechtel, W., & McCauley, R.N. (1999). Heuristic identity theory (or back to the future): The mind-body problem against the background of research strategies in cognitive neuroscience. In M. Hahn & S.C. Stoness (Eds.), *Proceedings of the 21st Annual Meeting of the Cognitive Science Society* (pp. 67–72). Mahwah, NJ: Lawrence Erlbaum Associates.

Bechtel, W., & Mundale, J. (1999). Multiple realizability revisited: Linking cognitive and neural states. *Philosophy of Science, 66,* 175–207.

Bechtel, W., & Richardson, R.C. (1993). *Discovering complexity: Decomposition and localization as strategies in scientific research.* Princeton, NJ: Princeton University Press.

Beer, R.D. (1995). A dynamical systems perspective on agent-environment interaction. *Artificial Intelligence, 72,* 173–215.

Berger, H. (1929). Über daas Elektroenkephalogramm des Menschen. *Archiv für Psychiatrie und Nervenkrankheiten, 87,* 527–570.

Bernard, C. (1865). *An introduction to the study of experimental medicine.* New York: Dover.

Bernard, C. (1878). *Leçons sur les phénomènes de la vie communs aux animaux et aux végétaux.* Paris: Baillière.

Berthollet, C.L. (1780). Recherches sur la nature des substances animales et sur leurs rapports avec les substances végétales. *Mémoires de l'Acadeâmie royale des sciences,* 120–125.

Berzelius, J.J. (1836). Einige Ideen über bei der Bildung organischer Verbindungen in der lebenden Naturwirksame, aber bisher nicht bemerke Kraft. *Jahres-Berkcht über die Fortschritte der Chemie, 15,* 237–245.

Bichat, X. (1805). *Recherches Physiologiques sur la Vie et la Mort* (3rd ed.). Paris: Machant.

Bickhard, M.H., & Terveen, L. (1995). *Foundational issues in artificial intelligence and cognitive science: Impasse and solution.* Amsterdam: North Holland.

Bickle, J. (1998). *Psychoneural reduction: The new wave.* Cambridge, MA: MIT Press.

Bickle, J. (2003). *Philosophy and neuroscience: A ruthlessly reductive account.* Dordrecht: Kluwer.

Biederman, I. (1981). On the semantics of a glance at a scene. In M. Kubovy & J. Pomerantz (Eds.), *Perceptual organization.* Hillsdale, NJ: Erlbaum.

Biederman, I., Mezzanotte, R.J., & Rabinowitz, J.C. (1982). Scene perception: Detecting and judging objects undergoing relational violations. *Cognitive Psychology, 14,* 143–177.

Bishop, M., & Trout, J.D. (2005). *Epistemology and the psychology of human judgment.* New York: Oxford University Press.

Blaxton, T.A. (1989). Investigating dissociations among memory measures: Support for a transfer appropriate processing framework. *Journal of Experimental Psychology: Learning, Memory, and Cognition, 15,* 657–668.

Bliss, T.V.P., & Collingridge, G.L. (1993). A synaptic model of memory: Long-term potentiation in the hippocampus. *Nature, 361,* 31–39.

Block, N. (1986). Advertisement for a semantics for psychology. In P. French, T. Uehling, & H. Wettstein (Eds.), *Midwest studies in philosophy* (Vol. 10, pp. 615–678). Minneapolis, MN: University of Minnesota Press.

Boas, M. (1952). The establishment of the mechanical philosophy. *Osiris, 10,* 412–541.

Bogen, J., & Woodward, J. (1988). Saving the phenomena. *Philosophical Review, 97,* 303–352.

Boogerd, F.C., Bruggeman, F.J., Richardson, R.C., Stephan, A., & Westerhoff, H.V. (2005). Emergence and its place in nature: A case study of biochemical networks. *Synthese, 145,* 131–164.

Bradley, D.C., Maxwell, M., Andersen, R.A., Banks, M.S., & Shenoy, K.V. (1996). Mechanisms of heading perception in primate visual cortex. *Science, 273,* 1544–1547.

Bransford, J.D., Franks, J.J., Morris, C.D., & Stein, B.S. (1979). Some general constraints on learning and memory research. In L.S. Cermak & F.I.M. Craik (Eds.), *Levels of processing in human memory* (pp. 331–354). Hillsdale, NJ: Erlbaum.

Braver, T.S., Cohen, J.D., Nystrom, L.E., Jonides, J., Smith, E.E., & Noll, D.C. (1997). A parametric study of prefrontal cortex involvement in human working memory. *Neuroimage, 5,* 49–62.

Brentano, F. (1874). *Psychology from an empirical standpoint* (A.C. Pancurello, D.B. Terrell, & L.L. McAlister, Trans.). New York: Humanities.

Brewer, J.B., Zhao, Z., Desmond, J.E., Glover, G.H., & Gabrieli, J.D.E. (1998). Making memories: Brain activity that predicts how well visual experience will be remembered. *Science, 281,* 1185–1187.

Britten, K.H., Shadlen, M.N., Newsome, W.T., & Movshon, J.A. (1992). The analysis of visual motion: A comparison of neuronal and psychophysical performance. *The Journal of Neuroscience, 12*(12), 4745–4765.

Broadbent, D. (1958). *Perception and communication.* London: Pergmanon Press.

Broca, P. (1861). Remarques sur le siége de la faculté du langage articulé, suivies d'une observation d'aphemie (perte de la parole). *Bulletin de la Société Anatomique, 6,* 343–357.

Brodmann, K. (1909/1994). *Vergleichende Lokalisationslehre der Grosshirnrinde* (L.J. Garvey, Trans.). Leipzig: J. A. Barth.

Brown, R., & Kulik, J. (1977). Flashbulb memories. *Cognition, 5,* 73–99.

Brown, S., & Schäfer, E.A. (1888). An investigation into the functions of the occipital and temporal lobes of the monkey's brain. *Philosophical Transactions of the Royal Society of London, 179,* 303–327.

Bruce, C., Desimone, R., & Gross, C.G. (1981). Visual properties of neurons in a polysensory area in superior temporal sulcus of the macaque. *Journal of Neurophysiology* (46), 369–384.

Bruner, J.S. (1991). *Acts of meaning: Four lectures on mind and culture.* Cambridge, MA: Harvard University Press.

Bruner, J.S., & Postman, L. (1949). On the perception of incongruity: A paradigm. *The Journal of Personality, 18,* 206–223.

Buckner, R.L. (1996). Beyond HERA: Contributions of specific prefrontal brain areas to long-term memory retrieval. *Psychonomic Bulletin and Review, 3*(2), 149–158.

Buckner, R.L. (2003). Functional anatomical correlates of control processes in memory. *Journal of Neuroscience, 23,* 3999–4004.

Buckner, R.L., & Schacter, D.L. (2004). Neural correlates of memories successes and sins. In M.S. Gazzaniga (Ed.), *The cognitive neurosciences III* (pp. 739–752). Cambridge, MA: MIT Press.

Bush, R.R., & Mosteller, F. (1951). A mathematical model for simple learning. *Psychological Review, 58*, 313–323.

Butler, A.B. (2000). Chordate evolution and the origin of craniates: An old brain in a new head. *The Anatomical Record, 261*, 111–125.

Cabeza, R. (1994). A dissociation between two implicit conceptual tests supports the distinction between types of conceptual processing. *Psychonomic Bulletin and Review, 1*, 505–508.

Callebaut, W. (1993). *Taking the naturalistic turn, or, how real philosophy of science is done.* Chicago, IL: University of Chicago Press.

Campbell, D.T. (1974). 'Downward causation' in hierarchically organised biological systems. In F.J. Ayala & T. Dobzhansky (Eds.), *Studies in the philosophy of biology*: London: Macmillan.

Cannon, W.B. (1929). Organization of physiological homeostasis. *Physiological Reviews, 9*, 399–431.

Carnap, R. (1936). Testability and meaning. Part 1. *Philosophy of Science, 3*, 420–468.

Carnap, R. (1937). Testability and meaning. Part 2. *Philosophy of Science 4*, 1–40.

Causey, R.L. (1977). *Unity of science.* Dordrecht: Reidel.

Cave, C.B., & Squire, L.R. (1992). Intact verbal and nonverbal short-term memory following damage to the human hippocampus. *Hippocampus, 2*, 151–163.

Chalmers, D.J. (1990). Syntactic transformations on distributed representations. *Connection Science, 2*, 53–62.

Chalmers, D. J. (1996). *The conscious mind.* Oxford: Oxford University Press.

Chomsky, N. (1956). Three models for the description of language. *Transactions on Information Theory, 2*(3), 113–124.

Christiansen, W.D., & Bickhard, M.H. (2002). The process dynamics of normative function. *Monist, 85*, 3–28.

Christiansen, W.D., & Hooker, C.A. (2000). Autonomy and the emergence of intelligence: Organized interactive construction. *Communication and Cognition — Artificial Intelligence, 17*, 13–157.

Church, B.A., & Schacter, D.L. (1994). Perceptual specificity of auditory priming: Implicit memory for voice intonation and fundamental frequency. *Journal of Experimental Psychology: Learning, Memory, and Cognition, 20*, 521–533.

Churchland, P.M. (1981). Eliminative materialism and propositional attitudes. *The Journal of Philosophy, 78*, 67–90.

Churchland, P.S. (1986). *Neurophilosophy: Toward a unified science of the mind-brain.* Cambridge, MA: MIT Press/Bradford Books.

Churchland, P.S., Ramachandran, V.S., & Sejnowski, T.J. (1994). A critique of pure vision. In C. Koch & J.L. Davis (Eds.), *Large-scale neuronal theories of the brain* (pp. 23–60). Cambridge, MA: MIT Press.

Churchland, P.S., & Sejnowski, T.J. (1988). Perspectives on cognitive neuroscience. *Science, 242*, 741–745.

Clark, A. (1997). *Being there.* Cambridge, MA: MIT Press.

Clark, A., & Chalmers, D. (1998). The extended mind. *Analysis, 58*, 10–23.

Clark, A., & Toribio, J. (1994). Doing without representing? *Synthese, 101*, 401–431.

Clarke, E., & Dewhurst, K. (1972). *An illustrated history of brain function.* Oxford: Sandford Publications.

Cohen, J. (2004). Information and content. In L. Floridi (Ed.), *Blackwell guide to the philosophy of information and computing* (pp. 215–227). Oxford: Blackwell.

Cohen, N.J., & Eichenbaum, H. (1993). *Memory, amnesia, and the hippocampal system.* Cambridge, MA: MIT Press.

Cohen, N.J., & Squire, L.R. (1980). Preserved learning and retention of pattern-analyzing skill in amnesia: Dissociation of knowing how and knowing that. *Science, 210,* 207–210.

Collier, J.O., & Hooker, C.A. (1999). Complex organized dynamical systems. *Open Systems and Information Dynamics, 6,* 241–302.

Corbetta, M., Miezin, F.M., Shulman, G.L., & Petersen, S.E. (1993). A PET study of visuo-spatial attention. *The Journal of Neuroscience, 13*(3), 1202–1226.

Corkin, S., Amaral, D.G., González, R.G., Johnson, K.A., & Hyman, B.T. (1997). H.M.'s medial temporal lesion: Findings from magnetic resonance imiaging. *The Journal of neuroscience, 17,* 3964–3979.

Cowan, N. (1995). *Attention and memory: An integrated framework.* New York: Oxford.

Cowey, A. (1964). Projection of the retina on to striate and prestriate cortex in the squirrel monkey *Saimiri Sciureus. Journal of Neurophysiology, 27,* 366–393.

Craik, F.I.M., & Lockhart, R.S. (1972). Levels of processing: A framework for memory research. *Journal of verbal learning and verbal behavior, 12,* 599–607.

Craik, F.I.M., & Tulving, E. (1975). Depth of processing and retention of words in episodic memory. *Journal of Experimental Psychology: General, 104,* 268–294.

Craik, K. (1943). *The nature of explanation.* Cambridge: Cambridge University Press.

Crammond, D.J. (1997). Motor imager: Never in your wildest dreams. *Trends in Neuroscience, 20,* 54–57.

Craver, C. (2007). *Explaining the brain: What a science of the mind-brain could be.* New York: Oxford University Press.

Craver, C., & Bechtel, W. (in press). Top-down causation without top-down causes. *Biology and Philosophy.*

Crowder, R.G. (1993). Systems and principles in memory: Another critique of pure memory. In A.F. Collins, S.E. Gathercole, M.A. Conway, & P.E. Morris (Eds.), *Theories of memory* (pp. 139–161). Hillsdale, NJ: Erlbaum.

Cummins, D.D., & Allen, C. (1998). Introduction. In D.D. Cummins & C. Allen (Eds.), *The evolution of mind* (pp. 3–8). Oxford: Oxford University Press.

Cummins, R. (1975). Functional analysis. *Journal of Philosophy, 72,* 741–765.

Cummins, R. (1983). *The nature of psychological explanation.* Cambridge, MA: MIT Press/Bradford Books.

Cummins, R. (2000). "How does it work?" versus "what are the laws?": Two conceptions of psychological explanation. In F. Keil & R. Wilson (Eds.), *Explanation and cognition* (pp. 117–144). Cambridge, MA: MIT Press.

Cushing, H. (1909). A note upon the faradic stimulation of the post-central gyrus in conscious patients. *Brain, 32,* 44–53.

Darden, L. (1991). *Theory change in science: Strategies from Mendelian genetics.* New York: Oxford University Press.

Darden, L. (2006). *Reasoning in biological discoveries.* Cambridge: Cambridge University Press.

Darden, L., & Maull, N. (1977). Interfield theories. *Philosophy of Science, 43,* 44–64.

Dawkins, R. (1976). *The selfish gene.* Oxford: Oxford University Press.

Dawson, G.D. (1951). A summation technique for detecting small signals in a large irregular background. *Journal of Physiology, 115,* 2P.

Deese, J. (1959). On the prediction of occurrence of particular verbal intrusions in immediate recall. *Journal of Experimental Psychology, 58,* 17–22.

Dennett, D.C. (1971). Intentional systems. *The Journal of Philosophy, 68,* 87–106.

Dennett, D.C. (1988). Quining qualia. In A. Marcel & E. Bisiach (Eds.), *Consciousness in contemporary science* (pp. 42–77). New York: Oxford.

Desimone, R., Albright, T.D., Gross, C.G., & Bruce, C. (1984). Stimulus-selective properties of inferior temporal neurons in the macaque. *Journal of Neuroscience, 4,* 2051–2062.

Deutsch, J.A., & Deutsch, D. (1963). Attention: Some theoretical concerns. *Psychological Review, 70,* 80–90.

Donders, F.C. (1868). Over de snelheid van psychische processen. Onderzoekingen gedaan in het Physiologisch Laboratorium der Utrechtsche Hoogeschool: 1868–1869. *Tweede Reeks, 2,* 92–120.

Donders, F.C. (1969). On the speed of mental processes. *Acta Psychologica, 30,* 412–431.

Dreher, B., Fukada, Y., & Rodieck, R.W. (1976). Identification, classification and anatomical segregation of cells with X-like and Y-like properties in the lateral geniculate nucleus of old-world primates. *Journal of Physiology, 258,* 433–452.

Dretske, F.I. (1981). *Knowledge and the flow of information.* Cambridge, MA: MIT Press/ Bradford Books.

Dretske, F.I. (1983). The epistemology of belief. *Synthese, 55,* 3–19.

Dretske, F.I. (1988). *Explaining behavior: Reasons in a world of causes.* Cambridge, MA: MIT Press.

Duffy, C.J., & Wurtz, R.H. (1991a). Sensitivity of MST neurons to optic flow stimuli. I. A continuum of response selectivity to large-field stimuli. *Journal of Neuroscience, 65,* 1329–1345.

Duffy, C.J., & Wurtz, R.H. (1991b). Sensitivity of MST neurons to optic flow stimuli. II. Mechanisms of response selectivity revealed by small-field stimuli. *Journal of Neuroscience, 65,* 1346–1359.

Duhamel, J.-R., Colby, C.L., & Goldberg, M.E. (1992). The updating of the representation of visual space in parietal cortex by intended eye movements. *Science, 255,* 90–92.

Dunbar, K. (1995). How scientists really reason: Scientific reasoning in real-world laboratories. In R.J. Sternberg & J.E. Davidson (Eds.), *Mechanisms of insight* (pp. 365–395). Cambridge, MA: MIT Press.

Düzel, E., Cabeza, R., Picton, T.W., Yonelinas, A.P., Scheich, H., Heinze, H.-J. & Tulving, E. (1999). Task-related and item-related brain processes of memory retrieval. *Proceedings of the National Academy of Sciences (USA), 96,* 1794–1799.

Ebbinghaus, H. (1885). *Über das Gedächtnis: Untersuchungen zur experimentellen Psychologie.* Leipzig: Duncker & Humblot.

Eichenbaum, H., Otto, T., & Cohen, N.J. (1993). Two component functions of the hippocampal memory systems. *Behavioral and Brain Sciences, 17*(3), 449–472.

Eliasmith, C. (1996). The third contender: a critical examination of the dynamicist theory of cognition. *Philosophical Psychology, 9,* 441–463.

Eliasmith, C. (1997). Computation and dynamical models of mind. *Minds and Machines, 7,* 531–541.

Elliot Smith, G. (1907). New studies on the folding of the visual cortex and the significance of the occipital sulci in the human brain. *Journal of Anatomy, 41,* 198–207.

Elman, J.L. (1993). Learning and development in neural networks: The importance of starting small. *Cognition, 48,* 71–99.

Elman, J.L., Bates, E.A., Johnson, M.H., Karmiloff-Smith, A., Parisi, D., & Plunkett, K. (1996). *Rethinking innateness: A connectionist perspective on development.* Cambridge, MA: MIT Press.

Enç, B. (1983). In defense of the identity theory. *Journal of Philosophy, 80,* 279–298.

Enroth-Cugell, C., & Robson, J.G. (1966). The contrast sensitivity of retinal ganglion cells of the cat. *Journal of Physiology, 187*, 517–552.

Estes, W.K. (1950). Towards a statistical theory of learning. *Psychological Review, 57*, 94–107.

Ettlinger, G., & Kalsbeck, J.E. (1962). Changes in tactual discrimination and in visual reaching after successive and simultaneous bilateral posterior parietal ablations in the monkey. *Journal of Neurological and Neurosurgical Psychiatry, 25*, 256–268.

Farah, M. (1995). The neural bases of mental imagery. In M.S. Gazzaniga (Ed.), *The cognitive neurosciences* (pp. 963–975). Cambridge, MA: MIT Press.

Felleman, D.J., & van Essen, D.C. (1991). Distributed hierarchical processing in the primate cerebral cortex. *Cerebral Cortex, 1*, 1–47.

Ferrier, D. (1873). Experimental researches in cerebral physiology and pathology. *West Riding Lunatic Asylum Medical Reports, 3*, 30–96.

Ferrier, D. (1876). *The functions of the brain.* London: Smith, Elder, and Company.

Ferrier, D. (1881). Cerebral ambylopia and hemiopia. *Brain, 11*, 7–30.

Ferrier, D. (1890). *The Croonian lectures on cerebral localisation.* London: Smith, Elder.

Ferrier, D., & Yeo, G.F. (1884). A record of the experiments on the effects of lesions of different regions of the cerebral hemispheres. *Philosophical Transactions of the Royal Society of London, 175*, 479–564.

Feyerabend, P.K. (1962). Explanation, reduction, and empiricism. In H. Feigl & G. Maxwell (Eds.), *Minnesota studies in the philosophy of science* (Vol. III, pp. 28–97). Minneapolis, MN: University of Minnesota Press.

Feyerabend, P.K. (1963). Mental events and the brain. *The Journal of Philosophy, 60*, 295–296.

Feyerabend, P.K. (1970). Against method: Outline of an anarchistic theory of knowledge. In M. Radner & S. Winokur (Eds.), *Minnesota studies in the philosophy of science.* (Vol. IV, pp. 17–130). Minneapolis, MN: University of Minnesota Press.

Feyerabend, P.K. (1975). *Against method.* London: New Left Books.

Field, H.H. (1977). Logic, meaning, and conceptual role. *Journal of Philosophy, 69*, 379–408.

Field, R.J., Koros, E., & Noyes, R.M. (1972). Oscillations in chemical systems. II. Thorough analysis of temporal oscillation in the Bromate–Cerium–Malonic acid system. *Journal of the American Chemical Society, 94*, 8649–8664.

Finger, S. (1994). *Origins of neuroscience.* Oxford: Oxford University Press.

Finger, S. (2000). *Minds behind the brain: A history of the pioneers and their discoveries.* Oxford: Oxford University Press.

Fitzpatrick, S.M., & Rothman, D.L. (1999). New approaches to functional neuroenergetics. *Journal of Cognitive Neuroscience, 11*, 467–471.

Flechsig, P.E. (1896). *Gehirn und Steele.* Leipzig: Veit.

Flechsig, P.E. (1920). *Anatomie des menschlichen Gehirns und Rückenmarks auf myelogenetischer Grundlage.* Leipzig: Thieme.

Flourens, M.J.P. (1846). *Phrenology examined* (C.D.L. Meigs, Trans.). Philadelphia, PA: Hogan and Thompson.

Fodor, J.A. (1968). *Psychological explanation.* New York: Random House.

Fodor, J.A. (1974). Special sciences (or: the disunity of science as a working hypothesis). *Synthese, 28*, 97–115.

Fodor, J.A. (1975). *The language of thought.* New York: Crowell.

Fodor, J.A. (1980). Methodological solipsism considered as a research strategy in cognitive psychology. *The Behavioral and Brain Sciences, 3*, 63–109.

Fodor, J.A. (1983). *The modularity of mind*. Cambridge, MA: MIT Press.

Fodor, J.A. (1987). *Psychosemantics: The problem of meaning in the philosophy of mind*. Cambridge, MA: MIT Press.

Fodor, J.A. (1990a). Psychosemantics or: Where do truth conditions come from? In W.G. Lycan (Ed.), *Mind and cognition: A reader* (pp. 312–338). Oxford: Blackwell.

Fodor, J.A. (1990b). *A theory of content and other essays*. Cambridge, MA: MIT Press.

Fodor, J.A. (1997). Special sciences: Still autonomous after all these years. *Philosophical Perspectives, 11*, 149–163.

Fodor, J.A., & Lepore, E. (1992). *Holism: A shopper's guide*. Oxford: Blackwell.

Fodor, J.A., & McLaughlin, B. (1990). Connectionism and the problem of systematicity: Why Smolensky's solution doesn't work. *Cognition, 35*, 183–204.

Fodor, J.A., & Pylyshyn, Z.W. (1988). Connectionism and cognitive architecture: A critical analysis. *Cognition, 28*, 3–71.

Fox, P.T., Raichle, M.E., Mintun, M.A., & Dence, C. (1988). Nonoxidative glucose consumption during focal physiologic neural activity. *Science, 241*, 462–464.

Freeman, W.J., & Skarda, C.A. (1990). Representations: Who needs them? In J.L. McGaugh, N. Weinberger, & G. Lynch (Eds.), *Brain organization and memory: Cells, systems and circuits* (pp. 375–380). New York: Oxford.

Freud, S. (1891). *Zur Auffassung der Aphasien*. Vienna: Beuticke.

Frith, C.D., & Friston, K.J. (1997). Studying brain function with neuroimaging. In M. Rugg (Ed.), *Cognitive neuroscience* (pp. 169–195). Cambridge, MA: MIT Press.

Fritsch, G.T., & Hitzig, E. (1870). Über die elecktrische Erregbarkeit des Grosshirns. *Arhiv für Anatomie und Physiologie*, 300–332.

Gabrieli, J.D.E. (2001). Functional neuroimaging of episodic memory. In R. Cabeza & A. Kingstone (Eds.), *Handbook of functional neuroimaging of cognition* (pp. 49–72). Cambridge, MA: MIT Press.

Gabrieli, J.D.E., Poldrack, R.A., & Desmond, J.E. (1998). The role of left prefrontal cortex in language and memory. *Proceedings of the National Academy of Sciences, USA, 95*, 906–913.

Gaffan, D. (2002). Against memory systems. *Philosophical Transactions of the Royal Society of London. Series B, Biological Sciences, 357*, 1111–1121.

Gaffan, D., Parker, A., & Easton, A. (2001). Dense amnesia in the monkey after transection of fornix, amygdala, and anterior temporal stem. *Neuropsychologia, 39*, 51–70.

Gall, F.J., & Spurzheim, J.C. (1810–1819/1835). On the functions of the brain and each of its parts: With observations of the possibility of determining the instincts, propensities, and talents, or the moral and intellectual dispositions of man and animals, by the configuration of the brain and the head (W. Lewis Jr., Trans.). Boston, MA: Marsh, Capen, and Lyon.

Gallant, J.L., Braun, J., & van Essen, D.C. (1993). Selectivity for polar, hyperbolic, and Cartesian gratings in macaque visual cortex. *Science, 259*, 100–103.

Galvani, L. (1791). *De viribus electricitatis in motu musculari commentarius*. Bologna: Ex typographia Instituti Scientiarum.

Gánti, T. (1975). Organization of chemical reactions into dividing and metabolizing units: The chemotons. *BioSystems, 7*, 15–21.

Gánti, T. (2003). *The principles of life*. New York: Oxford.

Garcia, J., McGowan, B.K., Ervin, F.R., & Koelling, R.A. (1968). Cues: Their relative effectiveness as a function of the reinforcer. *Science, 160*, 794–795.

Gennari, F. (1782). *De peculiari structura cerebri nonnullisque ejus morbis*. Parma: Ex regio typographeo.

Gibson, J.J. (1950). *The perception of the visual world*. Boston, MA: Houghton-Mifflin.

Gibson, J.J. (1966). *The senses considered as perceptual systems*. Boston, MA: Houghton Mifflin.

Gibson, J.J. (1979). *The ecological approach to visual perception*. Boston, MA: Houghton Mifflin.

Gibson, J.J., Olum, P., & Rosenblatt, F. (1955). Parallax and perspective during aircraft landings. *American Journal of Psychology, 68*, 372–385.

Giere, R.G. (1988). *Explaining science: A cognitive approach*. Chicago, IL: University of Chicago Press.

Giere, R.G. (1999). *Science without laws*. Chicago, IL: University of Chicago Press.

Giere, R.G. (2002). Scientific cognition as distributed cognition. In P. Carruthers, S. Stich, & M. Siegal (Eds.), *The cognitive bases of science*. Cambridge: Cambridge University Press.

Glennan, S. (1996). Mechanisms and the nature of causation. *Erkenntnis, 44*, 50–71.

Glennan, S. (2002). Rethinking mechanistic explanation. *Philosophy of Science, 69*, S342–S353.

Glickstein, M. (1988). The discovery of the visual cortex. *Scientific American, 259*(3), 118–127.

Glickstein, M., & Rizzolatti, G. (1984). Francesco Gennari and the structure of the cerebral cortex. *Trends in Neuroscience, 7*, 464–467.

Goldberg, M.E., & Robinson, D.L. (1980). The significance of enhanced visual responses in posterior parietal cortex. *Behavioral and Brain Sciences, 3*, 503–505.

Goldin-Meadow, S., & Wagner, S.M. (2005). How our hands help us learn. *Trends in Cognitive Sciences, 9*, 234–241.

Goldman-Rakic, P.S. (1987). Circuitry of primate prefrontal cortex and regulation of behavior by representational memory. In J.M. Brookhart, V.B. Mountcastle, & S.R. Geiger (Eds.), *Handbook of physiology: The nervous system* (Vol. 5, pp. 373–417). Bethesda, MD: American Physiological Society.

Goldman-Rakic, P.S., Funahashi, S., & Bruce, C.J. (1990). Neocortical memory circuits. *Cold Spring Harbor Symposia on Quantitative Biology, 55*, 1025–1037.

Golgi, C. (1873). Sulla struttura della grigia del cervello. *Gazetta Medica Intaliana, 6*, 244–246.

Golgi, C. (1898). Intorno alla struttura delle cellule nervose. *Bollettino della Società Medico-Chirurgica di Pavia, 13*, 3–16.

Goodale, M.G., & Milner, A.D. (2004). *Sight unseen*. Oxford: Oxford University Press.

Gould, S.J., & Lewontin, R.C. (1979). The spandrels of San Marco and the Panglossian paradigm: A critique of the adaptationist programme. *Proceedings of the Royal Society of London, Series B, 205*, 581–598.

Gratiolet, P. (1854). Note sur les expansions des racines cérébrales du nerf optique et sur leur terminaison dans une région déterminée de l'écorce des hémisphès. *Comptes Rendus Herdomadaires des Séances de l'Académie des Sciences de Paris, 29*, 274–278.

Gray, J.A., & Wedderburn, A.A.I. (1960). Grouping strategies with simultaneous stimuli. *Quarterly Journal of Experimental Psychology, 12*, 180–184.

Gregory, R.L. (1968). Models and the localization of functions in the central nervous system. In C.R. Evans & A.D. J. Robertson (Eds.), *Key papers in cybernetics* (pp. 91–102). London: Butterworth.

Griesemer, J.R., & Szathmáry, E. (2007). Gánti's chemoton model and life criteria. In S. Rasmussen, L. Chen, N. Packard, M. Bedau, D. Deamer, P. Stadler, & D. Krakauer (Eds.), *Protocells: Bridging nonliving and living matter*. Cambridge, MA: MIT Press.

Gross, C.G. (1968). Learning, perception, and the brain. *Science, 160*, 652–653.

Gross, C.G. (1998). *Brain, vision, and memory.* Cambridge, MA: MIT Press.

Gross, C.G. (2005). Processing a facial image: A brief history. *American Psychologist, 60,* 755–763.

Gross, C.G., Bender, D.B., & Gerstein, G.L. (1979). Activity of inferotemporal neurons in behaving monkeys. *Neuropsychologia, 17,* 215–229.

Gross, C.G., Bender, D.B., & Rocha-Miranda, C.E. (1969). Visual receptive fields of neurons in inferotemporal cortex of the monkey. *Science, 166,* 1303–1306.

Gross, C.G., Rocha-Miranda, C.E., & Bender, D.B. (1972). Visual properties of neurons in inferotemporal cortex of the macaque. *Journal of Neurophysiology, 35,* 96–111.

Gross, C.G., Schiller, P.H., Wells, C., & Gerstein, G.L. (1967). Single-unit activity in temporal association cortex of the monkey. *Journal of Neurophysiology, 30,* 833–843.

Grünbaum, A.S.F., & Sherrington, C.S. (1903). Observations on the physiology of the cerebral cortex of the anthropoid apes. *Proceedings of the Royal Society of London, 72,* 152–155.

Grush, R. (1997). The architecture of representation. *Philosophical Psychology, 10,* 5–24.

Grush, R. (2004). The emulation theory of representation: Motor control, imagery, and perception. *Behavioral and Brain Sciences, 27,* 377–396.

Haaxma, R., & Kuypers, H.G.J.M. (1975). Intrahemispheric cortical connections and visual guidance of hand and finger movements in the rhesus monkey. *Brain, 98,* 239–260.

Hacking, I. (1983). *Representing and intervening.* Cambridge: Cambridge University Press.

Hafting, T., Fyhn, M., Molden, S., Moser, M.-B., & Moser, E.I. (2005). Microstructure of a spatial map in the entorhinal cortex. *Nature, 436,* 801–806.

Hagler, D.J., & Sereno, M.I. (2006). Spatial maps in frontal and prefrontal cortex. *Neuro-Image, 29,* 567–577.

Hamman, S.B. (1990). Level-of-processing effects in conceptually driven implicit tasks. *Journal of Experimental Psychology: Learning, Memory, and Cognition, 16,* 970–977.

Harman, G. (1987). (Non-solipsistic) conceptual role semantics. In E. Lepore (Ed.), *New directions in semantics.* London: Academic.

Hartline, H.K. (1938). The response of single optic nerve fibers of the vertebrate eye to illumination of the retina. *American Journal of Physiology, 113,* 400–415.

Hartline, H.K. (1940). The receptive field of optic nerve fibers. *American Journal of Physiology, 130,* 690–699.

Haselager, P., de Groot, A., & van Rappard, H. (2003). Representationalism vs. anti-representationalism: a debate for the sake of appearance. *Philosophical Psychology, 16,* 5–23.

Hastie, R., & Dawes, R.M. (2001). *Rational choice in an uncertain world: The psychology of judgment and decision making.* Thousand Oaks, CA: Sage.

Haugeland, J. (1991). Representational genera. In W. Ramsey, S.P. Stich & D.E. Rumelhart (Eds.), *Philosophy and connectionist theory* (pp. 61–89). Hillsdale, NJ: Lawrence Erlbaum.

Haxby, J.V., Grady, C.L., Horwitz, B., Ungerleider, L.G., Mishkin, M., Carson, R.E., Herscovitch, P., Schapiro, M.B., & Rapoport, S.I. (1991). Dissociation of object and spatial visual processing pathways in human extrastriate cortex. *Proceedings of the National Academy of Sciences, USA, 88,* 1621–1665.

Hebb, D. (1949). *The organization of behavior.* New York: Wiley.

Hegarty, M. (1992). Mental animation: Inferring motion from static displays of mechanical systems. *Journal of Experimental Psychology: Learning, Memory, and Cognition, 18,* 1084–1102.

Helmhotz, H.V. (1867). *Handbuch der physiologischen Optik.* Leipzig: Voss.

Hempel, C.G. (1962). *Deductive-nomological vs. statistical explanation*. Paper presented at the In Feigl, H. and Maxwell, G., Minnesota studies in the philosophy of science, Vol. III. Minneapolis, MN: University of Minnesota Press.

Henschen, S.E. (1893). On the visual path and centre. *Brain, 16*, 170–180.

Henschen, S.E. (1903). La projection de la retine sur la corticalite calcarine. *La Semaine Medicale, 23*, 125–127.

Henschen, S.E. (1924). On the value of the discovery of the visual centre: A review and a personal apology. *Scandinavian Scientific Review, 3*, 10–63.

Hilborn, R.C. (2004). Sea gulls, butterflies, and grasshoppers: A brief history of the butterfly effect in nonlinear dynamics. *American Journal of Physics, 72*, 425–427.

Hinton, G.E., & Shallice, T. (1991). Lesioning a connectionist network: Investigations of acquired dyslexia. *Psychological Review, 98*, 74–95.

Hitzig, E. (1900). Hughlings Jackson and the cortical motor centres in the light of physiological research. *Brain, 23*, 545–581.

Holmes, F.L. (1992). *Between biology and medicine: The formation of intermediary metabolism*. Berkeley, CA: Office for History of Science and Technology, University of California at Berkeley.

Holmes, G.M. (1918). Disturbances of visual orientation. *The British Journal of Ophthalmology, 2*, 449–468.

Holmes, G.M. (1919). Lecture I. — The cortical localization of vision. *British Medical Journal, 2*, 193–199.

Holmes, G.M., & Horrax, G. (1919). Disturbances of spatial orientation and visual attention, with loss of stereoscopic vision. *Archives of Neurology and Psychiatry, 1*, 385–407.

Hooker, C.A. (1981). Towards a general theory of reduction. *Dialogue, 20*, 38–59; 201–236; 496–529.

Hubel, D.H. (1959). Single unit activity in striate cortex of unrestrained cats. *Journal of Physiology, 147*, 226–238.

Hubel, D.H. (1960). Single unit activity in lateral geniculate body and optic tract of unrestrained cats. *Journal of Physiology, 150*, 91–104.

Hubel, D.H. (1982). Evolution of ideas on the primary visual cortex, 1955–1978: A biased historical account. *Bioscience Reports, 2*, 435–469.

Hubel, D.H. (1995). *Eye, brain, and vision*. New York: Scientific American Library.

Hubel, D.H., & Wiesel, T.N. (1959). Receptive fields of single neurones in the cat's striate cortex. *Journal of Physiology, 148*, 574–591.

Hubel, D.H., & Wiesel, T.N. (1961). Integrative action in the cat's lateral geniculate body. *Journal of Physiology, 155*, 385–398.

Hubel, D.H., & Wiesel, T.N. (1962). Receptive fields, binocular interaction and functional architecture in the cat's visual cortex. *Journal of Physiology, 160*, 106–154.

Hubel, D.H., & Wiesel, T.N. (1965a). Binocular interaction in striate cortex of kittens reared with artificial squint. *Journal of Neurophysiology, 28*, 1041–1059.

Hubel, D.H., & Wiesel, T.N. (1965b). Receptive fields and functional architecture in two non-striate visual areas (18 and 19) of the cat. *Journal of Neurophysiology, 195*, 229–289.

Hubel, D.H., & Wiesel, T.N. (1968). Receptive fields and functional architecture of monkey striate cortex. *Journal of Physiology, 195*, 215–243.

Hubel, D.H., & Wiesel, T.N. (1970). Stereoscopic vision in the macaque monkey. *Nature, 225*, 41–42.

Hull, D.L. (1974). *The philosophy of biological science*. Englewood Cliffs, NJ: Prentice-Hall.

Hume, D. (1739). *A treatise of human nature*. London: John Noon.

Hyvärinen, J., & Poranen, A. (1974). Function of the parietal associative area 7 as revealed from cellular discharges in alert monkeys. *Brain, 97*, 673–692.

Ingle, D.J. (1973). Two visual systems in the frog. *Science, 181*, 1053–1055.

Jablonka, E., & Lamb, M. (1995). *Epigenetic inheritance and evolution*. Oxford: Oxford University Press.

Jackson, F. (1982). Epiphenomenal qualia. *Philosophical Quarterly, 32*, 127–136.

Jackson, J.H. (1863). Convulsive spasms of the right hand and arm preceding epileptic seizures. *Medical Times and Gazette, 1*, 110–111.

Jackson, J.H. (1868–1869/1931). Notes on the physiology and pathology of the nervous system. In J. Taylor (Ed.), *Selected writings of John Hughlings Jackson* (Vol. II, pp. 215–237). New York: Basic Books.

Jackson, J.H. (1870). A study of convulsions. *Transactions of the St. Andrew's Medical Graduates Association, 3*, 162–204.

Jackson, J.H. (1870/1931). A study of convulsions. In J. Taylor (Ed.), *Selected writings of John Hughlings Jackson* (Vol. 1, pp. 8–36). New York: Basic Books.

Jackson, J.H. (1873). On the anatomical and physiological localization of movements in the brain. *Lancet, 101*, 84–85, 162–164, 232–234.

Jackson, J.H. (1875). *On the anatomical and physiological localisation of movement in the brain*. London: J. and A. Churchill.

Jackson, J.H. (1884). Evolution and dissolution of the nervous system (The Croonian Lectures). *Lancet, 123*, 555–558, 649–652, 739–744.

Jacob, F., & Monod, J. (1961). Genetic regulatory systems in the synthesis of proteins. *Journal of Molecular Biology, 3*, 318–356.

James, W. (1890/1950). *Principles of psychology*. New York: Dover.

Jeannerod, M. (1994). The representing brain: Neural correlates of motor intention and imagery. *Behavioral and Brain Sciences, 17*, 187–245.

Johnson, K. (2004). On the systematicity of language and thought. *Journal of Philosophy, 101*, 111–139.

Kahneman, D., Slovic, P., & Tversky, A. (Eds.). (1982). *Judgment under uncertainty: Heuristics and biases*. New York: Cambridge University Press.

Kalatsky, V.A., Polley, D.B., Merzenich, M.M., Schreiner, C.E., & Stryker, M.P. (2005). Fine functional organization of auditory cortex revealed by Fourier optical imaging. *Proceedings of the National Academy of Sciences (USA), 102*, 13325–13330.

Kaneko, K. (1990). Clustering, coding, switching, hierarchical ordering, and control in a network of chaotic elements. *Physica D, 41*, 137–142.

Kapur, S., Craik, F.I.M., Tulving, E., Wilson, A.A., Houle, S., & Brown, G.M. (1994). Neuroanatomical correlates of encoding in episodic memory: Levels of processing effect. *Proceedings of the National Academy of Sciences (USA), 91*, 2008–2111.

Kauffman, S. (1971). Articulation of parts explanations in biology and the rational serach for them. In R.C. Bluck & R.S. Cohen (Eds.), *PSA 1970* (pp. 257–272). Dordrecht: Reidel.

Keil, F.C. (1989). *Concepts, kinds, and conceptual development*. Cambridge, MA: MIT Press.

Kelley, W.L., Miezin, F.M., McDermott, K., Buckner, R.L., Raichle, M.E., Cohen, N.J., & Petersen, S.E. (1998). Hemispheric specialization in human dorsal frontal cortex and medial temporal lobes for verbal and nonverbal memory encoding. *Neuron, 20*, 927–936.

Kelso, J.A.S. (1995). *Dynamic patterns: The self organization of brain and behavior*. Cambridge, MA: MIT Press.

Kemeny, J.G., & Oppenheim, P. (1956). On reduction. *Philosophical Studies, 7*, 6–19.

Kentridge, R.W., Heywood, C.A., & Milner, A.D. (2004). Covert processing of visual form in the absence of area LO. *Neuropsychologia, 42*, 1488–1495.

Kim, J. (1966). On the psycho-physical identity theory. *American Philosophical Quarterly, 3*, 227–235.

Kim, J. (1993). *Supervenience and the mind*. Cambridge: Cambridge University Press.

Kim, J. (1998). *Mind in a physical world*. Cambridge, MA: MIT Press.

Kirsh, D. (1991). Today the earwig, tomorrow man? *Artificial Intelligence, 47*, 161–184.

Klahr, D., & Simon, H.A. (1999). Studies of scientific discovery: Complementary approaches and convergent findings. *Psychological Bulletin, 125*, 524–543.

Klüver, H. (1928). *Mescal: The "divine" plant and its psychological effects*. London: Kegan Paul, Trench, & Trubner.

Klüver, H. (1948). Functional differences between the occipital and temporal lobes with special reference to the interrelations of behavior and extracerebral mechanisms. In L. Jeffress (Ed.), *Cerebral mechanisms in behavior* (pp. 147–199). Wiley: New York.

Klüver, H., & Bucy, P. (1938). An analysis of certain effects of bilateral temporal lobectomy in the rhesus monkey, with special reference to "psychic blindness." *The Journal of Psychology, 5*, 33–54.

Klüver, H., & Bucy, P. (1939). Preliminary analysis of functions of the temporal lobes in monkeys. *Archives of Neurology and Psychiatry, 42*(6), 979–1000.

Kolers, P.A., & Ostry, D.J. (1974). Time course of loss of information regarding pattern analyzing operations. *Journal of Verbal Learning and Verbal Behavior, 13*, 599–612.

Kolers, P.A., & Perkins, D.N. (1975). Spatial and ordinal components of form perception and literacy. *Cognitive Psychology, 7*, 228–267.

Kolers, P.A., & Roediger, H.L. (1984). Procedures of mind. *Journal of Verbal Learning and Verbal Behavior, 23*, 425–449.

Komatsu, H., & Wurtz, R.H. (1989). Modulation of pursuit eye movements by stimulation of cortical areas MT and MST. *Journal of Neuroscience, 62*, 31–47.

Kosslyn, S.M. (1994). *Image and brain: The resolution of the imagery debate*. Cambridge, MA: MIT Press.

Kuffler, S.W. (1953). Discharge patterns and functional organization of mammalian retina. *Journal of Neurophysiology, 16*, 37–68.

Kuhn, T.S. (1962/1970). *The structure of scientific revolutions* (2nd ed.). Chicago, IL: University of Chicago Press.

Kuipers, T.A.F. (2001). *Structures in science*. Dordrecht: Kluwer.

Kurylo, D.D., & Skavenski, A.A. (1991). Eye movements elicited by electrical stimulation of area PG in the monkey. *Journal of Neurophysiology, 65*, 1243–1253.

Landau, L. (1944). On the problem of turbulence. *Comptes Rendus d'Academie des Sciences, URSS, 44*, 311–314.

Langacker, R. (1987). *Foundations of cognitive grammar* (Vol. 1). Stanford, CA: Stanford University Press.

Laplace, P.S. (1812/1951). *A philosophical essay on probabilities* (F.W. Truscott & F.L. Emory, Trans.). New York: Dover.

Lashley, K.S. (1929). *Brain mechanisms and intelligence*. Chicago, IL: University of Chicago Press.

Lashley, K.S. (1950). In search of the engram. *Symposia of the Society for Experimental Biology, IV. Physiological Mechanisms in Animal Behaviour*, 454–482.

Lashley, K.S. (1951). The problem of serial order in behavior. In *Cerebral mechanisms in behavior* (pp. 112–136). New York: John Wiley and Sons.

Lavoisier, A.L. (1781). Mémoire sur la formation de l'acide nommé air fixe ou acide crayeux, que je désignerai désormais sous le nom d'acide du charbon. *Mémoires de l'Acadeâmie royale des sciences*, 448–458.

Lavoisier, A.L., & LaPlace, P.S.D. (1780). Mémoire sur la Chaleur. *Mémoires de l'Acadeâmie royale des sciences*, 35–408.

Lettvin, J.Y., Maturana, H.R., McCulloch, W.S., & Pitts, W.H. (1959). What the frog's eye tells the frog's brain. *Proceedings of the Institute of Radio Engineers, 47*, 1940–1951.

Levin, D.T., & Simons, D.J. (1997). Failure to detect changes to attended objects in motion pictures. *Psychonomic Bulletin and Review, 4*, 501–506.

Levy, W.B., Colbert, C.M., & Desmond, N.L. (1990). Elemental adaptive processes of neurons and synapses: A statistical/computational perspective. In M.A. Gluck & D.E. Rumelhart (Eds.), *Neuroscience and connectionist theory* (pp. 187–235). Hillsdale, NJ: Erlbaum.

Lewis, D. (1980). Mad pain and Martian pain. In N. Block (Ed.), *Readings in philosophy of psychology* (Vol. 1, pp. 216–222). Cambridge, MA: Harvard University Press.

Lewis, D. (2000). Causation as influence. *Journal of Philosophy, 97*, 82–197.

Leyton, A.S.F., & Sherrington, C.S. (1917). Observations on the excitable cortex of the chimpanzee, orang-utan and gorilla. *Quarterly Journal of Experimental Psychology, 11*, 135–222.

Liebig, J. (1842). *Animal chemistry: Or organic chemistry in its application to physiology and pathology*. Cambridge: John Owen.

Lisman, J.E. (1999). Relating hippocampal circuitry to function: Recall of memory sequences by reciprocal detate-CA3 interactions. *Neuron, 22*, 233–242.

Lissauer, H. (1890). Ein Fall von Seelenblindheit nebst einem Beitrag zur Theorie derselben. *Archiv für Psychiatrie, 21*, 222–270.

Livingstone, M.S., & Hubel, D.H. (1984). Anatomy and physiology of a color system in the primate visual cortex. *Journal of Neuroscience, 4*, 309–356.

Loftus, E.F. (1975). Leading questions and the eyewitness report. *Cognitive Psychology, 7*, 550–572.

Loftus, E.F., & Palmer, S.E. (1974). Reconstruction of automobile destruction: An example of the interaction between language and memory. *Journal of Verbal Learning and Verbal Behavior, 13*, 585–589.

Loomis, J., & Beall, A.C. (1998). Visually controlled locomotion: Its dependence on optic flow, three-dimensional space perception, and cognition. *Ecological Psychology, 10*, 271–285.

Lorenz, E.N. (1963). The predictability of hydrodynamic flow. *Transactions of the New York Academy of Sciences, 25*, 405–432.

Luria, A.R. (1973). *The working brain*. New York: Basic.

Lycan, W.G. (1972). Materialism and Leibniz' Law. *Monist, 56*, 276–287.

Lycan, W.G. (1979). Form, function, and feel. *Journal Philosophy, 78*, 24–49.

Machamer, P., Darden, L., & Craver, C. (2000). Thinking about mechanisms. *Philosophy of Science, 67*, 1–25.

MacKay, G., & Dunlop, J.C. (1899). The cerebral lesions in a case of complete acquired colourblindness. *Scottish Medical and Surgical Journal, 5*, 503–512.

Macmillan, M. (2000). *An odd kind of fame: Stories of Phineas Gage*. Cambridge, MA: MIT Press.

Maher, P. (1993). *Betting on theories*. Cambridge: Cambridge University Press.

Malach, R., Reppas, J.B., Benson, R.R., Kwong, K.K., Jlang, H., Kennedy, W.A., Ledden, P.J., Brady, T.J., Rosen, B.R., & Tootell, R.B.H. (1995). Object-related activity revealed by functional magnetic resonance imaging in human occipital cortex. *Proceedings of the National Academy of Sciences (USA), 92*, 8135–8139.

Malamut, B.L., Saunders, R.C., & Mishkin, M. (1984). Monkeys with combined amygdalo-hippocampal lesions succeed in object discrimination learning despite 24-hour intertrial intervals. *Behavioral Neuroscience, 98*, 759–769.

Mandik, P. (1999). Qualia, space, and control. *Philosophical Psychology, 12*, 47–60.

Mandik, P. (2005). Phenomenal consciousness and the allocentric-egocentric distinction. In R. Buccheri, A.C. Elitzur & M. Saniga (Eds.), *Endophysics, time, quantum and the subjective* (pp. 437–459). Singapore: World Scientific.

Marr, D.C. (1969). A theory of the cerebellar cortex. *Journal of Physiology, 202*, 437–470.

Marr, D.C. (1982). *Vision: A computation investigation into the human representational system and processing of visual information.* San Francisco, CA: Freeman.

Marshall, W.H., Woolsey, C.N., & Bard, P. (1937). Representation of tactile sensibility in the monkey's cortex as indicated by cortical potentials. *American Journal of Physiology, 119*, 372–373.

Marshall, W.H., Woolsey, C.N., & Bard, P. (1941). Observations on cortical somatic sensory mechanisms of cat and monkey. *Journal of Neurophysiology, 4*(1941), 1–24.

Martin, S.J., Grimwood, P.D., & Morris, R.G.M. (2000). Synaptic plasticity and memory, an evaluation of the hypothesis. *Annual Review of Neuroscience, 23*, 649–711.

Maturana, H.R., & Varela, F.J. (1980). Autopoiesis: The organization of the living. In H.R. Maturana & F.J. Varela (Eds.), *Autopoiesis and cognition: The realization of the living* (pp. 59–138). Dordrecht: D. Reidel.

Maunsell, J.H.R., & van Essen, D.C. (1983). The connections of the middle temporal visual area (MT) and their relationship to a cortical hierarchy in the macaque monkey. *Journal of Neuroscience, 3*, 2563–2586.

Maxwell, J.C. (1868). On governors. *Proceedings of the Royal Society of London, 16*, 270–283.

Mayr, O. (1970). *The origins of feedback control.* Cambridge, MA: MIT Press.

McCauley, R.N. (1986). Intertheoretic relations and the future of psychology. *Philosophy of Science, 53*, 179–199.

McCauley, R.N. (1996). Explanatory pluralism and the coevolution of theories in science. In R.N. McCauley (Ed.), *The Churchlands and their critics* (pp. 17–47). Oxford: Blackwell.

McCauley, R.N., & Bechtel, W. (2001). Explanatory pluralism and the heuristic identity theory. *Theory and Psychology, 11*, 736–760.

McClelland, J.L., McNaughton, B., & O'Reilly, R.C. (1995). Why there are complementary learning systems in the hippocampus and neocortex: Insights from the successes and failures of connectionist models of learning and memory. *Psychological Review, 102*(3), 419–457.

McCloskey, M., & Cohen, N.J. (1989). Catastrophic interference in connectionist networks: The sequential learning problem. In G.H. Bower (Ed.), *The psychology of learning and motivation* (Vol. 24, pp. 109–165). New York: Academic.

McCulloch, W.S., & Pitts, W.H. (1943). A logical calculus of the ideas immanent in nervous activity. *Bulletin of Mathematical Biophysics, 7*, 115–133.

McDermott, K.B., Jones, T.C., Petersen, S.E., Lageman, S.K., & Roediger, H.L. (2000). Retrieval success is accompanied by enhanced activation in anterior prefrontal cortex during recognition memory: An event-related fMRI study. *Journal of Cognitive Neuroscience, 12*, 965–976.

McNeill, D. (1992). *Hand and mind.* Chicago, IL: University of Chicago Press.

McNeill, D. (2005). *Gesture and thought.* Chicago, IL: University of Chicago Press.

Medin, D.L., & Smith, E.E. (1984). Concepts and concept formation. *Annual Review of Psychology, 35,* 113–138.

Merigan, W.H., & Maunsell, J.H.R. (1993). How parallel are the primate visual pathways? *Annual Review of Neuroscience, 16,* 369–402.

Merzenich, M.M., & Brugge, J.F. (1973). Representation of the cochlear partition on the superior temporal plane of the macaque monkey. *Brain Research, 50,* 275–296.

Meynert, T. (1870). Beiträgre zur Kenntniss der centralen Projection der Sinnesoberflächen. *Sitzungberichte der Kaiserlichten Akademie der Wissenshaften, Wien. Mathematish-Naturwissenschaftliche Classe, 60,* 547–562.

Miikkulainen, R. (1993). *Subsymbolic natural language processing: An integrated model of scripts, lexicon, and memory.* Cambridge, MA: MIT Press.

Miller, G.A. (1956). The magical number seven, plus or minus two: some limits on our capacity for processing information. *Psychological Review, 63,* 81–97.

Millikan, R.G. (1984). *Language, thought, and other biological categories.* Cambridge, MA: MIT Press.

Millikan, R.G. (1993). *White queen psychology and other essays for Alice.* Cambridge, MA: MIT Press.

Millikan, R.G. (1996). Pushmi-pullyu representations. In J. Tomberlin (Ed.), *Philosophical perspectives* (Vol. 9, pp. 185–200). Atascadero, CA: Ridgeview.

Milner, A.D., & Goodale, M.G. (1995). *The visual brain in action.* Oxford: Oxford University Press.

Minkowski, M. (1911). Zur Physiologie der Sepshäre. *Pflügers Archiv, 141,* 171–327.

Minkowski, M. (1913). Experimentelle Untersuchungen ber die Beziehungen der Grosshirnrinde und der Netzhaut zu den primaren optischen Zentren, besonders zum Corpus geniculatum externum. *Arbeiten aus dem Hirnanatomie Institut Zurich, 7,* 259–362.

Minsky, M., & Papert, S. (1969). *Perceptrons: An introduction to computational geometry.* Cambridge, MA: MIT Press.

Mishkin, M. (1954). Visual discrimination performance following partial ablations of the temporal lobe: II. ventral surface vs. hippocampus. *Journal of Comparative and Physiological Psychology, 47,* 187–193.

Mishkin, M. (1966). Visual mechanisms beyond the striate cortex. In R.W. Russell (Ed.), *Frontiers in physiological psychology.* New York: Academic.

Mishkin, M. (1982). A memory system in the monkey. *Philosophical Transactions of the Royal Society of London. Series B, Biological Sciences, 298,* 85–95.

Mishkin, M., & Pribram, K.H. (1954). Visual discrimination performance following partial ablations of the temporal lobe: I. Ventral vs. lateral. *Journal of Comparative and Physiological Psychology, 47,* 14–20.

Mishkin, M., Ungerleider, L.G., & Macko, K.A. (1983). Object vision and spatial vision: Two cortical pathways. *Trends in Neurosciences, 6,* 414–417

Mitroff, S.R., Simons, D.J., & Levin, D.T. (2004). Nothing compares two views: Change blindness can occur despite preserved access to the changed information. *Perception and Psychophysics, 66,* 1268–1261.

Moray, N. (1959). Attention in dichotic listening: Affective cues and the influence of instructions. *Quarterly Journal of Experimental Psychology, 11,* (56–60).

Morell, P., & Norton, W. (1980). Myelin. *Scientific American, 242,* 88–118.

Morris, C.D., Bransford, J.D., & Franks, J.J. (1977). Levels of processing versus transfer appropriate processing. *Journal of Verbal Learning and Verbal Behavior, 16*, 519–533.

Morris, R.G.M., Garrud, P., Rawlins, J.N.P., & O'Keefe, J. (1982). Place navigation impaired in rats with hippocampal lesions. *Nature, 297*, 681–683.

Moscovitch, M. (1989). Confabulation and the frontal systems: Strategic versus associated retrieval in neuropsychological theories of memory. In H.L. Roediger & F.I.M. Craik (Eds.), *Varieties of memory and consciousness: Essays in honor of Endel Tulving* (pp. 133–155). Hillsdale, NJ: Erlbaum.

Moscovitch, M. (1994). Memory and working with memory: Evaluation of a component process model and comparisons with other models. In D.L. Schacter & E. Tulving (Eds.), *Memory systems 1994* (pp. 269–310). Cambridge, MA: MIT Press.

Mountcastle, V.B. (1957). Modality and topographic properties of single neurons of cat's somatic sensory cortex. *Journal of Neurophysiology, 20*, 408–434.

Mountcastle, V.B., Lynch, J.C., Georgopoulos, A., Sakata, H., & Acuña, C. (1975). Posterior parietal association cortex of the monkey: Command functions for operations within extrapersonal space. *Journal of Neurophysiology, 38*(1975), 871–908.

Mundale, J. (1998). Brain mapping. In W. Bechtel & G. Graham (Eds.), *A companion to cognitive science*. Oxford: Basil Blackwell.

Munk, H. (1877). Zur Physiologie der Grosshirnrinde. *Berliner Klinische Wochenschrift, 14*, 505–506.

Munk, H. (1881). *Über die Funktionen der Grosshirnrinde*. Berlin: A. Hirschwald.

Murata, A., Gallese, V., Luppino, G., Kaseda, M., & Sakata, H. (2000). Selectivity for the shape, size, and orientation of objects for grasping in neurons of monkey parietal area AIP. *Journal of Neurophysiology, 83*, 2580–2601.

Murphy, G.L. (2002). *The big book of concepts*. Cambridge, MA: MIT Press.

Nagel, E. (1961). *The structure of science*. New York: Harcourt, Brace.

Nagel, T. (1974). What is it like to be a bat? *The Philosophical Review, 83*, 435–450.

Neisser, U. (1967). *Cognitive psychology*. New York: Appleton-Century-Crofts.

Neisser, U. (1979). The control of information pickup in selective looking. In A.D. Pick (Ed.), *Perception and its development: A tribute to Eleanor J. Gibson*. Hillsdale, NJ: Erlbaum.

Neisser, U. (1981). John Dean's memory: A case study. *Cognition, 9*, 1–22.

Neisser, U. (1982). *Memory observed: Remembering in natural contexts*. San Francisco, CA: W. H. Freeman.

Neisser, U. (1988). Five kinds of self-knowledge. *Philosophical Psychology, 1*, 35–39.

Neisser, U. (1989). *Direct perception and recognition as distinct perceptual systems*. Paper presented to the Cognitive Science Society 1989.

Neisser, U. (Ed.). (1987). *Concepts and conceptual development: Ecological and intellectual factors in categorization*. Cambridge: Cambridge University Press.

Neisser, U., & Harsch, N. (1992). Phantom flashbulbs: False recollections of hearing the news about the Challenger. In E. Winograd & U. Neisser (Eds.), *Affect and accuracy in recall: Studies of "flashbulb" memories* (pp. 162–190). New York: Cambridge University Press.

Neisser, U., Winograd, E., Bergman, E.T., Schreiber, C.A., Palmer, S.E., & Weldon, M.S. (1996). Remembering the earthquake: Direct experience vs. hearing the news. *Memory, 4*, 337–357.

Nersessian, N. (2002). The cognitive basis of model-based reasoning in science. In P. Carruthers, S. Stich, & M. Siegal (Eds.), *The cognitive basis of science* (pp. 133–153). Cambridge: Cambridge University Press.

Neurath, O. (1932). Protokollsatze. *Erkenntnis, 3*, 204–214.

Newell, A. (1973). Production systems: Models of control structures. In W.G. Chase (Ed.), *Visual information processing* (pp. 463–527). New York: Academic Press.

Newell, A., & Simon, H.A. (1956). The logic theory machine: A complete information processing system. *Transactions on Information Theory, 'IT-2(#3)*, 61–79.

Newell, A., & Simon, H.A. (1972). *Human problem solving*. Englewood Cliffs, NJ: Prentice-Hall.

Newport, E.L., & Aslin, R.N. (2000). Innately constrained learning: Blending old and new approaches to language acquisition. In S.C. Howell, S.A. Fish, & T. Keith-Lucas (Eds.), *Proceedings of the 24th Annual Boston University Conference on Language Development* (pp. 1–21). Somerville, MA: Cascadilla Press.

Nickles, T. (1973). Two concepts of intertheoretic reduction. *The Journal of Philosophy, 70*, 181–201.

Nisbett, R.E., & Wilson, T.D. (1977). Telling more than we can know: Verbal reports on mental processes. *Psychological Review, 84*, 231–259.

Noë, A. (2004). *Action in perception*. Cambridge, MA: MIT Press.

Noë, A. (2006). Précis of *Action in perception*. *Psyche: An Interdisciplinary Journal of Research of Consciousness, 12*(1).

Nolfi, S., & Parisi, D. (1993). Auto-teaching: Networks that develop their own teaching input. In J.L. Deneubourg, H. Bersini, S. Goss, G. Nicolis, & R. Dagonnier (Eds.), *Proceedings of the Second European Conference on Artificial Life*. Brussels: University of Brussels.

Nyberg, L., Cabeza, R., & Tulving, E. (1998). Asymmetric frontal activation during episodic memory: What kind of specificity? *Trends in Cognitive Sciences, 2*, 419–420.

O'Keefe, J.A., & Dostrovsky, J. (1971). The hippocampus as a spatial map. Preliminary evidence from unit activity in the freely moving rat. *Brain Research, 34*, 171–175.

O'Keefe, J.A., & Nadel, L. (1978). *The hippocampus as a cognitive map*. Oxford: Oxford University Press.

O'Regan, J.K., & Noe, A. (2001). A sensorimotor account of vision and visual consciousness. *Behavioral and Brain Sciences, 24*, (939–1031).

O'Reilly, R.C., & McClelland, J.L. (1994). Hippocampal conjunctive encoding, storage and recall: Avoiding a tradeoff. *Hippocampus, 6*, 661–682.

Oppenheim, P., & Putnam, H. (1958). The unity of science as a working hypothesis. In H. Feigl & G. Maxwell (Eds.), *Concepts, theories, and the mind-body problem* (pp. 3–36). Minneapolis, MN: University of Minnesota Press.

Palade, G.E., & Claude, A. (1949a). The nature of the Golgi apparatus. I. Parallelism between intercellular myelin figures and Golgi apparatus in somatic cells. *Journal of Morphology, 85*, 35–69.

Palade, G.E., & Claude, A. (1949b). The nature of the Golgi apparatus. II. Identification of the Golgi apparatus with a complex of myelin figures. *Journal of Morphology, 85*, 71–111.

Palmer, S.E. (1999). *Vision science: Photons to phenomenology*. Cambridge, MA: MIT Press.

Palmer, S.E., & Kimchi, R. (1986). The information processing approach to cognition. In T.J. Knapp & L.C. Robertson (Eds.), *Approaches to cognition: Contrasts and controversies* (pp. 37–77). Hillsdale, NJ: Erlbaum.

Panizza, B. (1856). Osservazioni sul nervo ottico. *Memoria, Instituo Lombardo di Scienze, Lettere e Arte, 5*, 375–390.

Pasteur, L. (1860). Mémoire sur la fermentation alcoolique. *Annales de Chimie, 3e Ser, 58*, 323–426.

Penfield, W., & Boldrey, E. (1937). Somatic motor and sensory representation in the cerebral cortex of man as studied by electrical stimulation. *Brain, 60,* 389–443.

Penfield, W., & Rasmussen, T. (1950). *The cerebral cortex in man: A clinical study of localization of function.* New York: Macmillan.

Perenin, M.-T., & Vighetto, A. (1988). Optic ataxia: A specific disruption in visuomotor mechanisms. I. Different aspects of the deficit in reaching for objects. *Brain, 111,* 643–674.

Petersen, S.E., & Fiez, J.A. (1993). The processing of single words studied with positron emission tomography. *Annual Review of Neuroscience, 16,* 509–530.

Petersen, S.E., Fox, P.T., Posner, M.I., Mintun, M., & Raichle, M.E. (1988). Positron emission tomographic studies of the cortical anatomy of single-word processing. *Nature, 331*(February 18), 585–588.

Petersen, S.E., Fox, P.T., Posner, M.I., Mintun, M., & Raichle, M.E. (1989). Positron emission tomographic studies of the processing single words. *Journal of Cognitive Neuroscience, 1*(2), 153–170.

Piattelli-Palmarini, M. (1994). *Inevitable illusions: How mistakes of reason rule our minds.* New York: Wiley.

Pitts, W.H., & McCulloch, W.S. (1947). How we know universals: The perception of auditory and visual forms. *Bulletin of Mathematical Biophysics, 9,* 127–147.

Place, U.T. (1956). Is consciousness a brain process? *British Journal of Psychology, 47,* 44–50.

Pohl, W. (1973). Dissociation of spatial discrimination deficits following frontal and parietal lesions in monkeys. *Journal of Comparative and Physiological Psychology, 82,* 227–239.

Pollack, J.B. (1990). Recursive distributed representation. *Artificial Intelligence, 46,* 77–105.

Popper, K. (1935/1959). *The logic of discovery.* London: Hutchinson.

Port, R., & van Gelder, T. (1995). *It's about time.* Cambridge, MA: MIT Press.

Posner, M.I., & Boies, S.W. (1981). Components of attention. *Psychological Review, 78,* 391–408.

Post, E.L. (1936). Finite combinatorial processes — Formulation I. *Journal of Symbolic Logic, 1,* 103–105.

Powell, T.P.S., & Mountcastle, V.B. (1959). Some aspects of the functional organization of the cortex of the postcentral gyrus of the monkey: A correlation of findings obtained in a single unit analysis with cytoarchitecture. *Johns Hopkins Hospital Bulletin, 105,* 133–162.

Pribram, K.H., & Bagshaw, M. (1953). Further analysis of the temporal lobe syndrome utilizing fronto-temporal ablations. *Journal of Comparative Neurology, 99,* 347–375.

Prinz, J.J. (2000). A neurofunctional theory of visual consciousness. *Consciousness and Cognition, 9,* 243–259.

Prinz, J.J. (2002). *Furnishing the mind: Concepts and their perceptual basis.* Cambridge, MA: MIT Press.

Prinz, J.J. (2004a). Embodied emotions. In R.C. Solomon (Ed.), *Thinking about feeling: Contemporary philosophers on emotion.* New York: Oxford University Press.

Prinz, J.J. (2004b). *Gut reactions: A perceptual theory of emotion.* New York: Oxford University Press.

Prinz, J.J., & Barsalou, L.W. (2000). Steering a course for embodied representation. In E. Dietrich & A.B. Markman (Eds.), *Cognitive dynamics.* Mahwah, NJ: Erlbaum.

Putnam, H. (1967). Psychological predicates. In W.H. Capitan & D.D. Merrill (Eds.), *Art, mind and religion* (pp. 37–48). Pittsburgh, PA: University of Pittsburgh Press.

Putnam, H. (1973). Meaning and reference. *Journal of Philosophy, 70,* 609–711.

Putnam, H. (1975). The meaning of 'meaning'. In H. Putnam (Ed.), *Mind, language, and reality: Philosophical papers of Hilary Putnam* (Vol. 2, pp. 215–271). Cambridge: Cambridge University Press.

Quine, W.V.O. (1964). Ontological reduction and the world of numbers. *Journal of Philosophy, 61,* 209–216.

Quine, W.V.O. (1969). Epistemology naturalized. In W.V.O. Quine (Ed.), *Ontological relativity and other essays.* New York: Columbia University Press.

Quine, W.V.O. (1973). *The roots of reference.* La Salle, IL: Open Court.

Quine, W.V.O. (1975). The nature of natural knowledge. In S. Guttenplan (Ed.), *Mind and language* (pp. 67–81). Oxford: Clarendon Press.

Radden, J. (1996). Lumps and bumps: Kantian faculty psychology, phrenology, and twentieth-century psychiatric classification. *Philosophy, Psychiatry, and Psychology, 3,* 1–14.

Raffone, A., & van Leeuwen, C. (2001). Activation and coherence in memory processes: Revisiting the parallel distributed processing approach to retrieval. *Connection Science, 13,* 349–382.

Raichle, M.E. (1998). Behind the scenes of functional brain imaging: A historical and physiological perspective. *Proceedings of the National Academy of Sciences, 95,* 765–772.

Raichle, M.E., & Mintun, M.A. (2006). Brain work and brain imaging. *Annual Review of Neuroscience, 29,* 449–476.

Rajah, M.N., & McIntosh, A.R. (2005). Overlap in the functional neural systems involved in semantic and episodic memory retrieval. *Journal of Cognitive Neuroscience, 17,* 470–482.

Ranganath, C., & Blumenfeld, R.S. (2005). Doubt about doubt dissociations between short- and long-term memory. *Trends in Cognitive Science, 9,* 374–380.

Ratcliff, G., & Davies-Jones, G.A.B. (1972). Defective visual localization in focal brain wounds. *Brain, 95,* 49–60.

Ratcliff, R. (1990). Connectionist models of recognition memory: Constraints imposed by learning and forgetting functions. *Psychological Review, 97,* 285–308.

Reber, A.S. (1967). Implicit learning of artificial grammars. *Journal of Verbal Learning and Verbal Behavior, 6,* 855–863.

Reichenbach, H. (1938). *Experience and prediction.* Chicago, IL: University of Chicago Press.

Reid, T. (1785). *Essays on the intellectual powers of man.* Edinburgh: Bell and Robinson.

Resnick, R.A., O'Regan, J.K., & Clark, J.J. (1997). To see or not to see: The need for attention to perceive changes in scenes. *Psychological Science, 8,* 368–373.

Richardson, R.C. (1979). Functionalism and reductionism. *Philosophy of Science, 46,* 533–558.

Richardson, R.C. (1981). Internal representation: Prologue to a theory of intentionality. *Philosophical Topics, 12,* 171–211.

Ringo, J.L. (1991). Neuronal interconnection as a function of brain size. *Brain, Behavior, and Evolution, 38,* 1–6.

Roediger, H.L., Buckner, R.L., & McDermott, K.B. (1999). Components of processing. In J.K. Foster & M. Jelicic (Eds.), *Memory: Systems, process, or function* (pp. 32–65). Oxford: Oxford University Press.

Roediger, H.L., Gallo, D.A., & Geraci, L. (2002). Processing approaches to cognition: The impetus from the levels of processing framework. *Memory, 10*, 319–332.

Roediger, H.L., & McDermott, K.B. (1993). Implicit memory in normal human subjects. In H. Spinnler & F. Boller (Eds.), *Handbook of neuropsychology* (pp. 63–131). Amsterdam: Elsevier.

Roediger, H.L., & McDermott, K.B. (1995). Creating false memories: Remembering words not presented in lists. *Journal of Experimental Psychology: Learning, Memory, and Cognition, 21*(4), 803–814.

Roediger, H.L., Weldon, M.S., & Challis, B.H. (1989). Explaining dissociations between implicit and explicit measures of retention: A processing account. In H.L. Roediger & F.I.M. Craik (Eds.), *Varieties of memory and consciousness. Essays in honor of Endel Tulving* (pp. 3–41). Hillsdale, NJ: Lawrence Erlbaum Associates.

Rolls, E.T., & Treves, A. (1998). *Neural networks and brain function.* Oxford: Oxford University Press.

Rorty, R. (1970). In defense of eliminative materialism. *The Review of Metaphysics, 24*, 112–121.

Rosch, E. (1973). Natural categories. *Cognitive Psychology, 4*, 328–350.

Rosch, E., & Mervis, C. (1975). Family resemblances: Studies in the internal structure of categories. *Cognitive Psychology, 7*, 573–605.

Rose, S.P.R. (1976). *The conscious brain.* New York: Vintage Books.

Rosen, R. (1991). *Life itself: A comprehensive inquiry into the nature, origin, and fabrication of life.* New York: Columbia.

Rosenblatt, F. (1962). *Principles of neurodynamics; perceptrons and the theory of brain mechanisms.* Washington, DC: Spartan Books.

Rosenblueth, A., Wiener, N., & Bigelow, J. (1943). Behavior, purpose, and teleology. *Philosophy of Science, 10*, 18–24.

Ruiz-Mirazo, K., & Moreno, A. (2004). Basic autonomy as a fundamental step in the synthesis of life. *Artificial Life, 10*, 235–259.

Ruiz-Mirazo, K., Peretó, J., & Moreno, A. (2004). A universal definition of life: Autonomy and open-ended evolution. *Origins of Life and Evolution of the Biosphere, 34*, 323–346.

Rumelhart, D.E., Hinton, G.E., & Williams, R.J. (1986). Learning representations by back-propagating errors. *Nature, 323*, 533–536.

Rumelhart, D.E., & McClelland, J.L. (1986a). On learning the past tenses of English verbs. In J.L. McClelland & D.E. Rumelhart (Eds.), *Parallel distributed processing: Explorations in the microstructure of cognition. Vol. 2. Psychological and biological models.* Cambridge, MA: MIT Press.

Rumelhart, D.E., & McClelland, J.L. (Eds.). (1986b). *Parallel distributed processing: Explorations in the microstructure of cognition. Vol. 1. Foundations.* Cambridge, MA: MIT Press.

Ryle, G. (1949). *The concept of mind.* London: Hutchinson's University Library.

Saffran, J.R., Aslin, R.N., & Newport, E.L. (1996). Statistical learning by 8-month-old infants. *Science, 274*, 1926–1928.

Salmon, D.P., & Butters, N. (1995). Neurobiology of skill and habit learning. *Current Opinion in Neurobiology, 5*, 184–190.

Salmon, W.C. (1984). *Scientific explanation and the causal structure of the world.* Princeton, NJ: Princeton University Press.

Schacter, D.L. (1987). Implicit memory: History and current status. *Journal of Experimental Psychology: Learning, Memory, and Cognition, 13*, 501–518.

Schacter, D.L., Curran, T., Galluccio, L., Millburg, W., & Bates, J. (1996). False recognition and the right frontal lobe: A case study. *Neuropsychologia, 34*, 793–808.

Schacter, D.L., Eich, J.E., & Tulving, E. (1978). Richard Semon's theory of memory. *Journal of Verbal Learning and Verbal Behavior, 17*, 721–743.

Schacter, D.L., Verlaellie, M., & Pradere, D. (1996). The neuropsychology of memory illusions: False recall and recognition in amnesic patients. *Journal of Memory and Language, 35*, 319–334.

Schäfer, E.A. (1888a). Experiments on special sense localisations in the cortex cerebri of the monkey. *Brain, 10*, 362–380.

Schäfer, E.A. (1888b). On the functions of the temporal and occipital lobes: A reply to Dr. Ferrier. *Brain, 11*, 145–166.

Schaffner, K. (1967). Approaches to reduction. *Philosophy of Science, 34*, 137–147.

Schaffner, K.F. (1969). The Watson-Crick model and reductionism. *British Journal for the Philosophy of Science, 20*, 325–348.

Schank, R.C., & Abelson, R.P. (1977). *Scripts, plans, goals, and understanding: An inquiry into human knowledge structures.* Hillsdale, NJ: Lawrence Erlbaum.

Schiffer, S. (1981). Truth and the theory of content. In H. Parret & J. Bouveresse (Eds.), *Meaning and understanding* (pp. 204–222). New York: De Gruyter.

Schneider, G.E. (1967). Contrasting visuomotor functions of tectum and cortex in the golden hamster. *Psychologische Forschung, 31*, 52–62.

Schneider, G.E. (1969). Two visual systems: Brain mechanisms for localization and discrimination are dissociated by tectal and cortical lesions. *Science, 163*, 895–902.

Schrödinger, E. (1944). *What is life? The physical aspect of the living cell.* Cambridge: Cambridge University Press.

Schwann, T. (1839). *Mikroskopische Untersuchungen über die Übereinstimmung in der Struktur und dem Wachstrum der Theire und Planzen.* Berlin: Sander.

Scoville, W.B., & Milner, B. (1957). Loss of recent memory after bilateral hippocampal lesions. *Journal of neurology, neurosurgery, and psychiatry, 20*, 11–21.

Searle, J.R. (1980). Minds, brains, and programs. *Behavioral and Brain Sciences, 3*, 417–424.

Sejnowski, T.J., & Rosenberg, C.R. (1986). *NETtalk: A parallel network that learns to read aloud,* Technical Report 86–01. Department of Electrical Engineering and Computer Science, Johns Hopkins University, Baltimore, MD.

Sellars, W. (1956). Empiricism and the philosophy of mind. In H. Feigl & M. Scriven (Eds.), *Minnesota studies in the philosophy of science. I. The foundations of science and the concepts of psychology and psychoanalysis* (pp. 253–329). Minneapolis, MN: University of Minnesota Press.

Semmes, J. (1967). Manual stereognosis after brain injury. In J.F. Bosma (Ed.), *Symposium on oral sensation and perception.* Springfield, IL: Thomas.

Sereno, M.I. (2001). Mapping of contralateral space in retinotopic coordinates by a parietal cortical area in humans. *Science, 294*, 1350–1354.

Shallice, T. (1988). *From neuropsychology to mental structure.* New York: Cambridge University Press.

Shallice, T., & Warrington, E.K. (1970). Independent functioning of verbal memory stores: A neuropsychological study. *Quarterly Journal of Experimental Psychology, 22*, 261–273.

Shannon, C.E. (1948). A mathematical theory of communication. *Bell System Technical Journal, 27*, 379–423, 623–656.

Shapiro, L. (2004). *The mind incarnate.* Cambridge, MA: MIT Press.

Shastri, L., & Ajjanagadde, V. (1993). From simple associations to systematic reasoning: A connectionist representation of rules, variables, and dynamic bindings using temporal synchrony. *Behavioral and Brain Sciences, 16*, 417–494.

Shepard, R.N. (1980). Multidimensional scaling, tree-fitting, and clustering. *Science, 210*, 390–397.

Shettleworth, S. (2000). Modularity and the evolution of cognition. In C. Heyes & L. Huber (Eds.), *The evolution of cognition* (pp. 43–60). Cambridge, MA: MIT Press.

Shiffin, R.M., & Atkinson, R.C. (1969). Storage and retrieval process in long-term memory. *Psychological Review, 76*, 179–193.

Simons, D.J., & Levin, D.T. (1998). Failure to detect changes to people during a real-world interaction. *Psychonomic Bulletin and Review, 5*, 644–649.

Singleton, J.L., & Newport, E.L. (2004). When learners surpass their models: The acquisition of American sign language from inconsistent input. *Cognitive Psychology, 49*, 370–407.

Skinner, B.F. (1971). *Beyond freedom and dignity.* New York: Knopf.

Smart, J.J.C. (1959). Sensations and brain processes. *Philosophical Review, 68*, 141–156.

Smolensky, P. (1990). Tensor product variable binding and the representation of symbolic structures in connectionist systems. *Artificial Intelligence, 46*(1–2), 159–216.

Smolensky, P. (1994). Constituent structure and explanation in an integrated connectionist/symbolic cognitive architecture. In C. MacDonald & G. MacDonald (Eds.), *The philosophy of psychology: Debates on psychological explanation.* Oxford: Blackwell.

Snyder, L.H., Batista, A.P., & Andersen, R.A. (1997). Coding of intention in the posterior parietal cortex. *Nature, 386*, 167–170.

Snyder, L.H., Batista, A.P., & Andersen, R.A. (2000). Intention-related activity in the posterior parietal cortex: A review. *Vision Research, 40*, 1433–1441.

Sober, E. (1997). Two outbreaks of lawlessness in recent philosophy of science. *Philosophy of Science, 64*, 458–467.

Sperling, G. (1960). The information available in brief visual presentations. *Psychological Monographs, 74*(498), 1–29.

Spinelli, D.N., & Pribram, K.H. (1966). Changes in visual recovery functions produced by temporal lobe stimulation in monkeys. *Electroencephalography and Clinical Neurophysiology, 20*, 44–49.

Squire, L.R. (1987). *Memory and brain.* New York: Oxford University Press.

Squire, L.R., & Knowlton, B.J. (1995). Memory, hippocampus, and brain systems. In M.S. Gazzaniga (Ed.), *The cognitive neurosciences* (pp. 825–837). Cambridge, MA: MIT Press.

Squire, L.R., & Zola-Morgan, S. (1991). The medial-temporal lobe memory system. *Science, 253*, 1380–1386.

Squire, L.R., & Zola, S.M. (1998). Episodic memory, semantic memory, and amnesia. *Hippocampus, 8*, 205–211.

Stampe, D. (1977). Toward a causal theory of linguistic representation. In P. French, T. Uehling, & H. Wettstein (Eds.), *Midwest studies in philosophy* (Vol. 2). Minneapolis, MN: University of Minnesota Press.

Sternberg, S. (1966). High-speed scanning in human memory. *Science, 153*, 652–654.

Sternberg, S. (1969). The discovery of processing stages: Extension of Donders' method. *Acta Psychologica, 30*, 276–315.

Suga, N. (1990). Biosonar and neural computation in bats. *Scientific American, 262*(6), 60–68.

Suppes, P. (1957). *Introduction to logic.* Princeton, NJ: Van Nostrand.

Tabery, J. (2004). Synthesizing activities and interactions in the concept of a mechanism. *Philosophy of Science, 71*, 1–15.

Taira, M., Mine, S., Georgopoulos, A.P., Murata, A., & Sakata, H. (1990). Parietal cortex neurons of the monkey related to the visual guidance of hand movements. *Experimental Brain Research, 83,* 29–36.

Talbot, S.A., & Kuffler, S.W. (1952). A multibeam opthalmoscope for the study of retinal physiology. *Journal of the Optical Society of America, 42*(12), 931–936.

Talbot, S.A., & Marshall, W.H. (1941). Physiological studies on neural mechanisms of visual localization and discrimination. *American Journal of Ophthalmology, 24,* 1255–1263.

Tanaka, K. (1996). Inferotemporal cortex and object vision. *Annual Review of Neuroscience, 19,* 109–140.

Tanaka, K., & Saito, A. (1989). Analysis of motion of the visual field by direction, expansion/contraction, and rotation cells clustered in the dorsal part of the medial superior temporal area of the macaque monkey. *Journal of Neurophysiology, 62,* 626–641.

Thelen, E., & Smith, L. (1994). *A dynamical systems approach to the development of cognition and action.* Cambridge, MA: MIT Press.

Thompson, R.F. (1999). Clinton Nathan Woolsey. *Biographical Memoirs, 76,* 360–374.

Tolman, E.C. (1948). Cognitive maps in rats and men. *Psychological Review, 55,* 189–208.

Touretzky, D.S., & Hinton, G.E. (1988). A distributed connectionist production system. *Cognitive Science, 12,* 423–466.

Treisman, A.M. (1964). Monitoring and storage of irrelevant messages in selective attention. *Journal of Verbal Learning and Verbal Behavior, 3,* 449–459.

Trevarthen, C. (1968). Two mechanisms of vision in primates. *Psychologische Forschung, 31,* 299–337.

Tsotsos, J.K. (1987). Image understanding. In S. Shapiro (Ed.), *Encyclopedia of artificial intelligence* (pp. 389–409). New York: Wiley.

Tulving, E. (1972). Episodic and semantic memory. In E. Tulving & W. Donaldson (Eds.), *Organization of memory* (pp. 381–403). New York: Academic.

Tulving, E. (1984). Multiple learning and memory systems. In K.M.J. Lagerspetz & P. Niemi (Eds.), *Psychology in the 1990s* (pp. 163–184). Elsevier.

Tulving, E. (1985). How many memory systems are there? *American Psychologist, 40,* 385–398.

Tulving, E. (1991). Concepts of human memory. In L.R. Squire, G. Lynch, & J.L. Weinberger (Eds.), *Memory: Organization and locus of change* (pp. 3–32). New York: Oxford.

Tulving, E. (1999a). Episodic vs. semantic memory. In R.A. Wilson & F. Keil (Eds.), *The MIT encyclopedia of the cognitive sciences* (pp. 278–280). Cambridge, MA: MIT Press.

Tulving, E. (1999b). Study of memory: Processes and systems. In J.K. Foster & M. Jelicic (Eds.), *Memory: Systems, process, or function* (pp. 11–30). Oxford: Oxford University Press.

Tulving, E. (2002). Episodic memory: From mind to brain. *Annual Review of Psychology, 53,* 1–25.

Tulving, E., Kapur, S., Craik, F.I.M., Moscovitch, M., & Houle, S. (1994). Hemispheric encoding/retrieval asymmetry in episodic memory: Positron emission tomography findings. *Proceedings of the National Academy of Sciences (USA), 91,* 2016–2020.

Tulving, E., Kapur, S., Markowitsch, H.J., Craik, F.I.M., Habib, R., & Houle, S. (1994). Neuroanatomical correlates of retrieval in episodic memory: Auditory sentence recognition. *Proceedings of the National Academy of Sciences (USA), 91,* 2012–2015.

Tulving, E., & Schacter, D.L. (1990). Priming and human memory systems. *Science, 247,* 301–306.

Tulving, E., Schacter, D.L., & Stark, H. (1982). Priming effects in word-fragment completion are independent of recognition memory. *Journal of Experimental Psychology: Human Learning and Memory, 8,* 336–342.

Turing, A. (1936). On computable numbers, with an application to the Entscheidungsproblem. *Proceedings of the London Mathematical Society, second series, 42,* 230–265.

Tversky, A., & Kahneman, D. (1974). Judgment under uncertainty: Heuristics and biases. *Science, 185,* 1124–1131.

Ungerleider, L.G., & Mishkin, M. (1982). Two cortical visual systems. In D.J. Ingle, M.A. Goodale, & R.J.W. Mansfield (Eds.), *Analysis of visual behavior* (pp. 549–586). Cambridge, MA: MIT Press.

van Essen, D.C., & Gallant, J.L. (1994). Neural mechanisms of form and motion processing in the primate visual system. *Neuron, 13,* 1–10.

van Essen, D.C., Maunsell, J.H.R., & Bixby, J.L. (1981). The middle temporal visual area in the macaque monkey: myeloarchitecture, connections, functional properties, and topographic organization. *Journal of Comparative Neurology, 199,* 293–326.

van Gelder, T. (1990a). Compositionality: A connectionist variation on a classical theme. *Cognitive Science, 14,* 355–384.

van Gelder, T. (1990b). What is the 'D' in 'PDP'? An overview of the concept of distribution. In S. Stich, D.E. Rumelhart, & W. Ramsey (Eds.), *Philosophy and connectionist theory.* Hillsdale, NJ: Lawrence Erlbaum Associates.

van Gelder, T. (1995). What might cognition be, if not computation. *The Journal of Philosophy, 92,* 345–381.

van Gelder, T. (1998). The dynamical hypothesis in cognitive science. *Behavioral and Brain Sciences, 21,* 615–628.

van Gelder, T., & Port, R. (1995). It's about time: An overview of the dynamical approach to cognition. In R. Port & T. van Gelder (Eds.), *It's about time.* Cambridge, MA: MIT Press.

van Gulick, R. (1993). Understanding the phenomenal mind: Are we all just armadillos? In M. Davies & G. Humphreys (Eds.), *Consciousness: Psychological and philosophical essays.* Oxford: Basil Blackwell.

van Leeuwen, C., Steyvers, M., & Nooter, M. (1997). Stability and intermittency in large-scale coupled oscillator models for perceptual segmentation. *Journal of Mathematical Psychology, 41,* 319–344.

van Orden, G.C., Pennington, B.F., & Stone, G.O. (2001). What do double dissociations prove? Inductive methods and isolable systems. *Cognitive Science, 25,* 111–172.

Varela, F.J. (1979). *Principles of biological autonomy.* New York: Elsevier.

Varela, F.J., Thompson, E., & Rosch, E. (1991). *The embodied mind.* Cambridge, MA: MIT Press.

Vargha-Khadem, F., Gadian, D.G., Watkins, K.E., Connelly, A., Van Paesschen, W., & Mishkin, M. (1997). Differential effects of early hippocampal pathology on episodic and semantic memory. *Science, 277,* 376–380.

Verrey, L. (1888). Hémiachromatopsie droite absolue. Conservation partielle de la perception lumineuse et des formes. Ancien kyste hémorrhagique de la partie inférieure du lobe occipital gauche. *Archives d'Ophtalmologie, 8,* 289–301.

von Bonin, G., & Bailey, P. (1951). *The isocortex of man.* Urbana, IL: University of Illinois Press.

Vygotsky, L.S. (1962). *Thought and language.* Cambridge, MA: MIT Press.

Wagner, A.D., Schacter, D.L., Rotte, M., Koutstaal, W., Maril, A., Dale, A.M., Rosen, B., & Buckner, R.L. (1998). Building memories: Remembering and forgetting of verbal materials as predicted by brain activity. *Science, 281,* 1188–1191.

Wallach, H., & O'Connell, D.N. (1953). The kinetic depth effect. *Journal of Experimental Psychology, 45,* 205–217.

Walsh, V., & Cowey, A. (1998). Magnetic stimulation studies of visual cognition. *Trends in Cognitive Sciences, 2*(3), 103–110.

Waskan, J.A. (2006). Models and cognition. Cambridge, MA: MIT Press.

Waugh, N.C., & Norman, D.A. (1965). Primary memory. *Psychological Review, 72,* 89–104.

Waskan, J.A. (1997). Directions in connectionist research: Tractable computations without syntactically structured representations. Metaphilosophy, 28, 31–62.

Werner, G. (1988a). Five decades on the path to naturalizing epistemology. In J.S. Lund (Ed.), *Sensory processing in the mammalian brain* (pp. 345–359). New York: Oxford University Press.

Werner, G. (1988b). The many faces of neuroreductionism. In E. Basar (Ed.), *Dynamics of sensory and cognitive processing by the brain* (pp. 241–257). Berlin: Springer-Verlag.

Westfall, R.S. (1971). *The construction of modern science.* New York: Wiley.

Wheeler, M.E., & Buckner, R.L. (2003). Functional dissociation among components of remembering: Control, perceived oldness, and content. *Journal of Neuroscience, 23,* 3869–3880.

Wheeler, M.E., Petersen, S.E., & Buckner, R.L. (2000). Memory's echo: Vivid recollection activates modality specific cortex. *Proceedings of the National Academy of Sciences (USA), 97,* 11125–11129.

Wheeler, M.E., Stuss, D.T., & Tulving, E. (1997). Toward a theory of episodic memory: The frontal lobes and autonoetic consciousness. *Psychological Bulletin, 121,* 331–354.

Wiener, N. (1948). *Cybernetics: Or, control and communication in the animal machine.* New York: Wiley.

Wiggs, C.L., Weisberg, J., & Martin, A. (1999). Neural correlates of semantic and episodic memory retrieval. *Neuropsychologia, 37,* 103–118.

Wilbrand, H. (1890). *Die hemianopischen Gesichtsfeld-Formen und das optische Wahrnehmungszentrum.* Wiesbaden: J. F. Bergmann.

Willingham, D.B., & Preuss, L. (1995). The death of implicit memory. *Psyche: An Interdisciplinary Journal of Research of Consciousness, 2*(15).

Wimsatt, W.C. (1972). Teleology and the logical structure of function statements. *Studies in the History and Philosophy of Science, 3,* 1–80.

Wimsatt, W.C. (1974). Complexity and organization. In K.F. Schaffner & R.S. Cohen (Eds.), *PSA 1972* (pp. 67–86). Dordrecht: Reidel.

Wimsatt, W.C. (1976a). Reductionism, levels of organization, and the mind-body problem. In G. Globus, G. Maxwell, & I. Savodnik (Eds.) *Consciousness and the brain: A scientific and philosophical inquiry* (pp. 202–267). New York: Plenum Press.

Wimsatt, W.C. (1976b). Reductive explanation: A functional account. In R.S. Cohen, C.A. Hooker, A.C. Michalos, & J. van Evra (Eds.), *PSA-1974* (pp. 671–710). Dordrecht: Reidel.

Wimsatt, W.C. (1981). Robustness, reliability, and overdetermination. In M.B. Brewer & B.E. Collins (Eds.), *Scientific inquiry and the social sciences: A volume in honor of Donald T. Campbell* (pp. 124–163). San Francisco, CA: Jossey-Bass.

Wimsatt, W.C. (1986). Forms of aggregativity. In A. Donagan, N. Perovich, & M. Wedin (Eds.), *Human nature and natural knowledge* (pp. 259–293). Dordrecht: Reidel.

Wimsatt, W.C. (1994). The ontology of complex systems: Levels, perspectives, and causal thickets. *Canadian Journal of Philosophy, Suppl., 20*, 207–274.

Wittgenstein, L. (1953). *Philosophical investigations*. New York: MacMillan.

Wong-Riley, M. (1979). Changes in the visual system of monocularly sutured or enucleated cats demonstrable with cytochrome oxidase histochemistry. *Brain Research, 171*, 11–28.

Woodger, J.H. (1952). *Biology and language*. Cambridge: Cambridge University Press.

Woolsey, C.N. (1943). "Second" somatic receiving areas in the cerebral cortex of cat, dog, and monkey. *Federation Proceedings, 2*, 55.

Woolsey, C.N., & Fairman, D. (1946). Contralateral, ipsilateral and bilateral representation of cutaneous receptors in somatic area I and II of the cerebral cortex of pig, sheep and other animals. *Surgery, 19*, 684–702.

Woolsey, C.N., & Walzl, E.M. (1942). Topical projection of nerve fibers from local regions of the cochlea to the cerebral cortex of the cat. *Bulletin of the Johns Hopkins Hospital, 71*, 315–344.

Wright, C., & Bechtel, W. (2006). Mechanisms and psychological explanation. In P. Thagard (Ed.), *Philosophy of psychology and cognitive science* (pp. 31–77). Amsterdam: Elsevier.

Wright, L. (1972). Explanation and teleology. *Philosophy of Science, 39*, 204–218.

Yue, G., & Cole, K.C. (1992). Strength increases from the motor program: comparison of training with maximal voluntary and imagined muscle contractions. *Journal of Neurophysiology, 62*, 1114–1123.

Zatorre, R.J., Halpern, A.R., Perry, D.W., Meyer, E., & Evans, A.C. (1996). Hearing in the mind's ear: A PET investigation of musical imagery and perception. *Journal of Cognitive Neuroscience, 8*, 29–46.

Zeki, S.M. (1969). Representation of central visual fields in prestriate cortex monkey. *Brain Research, 14*, 271–291.

Zeki, S.M. (1971). Cortical projections from two prestriate areas in the monkey. *Brain Research, 34*, 19–35.

Zeki, S.M. (1973). Colour coding of the rhesus monkey prestriate cortex. *Brain Research, 53*, 422–427.

Zeki, S.M. (1974). Functional organization of a visual area in the posterior bank of the superior temporal sulcus of the rhesus monkey. *Journal of Physiology, 236*, 549–573.

Zihl, J., von Cramon, D., & Mai, N. (1983). Selective disturbance of movement vision after bilateral brain damage. *Brain, 106*, 313–340.

Zola, S.M., Squire, L.R., Teng, E., Stefanacci, L., & Clark, R.E. (2000). Impaired recognition memory in monkeys after damage limited to the hippocampal region. *Journal of Neuroscience, 20*, 451–463.

Author Index

Subject Index